RAF BOMBER COMMAND
Reflections of War

RAF BOMBER COMMAND
Reflections of War

Volume 4
Battles with the *Nachtjagd*
(30/31 March–September 1944)

Martin W Bowman

Pen & Sword
AVIATION

First Published in Great Britain in 2013 by
Pen & Sword Aviation
an imprint of
Pen & Sword Books Ltd
47 Church Street, Barnsley, South Yorkshire S70 2AS

Copyright © Martin W Bowman, 2013

ISBN 978-1-84884-495-7

Typeset in 10/12pt Palatino by
Concept, Huddersfield

Printed and bound in England by
CPI Group (UK) Ltd, Croydon, CRO 4YY

Pen & Sword Books Ltd incorporates the Imprints of Pen & Sword
Aviation, Pen & Sword Family History, Pen & Sword Maritime, Pen & Sword
Military, Pen & Sword Discovery, Wharncliffe Local History, Wharncliffe
True Crime, Wharncliffe Transport, Pen & Sword Select, Pen & Sword
Military Classics, Leo Cooper, The Praetorian Press, Remember When,
Seaforth Publishing and Frontline Publishing.

For a complete list of Pen & Sword titles please contact
PEN & SWORD BOOKS LIMITED
47 Church Street, Barnsley, South Yorkshire, S70 2AS, England
E-mail: enquiries@pen-and-sword.co.uk
Website: www.pen-and-sword.co.uk

Contents

Acknowledgements

Gebhard Aders; Harry Andrews DFC; Frau Anneliese Autenrieth; Mrs
Dorothy Bain; Günther Bahr; Charlie 'Jock' Baird; Harry Barker; Irene
Barrett-Locke; Raymond V Base; Don Bateman; Steve Beale; A D 'Don'
Beatty; Jack Bennett; Andrew Bird; Peter Bone; Alfons Borgmeier; Jack
Bosomworth; Len Browning; Don Bruce; George Burton; Jim Burtt-Smith;
Maurice Butt; Philip J Camp DFM; City of Norwich Aviation Museum
(CONAM); Bob Collis; Jim Coman; B G Cook; John Cook DFM; Rupert
'Tiny' Cooling; Dennis Cooper; Ray Corbett; Coen Cornelissen; Leslie
Cromarty DFM; Tom Cushing; Hans-Peter Dabrowski; Rob de Visser;
Dr. Karl Dörscheln; J Alan Edwards; Wolfgang Falck; David G Fellowes;
Elwyn D Fieldson DFC; Karl Fischer; Søren C Flensted; Vitek Formanek;
Stanley Freestone; Ian Frimston; Prof. Dr Ing. Otto H Fries; Air Vice
Marshal D J Furner CBE DFC AFC; Ken Gaulton; Jim George; Margery
Griffiths, Chairman, 218 Gold Coast Squadron Association; Group Captain
J R 'Benny' Goodman DFC* AFC AE; Alex H Gould DFC; Hans Grohmann;
Charles Hall; Steve Hall; Jack F Hamilton; Eric Hammel; Erich Handke;
James Harding; Frank Harper; Leslie Hay; Gerhard Heilig; Bob Hilliard;
Peter C Hinchliffe; Neville Hockaday RNZAF; Werner 'Red' Hoffmann;
Ted Howes DFC; Air Commodore Peter Hughes DFC; John Anderson
Hurst; Zdenek Hurt; Ab A Jansen; Karl-Ludwig Johanssen; Wilhelm
'Wim' Johnen; Arthur 'Johnnie' Johnson; John B Johnson; Graham B Jones;
Hans-Jürgen Jürgens; Erich Kayser; George Kelsey DFC; Les King; Christian
Kirsch; Hans Krause; Reg Lawton; J R Lisgo; Chas Lockyer; Günther
Lomberg; Peter Loncke; George Luke; Ian McLachlan; Nigel McTeer;
B L Eric Mallett RCAF; Len Manning; The Honourable Terence Mansfield;
Eric Masters; Bernard 'Max' Meyer DFC; Cyril Miles; Colin Moir; Frank
Mouritz; Friedrich Ostheimer; Maurice S Paff; Simon Parry; Path Finder
Association; Wing Commander David Penman DSO OBE DFC; Richard
Perkins; Peter Petrick; Karl-Georg Pfeiffer; Eric Phillips; Vic Poppa; John
Price; Stan Reed; Ernie Reynolds; Peter Richard; Albert E Robinson;
Heinz Rökker; Squadron Leader Geoff Rothwell DFC; Fritz Rumpelhardt;

David M Russell; Kees Rijken; Eric Sanderson; Klaus J Scheer; Dr. Dieter Schmidt-Barbo; Karl-Heinz Schoenemann; Jerry Scutts; Johan Schuurman; Group Captain Jack Short; Leslie R Sidwell; Don L Simpkin; SAAF Assn; Albert Spelthahn; Dr Ing. Klaus Th. Spies; Dick Starkey; Squadron Leader Hughie Stiles; Mike 'Taff' Stimson; Ted Strange DFC; Maurice Stoneman; Ken Sweatman; Paul Todd; Fred Tunstall DFC; Hille van Dieren; George Vantilt; Bob Van Wick; Andreas Wachtel; Georg Walser; David Waters; H Wilde; John Williams; H J Wilson; Henk Wilson; Geoffrey and Nick Willatt; Dennis Wiltshire; Louis Patrick Wooldridge DFC; Fred Young DFM; Cal Younger.

I am particularly grateful to my friend and colleague Theo Boiten, with whom I have collaborated on several books, for all of the information on the *Nachtjagd* or German night fighter forces contained herein. And, aviation historians everywhere owe a deep sense of gratitude to his and all the other valuable sources of reference listed in the end notes; in particular, those by the incomparable W R 'Bill' Chorley, Martin Middlebrook and Chris Everitt and Oliver Clutton-Brock. Finally, all of the late authors' books, as listed, who are beyond compare. This book and its companion volumes are dedicated to their memory.

CHAPTER 1

The 'Night of the Big Kill'

It was a story of the perfect air ambush and Germany's greatest single defensive success in the grim cat-and-mouse game that was played out for nearly six years between the bombers and the fighters. The ground controllers had to guess where we were heading for and they guessed correctly. We were heading for the Stuttgart 'gap' – a small opening in the great flak belt. When we reached it there were hundreds of German fighters waiting in the brilliant moonlight to shoot down our heavily-laden bombers and they downed us by the score. Fifty miles from the target all hell was let loose. There were enemy fighters everywhere. We were sitting ducks with no cloud cover to shield us. We counted twelve of our aircraft going down in almost as many minutes, all of them in flames. Sometimes we could see two or three night fighters peeling away from one of our crippled bombers. Usually when we saw an aircraft going down or blowing up we reported it to the navigator, who made a brief note of the time and position; but on this raid it would have been a full-time job for him, so he told us to forget it.

Sergeant R E Holder, flight engineer, *G-George*, 460 Squadron RAAF,
Nürnburg raid 30/31 March 1944[1]

In the 1930s, Nürnburg – 90 miles to the north of Munich – had hosted the annual National Socialist rallies. Hitler called this Bavarian city on the River Pegnitz the 'most German of German cities'. It was here that the infamous Nürnburg Laws, the series of anti-Semitic edicts, were promulgated. But Nürnburg was more than just an important political target. By March 1944, with an estimated population of 426,000, of whom 220,000 were potential war workers, Nürnburg was high on the list of the British Cabinet's Combined Strategic Targets Committee, and several raids had been planned and then postponed. Nürnburg with Fürth was an important centre of general and electrical engineering with 50 factories and 46 other commercial plants. The famous Maschinen *Augsburg–Nürnburg* heavy engineering works produced land armaments of all kinds, from heavy tanks and armoured cars to Diesel engines. This factory had

1

become doubly important since many of the Berlin tank works had been destroyed in earlier raids and the huge MAN factory at Augsburg had also been all but destroyed. The G Müller works manufactured special ball-bearings for magnetos and the *Siemens Schuckertwerke* made electric motors, searchlights and firing devices for mines. The large Siemens factory in Berlin had been damaged during recent air attacks on the capital and the Nürnburg plant had therefore assumed a vital role in the German war effort.

Shortly after midday on Thursday 30 March 1944 the master teleprinter at High Wycombe sent out the first alert signal to the six Bomber Groups and Group commanders who were given the code name of the target: *Grayling*. This was in turn sent to stations and squadron commanders. Nürnburg would be a 'Maximum effort' – ten squadrons in 1 Group, eight squadrons from 3 Group, seven squadrons from No. 4, twelve from No. 5, nine from No. 6 and twelve squadrons from 8 Path Finder Force Group. Security was immediately put into force. All outgoing phone calls were blocked and those incoming were intercepted, cutting stations off from the outside world as preparations for the raid on Nürnburg began. This time it was definitely 'on' – unless there was a significant change in the weather forecasts. The weather did seem to be worsening, with a threat of snow and sleet that strengthened the feeling that the raid would eventually be scrubbed. Some thought that it might even be cancelled before the navigation briefing which always preceded the main crew briefing, but there was no such doubt in Harris's mind. At the pre-planning conference at High Wycombe the Commander-in-Chief announced that 795 RAF heavy bomber and 38 Mosquito crews were to be employed on the raid. On a huge wall map a line of red tape wheeling around marking pins traced the route that the bombers were to follow to and from their target. From a dead-reckoning position off the Naze where the force was to rendezvous, the tape streaked in a south-easterly direction to cross the Belgian coast near Bruges. With no change of course, it then went on to just short of Charleroi in Belgium; dangerously close to three known radio beacons which were used as gathering and waiting points for the night fighters: *Funk Feuers' Ida*, *Otto* and *Heinz*, close to the Ruhr. From there it stretched in a straight line that represented nearly 250 miles to the final turning point at Fulda, north-east of Frankfurt. At Fulda the force would swing on to a south-easterly heading for the bomb run on Nürnburg. But for two slight changes the return route the bombers were to follow after the raid was just about as direct as the outward course.

This planned route flew in the face of everything that had gone before. In the month leading up to Nürnburg Harris had decided that because of mounting casualties he must, whenever possible, avoid sending single streams of bombers on deep-penetration raids since such streams could be easily plotted by the Germans and intercepted before reaching their target. The alternative was to divide the striking force and send the two parts to different targets or send both to the same target but by different routes, thus confusing the enemy's air defences and making it more difficult for the German controllers to plot the raid. Yet the plan for Nürnburg was to send a large force on a long flight in what was virtually a straight line that was ideally suited to *Tame Boar* interception.

At 15.25 on the afternoon of the 30th, a weather Mosquito confirmed to Bomber Command that the outward flight in the moonlight had little chance of cloud cover and if the cloud seen over Nürnburg persisted it would rob the Path Finders of the ability to mark visually by moonlight. The deadline for announcing whether an operation was on or off was 16.00. A further forecast was handed to the deputy Commander-in-Chief Sir Robert Saundby at 16.40. It read: 'Nürnburg: Large amount of strato-cumulus with tops to about 8,000 feet and risk of some thin patchy cloud at about 15 to 16,000 feet.' Many years after the war, Sir Robert recalled:

> I can say that, in view of the met report and other conditions, every-one, including myself, expected the C-in-C to cancel the raid. We were most surprised when he did not. I thought perhaps there was some top-secret political reason for the raid, something too top-secret for even me to know. The conditions reported by the Mosquito were not passed down to the stations. Every effort was made to keep from crews the unpleasant fact that they were to fly a constant course through a well-defended part of Germany for 265 miles in bright moonlight with little chance of cloud cover. At a dozen stations Met officers forecast that there would be cloud cover at operational height. No one, not even the Path Finder squadrons, was told of the 'large amounts of stratocumulus' now forecast for Nuremburg.

Saundby was obliged to draw up a detailed flight plan for the operation in accordance with Harris's instructions but before doing so he contacted Path Finder Headquarters at Huntingdon on his 'scrambler' telephone and informed Air Vice Marshal Don Bennett DSO of the proposed route. Bennett was openly critical of the plan and he worked out an alternative route based on the Path Finder meteorological findings brought back earlier by the 'Pampa' weather observation flight by one of his 1409 Met Flight Mosquitoes flown from Wyton by Flying Officer T Oakes and his Canadian navigator, Flight Lieutenant 'Bob' Dale. Bennett's plan was replete with 'dog-legs' from the direct line of flight and other tactical feints aimed at confusing the enemy and making night fighter interception as difficult as possible. Bennett formulated the route backwards from the target and was influenced by his preference for down-wind attack rather than into wind to avoid 'creep back' from the aiming point (or bomb-loads being dropped short of the target). Because of the uncertainty of the weather he advocated using *Newhaven* and *Parramata* markers and *Wanganui* flares floating in the sky. Bennett's proposed Path Finder route found no favour with the majority of the main-force commanders who believed that a straight route would fool the JLOs into thinking that the bomber stream would suddenly veer off to attack some other objective than the one for which it seemed to be heading. The AOC 5 Group, Air Vice Marshal Sir Ralph A Cochrane, did not favour a dog-leg route because he believed it would only lengthen the flying time to the target and in turn greatly increase the risk of night fighter interception. The 'austere and humourless' baronet and the straight-talking Australian could not have been more different. Bennett said that Cochrane 'would have been the best Group Commander in Bomber Command had he done ten trips – or if he had done any trips, but his knowledge of flying and of ops was nil.'

The need for diversionary ploys had been made uncomfortably clear only a month earlier, when the attack on Leipzig on 19/20 February had cost 82 bombers: Bomber Command's highest loss rate to date. Forty-nine Halifaxes were to sow mines in the Heligoland area and 34 Mosquitoes of 8 Group would be employed on diversionary 'spoofs' to Aachen, Cologne, Kassel and other cities. Thirteen more Mosquitoes would strafe night fighter airfields at Twente, Volkel, Deelen, Juvincourt and Juliandorf, five more aircraft would fly RCM patrols and 19 Mosquitoes in 100 Group would carry out *Serrate* patrols.[2] Before the main force reached Nürnburg, nine Mosquitoes were to make a feint attack on Cologne between 23.55 hours and 00.07 hours. And a second force of 20 Mosquitoes would drop 'spoof' fighter flares, *Window* and TIs on Kassel between 00.26 hours and 00.28 hours in the hope that it would fool the JLOs into thinking that the main attack would be somewhere in the Ruhr.[3]

In the final analysis the Met men preferred their original forecast of wind speeds of up to 50 mph and the flight plan was therefore tailored to complement this assumption. By the 16.00 deadline the afternoon weather report showed no appreciable change. The only additional information was that on take-off visibility would be poor at most bases but not bad enough to prevent the bombers from getting airborne. Nos. 4 and 6 Groups were warned to expect a heavy, overcast sky over Germany with thick layers of cloud near to the target, and valley fog on return. Group Commanders were also told that they could expect large amounts of strata cumulus to 8,000 feet with a risk of patchy medium cloud at 15,000 to 16,000 feet. Bomb-aimers were warned that with a forecast wind speed of 60 mph at 21,000 feet over Nürnburg in direction 280° they would have to be quick with their bombing. And pilots were told that the wind speed was expected to increase to 70 mph over the French coast on the way home. At 00.59 hours two Mosquitoes were to mark Nürnburg with green target illuminators and eight other Mosquitoes would bomb the city one minute later. These aircraft were to release four bundles of *Window* per minute. The main force was also to use *Window*, dropping it at the rate of one bundle a minute and increasing it to two per minute when the planes were within 30 miles of the target. The duration of the attack would be from 01.05 hours to 01.22 hours, during which time Nürnburg was to be saturated with 3,000 tons of high explosives and incendiaries.

At Metheringham, 12 miles south-east of Lincoln, Pilot Officer 'Dick' Starkey and his crew on 106 Squadron had flown 21 operations. They had been scheduled to take part in a raid on Brunswick on the night of 29 March. However, four crews were on the last ten trips of their tours and it looked as though they would complete their tour at about the same time, so it was decided to stagger the remaining trips. Starkey's crew were therefore told to stand down for the Brunswick raid but this operation was then cancelled because the Met forecast was not good. On 30 March his Flight Commander told Starkey that his crew would be stood down. Starkey recalls:

I informed the lads of the order but as one man they said that as we had been a stand down crew for a cancelled operation one of the other crews should do so for the raid and they asked me to see the Flight Commander again. Although I had to decide whether or not to let the order stand, I agreed that we should be put on the Battle Order and gave my views to the Flight Commander. At first he said the order would not be reversed but after some thought he changed his decision.

Flight Sergeant C R 'Tubby' Holley of Southall was the rear-gunner in the Lancaster crew of Path Finder *D-Dog* on 156 Squadron at Upwood near Ramsey and captained by Squadron Leader Brooks, a former Hurricane pilot. Most of the crew were on their second tour of operations. Holley wrote:

Having just had a very welcome seven days' leave, I had to get up at 05.30 on 30th March to catch a train from Southall, which would get me to Kings Cross in time for the early train back to Huntingdon. After meeting our bomb-aimer and radar operator Flying Officer 'Blackie' Blackadder, a tall, well-built Birmingham man and our wireless operator Flight Lieutenant 'Robbie' Bagg we arrived at Upwood just after ten that morning to find to our intense disgust that we were down for 'ops' that night. Having just spent a hectic week on leave we were all feeling dead-beat and in need of a few days' rest. We cursed the clot who put off-leave crews on the 'blood-list'. We were not altogether happy either when we saw we were being routed on a few miles south of the Ruhr.

At Coningsby on 30 March Pilot Officer A E 'Ted' Stone on 61 Squadron had drawn his pay, travel vouchers and the Nuffield bounty for Pilot Officers and senior NCOs on operational leave and was about to go to his home in Bridgewater, Somerset. For seven days the regular Skipper and his crew of *N-Nan* could plan ahead comforted in the firm knowledge that they would see each dawn without remembering the odds against such likelihood. And with this confidence came a boisterous and carefree attitude. But just before Ted Stone and his crew left camp he was called into the CO's office where Wing Commander R N Stidolph asked him to delay crew leave for 24 hours and fly a maximum effort operation later that night. In return Stidolph promised that upon their return to Coningsby the following morning, he would have a 'sprog' crew fly Ted to the nearest airfield to his home. Stone agreed though he and every-one else at aircrew level did not know what the target of the maximum effort was. Coningsby dispatched 14 Lancasters altogether. Sergeant Len Whitehead, a mid-upper gunner on one of these Lancasters, had already taken part in the Leipzig raid on 19 February with a loss of 79 aircraft and the Berlin raid of 24 March with a loss of 75.

Flight Lieutenant Stephen Burrows DFC of Evesham, the flight-engineer on *Y-Yorker*, one of 16 Lancasters dispatched by 44 Squadron at Dunholme Lodge, was on his second tour of operations. *Y-Yorker*'s pilot was 27-year-old Wing Commander F W Thompson DFC AFC who was from Blackpool. Flying Officer William Clegg the 25-year-old bomb aimer was a bank clerk from Manchester. Another ex-clerk and fellow Mancunian, 23-year-old Pilot Officer Peter Roberts was the wireless-operator. The mid-upper gunner was 23-year-old Flight Sergeant Middleham who was a factory hand from Leeds. Flight Sergeant Tony Stancer, the 22-year-old navigator had been a London office clerk. Flight Sergeant J Hall the rear-gunner was a mill hand from Yorkshire. This crew would face added hazard in that they had been detailed to photograph and assess the bombing of Nürnburg after they had made their own bombing-run, which meant that they would have to fly back over the target while the raid was still on. Stephen Burrows adds: 'We were told it was to be a "maximum effort" deep into enemy territory and this shook us a bit since the Leipzig raid was still fresh in our minds. Although our crews were all second-tour types, we experienced the usual butterfly feeling in our stomachs. "Bloody hell!" remarks filled the air as crews entered the briefing room and saw the target map.'

Flight Sergeant Thomas N H 'Tom' Fogaty DFM, Skipper of a 115 Squadron Lancaster crew – average age 23 – operating from Witchford near Ely, recalled: 'Frankly, we were shaken when we saw that we were going straight to Nürnburg without any of the usual diversions; even though we were assured that there would be ten-tenths cloud cover for most of the way.'

Fogaty, who has been described by another man in his crew as 'a brave man but in a sense a very ordinary one, just a level-headed man from Devon,' had flown 13 operations. He had been awarded the DFM for bringing back a crippled Stirling in January after it had been attacked by a night fighter while bombing Brunswick. The bomber was hit in many places, one engine was rendered useless, the front and mid-upper turrets were put out of action and the aircraft became filled with smoke but Fogaty succeeded in evading the attacker and he reached Witchford, where he effected a masterly landing. In the first three months that 115 Squadron had operated Lancasters nearly 30 were missing or written off in accidents in one of the highest casualty rates in Bomber Command.

At Mildenhall 21-year-old Pilot Officer Oliver V Brooks, a Lancaster pilot on XV Squadron, and his crew, waited for the off. Brooks, who was from Hampshire where he was raised and educated, had left school at the age of 17 and worked for a short time as a temporary civil servant at the Royal Naval Armament Depot at Corsham near Bath in Wiltshire. A keen amateur boxer, he did not think his eyesight was good enough for pilot training and he considered becoming a RAF physical training instructor but he was accepted and in 1942 he honed his flying skills in the USA and Canada. In April 1943 Brooks formed his first crew at 12 OTU at Edgehill, a satellite to Chipping Warden, when their mount was the old Wimpy. Unfortunately, their time together was brief because Brooks had fractured his hand in a 'Wings For Victory' boxing tournament. The injury, which put him back two months, most likely saved his life. Crews were being fed into 3 Group, which at that time was operating Stirlings, and the 'chop' rate was very high. He had no idea what happened to his original crew and could only assume that they found another pilot.[4]

Brooks took a new crew with him when he resumed flying Wellingtons in July: Flight Sergeant Ken Pincott was navigator; Robert Allan Gerrard, who was engaged to be married, was the Canadian bomb aimer; Harry 'Whacker' Marr, air gunner and Les Pollard, wireless operator. Later, at 1651 HCU at Waterbeach, Sergeant C H 'Chick' Chandler the flight engineer and Ron Wilson the mid-upper gunner joined the crew. In February Sergeant Robert Edward Barnes replaced Pollard as wireless operator. Brooks' first operation on the Lancaster was on the night of 20/21 January when he took *O-Orange* to Berlin and back. This would be the aircraft they would fly on the Nürnburg operation.

The Path Finder Force was led by 23-year-old Wing Commander 'Pat' Daniels DSO DFC*, Commanding Officer of 35 PFF Squadron at Graveley, in *S-Sugar*. On hearing about the planned straight route he had warned that the force might well suffer 'the highest chop rate ever'. Daniels and Squadron Leader Keith Creswell DSO DFC, who flew *B-Beer*, were the primary visual markers, responsible for finding the target and marking it for their supporters in the Path Finder Force. Shortly after 18.00 hours –

three hours before 35 Squadron was due to taxi out at Graveley – Pat Daniels briefed the crews he was going to lead. He opened with a general pep-talk in which he emphasised the importance of the target they were going to attack and then he gave details of the types of flares and illuminators the Lancasters would carry and the precise times at which they would mark Nürnburg. With a billiard cue in his hand he went over the route, tapping the wall-map to indicate places along the course, which were dangerously close to heavily defended areas and he ended with a brief warning: 'Eight hundred aircraft are going to Nürnburg tonight and if we are to avoid collisions it's important that you keep to your heights. Be particularly alert and weave your aircraft into gentle banks so that the gunners can get a better chance of seeing any night fighters that may be around. Good luck and a good trip.'

At Waddington Squadron Leader Arthur Doubleday DFC RAAF gathered his crew together. Outwardly introspective, Doubleday never felt any different before an operation 'other than for 'waiting to go into bat [when] the fast bowler looked a lot faster from the fence but when you get there it's not so bad.' He had married Miss Phyliss Buckle at Beckenham, Kent in August 1943 after first flying 31 ops and completing his tour. The Doubledays had enjoyed four months of marriage before Arthur flew to Berlin on the first operation of his second tour. Arthur was now the 'B' Flight Commander on 467 Squadron RAAF in 5 Group. 'Look boys,' Doubleday said to his crew, 'it's on for young and old tonight. Just keep your eyes on the sky.'[5]

The first Lancaster off rolled down the runway at Elsham Wolds near Hull precisely at 21.16. The airfield's flare-path twinkled below, tiny blue ghostly needles of light, rapidly vanishing as the wispy, swirling cloud base embraced each aircraft. Then they broke out of the blanket of grey vapour. Some did not. At Skellingthorpe, where 19 Lancasters on 50 Squadron were dispatched, Flight Sergeant Geoff Bucknell crashed on take-off after a tyre burst and his Lancaster skidded out of control and was subsequently struck off charge. This Lancaster, in part funded from Andover's magnificent total of £232,787 raised in a 'Wings for Victory' campaign and which had completed 47 operational sorties, thus became the first aircraft lost on the operation. None of the Australian pilot's crew was injured. Bucknell and his crew later went to the Path Finders. All were killed on a daylight raid on Bois de Cassan on 6 August 1944 when they were shot down by flak near Paris.

Sergeant Ernest D Rowlinson of Northenden was the 22-year-old wireless operator on H-Harry on 50 Squadron flown by Flight Lieutenant George Charles 'Chas' Startin, an Australian from Tarbingar, Queensland. Rowlinson recalls: 'There was the usual back-chat among the crews but at the same time there was a feeling of tiredness amongst us. My crew had been on 50 Squadron only a fortnight yet this was to be our seventh night on flying duties and our fifth operation – one of which was on Berlin a few nights earlier.' At the briefing he remembered that there was surprise expressed by many when the curtain concealing the route was drawn aside to reveal that they would be flying just south of the Ruhr. But anxieties had been allayed to some extent when they were told that thick cloud cover was forecast for most of the way.

Flight Sergeant Les Bartlett, a bomb-aimer/front gunner on 50 Squadron, flew on the raid as a rear gunner: 'At 22.00 we taxied out and were first airborne. We crossed the enemy coast and it was eyes wide open.'

As soon as the intense bomber activity in the Norwich area was picked up by the forward *Würzburg* radars of the 1st *Jagdkorps* the German cathode ray tubes had lit up with hundreds of blips, each one representing a RAF bomber. The blips moved along an easterly heading and then converged over the northern part of the English Channel. The H_2S plotters reported the enormous stream, which was estimated at 'approximately 700 bombers' passing over the Belgian coast between the mouth of the Scheldt and Oostende between 23.10 and 23.50 hours. Of the original force of 782 heavy bombers that had taken off, 57 had already aborted with engine failure, oxygen supply problems and unserviceable radar sets and so on. At Lissett, East Yorkshire, twenty Halifaxes on 158 Squadron were dispatched but four turned back with mechanical problems. Only eight would complete the operation. Sergeant Reginald Cripps was the rear gunner on *L-Love* flown by 26-year-old Flight Sergeant Stan Windmill, six foot tall and an ex-policeman. Cripps recalls: 'To the north and south of the bomber stream there was much searchlight activity as we crossed the coast. Visibility was very good and the moon was coming out so we could easily see the numbers on the aircraft flying near us.'

Once airborne each of the bombers' four engines beat steadily and monotonously through the night sky with only the occasional pitch up when they hit the slip-stream of another aircraft ahead upsetting the smoothness of their flight. When the stream crossed the Belgian coast the first fighters of NJG1 and NJG4 were sent up from their bases in the Low Countries on the orders of 3 JD, commanded by ex-Battle of Britain pilot, *Generalmajor* Walther Grabmann at his HQ at Deelen. At Zeist *Generalleutnant* Josef 'Beppo' Schmidt's 1st Fighter Corps HQ was also immediately alerted. The Bavarian was a personal friend of Hermann Göring and only a year earlier had commanded the Hermann Göring *Panzer* Division in Tunisia. Schmidt had studied the British radio messages that had been intercepted by the German listening stations, and the radar blips confirmed that a raid in some strength could be expected with the Ruhr the likely target. Over the next hour a total of 246 single and twin-engined aircraft were concentrated in waiting areas, predominantly near Bonn (radio and light beacons *Ida*) and Frankfurt (radio and light beacons *Otto*).

As the blips on German radar headed over the Scheldt estuary to the Liège–Florennes line Schmidt's staff decided, correctly, that a smaller RAF formation in the southern sector of the North Sea approaching the Heligoland Bight must consist of mine laying aircraft. Jamming was carried out on a large scale but Mosquito 'spoof' attacks on Cologne, Frankfurt and Kassel were also identified for what they were because to the German defences they were apparently flying without H_2S. The heavies on the other hand could quite clearly be followed on radar by their H_2S bearings. As the bomber stream was clearly recognized from the start, the attempt was made to insert ('switch in') night fighters as far west as possible. All units of *3 Jagdkorps* at Deelen were switched in over radio beacon *Bonn*. *Generalmajor* Max Ibel's *2 Jagdkorps*, with its head-quarters in Stade, Hamburg, was brought near via radio beacons *Bonn* and *Osnabrück* and switched in by radio beacons *Bonn* and *Frankfurt* respectively. *1 Jagdkorps*, commanded by *Oberst* Hajo Herrmann at Berlin-Döberitz was brought near via radio beacons *Bonn* and *Harz* and switched in by a radar station north of Frankfurt, as was *7 Jagdkorps*, commanded by *Generalleutnant* Joachim Huth at Schleissheim near Munich. Single engined units from Oldenburg, Rheine and Bonn were directed via radio beacon Frankfurt to radio beacon *Nürnburg*. Night fighter units from Ludwigslust, Zerbst, Jüterborg and Wiesbaden were led directly to radio beacon *Nürnburg*.[6]

G-George, a veteran Lancaster on 460 Squadron RAAF was being flown on its 87th 'op' by Pilot Officer Neal of Melbourne, whose crew were on their eighth operation. Three more and if it made it back from Nürnburg, *G-George* would then be flown to Canberra to be exhibited in the Australian National War Museum. Aircraft on 460 also carried Australian names like *Anzac*, *Billabong Battler*, *Jumbuk*, *Kanga*, *Advance Australia* and *Jackass*. There was of course, *V-Victory*, with a kookaburra with a snake in its beak, and *K-Kitty* had a lion's head similar to the one that roars to introduce MGM movies.[7] *George* was reputed to have been flown by 29 different pilots and had 200 different men among its various crews. Neal's crew had the honour of flying this veteran Lancaster because *K-King*, their usual aircraft, was undergoing a major overhaul. The only other Australian on the crew was the navigator, Flight Sergeant W A Gourlay from Tasmania. The rest were Englishmen. One of them, Sergeant R E Holder the flight engineer, recalled:

As we crossed the coast at a height of 18,000 feet, climbing towards our operating band of 22,000 feet we saw a vast change in the weather. The sky in front of us was clear with hardly a trace of cloud. We expected the usual anti-aircraft fire from the coastal batteries but there was none. And we spotted many other bombers cruising along-side of us, though normally we never saw them until we neared the target.

The weather over Belgium and eastern France was 0/10ths to 4/10ths thin cloud while Holland and the Ruhr were cloudless. At Nürnburg there was 10/10ths cloud at 1,600 to 12,000 feet but the cloud veiled at 16,000 feet with generally good altitude visibility.

In the nose of *Y-Yorker* Tony Stancer studied his navigational charts, frowned, and leaned across his plotting-desk to take another reading from the *Gee* set in front of him. The former London office clerk quickly plotted it and then he flicked the switch on his oxygen mask that activated his intercom system and said: 'Navigator to Skipper. The Met forecast winds are all bull. Heavy tail winds have given us an incredible groundspeed. Unless we're to be well ahead of our ETA on the next turning point, we'll have to dog-leg. First dog-leg course coming up.'

Wing Commander Thompson asked if Stancer was quite sure of his calculations.

'Absolutely' replied Stancer.

Thompson then asked him whether the *Gee* set could be on the blink but Stancer assured his Skipper that he had checked and re-checked the set and that it was 'working perfectly'. Thompson knew he would now have to alter course 60° port for one minute and then swing 120° back: flying two sides of an equilateral triangle. It would lengthen their time to the first turning point, giving them two minutes to fly to a point they would otherwise have reached in half the time, but other aircraft would be doing the same thing and the collision risk would be high. The Wing Commander set the new course on his compass and swung the Lancaster in a gentle bank on to the first dog-leg. No sooner had he done so than Flight Sergeant Hall the rear-gunner reported on intercom: 'Unidentified aircraft coming towards us; port quarter.' Thompson was just about to throw the Lancaster into a violent corkscrew when he saw the massive shape of a Halifax as it zoomed 25 yards over the top of them.

'*Jeeze, that was close!*' someone gasped over the intercom.

Warrant Officer Jim McNab, a Scot among the Australians on 467 Squadron RAAF was not alone when he realised that the meteorological forecast was wrong. 'There was no cloud. It was so light that I could clearly read the squadron letters and identification numbers on the Lancasters flying next to us. One of our chaps said we were for it and he was right.'

'The forecast winds were not at all accurate and our navigator instructed the pilot to dog leg on at least two occasions' recalls Sergeant Len Whitehead. 'However, it was not as bad on this raid as it had been the week before on 24 March when we encountered a jet stream for the first time with winds far in excess of 100 mph, which caused the bomber stream to be spread over a vast area and was responsible for the heavy losses that night.'[8]

Squadron Leader Arthur William Doubleday adds: 'They started to fall within ten minutes of crossing the coast and from then to the target the air was not only of good visibility but seemed to be bright. The moon was really shining brightly although it wasn't a full moon.'

The first *Nachtjäger* reported making contact close to Liège, which was the start of a running battle that lasted 90 minutes until 01.30 hours. On the long 400 kilometre leg from Namur to the target, the *Nachtjagd* would shoot down 79 bombers. After the war General Schmidt said triumphantly, 'The flaming enemy aircraft served as flares, illuminating the bomber stream for the approaching German fighters.'

Wing Commander 'Pat' Daniels at the controls of *S-Sugar* had just made the course change at Charleroi when he saw before him a brilliant orange-coloured flash. Tracer hosed across off to port and then another dazzling splash of fire split the darkness. Moments later there was an explosion as a bomber blew up and was followed quickly by another. Daniels switched on his intercom and said: 'Skipper to navigator. Log on the chart two bombers going down in quick succession.' He then warned his gunners to keep a sharp look-out, telling them that as there was no flak to be seen the bombers must have been shot down by fighters.

The second of these was most likely the Lancaster flown by Flight Lieutenant Bruce Simpson DFC RAAF and crew on 467 Squadron RAAF at Waddington who were on their 22nd operation. They were attacked at Werbomont-Stoumont at 00.13 hours by *Oberleutnant* Richard Delakowitz of 7./NJG4 for the first of his two '*Lanki*' victories this night. Simpson and his whole crew bailed out before the Lancaster crashed and blew up near Spa in Belgium. The second victim, which crashed north-east of Spa eight minutes earlier, was the first of three Lancasters shot down by 26-year-old *Oberleutnant* Martin Drewes. The former *Zerstörer* pilot had transferred to *Nachtjagd* at the end of 1941 and had been appointed *Gruppenkommandeur* of III./NJG1 on 1 March. After taking off from Laon-Athies, Drewes headed for FF (*Funk Feuer*) *Ida* just south of Aachen, a route which crossed the bomber stream's path into Germany. His crew in the Bf 110 consisted of the *Bordschütze*, *Oberfeldwebel* Georg Petz and 24-year-old *Oberfeldwebel* Erich Handke, his *Bordfunker*. Handke has written:

There was no feeling of hate against the bomber crews. We knew that they also believed they were doing their duty. Our whole ambition was to get as many bombers down as quickly as possible so as to save the lives of civilians and prevent those senseless destructions.

We had been told by the running commentary that the bombers were about five minutes away. I hadn't even switched on the radar set when Petz poked me in the back and pointed, 'There he is up there, the first one!' As we came round we saw another straight away, about 200 metres directly above.

It was *N-Nan*, a 550 Squadron Lancaster flown by Flight Sergeant Arthur Harrington Jeffries CGM who was from Wantage, Berks. The crew were on their 19th operation. Handke continues:

> I switched on my set but we had dropped 2,000 metres behind in the turn and had lost them. When the set warmed up I saw three targets on it at once. I headed for the nearest and Drewes picked it up at 600 metres. Weather was marvellous – clear sky, half-moon, little cloud and no mist – it was simply ideal, almost too bright. It was a Lancaster flying nicely on a steady course so that when we were comfortably positioned underneath and from about fifty metres Drewes opened fire with the upward firing cannon at one wing which immediately caught fire. We followed the Lancaster for five minutes until it crashed below with a tremendous explosion.

Jeffries and three crew members were killed instantly in the explosion. The three survivors were thrown out as the Lancaster blew up, Sergeant S A Keirle sustaining very serious stomach, rib and leg injuries.

Handke continues:

> It was always a sinister feeling to hang only 30 to 50 metres under a Lancaster, always expecting fireworks: but nothing of the kind ever happened. I always navigated my pilot to approximately 200 metres below the enemy aircraft. When about 50 metres below the bomber's port wing we opened fire, aiming between the two engines into the fuel tanks; and then we dived directly to port to make sure that the burning aircraft did not hit us. With this kind of attack we always shot first, where in theory the tail-gunner should have spotted us first.

Ten minutes after Drewes had shot down his first victim of the night Handke saw another Lancaster. It was a 9 Squadron aircraft being flown by Flying Officer Jimmy Ling, a 23-year-old Scot from Newmilns, Ayrshire. The crew, who were on their 25th operation, had taken off from Bardney at 22.05 hours. Ling, who had made ten trips to Berlin, did not know that their Lancaster was above Drewes' Bf 110 and on the same course. Handke continues:

> We got fifty metres under it again but the cannon jammed after the second shot and could not be reloaded. The Lancaster must have been hit however, as it lost height quickly. But as we kept behind it, not having turned off in time, it must have spotted us, for suddenly it twisted into a corkscrew. We also dropped 600 metres. At 550 metres the Lancaster seemed to steady and we had to overcome the compulsion to attack in our old way – where one was exposed to the fire

of the tail-gunner. But we were already well used to the new tactics of firing into the wings, which did not endanger us so much when the bomber's load went off. At long last Drewes raised the nose of our fighter and fired a long burst with his front armament into the bomber's starboard wing, which burst into flame. For a second or so he forgot to dive away but there was no return fire from the rear-turret. The Lancaster's starboard inner engine dragged a banner of flame and its nose fell. As Drewes pulled away the Lancaster blew up, showering the sky with thousands of fiery fragments. I took a quick fix on my directional-finding gear and noted that the bomber had exploded in the air over the Vogelsberg area. Around us, bombers were dropping like flies sprayed with an insecticide gun.

Only one parachute came out of Ling's Lancaster. It was the navigator, Sergeant H Laws. The rest of the crew, including Sergeant Leonard Moss, who was 19 and from Moss Side, Manchester, and the tail gunner, Sergeant Italo Prada, a Londoner from St. Pancras, were killed. The Lancaster came down at Cleeburg, eight kilometres WNW of Butzbach.

After a while Handke spotted another bomber and navigated towards it. It was a 97 Squadron Lancaster, which was being flown by Flight Lieutenant Desmond Rowlands DFC of Kenton, Middlesex. His crew were mostly second-tourists who were on their third operation with the Path Finders. Flight Lieutenant Richard Algernon D Trevor-Roper DFC DFM, with his Oxford accent and Billingsgate vocabulary, had been a sergeant gunner at Swinderby before he was commissioned and became Guy Gibson's tail gunner on the Dams raid in May 1943. Handke continues:

> At 700 metres we could see it was another Lancaster. We were about to attack from the rear again when Petz announced that he had cleared the stoppage in our cannon. With the 'oblique' cannon working we could now attack from below and to the side of the bomber, with less risk of being seen. Drewes edged the night fighter closer and for a few seconds we were almost on parallel course. Unaware, the Lancaster flew on. Then Drewes raked it with a long burst aimed into the wing. Flames fanned from the engines along the fuselage to acknowledge the accuracy of his shooting. [Six bodies were later found near the main fuselage on the edge of a wood at Ahorn in the south-western suburbs of Coburg. The tail came down some distance away and Trevor-Roper's body was found in his rear turret.]

A minute after Drewes' third victim went down, 25-year-old *Oberst-leutnant* Helmut *Bubi* ('Nipper') Lent of *Stab*/NJG3 picked out a *Viermot*

THE 'NIGHT OF THE BIG KILL'

20–40 kilometres north of Nürnburg. Lent was eager to add to his score of 89 victories but he had been forced to wait on the ground at Stade until 23.40 hours before he was allowed to take off. And yet other pilots in NJG3 had by then already claimed seven kills. With Lent in the Bf 110 was *Feldwebel* Walter Kubisch, his 25-year-old *Funker*, a former black-smith and the son of a machine fitter, from Helbigsdorf in Saxony. The third member was *Leutnant* Werner Kark, a war correspondent and peace-time editor of *Oberdonau Zeitung*, a Hamburg newspaper, who flew as a trained *Bordmechaniker*. Kark, who had been attached to a series of front-line Luftwaffe units since 1940, flying many sorties as a full member of crew over England, Greece, Africa and Russia, made it a practice only to report from personal experience.

Lent's quarry at 01.21 hours, when the bombing was at its height, was a Halifax.[9] Kark's report of the night sortie, which included this graphic description of the shoot down, appeared in the *Oberdonau Zeitung* the next day:

> ... At the very moment that the *Funker* calls out to the pilot, 'There's one up there,' the aerial battle reaches a renewed climax. Below us the fires from the crashed bombers illuminate a thin covering of cloud. The flames of burning machines below it light it up blood-red. Around us it is as bright as day. Two, three, four combats have flared up very close to us. A fighter is just diving steeply down on its prey. To our starboard streams of tracer flash past our wings and above us we can make out the sharp outline of a Halifax swathed in flame from tail unit to cockpit. On our port side a bomber explodes in whirling fragments.
>
> Now we have picked up a prey of our own. Our foe seems to be overcome with fear. He is twisting and turning for his life in this inferno. But the *Oberstleutnant* doesn't let his victim off the hook. We follow him into a dive, pull up with him and go over on to the left wing, then the right one, so that everything in the cabin that is not fastened down floats up, ghost-like. Our target comes into our sights for a fraction of a second. Our pilot fires a long burst. Blood-red flashes streak from the barrels of our cannon. The shells hit his starboard wing, tear it off. For an instant, wreckage fills the air and then the bomber goes down vertically and hits the ground. There is a ball of fire on the earth, a thick black cloud of smoke from the explosion, the 87th night kill of *Oberstleutnant* Lent. When we get back to base the *Kommodore* is dissatisfied with himself and with the world. 'Our comrades shot too many down!' he says – and then laughingly adds that nevertheless tonight has been one of his great experiences with the *Nachtjagd*. We will never forget this night. Even less so will the British *Terrorfliegers*.[10]

'It was easy to approach bombers unseen', recalls *Oberleutnant* Fritz Brand, 'as we nearly always came in from below, where it was dark. Bombers did attempt to evade us by weaving and corkscrewing but we fighters stayed on their tails and flew in the same manner.'

'We always had the feeling that our task was worthwhile' asserts *Unteroffizier* Ulrich Hutze. 'We thought its success depended only on sufficient men and enough fuel. The night fighters came out of the dark like Indians and always had a feeling of superiority.'

Squadron Leader Keith Creswell was shocked by the number of flaming bombers he saw dropping from the sky and equally disturbed to see the 'bright sickle moon' being reflected by a carpet of cloud directly beneath him, which exposed his Lancaster to all and sundry. 'One would have been less embarrassed in Piccadilly Circus with one's trousers down,' he wrote later. 'The route was marked by burning or exploding aircraft and for the first time I was aware that great losses were taking place. I considered that my chances of returning were slim.'

Flight Lieutenant D F Gillam on 100 Squadron reported an unexpected hazard caused by freak weather:

We started leaving contrails at our allotted height of 19,000 feet. I decided to 'misinterpret' orders and get as much height as possible. We got up to about 22,000 feet, which was as high as we could get fully loaded. From there I could see a mass of contrails below us; they looked like a formation of American daylight bombers.

Another Lancaster pilot said:

As I looked down from my bomber, I could see the vapour trails of about a score of other bombers flying below me. That was the sort of night it was. Not only was there a moon to help the enemy but also their pilots could occasionally track us down from our vapour trails. We knew then that we would have to blast our way through to Nürnburg. All this was fairly early in the flight. Then to our port we saw our first combat. Tracer darted across the sky and an aircraft began to glow red in the night. Down it went in flames and my mid-upper gunner was sure that it was a fighter. Most of the fighters seemed to have been waiting for us on the outskirts of the Ruhr and it was here the battle began in earnest. While enemy searchlights raced across the gaps in the cloud in the hope of picking up any bomber that might have strayed off course, the fighters flew in to the attack. We found that they had already started dropping their flares; most of which were going down in clusters of three; and the fighters were laying them as close to our route as they possibly could. It wasn't safe to relax for a single moment.[11]

Flight Sergeant Les Bartlett continues:

As we drew level with the south of the Ruhr Valley, things began to happen. Enemy night fighters were all around us and in no time at all, combats were taking place and aircraft were going down in flames on all sides. So serious was the situation that I remember looking at the other poor blighters going down and thinking to myself that it must be our turn next, just a question of time. A Lancaster appeared on our port beam converging, so we dropped 100 feet or so to let him cross. He was only about 200 yards or so away on our starboard beam when a string of cannon shells hit him and down he went. We altered course for Nürnburg and I looked down at the area over which we had just passed. It looked like a battlefield. There were kites burning on the deck all over the place, bombs going off where they had been jettisoned by bombers damaged in combat and fires from their incendiaries across the whole area. Such a picture of aerial disaster I had never seen before and hoped never to see again.

On the way to the target the winds became changeable and we almost ran into the defences of Schweinfurt but we altered course just in time. The defences of Nürnburg were nothing to speak of; a modest amount of heavy flak, which did not prevent us doing our normal approach and we were able to get the Target Indicators dropped by the Path Finder Force in our bombsight to score hits with our 4,000lb 'Cookie' and our 1,000lb bombs.

Pilot Officer J Howell of Hobart, Tasmania said: 'We could see combats going on all round us. We spotted a FW 190 on our port side. It started to turn in underneath us but our mid-upper gunner had it well covered as it made a diving turn. Then the fighter tried again from the other side but before it could make the attack we cork-screwed into it and gave it the slip.'

Flight Sergeant Bob Whinfield of Newcastle-upon-Tyne, on his 13th trip as a Lancaster pilot on 619 Squadron, was fascinated by what he believed to be 'scarecrow rockets'; but they were Lancasters exploding, of which he said:

They came up like flares and hung in the sky. Then they burst and scattered on the ground, like clusters of incendiaries. The explosion of one of them as it hit the ground looked almost as if a one-thousand-pounder was going off. There was just one damned thing after another, all the way to the target and on the journey home. Tracer showed that air-combats were going on all the time and still more lights of various colours were being shot up as signals from enemy airfields as we passed overhead.[12]

Flight Sergeant Ronald Gardner the 19-year-old wireless operator from Tooting, London on 32-year-old Flying Officer Leonard Young's crew on 103 Squadron, whose 19th operation this was, recalled:

The fighters were waiting for us shortly after we crossed the coast, as if they already knew our target and route. And they were in force. Never have I seen so many gathered at one point during my tour of operations. We were attacked about three or four times but as soon as the fighters knew by our evasive action that we were alert they seemed to sheer off to look for less vigilant crews. Everything was fine until we left the coast. The clouds we had been flying in suddenly broke and the sky was absolutely clear and it was full of Me 109s and 110s. Normally, flying in the leading wave, we were seldom attacked by fighters until well into France or Germany. This raid was the only one in thirty operations when I could see in large numbers our fellow bombers. I counted fifteen of them being shot down within fifteen minutes of crossing the enemy coast. The losses I think were increased by pilots ramming their throttles through the gate to get more speed and burning their exhaust stubs off. Then they were lit up like Christmas trees and easy targets. Usually the fighters took at least half an hour to get amongst us. But this time they seemed to be waiting in strength ...[13]

Flight Sergeant C P Steedman, a Lancaster bomb-aimer of Parry Town, Ontario, Canada on his 26th operational flight, recalled:

We were on our run-up when we saw one particularly large explosion in the target area. At the time, the whole area was covered by cloud and the target was further obscured by the condensation trails left by our bombers; which criss-crossed over the target and caused a layer of haze through which we had to fly – but the light of this explosion flashed up in a bright orange glow. It lasted for some seconds.

Flight Sergeant Edgar Oberhardt RAAF of Maryborough, Queensland, Australia, a Lancaster rear gunner on 460 Squadron, reported:

We were going in to bomb when we saw a Junkers 88 about 350 yards away. I warned my Skipper and gave the fighter a burst as it came in from the port side. Then it went over to starboard. I had my guns trained on it as it snooped below. I saw tracer going through its fuselage and it soon made off. Other combats were going on near us at the same time. A shell from the Junkers went through our starboard wing, near the starboard inner engine and left a very large hole. A few minutes later, the engine began to get troublesome and we had to feather it. In the end it stopped altogether. We made our way home on three engines.[14]

Another Australian, Flight Sergeant Norman David L Lloyd of Winton, Northern Queensland, a Lancaster pilot on 460 Squadron RAAF recalled:

During our run-up, I was told that a fighter had seen us. It kept away until we had dropped our bombs and then came for us. It was a FW 190. My gunners were ready for it and after a sharp exchange of fire it made off. A few minutes later, another fighter took up the challenge. It was a better stayer than the first one and we didn't shake it off until it had followed us for about ten minutes.

Lloyd's luck and that of his crew were to run out on 3/4 May when they were shot down and killed coming home from Mailly-le-Camp.

Flight Lieutenant T R Donaldson of Brighton, Victoria, Australia, another Lancaster pilot, said: 'There were fighters all the way and they were making the most of the bright moon. I watched tracer flashing across the sky as, bomber after bomber fought its way to the target. The Germans were doing their damnedest to beat us off. Searchlights ... flak and fighters ...'

But Flight Lieutenant C G Broughan, a Halifax pilot from Sydney, Australia reported: 'There was cloud over the city but it was broken. Through the gaps we saw fires getting a firm hold. The Path Finders had marked out the area with sky and ground markers and though there had been scores of fighters along the route, there were not enough of them over the target to interfere seriously with the bombing.'

Nürnburg, as far as the *Nachtjagd* was concerned, was the 'night of the big kill'. Despite the British jamming the first interception of the bomber stream in the area south of Bonn was successful. From there on in the bomber stream was hit repeatedly and the majority of the losses occurred in the Giessen–Fulda–Bamberg area. A staggering 82 bombers were lost *en route* to and near the target.

Flight Lieutenant Reginald George 'Tim' Woodman on 169 Squadron, who with Flying Officer Pat Kemmis, his navigator-radar operator, were in a Mosquito night fighter supporting the operation, noted:

Instead of the bomber stream being five miles wide it was more like fifty. Some had already been shot down and before I reached to the far side of the stream they were being shot down on my left. Masses of *Window* were being tossed out of the bombers, which also jammed our radar. Twice we tried to turn *Serrate* contacts into AI contacts but, with all the bombers there, it was odds of twenty to one against it being a Hun. Twice I came up under bombers but turned away before the rear gunners saw me. 100 Group Mossies were Huns to the bomber boys. The third time we came up below a bomber the rear gunner spotted us, his tracer coming uncomfortably close whilst his pilot did a corkscrew. It was hopeless; we were doing more harm than good. Ahead the bombers were being shot down one after another, some going all the way down in flames, some blowing up in the air, the rest blowing up as they hit the ground. I counted 44 shot down on this leg to Nürnburg. What was happening behind I could only guess ... I was inwardly raging at the incompetence of the top brass at Bomber Command.

Woodman failed to add to his score of three victories but a 239 Squadron crew had better luck. Flight Sergeants J Campbell DFM and R Phillips on 239 Squadron picked up a Ju 88 on AI near beacon *Ida.* Campbell and Phillips attacked once but missed and lost their contact. A few minutes later they again found and attacked a Ju 88. It was a 4./NJG3 Ju 88C-6 piloted by *Oberleutnant* Ruprecht Panzer. His rear gunner was alert and put just seven bullets into the Mosquito, setting one the engines on fire. But this time Campbell and Phillips had not missed. One of the Jumo engines exploded and the Mossie crew were able to see the 88 fall all the way to the ground where it crashed and exploded 10 kilometres south-west of Bayreuth and only a short distance from beacon *Ida.* The Mosquito's engine fire was extinguished and the fighter nursed safely to West Raynham on one engine. Panzer, who was wounded in action, his *Bordfunker* and *Bordschütze* all bailed out safely.[15]

Oberleutnant Martin 'Tino' Becker, *Staffelkapitän*, 2./NJG6 took off from Finthen airfield near Mainz on a *Tame Boar* sortie with his *Bordfunker Unteroffizier* Karl-Ludwig Johanssen in a Bf 110 not yet fitted with *Schräge Musik.* Becker, whose current score stood at 19 victories and who eight nights earlier had shot down six bombers when Frankfurt had been raided, was guided by 3 JD into the bomber stream to the south of FF *Ida.* There they intercepted and shot down six bombers between 00.20 and 00.50 hours in *Zahme Sau* fashion. Becker's first victim, south-west of Cologne, was the 427 'Lion' Squadron Halifax flown by Squadron Leader Jack Montgomery Bissett DFM, a Canadian from St. Vital, Manitoba. This crew, who had previously flown a tour on 78 Squadron, were on their fourth operation of their second tour. Becker slid across into his favoured final attacking position and fired two bursts into the Halifax in rapid succession before either of the gunners could react. The Halifax reared up and climbed at a crazy angle for a few seconds and then slipped into a wild glide before turning over, its fuselage a mass of flames. The Halifax crashed at Herhahn, four kilometres NNW of Schleiden. Bissett and his crew were killed.

While Johanssen was recording that the Halifax had hit the ground between Lüttich and north of Frankfurt, Becker, who had seen the silhouette of another *Viermot* about 400 metres away, was already lining up his next victim. It was a Halifax III on 51 Squadron, which was being flown by Sergeant Jack Percival George Binder, who was from Moulton, Northants. Banking the 110 into attacking position, Becker kept the Halifax in sight but for some quick glances in his immediate vicinity. It was clear of other aircraft so he closed in and opened fire. He saw a flush of orange flame smear along its starboard wing. Another arm of fire reached from its outer engine as the Halifax went out of control and into a shallow cork-screw dive. Becker swung the 110 round and from close range pumped another withering burst into the stricken bomber. The nose of the Halifax went down and the bomber plunged almost vertically to the ground, south-east of Rosbach. All the crew, who were on their third operation, were killed. Johanssen recorded that the Halifax hit the ground at 00.23. As they looked down at the burning wreckage Becker and Johanssen saw six other bombers fall within seconds of each other.

Five kilometres north-east of Bad Hönningen at 00.33 hours the crack night fighter team picked out their third victim of the night. It was Lancaster *T-Tare* on 50 Squadron at Skellingthorpe, flown by 22-year-old Flight Sergeant Donald George Gray, from Ilford, Essex. That morning when he found out that he and his crew were 'on' Gray thought that 'at least it wasn't Berlin' and that this first operation 'might be an easy one'. Gray had been bored with his job as an RAF Training Command staff pilot and then a classroom instructor in navigation. He had wanted 'action' but his natural aptitude as a navigator had kept him off operational flying, until that is, he made himself enough of a nuisance by indulging in some unauthorized low flying, which resulted in a reprimand and a posting to a Conversion Unit. He had been promoted to Warrant Officer but the notification had not yet come through. The crew had not had leave for three months and had not been allowed to leave camp for 14 days after their arrival at Skelly, in case they were sent on a cross-country flying exercise. On Thursday evening, 29 March, some members of the crew decided to visit pubs in Lincoln and Gray was ordered to get them back as Wing Commander A W Heward wanted them for flying duties. Early on the morning of 30 March Gray escorted his wayward crew-members to the Orderly Room to see the CO only to be told that he was too busy to see them.

That same evening Donald Gray was sitting in the Sergeant's Mess having tea when a young WAAF reputed to be a 'chop-girl' began chatting to him. From that moment on he regarded the coming op with trepidation. At take-off time the friendly WAAF was at the forefront of well-wishers who had waved the Lancasters off. Soon after take-off Sergeant Bert Wright, the WOp, discovered that his *Fishpond* set (used to indicate enemy aircraft below the bomber) was not working properly. Then the intercom connection to the rear turret was found to be faulty and Sergeant Douglas Maugham, the rear gunner was given another helmet but Bert Wright reported that Maugham was losing consciousness. By this time they were at 22,000 feet, skirting the edge of the heavy flak defences south of Aachen. Sergeant Joseph Grant the flight engineer took a portable oxygen bottle and made his way to the rear. Within a couple of minutes Wright reported that the flight engineer too, was unconscious. *T-Tare* was now on course for Fulda, about 90 miles NNW of Nürnburg. Suddenly, Frank Patey the mid-upper gunner shouted that they were being attacked and he began firing. Becker set the starboard outer engine on fire. Within seconds of being hit the Lancaster, which was still carrying a 'Blockbuster', exploded over Waldbreitbach, a village in picturesque countryside, twelve kilometres east of the Rhine town of Sinzig.

When Gray gave the 'Bail Out!' order, Flight Sergeant Alan Campbell the navigator, one of two Australians on the crew, clipped on his parachute and left his compartment to make his way forward to the bomb-aimer's position in the nose of the Lancaster. Through the pilot's window he could see long tongues of blue and yellow flame streaming back from the starboard wing and reaching almost to the tail. The bomb-aimer, Flight Sergeant George Wallis, a fellow Aussie, was trying to open the escape hatch, but it would not move. As he threw up his hands in a gesture of failure there was a 'Whomp!' and Campbell was propelled forward, down the steps into the nose. He hit something hard. There was pressure, flame, disorientation and then – nothing. He opened his eyes. The stars were above: all was quiet, no sound and no sense of motion. Not certain whether he was clear of the aircraft, Campbell pulled the ripcord anyway. There was a jerk and he looked up and in the moonlight to see 'the glorious great canopy billowing above him!' Below Campbell was another parachute. Campbell landed in a quiet German countryside. The time by his watch was 00.30. Campbell had a cut head, facial scratches, swollen right arm, sore knee and a painful kidney. His parachute was tangled in bushes and Campbell gave up the task of getting it out of sight. He cut pieces off as souvenirs and headed west towards the Rhine. Then a figure loomed up. Campbell raised his hands, explaining he was an RAF navigator from a shot-down Lancaster. But the figure placed a hand on his shoulder and said: 'Don't panic Al, it's me, George!' It was Wallis, who had escaped through the shattered nose after the explosion. The two crewmen headed for the Rhine, but it was not long before they were spotted and escorted to a police station in Neuweid, on the east bank of the Rhine north of Koblenz. From there they were sent to the Interrogation Centre at *Dulag Luft* and finally to *Stalag Luft VI* at Heydekrug on the Baltic, where they arrived on Easter Sunday 1944 to await the end of the war and liberation.

Gray had also managed to get out and almost landed head first on an Autobahn. He was quickly captured by four elderly *Volksturm*. The other four members of the crew were killed.[16]

Becker and Johanssen's fourth kill, which followed at 00.35 hours, five miles north-east of Bendorf, was a 622 Squadron Lancaster flown by Pilot Officer John Sutton, who was from Newport on the Isle of Wight. The Lancaster crashed at Mönchengladbach, five kilometres east-south-east of Wetzlar. Sutton and his crew, who were on their 12th operation, were all killed.

Johanssen checked the fuel gauges and warned Becker that he had enough fuel left to keep him for one more kill but it would have to be a quick one.

Minutes later, Becker scored his fifth victory of the night. It was MH-Z^2, a Halifax on 51 Squadron, which was being flown by Flight Sergeant Edward Wilkins, an Australian from Maleny, Queensland. Becker gave the Halifax a five-second burst and the wing wheeled up and tilted over. Johanssen logged its time of impact on the ground 12 kilometres WNW of Wetzlar as 00.40 hours. All the crew, who were on their sixth operation, were killed. Although Becker now had little fuel remaining Johanssen picked up a blip on his radar screen almost at once and quickly guided Becker to the *Viermot* ten kilometres northwest of Alsfeld. It was MH-QZ, another 51 Squadron Halifax which was being flown by Flight Sergeant Geoffrey Graham Brougham RAAF of Marouba, New South Wales. The crew were on their first operation. Becker framed it in his sights and gave it a five-second burst. Brougham and four crew were killed with two men surviving to be taken prisoner. The Halifax crashed at Eisfeld, a small town on the east bank of the Werra, 19 kilometres NNW of Coburg. Johanssen logged its time of impact on the ground as 00.50. After returning to Mainz-Flinthen to re-fuel and re-arm, Becker and Johanssen took off on a second sortie, once more under *Himmelbett* control in *Raum* (Box) *Kauz* on the bombers' homeward track. South of Luxembourg they destroyed a Halifax III on 158 Squadron, which had been fired on over France by flak guns near Metz; *P-Peter* crashed at Eischen, 17 kilometres WNW of Luxembourg. Sergeant S Hughes, the pilot, and his crew who were on their eighth operation, were taken prisoner.

Next day 'Tino' Becker received news that he had been awarded the *Ritterkreuz*. 'There were such a lot of British bombers around that we could have knocked them down with a fly-trap' he said. He was decorated personally by the Führer at Hitler's HQ in East Prussia.[17]

Flight Lieutenant Burrows noted:

Combats appeared to be going on all around us, with aircraft blowing up as they received direct hits. Some exploded so close to us that *Y-Yorker* rocked alarmingly, as if every rivet would pop out from its socket. It was our duty to report each combat to the navigator, who logged the height, speed, time and position of it. But after the tenth was reported our Skipper told us to disregard them. The atmosphere was tense and I continued to report them. I was frightened out of my wits when Wing Commander Thompson dug me in the ribs and shouted, 'I said enough!' These conditions persevered for what seemed like ages. It was obvious to all of us that we were suffering alarming casualties with little or no cloud protection.

Jim Marshallsay DFC an experienced PFF pilot on 627 Squadron at Oakington was aloft in a Mosquito this night, as a *'Window* Opener' for the heavies with navigator Sergeant Nigel 'Nick' Ranshaw by his side as usual. Marshallsay recalls:

As we turned onto the 'long leg' we realized that something was going badly wrong. The moon was much too bright for the heavies. The expected cloud cover was not there. The Main Force was leaving persistent condensation trails, so there was a great white road in the air, leading into Germany. Combats soon broke out below us. As this was our 38th trip we knew what was happening to the heavies. First a long burst of tracer from the night fighter, then a ripple of flame from the wings of the Lanc' or Halifax. There was a short interval and then a massive explosion and fire on the ground. Nick logged the first few crashes but after we had seen 16 go down in six minutes, he stopped, preferring to use his time and eyes searching for fighters.[18]

Basil Oxtaby on 467 Squadron said that 'it was common to see four or five Lancasters or Halifaxes going down in flames, sometimes with three or four engines on fire, exploding on the ground. That made it even worse because when the aircraft exploded, there was a pool of light for hundreds of yards and the fighters above could see bombers silhouetted against that light.' After his gunners had reported something like 20 going down, Freddie Watts, a pilot on 630 Squadron, told them not to report any more because he did not think it was doing very much for the morale of the crew. Ken Pincott, the navigator on *O-Orange* flown by Oliver Brooks, was advised by his Skipper to stop recording the number of aircraft being shot down. 'I believe', says Pincott 'that I logged fifty such positions before reaching the target.' Flying Officer George Foley, sitting in his curtained-off and isolated H_2S position of a Path Finder Lancaster, was shocked to hear his pilot call over the intercom: 'Better put your parachutes on chaps, I've just seen the forty-second one go down.'

The navigator on *M-Mother* on 78 Squadron, one of 16 Halifaxes that had taken off from Breighton, had also given up logging bombers that had been shot down. The pilot was Squadron Leader Cooper DFC who was on his second tour of operations. Flight Sergeant Ramsden, the wireless operator, was a veteran of the Berlin raids and during the early part of these operations was usually completely absorbed by crossword puzzles in the *Daily Mirror*, but although Nürnburg meant relatively little to him as a target, for once he found it too unnerving to concentrate. Then he picked up two blips on his *Fishpond*, a second H_2S cathode ray tube indicator which showed other aircraft as spots of light. A night fighter was obviously circling a bomber. Then the blips disappeared from the radar screen.[19] Flight Lieutenant F Taylor, the squadron gunnery leader who had replaced the regular tail-gunner who had reported sick, confirmed that he had just seen a bomber going down in flames four miles to their port quarter. A little later Ramsden picked up a suspicious contact almost dead astern and it was closing rapidly from a range of half a mile. Ramsden warned the rear-gunner and Taylor fired his four Brownings at the angle given to him by the wireless operator. 'He's on fire! Going down to port!' Taylor shouted. Ramsden jerked back his blackout curtain and peered through the porthole to see a FW 190 as it hurtled under their wing tip in a mass of flames. Ramsden wrote later that 'another five seconds on that course and we could have thrown cream-puffs at him.'[20]

It seemed to Ernest Rowlinson on *H-Harry* that more and more shoot downs were being logged with each minute. He had never seen a bomber blown up before so he eventually decided to leave his radio compartment on the port side of the aircraft for a moment and take a look to satisfy his morbid curiosity. He had hardly stepped into the astrodome when a bomber ahead of him exploded in flames and commenced its death dive. Severely shaken by what he saw Rowlinson hurriedly returned to his compartment and quickly busied himself with his *Fishpond*. At once a blip appeared on the 8-inch diameter radar screen, small at first but growing bigger by the second. It was closing on *H-Harry*. Rowlinson alerted Startin on intercom to tell the Australian that a fighter was approaching fast from 4 o'clock on their port quarter. Sergeant E Hopkinson the rear gunner shouted for them to corkscrew to port. He had seen the enemy night fighter clearly enough to identify it as a Bf 110. The blip now filled Rowlinson's screen and he jumped nervously as Hopkinson fired his four Brownings, quickly followed by those of Sergeant Ernest McIlwine, *H-Harry*'s short and stocky Irish mid-upper gunner from Armagh. Hopkinson informed Startin that the 110, possibly hit, had broken off the attack. Startin brought the Lancaster back on course and warned the crew to keep a sharp look out. He then asked his Canadian navigator, Pilot Officer T Evans, who was standing in for the regular navigator who was on the sick list, to give him a new course to the target. Dismayed, Startin noticed that the moon was getting brighter.

Rowlinson's *Fishpond* now decided to go out and the screen went completely blank but he knew that the picture would fade if the rear escape-hatch accidentally opened and let in cold air to blow on the transmitter and cool the valves, so he went back to check. Sure enough, the escape-hatch door was wide open. Twice he tried to grasp the open door, missing it each time because the Lancaster lurched. The exertions of clambering around the weaving Lancaster to the hatch door and trying to shut it while using a portable oxygen bottle made it heavy going and he had left his parachute in his radio compartment, so one false move and he would have been whisked away into the night. On the third attempt Rowlinson got the door shut but the effort had exhausted him and he had to rest before returning to the nose of the aircraft.[21]

Sergeant R C Corker, a flight engineer in a Halifax on 578 Squadron at Burn was another who experienced a fighter attack: 'Without any warning at all, we were attacked from underneath; there was an enormous bang as a cannon shell exploded in the starboard-inner and four or five pieces caught me in the fleshy part of the bottom. The fighter shot across our nose and attacked another Halifax about 11 o'clock high from us. It blew up. He had made the two attacks in about 20 seconds.'

Squadron Leader Philip Goodwin, who had been married for just six weeks, was on his 47th operation flying as pilot of a PFF Visual Backer-up Lancaster on 156 Squadron and had just started his bomb run when the aircraft burst into flames. The night fighter's one long burst of cannon fire also killed Warrant Officer Victor Gardner DFM the rear gunner. Goodwin ordered Flying Officer W C Isted DFM the visual-marker-bomb aimer to dump the bomb load but not the TIs, in case they confused the following bombers. Goodwin was pressed flat against the roof of his cockpit watching the trees and snow on the ground revolving as the Lancaster spun. Luckily, he was wearing a seat-type parachute for the first time on operations and when the aircraft broke up he and Isted and two others on the crew were out before it was too late. The other three men on the crew died in the aircraft.

Pilot Officer 'Dick' Starkey and his Lancaster III on 106 Squadron crew continuously operated the 'banking search' looking for enemy aircraft coming up from below:

This was achieved by turning steeply to port for 15° to see if fighters were preparing to attack and then banking to return to the original course. Our *Fishpond* aircraft detector failed to work. We had been flying the long leg for many miles. When we were in a position 60 miles northwest of Nürnburg our luck changed. A fighter attacked with tracer and cannon fire, which hit the port main-plane and outer engine, flashed past outside the perspex covering of the cockpit and between my legs. I remember praying we would not go up in flames. However, within three or four seconds the port outer engine and main-plane were alight. It was always the one you didn't see that shot you down as in our case, and if *Monica* had been available we would have been aware of the fighter's approach. There was only one action to take; I gave the order to abandon aircraft.[22]

Starkey's Lancaster went down at Königsberg, eleven kilometres north-west of the centre of Giessen. He and his bomb aimer Sergeant Wally Paris were blown from the aircraft in the explosion and succeeded in opening their parachutes to land safely. The engineer, Sergeant 'Johnnie' Harris, who was from Biggleswade, Bedfordshire and who had handed Starkey a parachute from one of two in the rack at his side, must have been blown out like his pilot and the bomb aimer but his parachute had probably failed to open and he was killed. Sergeant Colin Roberts a Sheffield man and the crew's navigator, Sergeant Maitland 'Joe' Ellick the rear gunner, who was from Wallasey, Cheshire, Sergeant John 'Jock' Jameson of Stratford, London the mid-upper gunner and Sergeant George W 'Jock' Walker the wireless operator who was from Geddington, Northants, were killed by the burst of fire that Becker had slanted into the wing and which ran along the side of the aircraft.

Hauptmann Fritz Lau, now a Bf 110 night fighter pilot in II./NJG1 at Laon-Athies had also been kept waiting for the order to take off. It came at 23.00 hours. Lau and *Unteroffizier* Helmut Völler his *Bordfunker* and *Obergefreiter* Egon Reinecke his *Bordschütze* clambered aboard the Messerschmitt and in the pre-flight check that followed Lau cursed when he could see that the 110 had not been refuelled. A fuel bowser filled the tanks and when Lau finally got off the ground it was almost 23.54 hours. They flew for about 30 minutes until they saw an aircraft going down on fire. When they had reached about 5,500 metres Völler reported a contact on his radar set. Lau flew towards it and recognised it as a *Viermot*, whose pilot was weaving in 'crocodile line' at 20,000 feet. It was a Halifax.[23] Lau considered that the Halifax crew may have seen him but more likely the enemy pilot was weaving to fly through the many 'burn-ups' in the sky. Lau tried to get into an attack position but each time he thought he had got the *Viermot* in his sights, it moved out of them. At one moment he was 150 metres away, the next 200 metres. This continued for about two minutes. The Halifax weaved. Lau weaved. Gradually the German pilot came to the conclusion that he would lose him unless he did something quickly. He decided that the next time he got into a reasonably close position he would attack. The moment came when the Halifax, which was somewhat higher than the Bf 110, went into a gradual right-hand turn and Lau turned with him. The distance between them was now about 100 to 150 metres. Lau pulled in the stick, lifted the 110's nose and fired. Flames shot from the bomber and it went into a steep dive. Lau flew over the *Viermot* and he saw three of the crew bailing out. Before hitting the ground near Herbon-Seelbach south-west of Bonn the Halifax broke into two parts, of which one, the larger, again broke on impact so that in the end three parts of it were burning below. Only one man survived the bail out.

After he saw the first shoot-down Lau observed red flaming masses falling out of the sky almost every minute. When a German aircraft burned it flamed white. When an RAF aircraft burned, it burned dark red. There would be first an explosion on the ground as the *Viermot* hit and then bursts from the flames. A great row of these fires could be seen and they clearly marked out on the ground the course the bombers were flying. Lau was to see only two white 'burn-ups' this night.

Hauptmann Berthold *'Petz'* Ney of III./JG2 flying a Ju 88 claimed one of four 166 Squadron aircraft that failed to return to Kirmington, for his eighth victory. The Lancaster, one of 20 dispatched from Kirmington and which was flown by Flight Lieutenant F Taylor whose crew were on their 18th operation, went down at Weidenhahn, seven kilometres ESE of Herschbach. Two of the crew were killed. Taylor and four other crew members survived and they were taken prisoner. (In March 1945 Ney, who had 19 victories, was forced to bail out on his return from Operation *Gisela* over England when he could not find an airfield in the atrocious weather. He broke his back and never flew again.)[24]

The 14 Lancasters on 61 Squadron were experiencing varied fortune. It was normal for the gunners to report to the navigator when they saw an aircraft go down and give such details as to whether they saw any bail out, if it was flak, or if a fighter. On this occasion there were so many going down that Sergeant Len Whitehead's Skipper told them not to report, just concentrate on looking out for and avoiding attacks. He recalls:

It was difficult not to look at those going down but we knew we had to keep a careful watch. We would sometimes see some tracer fire and then a small flame which would quickly grow until it lit up the whole aircraft and then frequently would finish with a terrific explosion. Sometimes we were rather puzzled because we did not see any tracer fire and no flak; just the aircraft catching fire. It was not until years later that I learned that it was of course *Schräge Musik*. When using this no tracer was present so that it did not give away the form of attack. When an aircraft went down, or jettisoned the bombs, there would be a long line of incendiaries burning with bright silver and further illuminating the aircraft above.[25]

Near Cologne, *R-Robert* flown by Pilot Officer Donald Paul, passed night fighter-beacon *Ida* and was attacked by a Ju 88 night fighter. Over the next 15 minutes vigorous corkscrewing by the pilot and good work by the gunners managed to stave off two further attacks but during the defensive manoeuvres the Lancaster had lost altitude and suffered severe damage to two engines. Paul had to shut them both down. Still losing height and down to 10,000 feet the Skipper had no alternative but to jettison his bombs and turn for home. Later after throwing everything moveable out of the aircraft in order to maintain height and flying speed over the North Sea, Paul managed to land safely at Manston on the Kent coast.

The 'Gen Men' or 'Old Sweats' on *P-Peter* flown by Squadron Leader Edward Henry Moss DFC, an Oxford University graduate who had been a school master and whose crew were on their 20th operation, were all killed when shortly before midnight, *Hauptmann* Fritz Rudusch of 6./NJG6 flying a Bf 110 shot them down near Rimbach, north-west of Fulda. It was his first victory. A second followed just over an hour later when he destroyed a Halifax of 78 Squadron flown by Flight Lieutenant Harry McCormick Hudson RCAF, an American from Largo, Florida. The Lancaster crashed at Allendorf near Bad Kissingen and Flight Sergeant L Nugent was the only man to survive the shoot down.

German radar search equipment was proving very efficient and with it up to about four young and inexperienced crews could be directed into the bomber stream by older and more experienced night fighter crews. According to *Oberst im Generalstab* Janke, deputy commander and chief of staff of 7 JD, 'This equipment was used with much success by NJG6', who apart from 'Tino' Becker, accounted for about nine heavies on the Nürnburg raid.

NJG2 in 3 JD were equipped with the newer and faster Ju 88R-2 and had taken off from Quakenbrück at 23.41 hours with orders to patrol west of the Ruhr on a southerly heading. When almost at Aachen, *Oberleutnant* Günter Köberich with *Oberfeldwebel* Walter Heidenreich as *Bordfunker* and *Oberfeldwebel* Kramell as *Bordschütze*, picked up a contact five kilometres distant on the FuG 350 *Naxos Z* passive radar equipment. It was the first time that Köberich, who had a dozen victories, had flown the R-2 and the aircraft was one of the first to be fitted with *Schräge Musik*. Nearing Mainz at an altitude of 6,700 metres there was a shout of 'Lancaster! Lancaster!' from Köberich and Kramell. Almost dead ahead and slightly above them were two Lancasters flying in tight formation. The night fighter crew knew that they must be Path Finders. Both were from 156 Squadron. Köberich flew under the left hand Lancaster, which was being flown by Captain Finn Johnsen, a Norwegian from Bergen, and blasted the bomber's port wing with his side cannon from 80 metres range. All of the crew, who were on their 25th operation, were killed.

Köberich then flew crabwise under the second Lancaster, which was being flown by Warrant Officer John A 'Jack' Murphy, an Australian from Parramatta, New South Wales, whose crew was on their 19th operation of their second tour.

Heidenreich continues:

We acted quickly and the slanting cannons spoke again. *Blitz* fast there was a repetition of what had happened only a few seconds earlier. Now we saw two burning bombers flying side by side, still on their original course. We took up position 300 metres to the starboard of them and flew a parallel course. Number One Lancaster dipped towards the left and Number Two to the right, to crash north and south of the Rhine with mighty explosions. Even at our height it was light as day for a second or so. We logged these shoot-downs at 00.46 hours and 00.47 hours. We did not notice any of the crews bail out, although to us there was plenty of time for them to have done so because our cone of fire went into the wings. [Sergeant Lawrence W Woolliscroft the wireless operator, who had completed 42 operations, was the only one who survived, being thrown clear as the Lancaster exploded. He was on the run for four days, until exhausted, he gave himself up.] The crash-points were visible visiting cards. Cascades of technicoloured Christmas trees burned on the ground for a long time, showing beyond doubt that they were Path Finders; and it was especially rewarding to have got a pair of them so quickly. We believed we had intercepted the spearhead of the enemy bomber formation but despite intensive searching we did not pick up any other targets on our radar. In reality, we had caught two delayed Path Finders.

With fuel running out, Köberich landed at Kassel-Roth-Weston. It was to be the last operation for the German crew. A week later, on 8 April – Easter Sunday – B-17s attacked their base at Quakenbrück and laid seven carpets of bombs. Köberich, who on 1 April had been promoted to *Staffelkapitän*, was among the dead and Kramell was wounded. Heidenreich, who had gone on leave an hour before the attack, returned to duty as the victims of the raid were being laid out in a long row in the market-place of Quakenbrück to await burial.

Twenty-four-year-old *Oberleutnant* Dieter Schmidt, *Staffelkapitän*, 8./NJG1 took off from Laon-Athies and led his Bf 110s to radio-beacon *Ida*. Schmidt, who had 17 victories, was surprised even to have been ordered off in such bright moonlight and he could not help but think that it was a false alarm. But come they did:

Suddenly we are in the middle of them . . . course 120 to 150°. Ack-ack fire . . . Recognition signal. One shot down! Another! All the time more of them. I see one right in front of me. With my second burst of fire all I get is a miserable 'bum-bum'. The guns have jammed. I turn off course, change the magazines and test them again. Some go off but two cannon are completely out of action. My target has gone. Around us it is raining shot-down aircraft. Someone behind me. Swing away . . . to the right ack-ack is bursting furiously. All hell is let loose. Everywhere explosions and air-to-air tracer. Everywhere aircraft and bombs falling . . . a night the like of which I have never known. 00.45 hours, 5,700 metres. Attention! One on the left, 300 to 200 metres. Colossally huge, it flashes by us and I almost ram him.

We wheel to the right, pull up to him ... 100 metres, he twists ... even better target. I keep him just ahead, framed in my sights. Fire! He swings starboard and slides through my cone of fire. Immediately flames sweep along his fuselage and pour from his starboard inner engine. That should be enough. I come right past him. See it's a Halifax. He shoots back. I pull away and see the cockade and the recognition marking 'NP'. Then he is behind to the left, diving down. He hits the ground at 00.49, somewhere about 50 to 100 kilometres north-west of Würzburg ... in the mountains.

Schmidt's 18th victory was possibly NP-S (*S-Sugar*)[26] on 158 Squadron flown by Flight Sergeant Eric Ronald Fergus MacLeod RAAF of Townsville, Queensland. The crew were on their first operation and outbound at 20,000 feet when they were shot down, the Halifax crashing near Herborn-Seelbach. The only man to survive was Flying Officer A Shanahan RAAF who was badly injured and was taken prisoner but he never fully regained his health and died in Australia while still comparatively young.[27]

Hans Meissner of 2./NJG3, now a 25-year-old *Leutnant* credited with 14 *Viermots*, had taken off from Vechta in his Bf 110 and had steered a course straight for the spearhead of the bomber force. North-west of Frankfurt-am-Main his *Bordschütze* picked up a contact on his radar set and gave Meissner a bearing. The German pilot saw the exhaust fires of a *Viermot* in the distance and gave chase immediately. It was a Lancaster. Almost immediately the *Bordschütze* got another contact. The second bomber was also a Lancaster and Meissner spotted it about 1,000 metres ahead. Mentally he noted its position and then concentrated on the first Lancaster. From a distance of 150 metres and 50 metres below, Meissner coolly blasted the Lancaster with a burst of his fixed forward guns. He pushed the stick forward and slapped on left rudder as four streams of tracer hosed from the rear turret of the doomed Lancaster to slip past somewhere to his left. His steep turn once again brought the burning aircraft into his sights but Meissner was now ready to attack the second Lancaster, possibly the 97 Squadron Path Finder aircraft piloted by Flight Lieutenant Leonard Victor Hyde DFC whose crew was on their 29th operation. Alerted by the German's attack on the other Lancaster, Hyde hurled the aircraft into a corkscrew dive but Meissner was not to be outfoxed. As the great port wing of the Lancaster came upright when the pilot whipped it into a right-hand dive Meissner rolled the Bf 110 over on its back and shot it down virtually from above. Since the wing tanks were unprotected on the upper side by armoured plate the effect of his fire was 'devastating'. Hyde, who was from Shirley in Birmingham died in the inferno with his crew. Because of the excellent visibility it would have been possible for Meissner to continue. 'All hell was let loose for the enemy ... Burning aircraft made the night even brighter than it was before'; but he broke off the fight because he was 'nervous at the end'.

Oberleutnant Helmuth Schulte of 4./NJG5 and his crew of a Bf 110 at Parchim returned to base to file claims for four bombers destroyed to take his score to 11 victories. He recalled:

Night fighting in anger, inspired by a feeling of hate or because a comrade had been killed in a bombing raid, was not possible. In order to have any success and to stay alive it was essential that experience and concentration should be the first qualities in the flying, though it is true that the swashbuckling touch was often necessary as well. What was most important was to find the in-flying bomber stream – and in this the carefully-worked-out flight plan was vital. But very often it could only be worked out after take-off and even then it had to be altered. Also the business of getting the bomber into one's sights was often tedious. We sat well down under the bomber and then climbed slowly until we were within fifty to a hundred metres of it. Then I lined up and aimed between the two starboard engines. At the instant that I fired I would bank away to the left. Thus all the shots went from below into the fuel tanks of the bomber, which usually burst into flames immediately. Because we usually came from low down and from astern, we were rarely spotted by the British air-gunners and attracted no defensive fire. Being lower than the bomber, we could keep with it and observe it against the background of the night sky. If we managed to catch the head of the bomber stream, we used to hold back in order to more easily shoot down the waves of aircraft following.[28]

Schulte singled out his first victim using his *Schräge Musik* guns, which jammed after a few rounds so he finished off the crippled bomber with a long stream of cannon shells. It was the Lancaster piloted by Flight Sergeant Tom Fogaty. His crew in the last wave of the force had never seen so many aircraft going down. It seemed to Fogaty that the Bf 110s and Ju 88s had been waiting for them. But the Ruhr was behind them and they were now about 50 miles north-west of Mannheim at an altitude of 22,000 feet and 30 minutes from Nürnburg. But then it happened. Schulte fired a burst of cannon fire, which struck the Lancaster just as Sergeant E A Banham the rear gunner was shouting that his Skipper should cork-screw starboard. Fogaty at once flung the Lanc into a right hand dive. Sergeant V B 'Johnny' Dams the flight engineer, who had been keeping a close eye on the engine gauges, exclaimed as he saw the oil pressure beginning to fall on the starboard inner. Clearly they had been hit in that engine which, without oil pressure would quickly overheat. Dams, having reported this and received Fogaty's instruction to feather the starboard inner pulled the feathering toggle and watched anxiously as the engine coughed out a stream of blue-grey smoke before spinning slowly to a stop. Fogaty had in the meantime learned that they had lost the night fighter in their corkscrew manoeuvre and was bringing the Lancaster back on course, checking that no one had been hurt before trimming it to the heading on which it had been flying. There was an unhealthy smell of petrol and oil in the cockpit and when he checked his instrument panel he saw that the altimeter needle was falling steadily. Trimming the aircraft again, he fixed his eyes on the altimeter. They were losing height at the rate of 500 feet a minute: and the control column was sluggish and not responding as it should. In ten minutes they had lost 5,000 feet and the altimeter needle was still slicing back. Each additional minute was costing them a precious 500 feet in height. Fogaty thought that they were never going to reach Nürnburg. If they were to maintain any height at all they would have to jettison the bomb load.

Flying Officer J Ferris the Canadian bomb-aimer clicked down the bombing switches. If he had to jettison he would release the bombs live in the hope that they might hit something or someone. He called on Fogaty to open the bomb doors, confirmed that he had and pressed the bomb tit. That would release the photo-flash and lessen the risk of an explosion on board, he considered. Then he slammed the jettison bar across to clear any hang-ups. Fogaty knew that the bombs had gone when the control column kicked hard against his hands as the Lancaster ducked, freed from its load. He asked his navigator for a course to join the homeward track and began the turn. The Lancaster's rate of descent had been slowed to about 200 feet a minute by jettisoning the bombs; but its air-speed was also reduced as soon as it began heading into the high winds that had just been behind it. Fogaty swung them on to their new course and they were about 35 to 40 miles west of the target, maintaining a height of 15,000 feet, when the ground guns found them. They guessed it to be predicted fire for the heavy-calibre shells were bursting in neat groups around them, showering the night with a kaleidoscope of splintered ochre light. Shrapnel from the bursts rattled along the bomber's fuselage and it pitched and rolled in the blasts created by exploding shells.

After what seemed an eternity, although it was in fact only a few minutes, they were clear of the barrage and Fogaty asked his flight-engineer to check on what damage had been done. Dams made a quick inspection and reported nothing more serious than a few flak holes in the airframe. The bomber continued on three engines. It was now on its own – a solitary target which could be easily picked up by ground radar. Fogaty found that the controls were becoming increasingly difficult to handle and he was sure that something somewhere had been severed – but he had no idea what. Then, when they were 45 to 50 miles south-west of Stuttgart, something gave in the controls, the control column felt light and limp in Fogaty's hands and the bomber slipped into a shallow dive to starboard. Again the altimeter needle began to dip and the entire aircraft started to shudder in an alarming manner.

It was clear that far greater damage had been done to the Lancaster than had at first been thought. The altimeter showed that they were now down to 2,500 feet. They would never reach the enemy coast, let alone their base. There was only one solution. Fogaty called up his crew and told them to bail out. Ferris was the first to go. From the rear-turret Sergeant E A Banham shouted that he was stuck. Pilot Officer Jock Simpson the mid-upper gunner scrambled from his turret to go to Banham's assistance and made his way along the fuselage as the Lancaster skidded and lurched on its ever-quickening downwards course. Reaching the rear-turret, he began to turn it manually so that Banham could escape and was rewarded with the thumbs-up sign from the rear-gunner, who then tumbled into space. Simpson slipped on his own parachute, informed Fogaty that the rear-gunner had safely bailed out and then made his own exit. Flying Officer P H Paddon the navigator and Sergeant 'Jack' Lomas the wireless operator followed him.

Only Fogaty and Dams were left. Fogaty glanced at the altimeter and saw that they were down to 1,000 feet. If they were going to jump at all, it would have to be now. He unfastened his safety harness and motioned to Dams to hand him his parachute. Dams was waving his arms and pointing under the pilot's seat, indicating that his own parachute had become jammed under the seat by their earlier evasive action. Fogaty's reaction was instantaneous. 'Quick,' he called, 'Take mine. There's no time to lose.' The flight-engineer hesitated, knowing that his pilot would be left with no means of escape. Fogaty shouted at him again to take the parachute and jump. Dams put Fogaty's parachute on and jumped clear at just under one thousand feet.

Alone in the doomed Lancaster, Fogaty knew beyond doubt that he now had no chance of getting out, and with his safety straps undone, even if he accomplished the seemingly impossible feat of a crash landing he would certainly be hurled from his seat on impact. It was bad enough to have to land a crippled aircraft on a well-lit home base with an engineer to operate the throttle levers while the gunner kept the tail down. To make such an attempt single-handed in the middle of Germany in pitch blackness seemed impossible. But what alternative was there? If this was to be the end, at least he'd go out trying. The sound of his own breathing came to him over the intercom as he peered through the canopy and tried to find out what sort of terrain he was coming down over; but it was too dark for him to make anything out. Fogaty somehow managed to keep the Lancaster fairly straight as he lowered full flap. At 500 feet he switched on his landing lights and saw the ground rearing in front of him. Earth and sky seemed to merge as he struggled with the now almost-useless control column. He caught a glimpse of an orchard blurring beneath him and a stamp-sized patch which might have been a field. Twenty feet from the ground, seeing what looked like a carpet of snow, he cut the engines, braced his wrists behind the control column and prayed. An overwhelming, jarring pain lanced through his forehead as an avalanche of roaring sound consumed the Lancaster and he had a vague sensation of floating in a vacuum of utter darkness. And then – nothing.

Fogaty recalls:

> When I came to, I was lying in the snow fifty yards from the aircraft. I vaguely remember seeing a small fire in one of the engines. There were several people who looked like farmers around me and they took me to a farmhouse about a hundred yards away. None of them could speak English and I could not speak German. I was very confused. I had a huge bump on my forehead, a grazed leg and was minus one of my flying boots. After a short wait at the farmhouse, I was taken in a van to the police station of a nearby town. (My navigator remembers climbing a signpost which said 68 kilometres to Stuttgart, which he thought was north-east). I stayed, for what remained of the night, in a cell. The rest of the crew was brought in at intervals. The last to arrive was Jack Lomas. They were all surprised to see me – especially Johnny Dams. He couldn't believe that I had managed to land the Lancaster alone. The interrogating officer at *Dulag Luft* in Frankfurt later told me that I was shouting 'Voici ... voici ...' when I was found. Presumably, I must have thought I had landed over the French border.[29]

But though his commission came through while he was a PoW, Fogaty received no official acknowledgment from the Air Ministry for his courage in handing his parachute to a crew member and then going on to perform the fantastic and incredible feat of landing a crippled four-engined bomber single-handed in darkness and in unknown territory.[30]

Shortly after the attack on Fogaty's Lancaster, *Unteroffizier* Georg Sandvoss, Schulte's *Bordschütze*, picked up a contact 30 kilometres south-west of Eisenach. It was C8-B, a Halifax III on 640 Squadron at Leconfield flown by Flying Officer James Dutton Laidlaw RCAF whose crew were on their 21st operation. Schulte blasted the *Viermot* with his oblique guns, which were now working again. Laidlaw, who was from Kamloops, British Columbia received terrible wounds to his legs and just had time to order his crew to bail out before he died. The flight engineer was either killed outright or mortally wounded. The navigator, also badly injured, fell across the forward escape hatch and prevented others using it. Three other crew men managed to leave by the rear hatch but the seventh man on the crew, Flying Officer Martin M Corcoran, an Australian from Canungra, a little town in Queensland, refused to leave the injured navigator and although he had time to escape, was last seen by the side of his dying comrade.[31] The Halifax crashed and exploded near Wölferbütt, a village on the west bank of the Ochse just south of Vacha.

Unteroffizier Hans Fischer checked the guns and confirmed that the firing pins were unserviceable and when another Lancaster suddenly hove into their path north-west of Nürnburg, Schulte blasted it with his side guns. It was *E-Easy* on 57 Squadron at East Kirkby flown by Flight Lieutenant Eddie Tickler CGM, a member of the Tickler Jam Company, who had the words *The Jampot and the 7 Raspberries* painted below the cockpit. Tickler and Sergeants A Ferguson and W E Steeper USAAF bailed out and they were taken prisoner. The four others on the crew, who were on their 13th operation, went down with the aircraft, which keeled over and exploded near Bischwind-bei-Bamberg.

Schulte flew over Nürnburg and just south of the city he shot down his fourth victim of the night. It was another Halifax. A fifth victory eluded Schulte. First he had forgotten to reload and though he re-established contact and attacked again using his nose guns, the bomber plummeted into a steep corkscrew and escaped.[32]

Schulte recalls:

Night fighting was not enjoyable. It was a most bitter experience that broke many nerves and had few survivors. We had to withstand much anxiety. This was due less to the fighting itself, which took place in the dark and in which we had a better chance, than to the need to fly in bad weather in conditions under which normally no man would set foot in an aircraft. Night fighting was nerve-wracking; and the few who survived it had, above all things, flying skill and occasional luck.[33]

Pilot Officer Brooks was piloting *O-Orange* and recalls: 'As we approached the target Flight Sergeant Harry Marr, the rear gunner, reported a twin-engined fighter out on our rear port quarter, high. The enemy aircraft turned in towards us and dived, passing underneath us.' 'Chick' Chandler the flight engineer, who had seen the fighter emerge on the starboard side of the Lancaster, quickly warned the gunners over the intercom of the enemy fighter's position. Harry Marr rotated his turret to the starboard quarter and elevated his guns, as the Ju 88 executed a climbing turn into the same area. The enemy aircraft closed in and opened fire with cannon, the beauty of the illuminated stars of light leaving the fighter's nose belying their deadly intent. The Lancaster dipped its right wing as Oliver Brooks flung the aircraft into a corkscrew manoeuvre to starboard but not before some of the enemy shells hit along the main-plane as he recalls. 'We were hit in the number three tank on the port side. That was the small capacity (114 gallons) tank outboard of the outer. A shell went into it and exploded. It was in fact a brand new tank and had not been filled. If it had the results could have been disastrous. The enemy aircraft made just the one attack and disappeared, no doubt to seek other targets of which there were plenty.'

As the Lancaster dived to starboard, Harry Marr opened fire with his Browning machine guns. The Ju 88 continued in towards the bomber and then broke away to port. Sergeant Ron Wilson, whose sighting of the attacking fighter had been obscured by the Lancaster's tail-plane, saw the enemy aircraft as it broke away. He depressed his guns and fired off a short burst of 50 rounds before it disappeared from view; neither gunner saw the fighter again.

Brooks concludes: 'The target, if in fact it was the target, was not well marked at all. We bombed on a marker that appeared at our approximate ETA but we did not see much in the way of fires. It was clear from the way the bombs were falling all over the place that few people really knew where they were.'

Notes

1. *The Bombing of Nürnburg* by James Campbell (Futura 1973).
2. *Serrate* was designed to home in on *Lichtenstein* radar. See *Confounding The Reich* by Martin W Bowman. (Pen & Sword 2004).
3. Additionally, three *Oboe* Mosquitoes to Oberhausen and one Mosquito to Dortmund, and six Stirlings would lay mines off Texel and Le Havre.
4. See *Bomber Squadron: Men Who Flew with XV* by Martyn R Ford-Jones (William Kimber 1987).
5. In April W/C Doubleday DSO DFC took command of 61 Squadron, which he led with equal distinction. Just before taking up the appointment he was sent to London to attend a course. While there he arranged to meet his pregnant wife at the Regent Palace Hotel near Piccadilly Circus, where at 8 o'clock one morning a V-1 blew a hole in the side of the hotel and the blast knocked the Doubledays down a flight of stairs. The blast killed the twins that Phyllis was carrying. See *Chased By the Sun.*
6. Four Ju 88 units of 3JD (I./NJG2 at Langensalza and another from Langen-diebach, III./NJG2 at Twente and 10./NJG1 at Quakenbrück) were assembled at *FF Ida*, as were the He 219s of I./NJG1 at Venlo and 10 Bf 110s of I./NJG6 at Mainz-Finthen and several units of NJG4. Before midnight all these units were switched from *Ida* into the bomber stream, as far west as possible. Five Bf 110s of II./NJG6 took off from Echterdingen at around 23.30 hours and were directed to *FF Otto*, as were the 2JD *Gruppen* at Vechta (I./NJG3), Stade (III./NJG3) and Westerland (IV./NJG3) and from there into the bomber stream over the area NE of Giessen. 1JD contributed four *Gruppen* at Stendal (I./NJG5), Parchim (II./NJG5), Erfurt (IV./NJG5) and Werneuchen east of Berlin (NJGr.10), [whose aircraft often operated from Hangelar airfield near Bonn during night battles]; these were assembled over *Otto* and led into the bomber stream over the area between *Otto* and *Ida*. Finally, II./NJG1 at St-Trond were assembled over radar station *Bazi* (east of Wesel) before being guided on to radar station *Murmeltier* (at Malmédy) and directed into the bomber stream south of Aix la Chapelle. In addition to the twin-engined *Zahme Sau Gruppen* sent up by 1JD, elements of all three single-engined *Wilde*

Sau Geschwader were also employed. Twenty Bf 109s of I./JG300 were airborne from Bonn-Hangelar between 23.55 and 00.10 hours and flew to *Otto*, where they were joined by the FW 190s of II./JG300 from Rheine. Both *Gruppen* were then directed on to Frankfurt am Main. Here, they were soon ordered to land. The Bf 109s of III./JG300 at Rheine and Wiesbaden-Erbenheim were assembled by the 3JD controllers at *Leuchtfeuer* (light beacon) *Nordpol* (near Wittenberg, east of Dessau) and fed into the stream; these fighters were instructed to land in central Germany after accomplishing their mission. 2JD contributed one single-engined *Gruppe* (III./JG302) at Oldenburg, which was assembled at *FF Otto* but this unit was soon forced to land because the flight range of the aircraft was too limited. Finally, 1JD sent up three single-engined *Gruppen* (II./JG302 from Ludwigslust, III./JG301 at Zerbst and I./JG302 at Jüterbog) and assembled these *Wilde Säue* at light beacon *Nordpol*. These fighters only saw limited action, as they were ordered to land again after the attack on Nürnberg had begun. *Nachtjagd War Diaries. An operational history of the German night fighter force in the West* Vol. 1, by Dr. Theo E W Boiten, Vol. 2 by Dr. Theo E W Boiten and Roderick J Mackenzie. (*Red Kite*, Walton on Thames 2008).

7. *Chased By The Sun.*
8. See *Nachtjagd: The Night Fighter versus Bomber War over the Third Reich 1939–45* by Theo Boiten (Crowood 1997).
9. Which from research by Theo Boiten, was either MZ508 on 578 Squadron flown by F/Sgt Albert Edward Pinks of Barking, Essex, which went down nearing the aiming point to crash at Ermreus, 13 kms NE of Eerlangen, or LW429 flown by Flying Officer John Roy Taylor on 425 'Alouette' Squadron, which crashed at Tauchersreuth, 4 km NE of Heroldsberg. (Or, Taylor may have been shot down by a Ju 88 flown by *Feldwebel* Emil Nonnenmacher of III./NJG2). All of Pinks' crew, who were on their first operation, had been on the squadron just five days. They were all killed. Taylor, of Winnipeg and his crew who were on their 7th operation were all killed also.
10. *The Lent Papers* by Peter Hinchliffe (Cerberus 2003). *Oberst* Helmut Lent was the second highest scoring *Nachtjagd experte* of the war with a total of 102 *Nachtjagd* victories, including 61 *Viermots* and one Mosquito in 396 sorties and he was awarded the *Ritterkreuz* with *Eichenlaub, Schwerter* and *Brillanten*. Lent died on 7 October 1944 from injuries sustained two days earlier when he had an engine failure coming into land at Paderborn in a Ju 88 and crashed after hitting high tension cables. *Oberfeldwebel* Walter Kubisch, his *Funker*, who had suffered severe burns, internal injuries and extensive fractures, died during an emergency operation. A few hours later *Oberleutnant* Hermann Klöss the second *Funker* died from head injuries and the following morning *Leutnant* Werner Kark too died from similar causes.
11. Air Ministry Bulletin broadcast on 31 March.
12. Air Ministry Bulletin broadcast on 31 March. F/Sgt Robert Ford Whinfield, KIA 26/27 April 1944 on the operation to Schweinfurt.
13. Two Lancasters on 103 Squadron FTR from 16 Lancasters dispatched from at Elsham Wolds.
14. Oberhardt KIA 9/10 April 1944 when Lancaster JB734 flown by P/O Robert John Proud RAAF was lost on a *Gardening* operation to lay mines in the Baltic. All of the crew, five of whom were Australian, were killed.

15. See *Confounding The Reich* by Martin W Bowman. (Pen & Sword 2004) and *The Nürnburg Raid* by Martin Middlebrook. (Allen Lane 1973). Ten German aircraft were claimed shot down: 4 Ju 88s, 5 Bf 109 and FW 190 *Wild Boars* and 1 Bf 110.
16. Adapted from *Bail Out* by Paul Hutchinson, (Marshall Cavendish Ltd 1974).
17. The Halifax, which had been hit by flak near Metz, crashed at Eischen, 17 kilometres WNW of Luxembourg. Hughes and four of his crew were captured and taken prisoner. Two other men evaded capture.
18. *See At First Sight: A Factual and anecdotal account of No. 627 Squadron RAF.* Researched and compiled by Alan B Webb. 1991.
19. In 1943 'Bomber' Harris had supported a virtually private development by the TRE (Telecommunications Research Establishment) at Malvern, Worcestershire and his own RDF department to produce a 'picture' of the aircraft around the bomber on a second H_2S CRT indicator. With the help of Sir Robert Renwick a crash programme installed *Fishpond* on all H_2S aircraft by the end of 1943. *Bomber Harris; The Authorised Biography* by Dudley Saward (Cassell 1984).
20. Adapted from *The Bombing of Nürnburg* by James Campbell (Futura 1973). Ten night fighters were claimed shot down by RAF air gunners: four Ju 88s, three Bf 109s, two FW 190s and one Bf 110; eleven crew members were killed.
21. See *The Bombing of Nürnburg* by James Campbell (Futura 1973).
22. See *Legend of the Lancasters* by Martin W Bowman (Pen & Sword 2009).
23. Identified by Theo Boiten as either LK762 of 78 Squadron flown by Sgt Ronald Arthur Horton or LK795 of 76 Squadron flown by F/L Henry Coverley. Horton, who was from Leicester and three of his crew were killed. The three others were taken prisoner. The crew were on their first operation.
24. Bedridden for the next 51 years, he died in February 1996. See *Nachtjagd: The Night Fighter versus Bomber War over the Third Reich 1939–45* by Theo Boiten (Crowood 1997).
25. See *Nachtjagd: The Night Fighter versus Bomber War over the Third Reich 1939–45* by Theo Boiten (Crowood 1997).
26. Halifax III LW724.
27. *RAF Bomber Command Losses of the Second World War. Vol. 5 1944* W R Chorley (Midland 1997).
28. *The Bombing of Nürnburg* by James Campbell (Futura 1973).
29. Fogaty had crash-landed at Raidwangen, 4km south-west of Nürtingen. A second 115 Squadron Lancaster was lost when LL622 piloted by F/Sgt Ron Thomas of Redruth, Cornwall strayed 115 miles north of track on the homeward leg and was shot down by *Feldwebel* Hans Zeidler of 7./NJG1, crashing at Chimay, 5km SW of the historic battlefield at Waterloo. All the crew, who were on their first operation were killed.
30. Adapted from *The Bombing of Nürnburg* by James Campbell (Futura 1973).
31. See *The Nürnburg Raid* by Martin Middlebrook. (Allen Lane 1973). LW555, another 640 Squadron Halifax flown by P/O Charles Edward O'Brien, a Canadian from Toronto whose crew were on their fourth operation was, from research by Theo Boiten, possibly the aircraft shot down by *Leutnant* Hans Zettel of 2./NJG6, who claimed a Stirling at Montabaur at 0035 hours. They were all killed.

32. This Lancaster has been identified as the one flown by W/O Howard Hemming on 115 Squadron by Martin Middlebrook in *The Nürnburg Raid* (Allen Lane 1973). Sgt John Carter, the rear gunner, thought that the attack had been carried out 'in a half-hearted manner, possibly by a fighter flown by a pilot from a training unit.' Schulte and his crew were shot down by a Mosquito on 22/23 May 1944. Schulte and Fischer bailed out safely but Sandvoss was KIA. Schulte survived the war, being awarded the *Ritterkreuz* for 25 night victories in April 1945.
33. *The Bombing of Nürnburg* by James Campbell (Futura 1973).

CHAPTER 2

The Seats Were Empty

And should you weep for him, if so inclined,
Then mingle knowledge with your gift of tears,
Bare not your heart alone – unveil your mind
Upon the history of his nineteen years.

He kicked a ball in narrow London streets,
Then pedalled groceries round Walthamstow.
He learnt of love in cheaper Gaumont seats,
Set it to jazz-time on his radio.

He had a wife for seven magic nights,
His eyes grew softer in a small hotel.
They shared a dream of London, rich with lights
And all the things that Woolworths has to sell.

Against his shaggy head he brushed a sleeve,
Within the barber's shop considered 'pride',
Bought contraceptives in the hope of leave,
Then flew to Nürnburg that night and died.

'Requiem for a Rear Gunner' by Walter Clapham. Flight Sergeant
William Paterson Clapham on 'Turkey' Laird's crew was KIA on
30/31 March 1944.

Squadron Leader E N M 'Neville' Sparks DFC AFC, one of the Path Finders
on 83 Squadron, looked on horrified at the shambles over Nürnburg:

As was the custom, we left England after the stream had gone
and highly laden we passed them on the way. We were flying at
19,000 feet and the Main Force were 3,000 feet above us. Contrary to
the forecasts there was no layer cloud in which they could hide from
enemy fighters. They were clearly visible, glinting in the moon light.
The forecast was for the moon to be at about half its full strength.

41

In fact it was about as bright as it could be. The night too was as clear as a bell – no clouds – with fantastic visibility. Anyway, we were catching up with the force on the second leg of the trip – the 250 miles between Charleroi and Fulda – when the slaughter began. We had an incredible view. In the sixty or ninety minutes after midnight we saw sparkles of cannon fire; some distant and some almost directly above us, followed by explosions, fires, plunging planes and a scattering of fires on the ground as far as the eye could see. I saw three planes blow up as they collided and one of them, a Path Finder, blazed like a torch as its flares ignited.

The Halifax III piloted by Squadron Leader 'Turkey' Laird DFC RCAF on 427 'Lion' Squadron and the Lancaster flown by Flight Sergeant Eric Pickin on 622 Squadron collided in the south-east corner of Belgium and plunged into the ground near Rachecourt in Luxembourg. George Johnstone Laird's crew had averaged 15 operations. Pickin, who was from Witney, Oxfordshire and his crew, were on their 5th operation. Four of the crew bailed out but one had hit a tree and he was killed. The bodies of the other three were found near their aircraft, their parachutes unopened. 'Turkey' Laird's rear gunner Pilot Officer John Moffat RCAF had watched helplessly as the Lancaster hit them very close to his turret. The starboard rudder was torn off in the collision and a large hole made in the top of the fuselage near the tail turret. Moffat had great difficulty in getting his parachute as it was tangled with the tail control wires, which were all broken. Normally, he would have been occupying the mid-upper-turret, which was crushed in the collision. He was doubly lucky because by the time he jumped the Halifax was down to 1,000 feet, yet he survived. Laird, who was from Winnipeg, and four of his crew were found in the wreckage. Flying Officer John Morrison DFC the flight engineer was found horribly injured hanging from a tree. He was to die three weeks later on 20 April at Arlon hospital and was buried with full military honours in the communal cemetery. Moffatt meanwhile, evaded capture.[1]

At a quarter to one, the leading bombers reached the end of the long leg at Fulda 50° 32' north, 10° 36' east and started to turn south to Nürnburg. The 220 miles from Liège to the last turning-point was by now clearly marked by the blazing remains of 41 Lancasters and 18 Halifaxes. It is unlikely that a single hour, before or since, has seen a greater rate of aerial destruction. By the time the Main Force reached the target area they would be missing 79 aircraft, a figure exceeding the Leipzig total of six weeks earlier.

The target was now 75 miles to the south; without the tail wind, this would be a 20-minute flight. The turning-point was a tricky one, above the forests of Thuringia with no recognizable feature or nearby town. Most of the aircraft turned well to the north of the right place and slightly short of it. As the leading Path Finders flew past the searchlights of Bamberg, 30 miles north of Nürnburg, they were confronted by a thick blanket of cloud, less than 2,000 feet at base and extending up to 11,500 feet. Pat Daniels was the first in the Path Finder force to orbit the target, which was covered in 7/10ths cloud. Not only was Nürnburg covered by heavy broken cloud but the winds from the west had suddenly increased in velocity and were blowing the big bombers sideways to the east. So, instead of flying over Erlangen and on to Nürnburg, some of the Path Finders had crossed another small town (Forchheim) and then approached Lauf, much smaller than the real target but with similar characteristics on the H_2S radar screens, being situated on a river and surrounded by woods.

Mosquitoes on 627 Squadron opened the activities of the Primary Marking Force at two minutes to one, off-loading 500-pounders and *Window* at the rate of four bundles a minute to disrupt the 100-plus radar-predicted flak guns known to be defending the city. Jim Marshallsay recalls:

> *Window* Opening meant that we had to be over the target before the first of the Marker aircraft and scatter *Window* to confuse the radar defences. We threw out our *Window*, dropped our four 500lb bombs and circled to watch the attack develop but little could be seen except for a few *Wanganui* flares. Nick said, 'We're going straight home.' And that is what we did. We turned the aircraft's nose towards Oakington and left at a great pace.[2]

Sergeant Ernest Rowlinson, the wireless operator on Lancaster *H-Harry*, which had earlier been attacked by a night fighter, was relieved to see the target when they arrived over Nürnburg shortly after 01.09 hours. Flight Sergeant Keith Gilbert 'Ben' Lawrence the 22-year-old bomb aimer brought *H-Harry* on to the bomb run at a height of 19,000 feet but *H-Harry* was coned and Startin immediately dived. They went left and then right and everything that was not bolted on flew around inside the Lancaster. By the time Lawrence called on Startin to open the bomb doors *Harry* was down to 8,000 feet!

'There it is Skipper – straight ahead. Keep her steady. Steady – right; right; hold it – ste-ady.'

Eight seconds to go. With only three seconds to go Lawrence called 'Steady – hold it . . .' and then, 'Bombs gone.' There was relief in his voice.

Rowlinson meanwhile was watching his *Fishpond* when another blip showing a fighter approaching from the port quarter, appeared on his screen. He alerted the gunners and Hopkinson in the rear turret spotted the fighter almost at the same instant, and he and McIlwine in the mid-upper turret fired immediately. The fighter disappeared and

Startin weaved and corkscrewed *H-Harry* until they were well clear of the target.[3]

At 01.05 hours the first of the Path Finder *Wanganui* vivid red sky-markers went down on their parachutes and were interspersed with clusters of emerald-green stars and red TIs, which fell over the city 'like fiery Christmas trees.' These were followed by more red flares, while down below anti-aircraft guns blazed away with red-orange flashes. It looked like the clouds were on fire. A minute later, more red flares were released, 'this time shooting out clusters of yellow stars from their centres.' And at 01.07 hours the six 'visual' PFF Lancasters swept in and released ground markers through the centre of the *Wanganui* flares, followed a minute later by a strong formation of blind-sky marker Lancasters which dropped its candelabras among the still-twinkling illuminators of the leaders. Behind them came more visual markers, who unloaded further clusters of TIs, and at 01.09 hours both sky and ground were exposed to yet more flares as the PFF force's supporters droned over the target.[4] Daniels made three orbits of Nürnburg in all. He saw that some of the Main Force bombers, which had arrived earlier than they should have, were levelling out for their bomb runs. At 01.10 hours the first wave of the Main Force Lancasters and Halifaxes fanned out over Nürnburg on a broad front. Some of the bombers were operating on misjudged wind-speeds and their bombs overshot the city. Others completely missed the city with their bombs. During the first five minutes only 33 aircraft bombed.

Pilot Officer J Cotter flying a Halifax was on his 30th op; his navigator was only on his first or second trip. 'With the heavy fighter attacks, the navigator could not have had a more unfortunate introduction and eventually he was unsure of his position. Before we were due at Nürnburg, we saw Path Finder markers going down just off our track. We had not been briefed on any diversionary target here and I just thought we were lucky that we'd got to Nürnburg and so we bombed. Not one of us queried the target.'

Pat Daniels swept *S-Sugar* across the city for its third circuit of the target and he noted with anxiety that the bombing was becoming increasingly erratic. Whirling mists and curling peaks of dense vapour were obscuring the markers and spoiling the accuracy of the bomb aimers. Altogether, 512 aircraft bombed in the Nürnburg area; what had happened to the other 119 bombers that should have done so? Forty-eight crews would take back clear bombing photographs – of Schweinfurt! Damage was done to all three of the ball-bearing plants. Thirteen other bombers released their loads when they realized they were lost; these fell on unspecified targets, including Bamberg and a small town 60 miles north. Daniels, having spent nearly 25 minutes over Nürnburg, swung *S-Sugar* in a broad arc and headed for home. There was nothing more that he could do and he needed every precious drop of fuel if he were to make Graveley. Keith Creswell in *B-Beer*, the leader of the primary visual markers, soon followed him. He too had a strong feeling that the attack was not as successful as it might have been. On his first quick circuit of the city he knew that the 60 mph winds encountered had dispersed many of the sky-markers and as a consequence, the bombing 'was poorly concentrated and very spasmodic.'

By 01.08 hours 65 Path Finders and Supporters had done their best but the conditions were hopeless. Instead of a clear and vividly marked target for the Main Force bomb-aimers due to arrive at 01.10, there was one group of sky-markers over Nürnburg and another group ten miles to the north-east near Lauf, both being blown eastwards and falling towards the clouds. Seeing two groups of markers, the Main Force crews were understandably confused; so were the Backers-up among them whose duty it was to renew the sky-markers. They managed to re-mark the group over Lauf, which now gave off the most light and attracted by far the greater number of bombs. Some of the later Path Finders placed their markers accurately over Nürnburg but the damage had been done and soon there was a ragged line of sky-markers more than ten miles wide. The wrecks of nine aircraft shot down on their bombing runs formed a long straight line from Bamberg to Lauf. The creep-back started early and soon measured 15 miles.

Warrant Officer Jim McNab RAAF who was on a Lancaster on 467 Squadron RAAF, recalls:

Nürnburg was the only place covered by cloud. I could see Lancasters being shot down by anti-aircraft guns and fighters. I don't think there was any question of a leakage of information. As far as we could make out, it was the bright moon which was the death-blow for our planes. It was so light that I could clearly read the squadron letters and identification numbers on a Lanc flying next to us. One of our chaps had said we were for it and was he right! Nürnburg was the only place covered by cloud. I saw Lancasters being shot down by anti-aircraft guns as well as fighters.

Flight Lieutenant W D Marshall on the same squadron recalled: 'We were late getting to the target and I don't think we got a good bombing photo because we were chased by a German fighter and then a very twitchy Lancaster gunner tried hard to shoot us down.' Flight Lieutenant Milton Smith, another Australian on the squadron said, 'The section of the route from Aachen to the target was reminiscent of a battlefield of burning aircraft. It was very noticeable in the last half-dozen trips that so many aircraft were seen going down in flames from operational height. I would suggest that the enemy was using a new type of ammunition.[5]

Flight Sergeant Brian Soper, who six days earlier had flown his 11th raid on Berlin on Arthur Rew's crew, thought that Nürnburg was probably the most frightening of all his raids on Germany:

> It was a clear moonlit night as we were climbing to bombing height. We realised that we were all showing heavy vapour trails. Most of the weather forecast, including wind-speed, was apparently wrong. There were many night fighters about and we saw several aircraft blow up. Because it was so light we also saw aircraft where the crews were bailing out. We had seen Lancs blow up before, but never in so much detail. The pilots changed height several times to try to lose the vapour trails because the night fighters were just sitting above and picking them off from the vapour trails. We also saw what we had been told were 'scarecrows', a device which exploded between 18,000 and 20,000 feet with a lot of smoke and flame but were otherwise harmless. We found out a year or two later that, as we suspected, they were just other exploding bombers. There was so much going on during that first leg of the route, that it was difficult to tell whether aircraft were mostly lost to flak or to night fighters. Some of those shot down must have been pathfinders since some burning on the ground contained ground TI colours. We suspected that the early part of the route may have been known to the Germans. As we continued to gain height up to 22,000 feet – flying at approximately 155mph, we lost some of the vapour trails and felt a little safer although it was still very clear. Most of the losses were around the Ruhr area on the first long leg out: Frankfurt, Cologne etc. There was a lot of flak, but I think that the losses were mostly due to the night fighters.

Lancaster *E-Easy* on 625 Squadron approached Nürnburg with its rear-turret out of action. A mechanical fault had developed and although the turret could still be turned its guns would not fire. By the time the crew had discovered this it was too late to go back. But luck was with them. Despite the many combats that raged around them, they reached Nürnburg without being attacked. Flight Lieutenant N R Truman DFC the flight engineer says:

> We began our bombing-run at 20,000 feet, and were aghast to see masses of vapour trails from the bombers ahead of us, which plainly showed our track to the fighters. We became increasingly conscious of very considerable fighter activity. Everywhere one looked there were unmistakable signs of air-to-air firing. With our rear-turret useless, we decided to get in and out fast. Once we had dropped our bombs we increased power and began to gradually shed height to

give us greater speed. It was contrary to our briefing orders but we were determined to get away from those tell-tale vapour trails. And it was a tactic that paid off, for *E-Easy* again had the phenomenal luck of reaching the coast unscathed.

Navigator Flight Lieutenant Fred Hall who had escaped death on 3 November when *Betty the Heffulump* had crashed on an air test, was now on Flight Lieutenant R J Bolt's crew on *J-Johnny* on 76 Squadron:

I had made my first trip of 8 hours to Nürnburg on 27 August 1943. My 26th on the 30th March 1944 was rather more spectacular. I had never seen so many aircraft attacked, on fire and falling or so many attacks by fighters so early in a trip. I felt sure that my 26th trip was going to be my last. We were in the last wave and fighters were seen to be up in strength as we crossed the Rhine. Aircraft were continually falling out of the sky on fire and I gave up logging them. One minute after leaving the target we were shattered as cannon fire suddenly hit us from underneath putting the starboard inner engine out of action. The navigation table was covered in debris, the wireless set hit, the starboard wing, bomb bay and fuselage on fire. The pilot dived twice to put out flames and we all tackled the fires with extinguishers, eventually successfully. As if this was not enough, 12 minutes later we were approached by a fighter from dead astern, but we took evasive action and he passed 50 yards over the tail receiving full blasts from both gunners.

Lack of sleep was beginning to tell on the crew of *D-Dog* a primary blind-marker Lancaster on 156 Squadron. In the rear turret, 'Tubby' Holley could hardly keep his eyes open. On the flight south of the Ruhr the crew observed several combats and Holley reported four or five bombers going down in almost as many minutes. 'Robbie' Bagg, who was on his second tour of operations, then picked up on *Fishpond* his first blip about one mile to port of them. Holley peered into the darkness but could see nothing. A moment later Bagg reported that there was another fighter two miles to starboard but again Holley failed to see them. The blips then vanished from the screen and the gunners were informed that the fighters had gone. It was just as well because Holley's guns were not working. The weary tail gunner was fervently hoping that they would soon reach Nürnburg but then Bagg announced on intercom that he had picked up more fighters on his screen. Again Holley was unable to get a visual on them and they did not attack the Lancaster. Finally, *D-Dog's* navigator, Flying Officer Jones, said on intercom that he was setting the course for the run in to the target. 'Blackie' Blackadder the bomb aimer lifted the bombing tit from its socket as he watched the outskirts of

Nürnburg appear on the screen of his H_2S scanner. Recalling the bomb run, Holley said:

> The flak was moderate but even the thought of a fighter on our tail was not worrying me all that much, as I was so tired. Somehow or other, I just about managed to keep the turret swinging, looking out now and them at the searchlights. 'Blackie' released our target indicators, the 'cookie' and other bombs with the aid of H_2S. And then came the worst part as we flew straight and level over the target with our camera whirring. Now and then the Lancaster pitched and rocked from the concussion of bursting anti-aircraft shells. Next minute we were turning on to our course for the homeward journey. Before long and in spite of all my efforts to stay awake, I felt my eyes closing. I don't suppose they were shut for more than a few seconds, for as my head dropped forward on to my chest I woke up and stared out of the turret, searching for fighters. And so it went on. As I came out of a doze, I would stare into the darkness and then my head would go down and I'd drop off.

Sergeant R E Holder on *G-George* recalls:

> During the heat of the battle we began to wonder when our turn would come. All the time tracer fire was criss-crossing the sky. Bombers were taking violent evasive action so one didn't really know what was actually happening. But if a red glow appeared, we knew it was one of ours. Over the target it was chaotic. Bombers were sweeping in from all directions, unloading their bombs and getting out as fast as they could. It was obvious that the stream was disorganised before it ever reached Nürnburg. The run-in was nerve-racking as we had to watch for other bombers suddenly swerving across our track. But with luck or perhaps skill on our bomb-aimer's part we made a perfect run over the target. The ack-ack was fairly intense but I thought they were firing at random. Yet even over the city the fighters were mixing it with us. After we dropped our bombs our pilot shouted over the intercom for us to get the hell out of it and rammed the throttles through the gate. He screamed into a dive and the Lancaster shuddered with the speed of it. This worried me as I had to watch our fuel consumption and such action burned it up. The bomber gunners put up a brave show against terrific odds. At one period near the target we saw one Lancaster on fire from nose to tail, yet the gunners were still firing until it eventually blew up. I was amazed that there were not more collisions over the target. One bomber missed our tail by inches and our rear-gunner coolly remarked that if he had thrust out his hand he could have shaken hands with its pilot. Before this hellish action we had bombed many

big German cities such as Berlin, Essen, Frankfurt and Stuttgart but this was our first real experience of encountering the full fury of the enemy's fighter force and it was terrifying.[6]

Leutnant Hans Schäfer and his 7./NJG2 crew of *Unteroffizier* Manter his *Funker* and *Obergefreiter* Klietmann, *Bordmechaniker* had taken off from Twente in their Ju 88 at 23.21 hours in search of their first *Abschuss*. At 00.17 hours Schäfer destroyed the first of two Lancasters and a Halifax before landing back at their home base again at 01.49 hours. Their second victim, ten kilometres northwest of Giessen on the extended outward leg, was probably *C-Charlie* on 635 Squadron flown by Flight Lieutenant Hugh Julian Langdon Webb of Beaconsfield, Buckinghamshire, whose crew were on or around their 20th operation; there were no survivors.

The Halifax that fell to Schäfer's guns was possibly *X-X-Ray* on 166 Squadron flown by Flight Sergeant Roy Barton Fennell and was reported to have crashed on an airfield near Giessen. Fennell, from Bromham, Wiltshire and all except one of the crew, who were on their 13th operation, were killed. Schäfer noted in his *Flugbuch* that his first two victims put up a very weak defence but that he was subjected to 'very strong defensive fire' from his third victim. Schäfer and his crew all survived the war with 12 confirmed and one unconfirmed, victories.[7]

Twenty-three year-old *Leutnant* Wilhelm Seuss, pilot of a Bf 110 in 11./NJG5 at Erfurt near Weimar in Saxony had been due for leave and had thought that he would not be flying at all this night. The moonlit night had seemed to confirm it but he and his comrades had been ordered off at 23.17 hours with orders to fly west. With him in his Bf 110 were *Bordfunker* Bruno Zakrzewski, and Fritz Sagner his *Bordschütze*. At an altitude of 6,000 metres the fighters levelled out in the neighbourhood of Frankfurt and were anxiously watching their fuel gauges as the pilots orbited for 15 minutes. Then at about 00.15 hours they noticed lights in the sky. Seuss estimated that it was in the region of Giessen that the bombers had a turning point where they would change course. Visibility at the altitude at which they were flying was so good that they could even see burning aircraft a great distance away. Seuss flew for about 10 to 15 minutes in a northerly direction and reached the main bomber stream. The heading on which they were flying was readily distinguished because of the wrecks burning on the ground.

Bruno Zakrzewski obtained a number of good fixes but each time Seuss had to break off the action as other night fighters were attacking the same aircraft. Then at about 00.52 hours, north of Fulda, Zakrzewski got another contact on his radar screen. Zakrzewski nursed his newfound quarry on his set and called out, 'Target ahead ... climb a bit ... steady. Left ... left ... a little higher. Easy ... 1,000 metres ... 800 metres ... 600 metres ...' At 400 metres Seuss saw the *Viermot* ahead. It was a Lancaster on 103 Squadron which was being flown by Pilot Officer Robert Richard

Jack Tate of Loughton, Essex whose crew were flying their first operation. Seuss brought his Messerschmitt below and to the port of Tate's Lancaster until its port wing was ringed in the sights of his side guns and he fired. Seuss assumed that at least some of the crew were able to save themselves by parachute because the Lancaster caught fire slowly – but there were no survivors. The shoot-down was logged at about 25–30 kilometres north-west of Schweinfurt.

Keeping a sharp look-out, Seuss flew quite near to the searchlights and his crew was able to see another bomber catch fire and dive to the ground. It had been caught in the beams. Later, they learned that it was one of two Lancasters that had been shot down by their *Kommandeur Hauptmann* Gustav Tham.[8] Seuss then told Sagner to change the ammunition drums on the oblique guns. Meanwhile, Zakrzewski was able to lead his pilot on to another *Viermot* at 22,000 feet and drawing close to the final turning point. It was another Lancaster, a 514 Squadron aircraft,[9] which was flown by Pilot Officer Donald Charles Cameron Crombie of Ascot, Queensland and his crew who were on their 14th operation. In his excitement Sagner took longer than usual to change the drums and Seuss had to shadow the Lancaster, keeping 120 metres beneath it while he followed all its movements. Without warning, Crombie corkscrewed, although Seuss was certain the crew had not seen them. At the moment he decided to attack from behind using the horizontal guns. Sagner reported that the oblique guns were now working. Seuss tried again to land his shots between the two port engines but the Lancaster suddenly swerved to port so that his fire landed in the port and starboard wings. Both wings burst into flames and the Lancaster dived sharply. This shooting-down was probably south-east of Schweinfurt. Crombie and four of the crew were killed. Sergeant James McGahey, the flight engineer, who was from Exeter, died going to the aid of the rear gunner, Sergeant Roy Hill, who was trapped in his turret. McGahey was deeply religious and also a scoutmaster and carpenter who had worked on churches and cathedrals in the Devon area. A talented musician, he played the piano and accordion amongst other instruments. He surprised his whole family when he volunteered for the RAF, as they were expecting him to be a conscientious objector. His brother, Frederick, remembers the whole family being shocked when Jim once came home on leave wearing sheepskin flying boots, a breach of regulations but the winter of 1943–44 was the coldest on record and he was determined that his feet shouldn't get cold! Frederick believed that Jim was 'led astray' by another member of the crew, the Canadian, William Earle Brown, from Calgary, Alberta who apparently was a bit of a rascal! Flight Sergeant C Payne a Londoner from Stratford and fellow Londoner, Sergeant M J Tyler of Wembley were the other two men who died. The Lancaster crashed with a full bomb load just outside the Bavarian village of Eichenhausen, a district of Bad Neustadt.[10]

Seuss's third shoot-down was *L-London*, the 408 'Goose' Squadron RCAF Lancaster piloted by Flying Officer J G White RCAF and an eight-man scratch crew, some with 20 to 25 operations flown, which included fellow Canadian, Flight Sergeant J R Hughes who was aboard to gain operational experience. Seuss, who was again led on to the target by his *Bordfunker*, believed that he must have hit an important point in the fuselage, because the aircraft burst into flames and threatened to drop down upon their 110. He immediately threw his fighter into a steep dive and lost at least 1,000 metres before the machine answered to the controls again. The shooting-down took place south of Bamberg and the Lancaster crashed in the village of Simmershausen, three kilometres NE of the small town of Hilders, with the loss of three of the crew, all gunners. White's Lancaster was the only one of the dozen dispatched from Linton-on-Ouse that failed to return.

The Halifax flown by Pilot Officer Christian M Nielsen RCAF on 433 'Porcupine' Squadron at Skipton-on-Swale became Seuss's fourth and final victim of the night when it was shot down at Friesen just before its bombing run south of Bamberg. 'The Mad Dane', as Neilsen was known, was an American citizen of Danish extraction. He and two of his crew, all of whom were on their 27th operation, were taken prisoner. The five others, including Flight Sergeant William Francis Rost RCAF who was making his 'second dickey' trip, and Sergeant Christopher Witton 'Chris' Panton the flight engineer who was from Old Bolingbroke in Lincolnshire and who wanted one day to become a pilot, were killed.[11]

After this and especially after the steep dive, Seuss was feeling very exhausted. He also had to look for a landing strip as they had already been two hours in the air. They picked up the *Leuchtfeuer* (light and radio-beacon) of their base, took a northerly course and landed at Erfurt at 01.55 hours. When most of the crews were back and the night fighters housed in the hangars, a long-range Mosquito Intruder flew low over Erfurt and raked the hangars with long bursts of fire. Ironically, Seuss's Messerschmitt, which was unscathed by its four combats, was among the machines hit. Its radiator cooling system and propeller were damaged.[12]

Returning to base, *Leutnant* Hans Raum of 9./NJG3, who claimed three Lancasters and a Halifax for his 9–12th confirmed victories (his fourth *Viermot* remains unidentified),[13] was shot down and injured by a Mosquito Intruder near Roth an der Sieg. Helmuth Schulte recalls:

Before the Nürnburg raid there had been an easing off in the British long-range night fighter attacks on the aerodromes. These attacks were often unpleasant and brought us many losses but they were not decisive. This was because usually bad weather prevailed and this went against the long-distance night fighters. But after the Nürnburg raid the bombers, when they eventually came back, were protected by these long-range fighters, which caused us very heavy losses. Above all, we could hardly ever fly on a direct course without running into the danger of being caught by a long-range British night fighter.[14]

Hauptmann Ernst-Wilhelm Modrow of 1./NJG1 at Venlo, north-east of Düsseldorf, had taken off in a Heinkel He 219 *Uhu* ('Owl') with orders to hunt down the dreaded *Moskitoes*.[15] The experienced pre-war Lufthansa pilot spent two hours vainly patrolling the Scheldt Estuary and the Zuider Zee without seeing any sign of the Mosquitoes or *Viermots*. Modrow had joined the ranks of the night fighters in October 1943 and had yet to score a victory. He landed back at Venlo to find that the other night fighters there had gone into action against strong bomber formations approaching southern Germany. It was too late for him to join them so he was ordered to intercept the bombers on their homeward flight. After taking off, his *Bordschütze* picked up an SN-2 contact over France. It was the Halifax III on 640 Squadron flown by Warrant Officer David Warnock Burke RCAF who was heading home to Leconfield at the end of what was their fifth operation. The Canadian, who was from London, Ontario, never made it. Modrow hit the bomber in the starboard wing with a burst of his six wing and nose cannon and it exploded. Momentarily blinded by the glare he banked into a steep starboard turn and right into the sights of the rear gunner of the Halifax. Most of the return fire was deflected by the Owl's strong undercarriage and he watched as the bomber went down and crashed near Abbeville. Burke and the crew – one Scotsman, one Irishman and four Englishmen – perished.

Modrow's *Bordschütze* announced another contact and he headed towards it, fastening onto a *Viermot* with the dawn beginning to come up faintly behind them. It was the 158 Squadron Halifax flown by Flight Sergeant Albert Brice, who was from Stoneycroft, Liverpool, and most of whose crew was on their fourth operation. This time Modrow's kill was quick and the bomber crashed in flames at Caumont, north of Dieppe. Brice and four of his crew were found dead in the aircraft. One other who did bail out was also killed. The only survivor was Sergeant Kenneth Dobbs the wireless operator who had not been detailed to fly and was going home but who had popped into the flight office 'just to see what was going on'. Brice's crew was a wireless operator short – he had gone sick – and Dobbs said 'he'd go'. Modrow continued his search but finding no further victims he eventually turned on course for Venlo. The time was now 06.00 hours and the dawn was coming up fast.[16]

Oberfeldwebel Rudolf Frank of 3./NJG3 flying a Bf 110G-4 had taken off from Vechta with his *Bordfunker Oberfeldwebel* Hans-Georg Schierholz but minus his usual air-gunner, *Feldwebel* Heinz Schneider, who had been replaced by a young pilot fresh from training to gain combat experience. Frank, who was flying his 176th night sortie, landed back at Langendiebach near Hanau with claims for three *Viermots* destroyed.

Frank despatched his first victim, a Halifax,[17] which he identified as a Lancaster, using his oblique guns. With one burst he set the bomber's fuel tanks ablaze to send it crashing down at Vogelberges at 00.01 hours. Seventeen minutes later a Lancaster fell to Frank's guns in the same manner as the Halifax, in the region north of Fulda.

Thirty-four minutes later Schierholz picked up a new contact. It was a Halifax. On instructions from *Generalmajor* Max Ibel's 2 JD headquarters in Stade they flew for about five minutes with the bomber in order to determine its course and altitude before receiving instructions to attack. Frank employed the same tactics as before and the Halifax crashed in flames in the region of the Rhön.[18]

Scores of night fighters landed at Langendiebach. *Hauptmann* Fritz Lau of II./NJG1 put his Bf 110 down and went off to report his claim for a Halifax shot down. It could have been more but *Unteroffizier* Helmut Völler had been unable to pick up the rearguard of the bomber force on his radar set. Lau would finish the war as a Hauptmann with 28 night victories and the coveted *Ritterkreuz*.

Oberleutnant Dieter Schmidt examined his Bf 110 after landing at Langendiebach and found to his horror some human hair and flesh stuck to the port propeller boss of the aircraft after shooting down the Halifax.[19]

Flight Sergeant Les Bartlett on 50 Squadron concludes:

To reach the coast was a binding two-hour stooge. The varying winds were leading us a dance and we found ourselves approaching Calais instead of being 80 miles further south, so we had a slight detour to avoid their defences. Once near the enemy coast it was nose down for home at 300 knots. Even then we saw some poor blokes 'buy it' over the Channel. What a relief it was to be flying over Lincoln cathedral once more. Back in debriefing we heard the full story of the Squadron's effort. It was the worst night for the Squadron.

Sergeant Ernest Rowlinson, *H-Harry*'s wireless-operator adds:

The de-briefing took much longer than was usual. Of the fourteen aircraft that took off from our squadron only eight returned and the interrogation officers particularly questioned the gunners, they wanted to know everything – the times and positions of combats and the manner in which aircraft went down. Not only were the individual crews alarmed but also the top brass. They seemed to think that slackness on the part of the aircrews was to blame for a large percentage of the losses. The immediate result was a general tightening up on discipline and an increase in 'bull', which did not go down at all well with the crews. Apart from the bright moonlight, I think fatigue played a big part in the Nürnburg casualty rates. The

mental and physical strain of operating every other night was very
much greater than was realised at the time by both the individual
and the authorities.

As Wing Commander Thompson's crew of *Y-Yorker* on 44 Squadron
neared the French coast at Dieppe they saw two anti-aircraft guns about
a mile apart sending up cones of fire that crossed at 10,000 feet. A few
seconds later a bomber was caught in the crossfire and fell in flames. The
429 'Bison' Squadron RCAF Halifax flown by Flying Officer James Henry
'Jimmy' Wilson RCAF from Moose Jaw, Saskatchewan had been attacked
and badly damaged near Stuttgart and was set on fire. His Canadian
flight engineer extinguished the fire by chopping a hole in the side of the
fuselage and kicking out two blazing magnesium flares that were carried
for a landing on the sea. Wilson made it to the coast and ditched in the
English Channel where the nose section broke away, taking the pilot
to the depths. The rest of the crew survived the ditching and they were
picked up following a tense operation involving Spitfire, Tempest, Sea
Otter and Walrus aircraft and two RAF HSLs from Newhaven, which
found them drifting 25 miles off the Normandy coastline.

That was bad luck, but *Y-Yorker*, which dived rapidly and cleared the
coast at 100 feet, seemed to have had more than its fair share of good
fortune. After the crew had made the change of course at Charleroi for
the 250-mile leg to Fulda they had narrowly missed colliding with
another Lancaster. North of Frankfurt *Y-Yorker* had been caught by the
searchlights and two and then three held them in the beams. They were
helpless but the anti-aircraft guns had remained silent. At the target,
when Flying Officer Bill Clegg, *Yorker's* experienced bomb-aimer was
ready to bomb, he had noticed that other Lancasters above, below and
on each side of their bomber were making their runs and some were in
the way, so he asked Thompson to go around again. As the second run
began Clegg noticed that the cloud veiling Nürnburg was now gradually
thinning and then he saw a dying TI below so he thumbed forward
the drift handle of his Mk. XIV bombsight, slapped down his selector
switches and fused his bombs. Thompson had just seen the light-appear
on his panel to confirm that the bomb-doors had opened when out of
the night another bomber side-slipped in front of *Y-Yorker*. Thompson
jabbed on right rudder, dropped the nose of the Lancaster and cursed the
black shape that now flashed past above them. Inexperienced crews
bombed short so the Path Finders would place their markers right at the
far end of the target. Panicky bomb aimers had a tendency, when they
saw all the flak and searchlights, to drop their bombs quickly and get the
hell out of it, so raids always tended to creep back. Clegg did not blame
them but he refused to panic and he refused to let his bombs go at
random. He stretched himself along his bombing mat a third time and
got the bombs away. Bombs gone, Thompson dropped to 10,000 feet to

begin a straight run across Nürnburg with cameras running. Burrows the flight engineer glanced out over *Y-Yorker's* starboard wing. Horrified, he saw another Lancaster coming straight at them.

'Dive! Dive!' he screamed over the intercom.

Thompson, who had by then been flying for four hours and had amazingly already avoided a collision with a Halifax, had reacted equally fast and again there was no collision. They flew on home to Dunholme Lodge on three engines.

Squadron Leader Neville Sparks' navigator, 'Doc' Watson, marked 57 ticks in his log on the way to Nürnburg. Sparks recalled:

Each tick was a four-engined bomber we had seen shot down by German fighters. It looked like an ambush from where we were watching. It was the most terrible thing I have ever seen. I'm pretty certain we brought back a good photo of the target. 'Strobe' Foley my bomb-aimer was wizard at operating the H_2S set. I know he identified Nürnburg correctly. On the way back, a powerful head-wind blew up, unpredicted at briefing but, by getting down to 10,000 feet we got home before the CO. We flew straight across and saw nothing but a row of six flares several thousand feet above, which indicated that enemy fighters were still searching for the survivors from the main attacks. We were diverted to Downham Market and I rushed to the CO there who happened to be my cousin 'Lofty' Cousins to tell him that we had seen planes fall from the sky like pigeons dipped in lead. 'Doc' Watson showed his log to the CO who immediately got on to the AOC and told him it had been a 'killer' raid. We did not know then that it was the worst in the history of the RAF but we were pretty sick about what we had witnessed. There were rumours about a leak but how could you tell what was true? It certainly looked like an ambush from where we were watching. It was the most terrible thing I had ever seen, the more so as it had a certain wild, primitive beauty about it.

Only ten crews on 61 Squadron at Coningsby reported bombing the target. One of them was Ted Stone, who now took up his CO's promised flight home and he headed for Bridgewater a few hours after the de-briefing. *Mickey the Moocher* made it back after running into problems returning over the North Sea, having encountered stormy conditions off the north Norfolk coast. The Lancaster was struck by lightning on the front turret causing Pilot Officer John Forrest to lose control and the aircraft plummeted towards the sea. While in a blinded and shocked state the Australian pilot ordered the crew to bail out while he tried to pull the aircraft out of the dive. Forrest managed to regain control at 1,000 feet and he immediately countermanded the order to bail out but it was too late to save the lives of the mid-upper gunner, Flight Sergeant

Harold W Pronger, who was from Bundaberg, Queensland and the wireless operator, Sergeant Len Darben, a Londoner from Walthamstow. They had already taken to their parachutes and they both drowned.[20]

At Coningsby, of *Q-Queenie* there was no sign. Pilot Officer Desmond 'Denny' Freeman RAFVR had crash-landed his crippled Lancaster at Foulsham airfield in Norfolk where the starboard wingtip dug into the ground after the right undercarriage failed. One of the crew had been peppered with small pieces of shrapnel in his back and just under the scalp. Two more were so badly injured that they never flew again on operations.[21] At Bardney there was no word from Ling's Lancaster, which had been shot down. There were no other 9 Squadron losses, though Flying Officer Ronald 'Ginger' Craig's *G-George* and Pilot Officer Harry Forrest's *V-Victor* were attacked by night fighters and only just escaped. Flight Sergeant Bernard Thomas Utting, the 22-year-old mid-upper gunner in Forrest's crew, was killed. At Lissett four Halifax aircraft were missing and one was damaged.[22]

Squadron Leader Creswell, knowing beyond doubt that *B-Beer*, which had been holed in one of the petrol tanks by a shell, could never make Graveley, was ready to land anywhere and so his only option was to head for the nearest coastal airfield, the Fleet Air Arm station at Ford. As if things were not bad enough, mist and fog now engulfed them in swirling eddies. When he reached the airfield there simply was not enough fuel for circling first: it had to be a straight, flat approach.

He wrote afterwards:

We left a rather badly damaged aircraft on the runway with a burst tyre, half the elevator shot off, and a hole one could crawl through in the port wing. Why she didn't blow up I shall never know. I found out later that a cannon shell had lodged in the armour-plating of my seat, the firing pin having been bent over during its passage through the fuselage … How lucky can one be!

In fact Creswell had been doubly lucky. During an attack by a night fighter he had had an intuitive flash, ignoring his gunners' call to cork-screw to port when the fighter attacked them. Creswell said, 'I suddenly thought that the bastards always reckoned on one turning to port, so I whipped the aircraft over to starboard. It just goes to show how thin one's life-thread is.'

At Metheringham, where 17 Lancasters on 106 Squadron had taken off, four were missing. Aside from Pilot Officer Starkey's crew there was no word from *C-Charlie* flown by Flight Sergeant Thomas William J Hall DFM whose crew had flown just one operation. The Lancaster had exploded near Berghausen. *J-Jig* flown by Pilot Officer Wilf Moxey, an Australian from Miranda, NSW, drifted well north of track while making for home and was shot down over Belgium by *Leutnant* Fred Hromadnik of 9./NJG4 for the first of his three *Abschüsse* of the night.[23] None of Moxey's crew, including Sergeant Julian Pelham MacKilligin, an 18-year-old gunner who is believed to have completed 15 or 16 operational sorties, survived.[24] Word was finally received that Flying Officer Ernest Richard 'Dickie' Penman had crash landed his Lancaster at Manston without injury to the crew. This crew would survive for just over another month before being killed in action on the operation to Salbris on 7/8 May.

In all, fourteen bombers crashed or crash-landed in England. Pilot Officer James Brooks' Halifax, one of 17 dispatched by 51 Squadron at Snaith, crashed into a wood near Stokenchurch, 16 miles south-east of Oxford. Brooks, from Bo'ness, West Lothian and all the crew, who were on their 19th operation, were killed.

At Snaith no word was received from five other Halifaxes. Four of them had been shot down by night fighters. Forty-two men were missing, seven of them prisoners in Germany.

On 101 Squadron at Ludford Magna six ABC Lancasters were missing, and *X-X-Ray* flown by Flight Sergeant Edwin Robert Thomas who was from Forest Gate, London, crashed near RAF Welford, Berkshire, an American Troop-Carrier base. All the crew, who were on their 5th operation, and the Australian special operator, were killed. *K-King* flown by Pilot Officer Albert Lander RNZAF and *H-Harry* flown by Pilot Officer Donald James Irving RAAF from Innisfail, Queensland were shot down on the outward flight. All of Irving's crew, who were on their 9th operation, were killed. Lander was at 18,000 feet when intercepted by a night fighter, possibly that of *Unteroffizier* Bruno Rupp of 4./NJG3. Following a brief engagement, the Lancaster exploded near Dillenburg. Lander and Sergeant W G Clapp were thrown clear. Both were seriously injured. The other six men on board were killed.

The 4,000 pounder in the bomb bay of *J-Johnny* flown by Sergeant Clyde Harnish RCAF from Halifax, Nova Scotia exploded. He and two of his crew were killed. Pilot Officer Rex Cond the special operator only lived for a few hours after the crash. The four other crewmembers survived to be taken prisoner although one was badly beaten up by irate villagers. *R-Robert* flown by Pilot Officer 'Jimmy' Batten-Smith DFC whose crew were on their 22nd operation, crashed near the autobahn at Röthenbach killing all seven crew and the specialist operator. Flight Sergeant Gerald Tivey of Melbourne, Derbyshire was hit by flak at Koblenz and crashed near the village of Rubenach. All the crew, who were on their 10th operation, and the special operator, were killed.

On *L-London* Pilot Officer William Ian Adamson DFC and three of his crew were killed in the aircraft. Two others bailed out and were taken prisoner. Sergeant Don Brinkhurst, the mid-upper gunner, got out of his turret and helped Flying Officer Norman Marrian, the special operator, out of his seat after their Lancaster was hit by fire from a Halifax. The SO's parachute had been damaged so they both agreed to go down on Brinkhurst's parachute. During the descent Marrian slipped out of Brinkhurst's arms and he was killed. Brinkhurst reached Switzerland but later in the year crossed back into France and subsequently returned to the Squadron and completed a further 20 operations.[25]

Squadron Leader Maurice McCreanor on 578 Squadron at Burn, which had dispatched 11 Halifaxes, tried to put his Halifax III down at RAF Silverstone in Northamptonshire at the end of what was their 15th op, but in the poor visibility they failed to see the masts of the Assisted Safe Landing equipment and *S-Sugar* crashed into playing fields nearby. McCreanor, who was from Macclesfield in Cheshire and six of his crew, including Sergeant Alex McLennan, the 'second dickey', were either killed outright or died later. There was only one survivor.

American pilot, First Lieutenant Max Dowden on 625 Squadron who was from Santa Cruz, California and had joined the RCAF before Pearl Harbor following a broken engagement, also tried to put his Lancaster down at Silverstone but he was refused permission and he was diverted to Bovingdon in Hertfordshire. They got down to 500 feet without reaching the airfield and the crew got into their crash positions. Dowden made a brilliant wheels-down landing in a small field and rumbled across a field on the Duke of Bedford's estate at Little Chalfont. A wagon from the American base picked them up and took them to Kings Cross station to get back to Kelstern.

Flight Lieutenant A H MacGillivray RCAF, pilot of *Z-Zebra*, one of 20 Lancasters on 7 Squadron dispatched from Oakington, was diverted due to fog and he crash-landed at Feltwell, hitting a concrete pill box in the process. A fire broke out but the crew was able to evacuate the wreckage of the Lancaster without injury. Two other 7 Squadron Lancasters failed to return home. Outbound, 38-year-old Squadron Leader Colin Howard Wilson DFC of Bowden, Cheshire and his crew who were on their fourth operation, were shot down in an attack by a night fighter, possibly flown by *Leutnant* Günther Wolf of 9./NJG5 in the Fulda area. All seven crew died when the bomber exploded. One of the dead was Sergeant Wycliffe Jenkins the 19-year-old flight engineer of Rainham, Essex. The only complete body was that of Sergeant Frank Fuller the 20-year-old rear gunner who was found lying near an engine at the crash site at Ober-Moos.

Shortly before reaching the aiming point at 01.25 hours Flight Lieutenant Stanley Evans of Leicester and his crew, who were on their 26th operation, were shot down by a Bf 109G-6 flown by *Leutnant* Kurt Gabler, *Staffel-kapitän* of 9./JG300. In the exchange of fire, both aircraft went down. All the Lancaster crew were killed, while the *Wild Boar* pilot bailed out safely at Gutenburg near Gräfenberg.[26]

Flight Sergeant Jack Ward, a former 'Mountie', crashed his Halifax into a small farm building three miles from RAF Cranwell. Incredibly, there were no causalities. *S-Sugar* a Lancaster III on 619 Squadron crashed at Woodbridge and was consumed by fire but none of Sergeant John

Parker's crew was hurt, though all were killed later on operations before the year was out.[27]

Six Lancasters on 514 Squadron failed to land back safely at Waterbeach, from where 19 Lancasters had been dispatched earlier that night. Warrant Officer 'Bill' McGown was diverted on his return to RAF Stradishall but this airfield was also fog-bound and despite several attempts the Glaswegian could not land there. Finally, two men bailed out at 1,000 feet into the fog before McGown crash-landed near Sawbridgeworth. There were no casualties. Bill McGown and his crew were later shot down on the night of 7/8 June on the operation to Massy-Palaiseau.[28]

514 Squadron Skipper, Pilot Officer Evan Chitty, was baulked on finals at Waterbeach by another aircraft and crash-landed heavily while attempting to go around again. Two of the Australian's crew were killed and four others injured. Chitty and his crew were later killed on the daylight raid on Caen on 30 July.[29]

At Holme-on-Spalding Moor, where 14 Halifaxes had been dispatched by 76 Squadron, the clock in the big briefing room ticked on. On the ops board in the column headed 'Time Down' were four blank spaces; *J-Johnny*, *P-Peter*, *W-William* and *X-X-Ray*. Nothing could happen to *P-Peter* could it? Flight Lieutenant Henry Coverley was on his second tour. The Intelligence Officer looked at his watch and checked it with the clock. Hopefully *P-Peter* aka *Roger De Coverley* and *W-William* and *X-X-Ray* had all made an emergency landings at 'dromes on the southeast coast; the telephone, at his elbow, would ring in a moment confirming it. The room was crowded and there was acute expectancy in the air. Crews who were down were hanging about, deliberately taking their time over mugs of tea, forgetting the hot flying suppers waiting for them in the messes. As the minutes ticked by, many considered the chances of the three crews bailing out and spending the rest of the war as a PoW or lobbing down somewhere in the drink off the coast. It was the best that they could hope for.

P-Peter, *W-William* and *X-X-Ray* were all shot down by Bf 110s employing *Schräge Musik* attacks.

Henry Coverley and five of his crew, who were on their 9th operation, bailed out before *Roger De Coverley* crashed near the town of Hamm but Sergeant George Edwin Motts the flight engineer, who was from Lincoln, died when he evacuated the Halifax with his parachute on fire. Coverley walked for 30 miles and evaded capture for four days before being caught crossing a bridge over the Rhine. One by one the other five men on the crew were rounded up and sent to prison camps.[30]

After being shot down in flames two men on Flying Officer Gordon Charles George Greenacre's crew bailed out of *W-William* and were taken prisoner. The pilot, from Wroxham in the heart of the Norfolk Broads who was on his second tour on the Squadron, and four of his crew, all of whom were on their 21st operation, were killed.

There was just one survivor on *X-X-Ray*, which went down at Daubhausen, 12 kilometres Northwest of Wetzlar. Squadron Leader Kenneth Arthur Clack DFM, who was from Harrow Weald, Middlesex and six of his eight-man crew, who were on the fourth operation of their second tour, were killed. Sergeant G L Edwards the mid-upper gunner was taken prisoner.

Wyton had dispatched 14 Lancasters on 83 Path Finder Squadron, each carrying four flares to drop visually to build up those dropped earlier by other Path Finders, and a 8,000lb bomb for good measure. All aircraft returned safely although Warrant Officer Ken Lane experienced severe difficulties when they arrived back over their base in atrocious weather conditions with a snowstorm giving nil visibility. Several attempts to approach were made but each time the runway was lost. Fuel was running low when Lane finally got the Lancaster down on one last attempt after a near-stall at little over 65 knots, which had almost resulted in a crash. The Aerodrome Control Pilot in his caravan claimed later that he had not seen an aircraft actually land, although he had heard some frightening noises. There was no sign of life on the station and the duty officer had to be roused to de-brief them, much to his disgust.

On the wireless next morning Ken Lane heard the sombre news that 95 aircraft were missing but he knew that others would probably have run out of fuel and crash-landed but he never heard the final toll. For him it was the night when the Lancaster performed the impossible.[31]

On 156 Squadron 'Tubby' Holley on *D-Dog* had vaguely heard the navigator's call that they had crossed the French coast before dropping off to sleep and he had woken again after they had crossed the English coast. Gradually, Squadron Leader Brooks brought the Lancaster down through thick cloud on to the course given him by his navigator for their base at Upwood. Flying Officer Jones then read off a new set of fixes from the *Gee* box and announced that they were over the base. The bomber was now down to 900 feet but still the cloud was solid. Brooks sliced off more height, until his altimeter showed that they were at 300 feet and told his crew that he would take the Lancaster a little lower to try to get under the cloud base. He could see nothing outside but thick, smothering vapour. Jones, after taking another fix, warned that they were getting away from Upwood and gave Brooks a course alteration that would take them back over their base. They were now at a height of 200 feet and Brooks' right hand gripped the throttle levers firmly in readiness to give the engines more power should it be necessary to climb hurriedly. He fully realised the danger of attempting to fly lower with visibility nil but there was no alternative. 'I'm not going to call up control,' he told the crew. 'They'll only divert us. Hang on and keep your fingers crossed.' He then slammed open his side-panel as an aid to vision and was amazed to be showered with snow. 'Christ!' he shouted. 'This isn't cloud. It's a bloody snowstorm! No wonder I can't see a thing; the blasted wind-screen's covered with thick snow.'

Moments later his voice came to them again and though it was calm they detected in it an underlying tone of caution. 'We're down to a hundred feet. We can't go much lower without hitting something, that's for sure.' He then dropped the port wing gently and peered out of the side window in the hope of glimpsing the tall chimneys of an old brickworks that was near Upwood. But before he could take in anything his flight engineer, Sergeant Sabin, called out that he thought he had seen some Drem lights (the guide-lights that marked the perimeter of an airfield) to their starboard. Brooks hauled the Lancaster into a steep right-hand turn and saw the faint, flickering lights of Upwood. In that instant the aircraft pitched wildly and Brooks froze in his seat as another Lancaster slid a few feet above them, blasting *D-Dog* with its slipstream.

'*Jee-zus!*' someone gasped over the intercom. 'Did you see that?'

Holley recalls:

We all thought we'd had it. Brooks took the Lancaster down to 70 feet and ordered the engineer to drop the undercarriage. 'We'll follow the Drem lights round and swing on to the runway as soon as it shows up through this muck,' he announced. But it wasn't as simple as it sounded. On our first trip round we were too close and crossed the runway at right-angles. On our next circuit we missed it completely. I had my turret facing port and when on our next orbit the engineer shouted 'Hard to port' Brooks banked so steeply that I found myself looking straight down at the deck. A moment later he straightened *D-Dog* and told us, 'OK, I've got it ... Stand by to cut engines ... *Cut!*' The next moment we hit the tarmac with quite a thump. Brooks swung the aircraft sharply to face the direction from which we had landed. This rather unorthodox procedure had the effect of pulling us up more effectively and more quickly than any application of the brakes would have.

Ours was the first and only aircraft to land at Upwood whilst the snow was falling. Half an hour later, when we had completed our interrogation of the raid, four more bombers from the squadron landed. The majority had called up earlier and had been diverted to other airfields. We soon learned how lucky we had been. Usually, one of the hottest spots on an operation was to be in the first wave with the fighters doing their utmost to prevent the Path Finders getting to the target and illuminating the aiming point. On this occasion we had been extremely fortunate in being in the role of primary markers. While I had seen a mere four or five aircraft going down as we flew south of the Ruhr, several of my colleagues who had been further back in the bomber stream were attacked. According to their tote, over 40 bombers had got the chop in that area.

I doubt if I would have dozed so well on the way back had I realised things were so dicey. I was even more shaken when I heard that four of our own squadron Lancasters had gone down.[32]

Flight Sergeant Brian Soper recalls:

We eventually had found the target and bombed on red/yellow TI markers. I shall never forget the searchlight cones on the way back and particularly a Mossie, which was caught by the master search-light and then coned, very near us. While those unlucky blokes were getting the attention we managed to clear the area, a searchlight just crossing us a few times and with a constant barrage of flak. On the route home, at around Saarbrücken, we lost the port inner engine. Losing oil and overheating we had to shut off and feather the engine. I later had to cross feed the petrol to maintain a balance of fuel and weight. This also meant being extra alert for fighter attacks. We subsequently arrived back at Wickenby and made a successful landing on three engines.[33]

Some squadrons returned relatively unscathed. Sixteen Halifaxes on 576 Squadron had taken off from Elsham Wolds and only one was lost. Flight Lieutenant P E Underwood and crew, who were on their sixth operation, were flying at 20,500 feet on the outward leg when they were shot down by a night fighter at Oberweid, 25 kilometres ENE of Fulda. Underwood and one of his crew bailed out successfully but the other five members were killed. At Skipton-on-Swale only the one Halifax on 433 'Porcupine' Squadron from a dozen that had left the station earlier failed to return but Flight Sergeant Reinell had flown his Halifax for nearly two hours with a raging fire in the starboard wing. He only just made it to Manston where 32 square feet of the wing's aluminium skin had been burnt away.

Flight Sergeant T A Lloyd on 550 Squadron at North Killingholme landed his badly damaged Lancaster at Ford on the south coast of England minus three of his crew. The Lancaster had been attacked by a night fighter on the homeward leg just south of Paris. With the trimming tabs shot away Lloyd struggled to keep control of the bomber but he managed to shake off the fighter. Five minutes later a second attack set the bomb bay and fuselage on fire and he gave the order for the crew to bail out. The mid-upper gunner, bomb aimer and rear turret gunner bailed out. Before the rest could follow, the aircraft went into a dive which helped to extinguish the fires. The bomb aimer and the rear gunner were captured but 30-year-old Sergeant J G Pearce the mid-upper gunner evaded, and helped by the Resistance, made it home via Gibraltar in June.

Two other Lancasters on 550 Squadron failed to return.

Three of the eleven Lancaster Path Finder aircraft that were lost on the raid were on 635 Squadron at Downham Market in Norfolk where earlier, fourteen aircraft had been dispatched. Flight Lieutenant Charles Anthony Lyon of Whitley Bridge, Yorkshire, crashed at Erksdorf near Neckartzenlingen with the loss of all the crew. They were on their 16th operation.[34]

Wing Commander 'Pat' Daniels was the first to land at Graveley, where he found Air Vice Marshal Bennett who usually drove over from his headquarters in Huntingdon, waiting for him in the de-briefing room. Daniels said bitterly, 'Bloody hell! Why did we have to go that way?' On hearing the details Bennett was inclined to be sceptical; not wanting to believe that the operation could have been such a disaster but he knew that Daniels was not prone to exaggeration. To appease Daniels, Bennett took him over to the big wall map and while he drank his tea from a dirty cup – 'it still tasted very good after seven and a half hours flying' – he talked of the future targets in the south of Germany, which had so far been untouched. Daniels recalls:

He pointed out to me, in confidence the targets that we would have to attack there and explained that they were lightly defended. 'There were some big ones, which would have to be done soon', he said. Munich was one of them and it was finally done successfully. However, I thought the difficulty after this night's show would be to get there, especially in bright moonlight. We had climbed that night through cloud over the sea and when we got above it there was bright moonlight. Although there was thick cloud over the target, it was the brightest moonlight I could remember flying in. I again stressed to Bennett that on this raid there was a large number of sightings of aircraft blowing up. Most of them were brought down by fighters. There was also a large number of scare-shells sent up to simulate an aircraft exploding and they were very good imitations. But I soon found out that in many cases they were, in fact, bombers blowing up. The fighter attacks on the bombers usually started a small fire in the fuselage or wing, which was spread by the slip-stream and wind to the fuel tanks and bombs. Then everything went up. Often, though, it was difficult to be sure whether it was a bomber exploding or a scare-shell.

Squadron Leader Arthur William Doubleday DFC RAAF was first back at Waddington and Sir Ralph Cochrane called him up to the control tower: 'He asked, "How did it go?" I said, "Jerry got a century before lunch today." He didn't quite – he got 95.'

Much to his relief, Doubleday's great friend, Squadron Leader Bill Brill DFC RAAF, who was also on his second tour and had been his best man at his wedding to Phyllis Buckle on 14 August 1943, finally touched down at Waddington one hour after the rest of 463 Squadron had landed. In clear sky with the cloud below him Brill had seen a violent explosion and a sheet of flame as a bomber exploded in front of him. As he flew through the cloud of smoke and flying debris something 'solid' had hit his Lancaster. Brill flew on and bombed on a *Wanganui*. As he slowly pulled away with the port outer engine stopped and the rear gun turret out of action he was attacked by a fighter but he turned towards the fighter and the cannon fire went wide. The enemy pilot broke off the attack and did not return, which was fortunate because the port inner engine suddenly stopped. Brill told the crew to get ready to bail out but then one of the engines, its propeller wind-milling uselessly, coughed and spluttered back to life and the Lancaster flew slowly home to Waddington. Later, part of a belt of .303 ammunition was found in the wing of Brill's Lancaster. It had cut the oil lines to the outer engine.[35]

At Melbourne Pilot Officer J D Whiteman on 10 Squadron told his 4 Group Commander, Air Vice Marshal C Roderick Carr, a New Zealander, 'I did not think that we were going to reach the bloody target let alone return to base.' Doubtless Carr's entourage – two American colonels and the station and squadron commanders who had also arrived to attend the debriefing – were well aware now of how crews felt about the debacle that had unfolded.

Against all the odds *Y-Yorker* was one of 14 Lancasters that returned to Dunholme Lodge. Wing Commander Thompson's crew went straight to the interrogation room where Flight Lieutenant Burrows the flight-engineer was surprised to see the imposing 6-foot-six figure of their station commander, Air Commodore 'Poppy' Pope standing beside the station commander, Group Captain Butler. Both of these officers asked him how the operation had gone. Burrows stated that he thought that Bomber Command had lost about 100 aircraft and he was told not to be ridiculous. They turned to the doctor and remarked, 'Send this crew on leave. It's time they had a rest.'

Burrows adds:

The de-briefing was very quiet and the atmosphere was electric. It certainly appeared to me that Jerry was waiting for us and there were rumours that the raid had been leaked. In fact, it was said quite openly during interrogation – with lots of derogatory remarks being made. We on 44 Squadron had lost seven aircraft and we noticed at breakfast that many seats were empty. There were plenty of fried eggs to spare. They had been cooked for crews who never returned.[36] That evening we consumed gallons of ale.

E-Easy on 57 Squadron was not the only loss at East Kirkby: three Lancasters on 630 Squadron were shot down by night fighters on the outward flight. *S-Sugar* was flown by Pilot Officer Ronald Leslie Clark from Parkdale, Victoria and his crew who were on their first operation. Only Sergeant R I Smith the bomb-aimer survived and he was taken prisoner. *T-Tommy* piloted by 31-year-old Flying Officer John C 'Jock' Langlands whose crew were on their third operation, was shot down at 20,000 feet fell and out of control near Ruhla. The tall and slim Langlands who had been an Edinburgh policeman, calmly kept the Lancaster level as the men in the front of the aircraft bailed out. Pilot Officer H B 'Benny' Bryans the bomb aimer from Leicester could not get the forward escape hatch open so 23-year-old Sergeant Norman 'Hermann' Goring the flight engineer from Hull, went down and dragged it up. He pushed out Bryans and then he too jumped out into the night. Flying Officer Bob Guthrie the navigator, who had just turned 21 and was from Reading, followed. Langlands was the last to leave; Sergeant Geoff Jeffery the 22-year-old wireless operator from Sevenoaks in Kent, and both gunners, went down with the aircraft. The rear gunner, Flight Sergeant Alan Drake, a married man from Wigan in Lancashire was a veteran of ten years' service and had been an armourer before becoming an aerial gunner. Sergeant Harry 'Bud' Coffey the 21-year-old mid-upper gunner was from Saint John, New Brunswick.

H-Harry flown by Pilot Officer Allan George Garth Johnson of Nassau in the Bahamas, whose crew were on their 16th operation, was probably shot down by *Feldwebel* Ernst Reitmeyer of 1./NJG5 north-west of Nürnburg. The Lancaster crashed at Altendorf on the east side of the Donau–Regnitz Kanal. Johnson and Ernest Arthur Farnell, from Sevenoaks in Kent, Arthur Henry McGill who was from Bristol and Bill France from Malin Bridge, Sheffield, were killed; the three survivors being taken prisoner.

At Binbrook, where 24 Lancasters including the veteran *G-George* had taken off, three Lancasters on 460 Squadron RAAF were missing. Pilot Officer Peter Robert Anderson, an Australian from Halbury, South Australia whose crew were on their fifth operation, had been lost to the Rhine flak nearing Koblenz on the outward flight. South of Cologne Squadron Leader Eric Arthur Gibson Utz DFC* RAAF, a grazier from Armidale in the 'New England district' of New South Wales was attacked again and again by a single-engined night fighter, which hit the fuel tank and set the bomber on fire 'like a great white torch in the sky'. The Lancaster exploded in the air killing everyone except Pilot Officer R J McCleery RAAF the navigator who was blown out and who survived. Badly injured in one leg, McCleery was treated by a local village doctor but his leg had to be amputated later. The Lancaster crashed between Fulda and Gersfeld (Rhön). Utz and the bodies of the other five members of his crew – most were on their 18th operation of their second tour – were recovered from deep snow the following day.[37] Another Lancaster, flown by Flight Sergeant Charles Haley Hargreaves RAAF of Gordon, New South Wales was shot down near the target by *Unteroffizier* Günther

Schmidt of 8./NJG2.[38] All of the crew, who were on their fourth operation perished. Pilot Officer Neal's crew of *G-George* had not been fooling themselves that the run-in on Nürnburg would be easy but they had been comforted by the knowledge that their Lancaster had had the phenomenal luck to come through 86 operations, and trusted that Nürnburg would be the 87th. It was. *G-George* was one of those that made it back. On 22 April, after its 90th and last operation the previous day, *George* was officially retired from operations. In October the veteran Lancaster was on its way to Australia.

R-Robert, a Path Finder on 83 Squadron at Wyton was a visual-marker and it reached the target area without being attacked by night fighters, but the crew saw many bombers going down in flames behind them. Navigator Flying Officer Davidson counted over 50 of them before the pilot, Flight Lieutenant Hellier, told him to stop logging them and concentrate on his navigation instead. Flight Sergeant Frank Wildman DFM *R-Robert*'s flight-engineer, wrote:

We were one of the first aircraft over Nürnburg and the target was not particularly 'hot' at that stage, as far as we were concerned. In fact, we thought it rather quiet on the bomb-run after having done 11 sorties to Berlin during the previous month. But we felt that something was really happening behind us. This made us a bit apprehensive about the return trip, yet it turned out to be uneventful. As we neared Wyton we were diverted because of fog to Downham Market, where an estimated seven squadrons landed. There were all sorts of rumours flying about but no official explanation was ever given to us for the high losses. We were one of the first aircraft to land at Downham Market so there was not a hint at our de-briefing of the large numbers of bombers that had not returned. Crews who landed there could not be sure how their squadrons had fared because of the number of diversions. The shock came when the official figures were announced.

Max Dowden's crew arrived at Kings Cross station in the American wagon carrying their flying equipment and the machine guns from their Lancaster. As they walked up the ramp they were staggered to see the *Daily Express* placard saying '96 Down'. The Air Ministry 39-word communiqué broadcast by the BBC said, 'Last night aircraft of Bomber Command were over Germany in very great strength. The main objective was Nürnburg. Other aircraft attacked targets in western Germany and mines were laid in enemy waters. Ninety-six of our aircraft are missing.' In a subsequent communiqué the Air Ministry amended the number of missing aircraft to 94 but this took no account of the bombers that came down in the sea on the homeward flight or crashed in England.[39] It was the worst Bomber Command loss of the war and more aircrew had been killed in one night than in whole of the Battle of Britain. 'It was possible to plot your course to the target' reported *Oberleutnant* Fritz Brandt 'by the number of wrecked aircraft, which we could see next day. They ran in a smouldering line across half of Germany.'

On 27 June it was announced in the London Gazette that Pilot Officer Cyril Joe Barton on 578 Squadron, the pilot of *Excalibur*, a Halifax, which crashed near Ryhope Colliery in County Durham, killing Barton and a local miner on his way to work, had received the posthumous award of the Victoria Cross. Barton's citation read:

> On the night of 30 March 1944 Pilot Officer Barton was captain and pilot of a Halifax aircraft detailed to attack Nürnburg when, 70 miles short of the target, the aircraft was attacked by a Junkers 88. The first burst of fire from the enemy made the intercommunication system useless. One engine was damaged when a Messerschmitt 210 joined the fight. The bomber's machine guns were out of action and the gunners were unable to return the fire. The two fighters continued to attack the aircraft as it approached the target area and, in the confusion caused by the failure of the communications system at the height of the battle, a signal was misinterpreted and the navigator, air bomber and wireless operator left the aircraft by parachute. Barton now faced a situation of dire peril. His aircraft was damaged, his navigational team had gone and he could not communicate with the remainder of the crew. If he continued his mission, he would be at the mercy of hostile fighters when silhouetted against the fires in the target area, and if he survived, he would have to make a four-hour journey home on three engines across heavily-defended territory. Determined to press home his attack at all costs, he flew on and reaching the target, released the bombs himself. As Barton turned for home the propeller of the damaged engine, which was vibrating badly, flew off. It was also discovered that two of the petrol tanks had suffered damage and were leaking. Barton held to his course and, without navigational aids and in spite of strong head winds, successfully avoided the most dangerous defence areas on his route. Eventually he crossed the English coast only 90 miles north of his base. By this time the petrol supply was nearly exhausted. Before a suitable landing place could be found, the port engines stopped. The aircraft was now too low to be abandoned successfully and Barton therefore ordered the three remaining members of his crew to take up their crash stations. Then, with only one engine working, he made a gallant attempt to land clear of the houses over which he was flying. The aircraft finally crashed and Barton lost his life but his three comrades survived. Barton had previously taken part in four attacks on Berlin and fourteen other operational missions. On one of

these, two members of his crew were wounded during a determined effort to locate the target despite appalling weather conditions. In gallantly completing his last mission in the face of almost impossible odds, this officer displayed unsurpassed courage and devotion to duty.

Returning to Skellingthorpe Sergeant Albert Handley on 50 Squadron, whose crew was on only their second operation, finally landed at Winthorpe near Newark where the Lancaster ran off the runway, tipped onto its nose and came to a stop. Fortunately no one was injured. Later promoted to Pilot Officer, Handley was killed, along with his crew, in May on the almost equally disastrous raid on Mailly-le-Camp.

Lastly, the Lancaster flown by Flight Sergeant A F T L'Estrange on 12 Squadron was returning to Wickenby over Cambridgeshire when at 04.33 hours it was attacked by a Ju 88 intruder flown by *Oberstleutnant* Wolf Dietrich Meister of *Stab*/KG51 *Edelweiss*, who mistook his prey for a B-17 Fortress. Meister was aided in his interception by the bomber crew who had relaxed and thinking that they were finally 'home and dry' had switched on their navigation lights. Sergeant A Davenport, the tail gunner even put on the light inside his rear turret. Without warning, Meister fired two long bursts of cannon fire into the Lancaster from dead astern. The second of these wounded Davenport and caused extensive damage to the Lancaster. L'Estrange managed to reach Wickenby where he put the badly damaged Lancaster down on the runway but collided with another Lancaster. There were no casualties in either aircraft and at last they 'were home'.

Limping home with the starboard inner engine out of action and fuel disappearing fast from a broken fuel pipe, *J-Johnny*, Flight Lieutenant Bolt's Halifax on 76 Squadron, had no hope of making it back to Holme-on-Spalding Moor. Bolt instead made straight for the nearest part of the French coast, crossed the Channel safely and headed for Ford. Fred Hall says:

But this airfield was full of circling aircraft and so we continued on to Tangmere. The engineer had to take an axe to the undercarriage up lock housing to manually release the jammed starboard leg. We landed, but swung off the runway as the tyres were burst. A fuel check after landing showed that we had only five minutes' fuel remaining. The Squadron Engineer flew down from Holme-on-Spalding Moor the following morning to confirm that the aircraft was beyond repair; indeed, he couldn't understand why the starboard wing had not folded. But our only injury was found the following morning when the wireless operator discovered his cigarette case had been flattened by a cannon shell and he had a bruise on his right hip!

Hall and his pilot were awarded immediate DFCs. *J-Johnny* was written off.

Replacements now began trickling onto the windswept airfields where their reception was determined by the events of the night before. Peter O'Connor, a 22-year-old Australian navigator, arrived on 44 Squadron at Dunholme Lodge where he and his crewmates were ushered into a Nissen hut but personal belongings indicated that all space was taken. They asked the guard what the story was.

'They went off last night; they won't be back' he said. 'They're your beds.'

O'Connor, who had completed his education at Sacred Heart College in Adelaide and would before each op, pay a visit to the priest who heard his confession, walked around the airfield and found people 'stunned' and 'dazed' and 'WAAFs crying all over the place.'

'We were like strangers at a funeral.'[40]

In Canada Peter Bone made no mention of the debacle in his diary but he must have been aware of it because an Air Ministry press release, while not going into details, followed the normal procedure and noted the losses.

He recalls:

Perhaps I just didn't want to think about what could well be facing me in a few months' time. Next day the sailing draft list was read out and both Geoff and I were on it. What good fortune! A few days later, as the morning sun came up I was on gun duty on the *Pasteur* watching the Canadian coastline slowly disappear over the horizon. Aircraft of the Royal Canadian Air Force circled above us and then wagged their wings in a final 'Godspeed' before disappearing too. The next coastline we would see would be that of dear old Britain. Although the Atlantic was choppy, it remained relatively calm but I succumbed to seasickness as soon as we reached open water and spent another wretched week hanging over the rail, even when I was supposed to be keeping a lookout for *U-boats*. It was a great relief to see the coastline of Northern Ireland appear, then that of Scotland and then the port of Liverpool. It was early April and as the troop train clattered its way south that sunny morning, I looked out at the pink blossom in the placid green fields and thought of Browning's poem, '*Oh to be in England, now that April's there.*'

Notes

1. He and Sgt William Jones on the crew of F/Sgt S Hughes on 158 Squadron (who were all captured) were taken in by the Resistance and hidden in a house. But during a raid by about 80 German soldiers they were shot at as they jumped from a top floor window. Bill Jones was hit in the leg and

apprehended. Moffatt, who was not wearing his boots, got away. Jones was later tortured before finally being sent to *Stalag Luft VII* at Bankau. Albert Paul, their brave Resistance saviour, was later shot by the Germans. After many close shaves and fighting with the Resistance, Jim Moffatt met up with the American advance and he was flown to England in September. See *RAF Evaders: The Comprehensive Story of Thousands of Escapers and their Escape Lines, Western Europe, 1940–1945* by Oliver Clutton-Brock (Grub Street 2009).

2. See *At First Sight: A Factual and anecdotal account of No. 627 Squadron RAF.* Researched and compiled by Alan B Webb. 1991.

3. *The Bombing of Nürnburg* by James Campbell (Futura 1973).

4. *The Bombing of Nürnburg* by James Campbell (Futura 1973).

5. F/L Milton Frederick Smith DFC was killed on 17 June 1944 serving on 1660 HCU.

6. *The Bombing of Nürnburg* by James Campbell (Futura 1973).

7. Theo Boiten. Also, 166 Squadron lost the Lancaster flown by P/O Walter Henry Burnett to another night fighter, flown by *Unteroffizier* Johann Werthner of 7./NJG2 10km S of Eitorf. The crew, most of whom were on their 16th operation, never saw the fighter and the rear turret was disabled in the first pass. Subsequent passes set the engines on fire and Burnett, from Stanmore, Middlesex ordered everyone to bail out. The mid-upper gunner stayed to help the rear gunner and it is believed that Burnett, knowing that they were still on board, elected to ride the aircraft in. All three died; the five other men survived and were taken prisoner. A fourth Lancaster in 166 Squadron, flown by F/L Gordon Arbuthnot Proctor, a Londoner from Clapham Common, was shot down by a night fighter (possibly *Leutnant* Günther Wolf of 9./NJG5) and crashed 400 metres SE of Michelsrombach with the loss of all the crew. They were on only their second operation.

8. From research by Theo Boiten these were two 207 Squadron Lancasters at Spilsby: LM436 flown by P/O Bertram Challis Riddle of Fairlie, Canterbury, New Zealand and ND568 flown by P/O Jack Hardy Thornton RCAF from Hamilton, Ontario. Riddle and all his crew, who were on their 5th operation, were killed. Thornton's Lancaster was hit nearing the target and crashed near Schweinfurt. All the crew, who were on their 11th operation, were also killed.

9. DS836.

10. WO2 William Earle Brown was KIA on 21/22 May 1944 on the operation on Duisburg.

11. Chris Panton had two younger brothers, Fred (13) and Harold (11). In 1981 the Panton brothers bought the airfield at East Kirkby and seven years later purchased Lancaster X NX611. Fully restored, *Just Jane*, as the aircraft is named, can be taxied on all four engines and may be viewed at the Lincolnshire Heritage Centre.

12. The Intruder, which was identified by Martin Middlebrook in *The Nürnburg Raid*, was a 605 Squadron Mosquito flown by F/L Peter Garner and Flying Officer Duncan who had patrolled Erfurt for over an hour before they saw German fighters starting to land there. They fired 89 cannon shells and 54 machine gun bullets, and strikes were seen on two fighters in the hangar. F/L Garner was killed at Yeovil in 1948 while flying as a test pilot on the Westland Wyvern.

13. The first was possibly Lancaster LL738 on 514 Squadron 20km SE of Bonn. [P/O Garth Stewart Hughes DFC RAAF and his crew were on their 19th operation. F/Sgt A D Hall RNZAF was the only survivor]. Raum's third victim was Halifax LW537 on 51 Squadron [flown by Flying Officer Malcolm Mason Stembridge of York whose crew were on their 6th operation. Stembridge and Sgt John Docherty Goskirk of Innerleithen, Peebleshire, were killed]. Raum survived the war as *Staffelkapitän* of 9./NJG3 with 14 to 17 victories. (From research by Theo Boiten).

14. *The Bombing of Nürnburg* by James Campbell (Futura 1973).

15. The Heinkel He 219 *Uhu* (Owl) might have turned the tide for *Nachtjagd* had it been introduced in quantity. Fast (670 km/h at 23,000ft), manoeuvrable and heavily armed with four or six forward firing cannon and a twin 30mm Mk.108 *Schrage Müsik* installation, the *Uhu* was *Nachtjagd's* only aircraft capable of meeting the Mosquito on equal terms. But by the time the first He 219A-6 Mosquito hunters (with all engine and ammunition, tank armour and oblique armament removed) were delivered, use of the *Uhu* against the 'Wooden Wonder' had officially been banned. He 219 production ceased in favour of the Ju 88G (Gustav) series by January 1945.

16. Modrow claimed 34 night kills in 109 sorties between March 1944 and January 1945 and he was awarded the *Ritterkreuz*. In the period 12 June 1943–2 July 1944 twenty *Uhu* pilots destroyed 111 Bomber Command aircraft including seven Mosquitoes. Modrow was the top-scoring pilot in this period with 25 victories. *Night Airwar; Personal recollections of the conflict over Europe, 1939–45* by Theo Boiten. (Crowood Press 1999).

17. From research by Theo Boiten, possibly LW647 [the 76 Squadron Halifax piloted by F/O Gordon C G Greenacre].

18. Rudolf Frank, 45 night victories in NJG3, *Ritterkreuz* with *Eichenlaub* was KIA on 26/27 April 1944 when he crashed after being hit by debris from a 12 Squadron Lancaster. He was posthumously promoted to *Leutnant* at the end of April on Hitler's birthday.

19. *Hauptmann* Dietrich Schmidt ended the war with 40 night victories in NJG1. He was awarded the *Ritterkreuz*.

20. F/L John Augustus Forrest RAAF was KIA on 24/25 June 1944 on the operation on Prouville.

21. Freeman was awarded the DFC and Jimmy Chapman the WOp/AG the Conspicuous Gallantry Medal (CGM). F/O Denny Freeman and four of his crew were killed in action on 24 September when his Lancaster was hit by flak and crashed into the sea during the operation to attack strong-points at Calais. After recovering from his wounds Jimmy Chapman had returned to operations with 61 Squadron at Skellingthorpe where he flew ops alongside 35-year-old F/Sgt Arthur Sherriff, the crew's air gunner who had been awarded the DFM for his actions on the same raid. Both men were killed on 1 February when their Lancaster, which was flown by S/L Hugh Horsley, lost all four engines on take-off and crashed, killing everyone except the rear gunner. See *Legend of the Lancasters* by Martin W Bowman (Pen & Sword 2009).

22. Apart from those already mentioned, HX349 flown by S/L Samuel Davis Jones DFC who was from Saul in Gloucestershire, had been hit by flak at Westerburg. The crew were on their 12th operation of their second tour. Jones

and F/Sgt Kenneth Arthur Bray, who was from Helston in Cornwall, were killed. The five others who bailed out successfully were taken prisoner. P/O Ronald Henry 'Ginger' Craig was KIA on 24/25 June on the operation to Prouville.

23. Wilfred George Moxey and all of his crew were KIA, their Lancaster crashing at Villers-Deux-Eglises (Namur). Hromadnik next shot down Halifax LV899 of 78 Squadron flown by WO2 Fred Topping RCAF 24 km NW of Charleville. Topping, from Prince Albert, Saskatchewan and crew were on their third operation. They were all killed. Hromadnik's third victory was R5734 *V-Victor* on 61 Squadron, 3½ km NE of Namur. P/O James Arthur Haste RAAF from Maylands, South Australia and crew who were on their 8th operation were killed. (Theo Boiten).

24. ND585 crashed at Villiers-deux-Eglises (Namur), 4 km WSW of Philippeville at 02.52 hours. JB566 flown by F/Sgt Hall crashed with the loss of all except two of the crew.

25. P/O William Ian Adamson DFC of Bathgate, West Lothian and four of the crew were killed. DV264 went down near the small town of Gemund, 5 km NNE of Schleiden.

26. Theo Boiten.

27. Sgt John Harold Woodcock the rear gunner, KIA on the operation to Salbris on 7/8 May. P/O John Parker, who was from Northern Ireland and the other five men in the original crew, KIA on the operation to Kiel on 23/24 July.

28. P/O William L McGown and W/O A N Durham RAAF evaded capture. Two crew were PoW; 3 KIA.

29. Three other Lancasters on 514 Squadron at Waterbeach FTR. LL696 flown by F/O P J K Hood was believed shot down while on the final leg. Hood and five of his crew, including his rear gunner Technical Sgt M G Lanthur USAAF bailed out successfully and were taken prisoner. Sgt Clarence Dunkin Fraser Mackenzie, a Glaswegian, was killed. The crew were on their 16th operation. LL738 flown by P/O Garth Stewart Hughes DFC of Turramurra, NSW was shot down by a night fighter, possibly *Leutnant* Hans Raum of 9./NJG3. Hughes and five of the crew, who were on their 19th operation, were killed. JI-J² LL698 flown by F/Sgt Fred Gregory of Tottenham, London and his crew, who were on their 8th operation, were shot down by a night fighter, possiblythat of *Unteroffizier* Lorenz Gerstmayr of 4./NJG3 who claimed a *Viermot* SE of Bonn. Only one of Gregory's crew survived.

30. Sgt David M Bauldie, the rear-gunner who was from Dunfermline, Fifeshire was amongst a large group of airmen killed on 19 April 1945 in an attack on their PoW column by Typhoons.

31. *The Lancaster at War* by Mike Garbutt and Brian Goulding (Ian Allan 1971).

32. *The Bombing of Nürnburg* by James Campbell (Futura 1973). Apart from the three crews on 156 Squadron already mentioned, a fourth Lancaster FTR when P/O L Lindley and his crew who were on their 19th operation, were shot down by a night fighter. Lindley was the only survivor. His crew included Sgt John Esprey Bates, a southern Irishman from Dublin and Sgt Bankole Beresford Vivour, a Nigerian.

33. 'At the end of the tour most of the crew were awarded the DFM, (including myself). Arthur, the pilot, had been commissioned by this time and qualified for the DFC. Bill Redding, "Wild Bill", (who wasn't at all wild), was the only

one to be chosen to receive his medal at the palace. The rest of them got them through the post. The crew split up after leaving Wickenby although most of them came to my wedding with Mary on 10 June 1944. We had quite a problem sorting out arrangements, since all travelling was restricted because of D Day.'

34. One of the two other 635 Squadron Path Finders lost was JB706 F2-T *T-Tommy* piloted by F/L J H Nicholls DFC and crew who were on their 35th operation, which was shot down by the Westerburg flak. Nicholls and four of his crew survived and were taken prisoner.

35. *Chased By The Sun*. Doubleday and Brill, were farmers from Wagga Wagga, New South Wales, whose wartime careers marched almost in step, typifying many famous Australian air partnerships. After volunteering for the RAAF they were called up together in 1940 and thereafter their promotions were simultaneous. When they became wing commanders, Brill commanded 463 Squadron RAAF and Doubleday 61 Squadron RAF. Each was awarded the DFC and DSO. Brill added a bar to his DFC later. Both were original members of 460 Squadron RAAF. Bill Brill's younger brother Vic who was a pilot on 463 Squadron RAAF also flew the Nürnburg raid.

36. Sixteen Lancasters had taken off from Dunholme Lodge. ND795 flown by P/O Trevor George William Charlesworth who was from Shareshill, Staffs, was shot down near the final turning point and crashed at Unteressfeld with the loss of Charlesworth and five of his crew, who were on their 7th operation. There was only one survivor. ME629, flown by P/O Charles Albert Frost who was from Birkenhead, Cheshire and his crew who were on their sixth op, was lost also. There were no survivors.

37. *The Nürnburg Raid* by Martin Middlebrook (Allen Lane 1973).

38. 3km W of Gräfenberg. From research by Theo Boiten.

39. Sixty-four Lancasters and 31 Halifaxes (11.9% of the force dispatched) were lost. It took the German night fighter arm's total for March to 269 RAF bombers destroyed.

40. *Chased By The Sun*.

CHAPTER 3

The Fruits of 1944

Aunt Kitty was crying. Uncle Chris was stoic as ever. Their only son,
George, had been declared officially missing in action. He was likely dead,
they realized but clung to the hope he would turn up in a prison camp when
the war ended. His bags were sent home from his squadron headquarters
in Yorkshire. Aunt Kitty took the suitcases up to George's room and left
them there. They were never opened. She still clung to the hope that George
would be found when the war ended. The hope remained through 1946
when newspaper reports of long lost soldiers and airmen continued to crop
up. Aunt Kitty could never accept George's death. So the ghost of George
Freeman became part of my childhood years ...

Alan Skeoch, a history teacher and cousin of Sergeant
George Freeman, mid-upper-gunner, Halifax XH313,
KIA 27/28 May 1944.

Nürnburg was – as Winston Churchill recorded in his history of the war
– 'proof of the power which the enemy's night fighter force, strengthened
by the best crews from other vital fronts, had developed under our
relentless offensive.' The raid brought, for a brief period, the virtual
cessation of heavy attacks because without 'radical and remedial action'
the prospect of sustained and massive long-range operations deep into
Germany was impossible. Yet the previous December, when Harris wrote
to the Air Ministry saying he expected in the next three months to have
40 Lancaster squadrons that would be able to drop 13,850 tons of bombs
a month, sufficient to destroy between 40 and 50 per cent of the principal
German towns, he had concluded that 'from this it appears that the
Lancaster force alone should be sufficient but only just sufficient to
produce in Germany by 1 April 1944 a state of devastation in which
surrender is inevitable.' After Nürnburg the night fighters were largely
given a three-week respite before the next big raid though Aachen was
bombed on 11/12 April by over 340 Lancasters and Cologne was hit by
almost 380 aircraft on 20th/21st. 5 Group was unleashed against three

74

targets in Germany in quick succession – Brunswick on 22/23 April, Munich two nights later and Schweinfurt on 26/27 April.

The large scale raid on Munich on 24/25 April was really in the nature of an experiment to test marking a target from low altitude by 617 Squadron. What the Lancasters had to do was lay a concentrated carpet of hooded flares, the light from which would be directed downwards onto the target, making it as bright as day. The small force of Mosquitoes would orbit, find the aiming point and then mark it in a shallow dive with 500lb spot-fires. Marker Leader would assess the position of the spot-fires in relation to the aiming point and would pass this information to a 'Master of Ceremonies' (MC) in one of the Path Finder Lancasters. The MC would then take over and direct the Main Force Lancasters in their attack on the target.[1]

The 26/27 April Schweinfurt raid was a failure. The low-level marking was inaccurate and unexpectedly strong head winds delayed the Lancaster marker aircraft and the Main Force. As a consequence, much of the bombing fell outside the city. German night fighters carried out fierce attacks throughout the period of the raid, which resulted in the loss of 21 Lancasters.

The bombing of German cities was one thing but grave doubts existed at the highest level as to the accuracy of bombing transportation targets in France in the run-up to D-Day. Allied forces required destruction of the French railway system leading to the invasion beaches on the coast of Normandy, and *Luftwaffe* airfields in the Low Countries and France. The best method of doing this was by employing heavy bombers but Winston Churchill was adamant that French lives must not be lost needlessly.

On Easter Sunday, 9 April, scores of Halifax, Stirling and Lancaster crews carried out air tests in readiness for the night's Main Force raids on the goods station at Lille-Délivrance, close to the border with Belgium, and the rail yards at Villeneuve-St-Georges near Paris. La Délivrance was surrounded mainly by housing areas and commercial premises but it was felt that by using a combination of the new low-level marking by 11 Oboe-equipped Mosquitoes and a Master Bomber the bombing would be accurate enough to avoid unnecessary casualties. A further 103 Lancasters of 1 and 5 Groups were detailed to lay mines off Danzig, Gdynia and Pillau in the Baltic. In total, 697 sorties would be flown on the night of 9/10 April.

In Norfolk and Suffolk, just over 100 Liberators of the US 2nd Bomb Division, 8th Air Force, began assembling for raids on enemy airfields and an assembly plant at Tutow in Germany. As they climbed for altitude over Norfolk at around 09.00 hours, two of the American bombers collided in undercast at 8,000 feet over Foulsham airfield where Halifax aircraft on 192 Squadron in 100 Group were preparing for the Bomber Support operation for the raid on Paris later that evening. Maurice Flower's crew were taxiing up to the end of the runway. On the right hand side of them was the 4,000lb bomb dump. He recalls:

> They were like 50-gallon drums, all stacked up. We'd just been given the go-ahead for take-off, the runway was clear and it was a beautiful sunny day. There was one cloud over our airfield and two of the Liberators flew into this cloud and collided. Their bombs dropped all around us. One hit the 4,000lb bomb dump on our right hand side. I wasn't scared; I was just fascinated to watch this 4,000lb bomb. It rolled in from behind the starboard wing, went right through and then disappeared. Then it appeared in front and it just rolled gently across and came to a rest on the left hand side of the runway. I never thought about it exploding but if it had gone up, they wouldn't have seen us again! All the bodies dropped around our aeroplane. There was one bloke parachuting down who'd had his legs blown off and he died on the way down. Bodies just fell all around us. A WAAF appeared in a little Bedford van and she went round covering all their faces. She was fantastic; just getting on and doing that; only a young girl.[2]

At Lille, over 230 bombers, mostly Halifaxes, got their bombs away but the yards were hit by just 49 bombs, which destroyed 2,124 of the 2,959 goods wagons in the yards; the rest falling outside the railway area killing 456 French civilians. In the suburb of Lomme more than 5,000 houses were destroyed or damaged.[3] According to the Bomber Command Operational Research Section 875 of the 3,335 bombs dropped had fallen into the designated target area and that it was the 'best centred of all the marshalling yard attacks to date'. It was an inescapable fact that over 2,000 bombs had fallen into mostly urban areas. It was much the same story at Villeneuve-St-Georges where 400 houses were damaged or destroyed and 93 French civilians killed and 167 injured.

Just one Lancaster failed to return from the operation on Lille and one Halifax was abandoned after colliding with another Halifax near Thirsk while forming up for the operation on Villeneuve-St-Georges. Night fighters were active over Denmark and nine Lancaster minelayers including three on 460 Squadron RAAF at Binbrook were shot down. *G-George* on 103 Squadron at Elsham Wolds, which was tasked to lay mines in Danzig Bay, was intercepted by *Oberleutnant* Günter Rogge of 2./NJG 3 at 18,600 feet while crossing the Jylland peninsula on the return flight and was severely damaged. Pilot Officer Jim Nimmo RAAF ordered the crew to bail out but only Flight Sergeant Keith F Clohessy RAAF the rear gunner and Flight Sergeant John Smith RAAF the mid-upper gunner managed to get out of the Lancaster before it exploded in the air at 03:49 hours. A major part of the fuselage fell close by the hospital in Brande while the front end fell in a field at Dørslunde. The body of Pilot

Officer Arthur T Thornton RAAF the navigator was found 300 feet from the front end. The bodies of Sergeant James M Roberts the flight engineer, Flight Sergeant Jack Bernaldo the bomb aimer, Jim Nimmo and the W/Op Pilot Officer Thomas W Bradley, were found in fields nearby. They were all laid to rest in Fovrfelt cemetery in Esbjerg on 15 April.

John Smith landed in a field belonging to Harry Svarre, of Nørre Hygildgaard farm. The parachute got caught in some high trees 500 metres south of the farm. He released his harness and fell to the ground. He then started walking away from the landing place heading west. After having walked about five kilometres he hid in some scrub and lay down to sleep. He was awoken by a German soldier who jabbed him in the stomach with a pistol. Smith was next taken to Brande and placed in the school which had been occupied by the *Wehrmacht*. In the bicycle shack he saw the bodies of his dead comrades. The next day he was sent by train to *Dulag Luft* for interrogation and into captivity.

Keith Clohessy landed about two kilometres west of the front end of the fuselage. He had lost one boot and his right knee was twice its normal size. He moved on and after a while rested in a small wood. Next day he got in touch with some Danes but due to the language problem they found it hard to communicate. A farmer, however, showed up with a pair of old boots and a long black overcoat, which he gave to Clohessy. He started walking and in the evening he sought shelter in a small farm where he entered the loft of a chicken coop and washing house. He continued walking the next morning but he was arrested by a Danish police constable and handed over to the *Wehrmacht* and taken to Brande where he met Smith and followed him to *Dulag Luft*.

Despite the casualties to French civilians at Lille and amid protests from the Vichy regime, attacks on marshalling yards continued unabated, with the next raids going ahead on the night of 10/11 April. Pilot Officer William 'Bill' Alliston sat in the mid-upper gunner's turret of *J-Johnny*, a Halifax on 10 Squadron at Melbourne, Yorkshire, as the big aircraft thundered off down the runway. In the navigator's seat Flying Officer M S 'Junior' Steele gave Flight Lieutenant William George Barnes DFC the pilot his course. The target was the marshalling yard at Tergnier, 70 miles north of Paris, one of five sets of railway yards in France and Belgium that were hit by Bomber Command this night. In all, 157 Halifaxes of 4 Group and ten PFF Mosquitoes were dispatched to Tergnier, which lay on the important Liège–Paris line and would offer German army units a route towards Normandy from Metz and south-west Germany. In addition to the marshalling facilities Tergnier contained very large carriage and wagon repair sheds and trans-shipment sheds and an engine depot containing about 90 locomotives. Crews could not help noticing that Tergnier was dangerously close to the *Luftwaffe* bases at Laon-Athies and Montdidier.

A brilliant full moon provided perfect visibility for enemy fighters as the attackers crossed the French coast but their flight, until they were well inland was strangely peaceful – a matter which Alliston, who was on his 28th operation, instinctively distrusted. His eyes ranged the whole arc of the sky beyond his Perspex turret cover but saw nothing untoward until the aircraft turned on to its bombing run. Then, as so often happened, an enemy fighter materialized from nowhere at all to attack the bomber's vulnerable belly. The first thing anyone knew about its presence was a shattering burst of cannon shells, which crashed into the starboard wing. In the same instant a stray shell exploded in Alliston's turret, splitting the Perspex cover, which then whipped off into the slip-stream. The blast hit the half-dazed Alliston and tore his flying helmet half off so that the straps wrenched at his throat. He grabbed for it and with difficulty, clawed it back on to his head in time to hear the pilot saying on intercom, 'Sorry chaps – bail out. Come on, bail out everybody!'

Alliston climbed down from the turret seat and staggered up the fuselage towards the nose of the aircraft. As he did so, he realized that it had lurched over and was in a spin with a roaring furnace streaking back from the starboard wing. He made for the escape hatch and caught a glimpse of his pilot still fighting with the controls so that his crew could get out. In the strange freakishness of war Alliston had no memory of what happened after that moment until he was floating down the dark sky with his parachute fully open above his head. His first conscious realization was that his left boot and sock were missing. Next, that he was swinging so wildly that he feared his parachute would collapse and spill its vital cushion of air. Next he saw the aircraft blazing fiercely below in what appeared to be a shallow lake. And he seemed to be about to land squarely in the flames. However, he missed the blaze and landed heavily, biting his tongue violently. The 'lake' proved to be nothing but an illusion. He was lying in the middle of a ploughed field brightly illuminated by the burning wreckage.

He staggered to his feet and began scraping a hole to bury his para-chute and harness. His flying suit, he discovered, was ripped all over as by razor slashes. A burning pain throbbed in one of his legs, and above his eyes and round the back of his head were deep cuts. Alliston made for a nearby wood as best he could. As he went he heard someone blundering through the bracken close by and found himself face to face with 'Junior' Steele the navigator who whispered questions as to how the rest of the chaps had got on. Alliston, his tongue swollen so that it seemed to fill his mouth, could only answer vaguely by signs. From that moment onwards he and Steele kept together and passed through a series of fantastic adventures. For three weeks Alliston kept himself alive by eating grass and drinking water from ditches. (After the war he had to have an operation to remove a stone embedded in his throat.) They made their way into a village and although it was then about midnight, took the chance of knocking on a door. A strange providence seemed to have made them choose that one cottage out of the 200 in the village. For there they found that their wireless operator, Flight Lieutenant D F Coller DFC, had also chosen the cottage for his first bid for help and was there to shake hands with them. A Polish charcoal burner took them to his boss, a veterinary surgeon – and a member of the Resistance. Once Alliston's wounded knee had been cleaned up, arrangements were made to send the men to Paris. The journey to the capital was made in a cart of potatoes and hay. It was stopped on the way and a German soldier prodded the load. Alliston was treated at a hospital in Paris where all the staff in the operating theatre were resistance workers. He was taken to the house of Maurice Dupuis who was an enthusiastic member of the underground movement. The Dupuis family hid them, looked after their wounds and fed them, found them clothes and false identity cards. Later, Dupuis paid for his philanthropy with his life. After his wards had left him his activities were discovered by the Germans and he was transported to the notorious Dachau camp where he was tortured and finally died of typhus.

When they were well enough to move Coller decided that he would become one of the resistance movement and stay in France, since his knowledge of the RAF might prove valuable, which indeed it did throughout the remainder of the war. Alliston and Steele decided to try to get back. While arrangements for a train journey with two other airmen to the Spanish border were made, Alliston stayed at the home of a French couple. The wife, Mimi, passed him off as her deaf-and-dumb brother and made him walk round the streets of Paris with his head held high, even in the presence of German soldiers. The train to freedom was stopped by the Germans who removed the engine. When a French guard asked for his ticket, knowing hardly any French Alliston replied *Oui*. The guard whispered *Bon chance*. Because the train was late the monk who had arranged to meet them and get them over the Pyrenees into Spain was not at the station and the airmen had no alternative but to start climbing. They risked capture by asking for shelter at an isolated house but it was owned by an Englishwoman whose French doctor husband had been murdered by the *Nazis*. The ordeal did not end in Spain. The military police put Alliston in prison where he lay ill for months. It was through the intervention of the British Ambassador, Sir Samuel Hoare, that he was released and sent to hospital in England. Subsequently Alliston and Steele were given leave and they both returned to operational flying. Pilot Officer Alliston was later awarded the DFC. The rest of the gallant crew, with the exception of Sergeant Gordon Charles Howell the rear gunner and the pilot who were killed, were taken prisoner and repatriated after the war. It seems clear that the pilot gave his own life by staying with the aircraft too long in order that they might have a chance of survival.

Altogether, ten Halifaxes were lost from the 157 aircraft that set off to attack Tergnier, mostly in the Poix and Montdidier areas.[4] About 144 Halifaxes bombed the target in two waves but the marking in the second wave was not accurate and the majority of Halifaxes bombed houses west of the target. Most of the blame was placed on the poor service-ability of *Oboe* equipment but it was also discovered that the position of the southern Aim Point had been incorrectly calculated because of an error in the photographic scale which had accompanied the Target Illustration print. The result of the latter error led to both phases of the attack being centred mostly round the same Aim Point.[5]

Just over 120 Halifaxes of 6 Group and ten Path Finder Mosquitoes that went to Ghent returned to England after bombing the Merelbeke-Melle railway yards on the main line to Brussels. One Halifax, which was hit by flak on crossing the enemy coast, turned back and was abandoned over Suffolk and crashed near Ipswich. The Merelbeke-Melle yards were badly damaged but over 1,500 houses were also hit and 428 Belgian civilians were killed and 300 injured.

Some 148 Lancasters and 15 Mosquitoes hit the corner of the railway yards at Laon. A Lancaster on 622 Squadron at Mildenhall failed to return. The railway yards at Aulnoye on the east bank of the River Sambre and 30 miles northwest of St-Quentin were attacked by 132 Lancasters of 1 Group and 15 Path Finder Mosquitoes. Aulnoye had earlier been attacked on 25/26 March but the Path Finders had been unable to mark the yards accurately and most bombs had fallen wide of the target. This time 287 bombs hit the yards and the engine shed was hit, putting 30 locomotives out of action, although 340 houses were destroyed or damaged and 14 civilians were killed. All seven Lancasters that were lost were shot down in 46 minutes by *Hauptmann* Helmut Bergmann, *Staffelkapitän*, 8./NJG4, operating from Juvincourt, (his 17th–23rd kills).

Another 180 Lancasters of 5 Group attacked the railway yards at Tours. *U-Uncle* on 9 Squadron piloted by Warrant Officer Colin Albert Peak RAAF was hit by flak and crashed at St-Pierre-des-Corps in the south-east suburbs of Tours with the loss of all the crew including the bomb-aimer, Flying Officer John Enoch 'Pappy' Wilkes USAAF from Barrington, Rhode Island. The seven bodies were buried at Nantes. Wilkes, who was on his 15th op, was later re-interred in the US Military Cemetery at St-Laurent-sur-Mer (Calvados).[6]

On 11/12 April, 352 heavies and Mosquitoes raided Aachen, for the loss of nine aircraft. Crews were then stood down for a week and the next Main Force operations took place on the night of 18/19 April when rail yards at Rouen, Juvisy, Noisy-le-Sec and Tergnier were bombed by four separate forces, and 168 aircraft dropped mines off Swinemünde and in Kiel Bay and off the Danish coast.

The Dam Busters provided 19 Lancasters and all four Mosquito aircraft of the Marker Force for the attack by 209 Lancasters of 5 Group on the

Juvisy marshalling yards in the southern suburbs of Paris near Orly Airport. Three Mosquitoes of 8 Group carried out high-level *Windowing*. Tom Bennett, navigator in the 617 Squadron Mosquito flown by Gerry Fawke, recalls:

Some PFF captains, not briefed for the operation travelled in 617 Lancasters to act as observers of the new technique. Flares were dropped to the north of the target but illuminated the Arc de Triomphe. This enabled Gerry to position his Mosquito correctly for a marking dive and he laid the red spot fires precisely on the aiming point. Cheshire dived to back-up this initial marking but his stores hung up again. However, his observation at low-level made him decide that the markers were perfectly placed and he instructed the other two marker Mosquitoes to refrain from back-up. The Lancaster force was given bombing clearance as it approached the target. The 617 Squadron Lancaster force spearheaded the bombing, each carrying a load of 14 1,000lb bombs or a mixed high explosive and incendiary load. Their bombs burst laterally along the narrow bottleneck of the marshalling-yard, successive loads supplementing and adding to damage already wreaked on the target. It appeared to the watching Mosquito crews that this initial bombing had torn the heart out of the target. The remainder of the bombing spread this wholesale damage to the rest of the area but Cheshire reported 'two wild sticks' in his debriefing report. Sadly, these loads, a mix of instantaneous fused and delayed action bombs caused distressing casualties in the civilian areas in which they fell.

Some 273 Lancasters of 1, 3 and 8 Groups claimed a concentrated attack on the railway yards at Rouen with much destruction being caused. Mindful of the poor results of the 10/11 April raid, marking instructions for the return raid on Tergnier included the use of 24 Lancasters of 8 Group for visual marking, illuminating, support and back-up. The Master Bomber, 23-year-old Wing Commander John Fraser Barron DSO DFC DFM, RNZAF, a New Zealander from Dunedin, one of three visual markers on 7 Squadron, with the radio call sign 'Stinkbow', controlled the raid using VHF radio. Barron was just 19 when he joined the RNZAF in July 1940; a slight, modest boy, only 5 feet 6 inches in height. He arrived in England as a sergeant pilot in March 1941 and within three years had become one of the PFF's veteran leaders.[7] The attack began as planned but again the Mosquitoes suffered poor serviceability of their *Oboe* equipment and of the eight detailed to attack, three only released their TIs, creating an MPI further to the west of those of the previous raid.[8] Fifty railway lines were blocked but here too, bombing fell on housing areas south-west of the railway yards and caused a number of French casualties. At Noisy-le-Sec the marshalling yards were so well hit that they were not completely repaired until six years after the end of the war, but 750 houses were destroyed and more than 2,000 damaged, and 464 French civilians were killed. Aircraft losses were relatively light. A Lancaster on 9 Squadron was lost on the operation on Juvisy marshalling yards and a 57 Squadron Lancaster came down at 01.00 hours while returning to East Kirkby, at Chapelbridge near Whittlesey in Cambridge-shire with the loss of all eight crew. Four Halifaxes were lost on the raid on Noisy-le-Sec, six more on Tergnier, including two that collided in the air and crashed at Seraucourt-le-Grand in the Aisne. Flying Officer William Adrian Hughes RCAF, an American from Hollywood, California who was on his 10th sortie, and his crew on *K-King* on 158 Squadron at Lissett, and Sergeant Colin Shackleton's crew on 51 Squadron at Snaith, who were flying their first op, all died.

No aircraft were lost on Rouen but three Lancasters were shot down on their return over eastern England by Me 410A-1 intruder aircraft of KG51 *Edelweiss* at Soesterberg airfield in the Netherlands. At Witchford 115 Squadron had sent 26 Lancasters to attack Rouen and, in the early hours of 19 April they began returning to their base near Ely. At 02.09 hours the undercarriage of Sergeant Lemoine's Lancaster collapsed when it was three-quarters of the way along the runway and temporarily prevented other aircraft from landing. Pilot Officer John Birnie was the pilot of one of the circling aircraft and, just one minute after Lemoine's Lancaster had crashed, he was shot down by an intruder of KG51. A second Lancaster, piloted by Flight Lieutenant Charlie Eddy MBE, an Australian serving in the RNZAF, met a similar fate. Both aircraft fell close to the airfield giving none of the crew members time to escape. *Oberleutnant* Claus Breissner of 5./KG51 and *Major* Dietrich Puttfarken, *Staffelkapitän* of 1./KG51 claimed the two aircraft. Puttfarken and his *Bordfunker Oberfeldwebel* Willie Lux were killed three nights later, on 22 April, when over Norfolk and Suffolk they attacked B-24 Liberators of the US 2nd Air Division returning from raids on the Continent. They are thought to have crashed in the North Sea. Puttfarken, who was born in Hamburg and had been awarded the *Ritterkreuz* for completing 250 combat sorties, would have been 24-years old on 30 April. A Lancaster flown by Pilot Officer Joseph Patrick Cosgrove RCAF, one of 13 on 625 Squadron that were dispatched to Rouen, was shot down by *Leutnant* Wolfgang Wenning, St.III/KG51. Cosgrove was com-pleting his landing circuit at Kelstern when his Lancaster was seen to burst into flames and crash close to the airfield, killing all seven crew.[9] Wolfgang Wenning and *Feldwebel* Gustav Delp, his *Bordfunker*, were killed on 27 April when they collided with an Oxford near Church Lawford airfield and crashed at Frankton near Rugby.[10]

On 20/21 April, 247 Lancasters of 5 Group and 22 Mosquitoes of 5 and 8 Groups visited the marshalling yards at La Chapelle, just 600 yards northeast of the Gare du Nord. This time the attack was made in two waves, eight Mosquitoes performing *Windowing* duties for each wave.

The 14 Lancasters of 617 led in the first wave, whose aiming point was marked by Wing Commander Leonard Cheshire and Gerry Fawke. Dave Shannon and 'Terry' Kearns marked the aiming point for the second wave one hour later. A delay in the rather complicated PFF target illuminating procedure led to a profusion of flares being dropped together instead of being spaced to afford six minutes of maximum illumination for target identification and marking. However, Cheshire found and marked the aiming point without further delay and his accurate spot fires were adequately backed up by Fawke. The bombing, even more concentrated than at Juvisy, ensured that maximum damage was done to that part of the yard. The resultant fires were a beacon that beckoned in the second wave. Shannon and Kearns had no difficulty in locating the new aiming-point, which was marked and then heavily bombed. Subsequent reconnaissance revealed that both these yards had been dealt a devastating blow from which they never fully recovered until after the war. A block of tenement buildings on the fringe of La Chapelle had been razed to the ground and this caused some soul-searching until it was confirmed that its occupants had been a *Luftwaffe* regiment.

Tom Bennett recalls:

The reactions of the various PFF 'observers' who flew on 617 Squadron aircraft on these two operations baffled and disconcerted the 617 crews. Very little credit was given for the accurate marking and bombing, confirmed by the reconnaissance photos. Instead, almost to a man, they chose to 'parrot' the earlier objections to the technique that AVM Bennett had put forward, adding that it would be a different story entirely when the technique was used against targets in Germany. They claimed that a heavy price would be paid on such operations and the technique would prove unworkable. One Australian 'observer' who had flown with an Australian-captained 617 crew was so caustic and patronising in his verbal post-operation verdict that a 'civil war' almost broke out on the dispersal as the 617 captain moved menacingly towards him. Fortunately, the crew members recognised the signs and took station firmly between the two Australians, managing to soothe their captain's ruffled feathers and avoiding the threatened fisticuffs. Cheshire was pleased with the way the other 5 Group squadrons had welcomed and absorbed the new procedure. Its straightforward nature, with one accurately-marked aiming-point to bomb, requiring no personal assessment of which ground-marker was probably the most accurately laid, held great appeal for the crews. It meant a smooth bombing-run on a specific point and more accurate bombing.

Towards the end of April a series of deep penetration raids into Germany were mounted again, to which 1 *Jagdkorps* replied with successful *Tame*

Boar operations. On six nights from 21–28 April, 1,407 night fighter sorties were dispatched, which resulted in claims for 135 bombers destroyed. On 20/21 April, when Main Force targets included Cologne and four rail targets in France and Belgium, the 1,555 sorties flown was a new record.[11] Flight Sergeant Brian Soper flew on the Cologne raid, a short trip at just under five hours:

> Cologne, like Frankfurt, was well known for its many searchlights. This particular night the pathfinder markers were about eight minutes late and we were hanging around waiting for them to go down. There was 10/10 cloud up to 15,000 feet. Eventually they appeared and we bombed mainly on red-yellow sky markers at about 21,000 feet. The main danger on cloudy nights was that searchlights below the cloud made an illuminated white blanket above which the Lancs made a black silhouette. Two thousand feet above this sat the night fighter waiting to pick us off, of which we often only became aware as the stream of tracer bullets passed by and the dive and corkscrew started. Our bombing time over the target was 02.09 hours and the air speed 170 mph.

Four bombers failed to return from the raid on Cologne and eight bombers were lost in the attacks on the rail targets. The stress and tension was also too much for some who returned. Dennis 'Lofty' Wiltshire, a flight engineer on Lancasters on 90 Squadron had his tour ended abruptly when he cracked mentally during the operation to Cologne:[12]

> As always the crew of *G-George* were anxious, alert and apprehensive. A Bedford 2-ton truck with drop tail-board and canvas hood took us out and with Mae Wests, 'chutes etc, we clambered aboard our aircraft and, with a little banter, took up our respective positions. I shared the flight deck with Leslie the Skipper and I went through our respective pre-flight checks: Fuel cocks open (or closed) as appropriate, main engine switches 'OFF' – all the usual routine. We were given the all clear to 'START'. Each engine in turn burst into life, over-rich combustion gasses belching from the exhaust stubs. The earth seemed to tremble into life with us. It was pitch black outside. 'Maps' (Reg, the navigator) had his map table illumination 'ON'. There was very subdued light from the instrument panels. We could see the various ground crew struggling to pull away the 'trolley accs' (starting battery trolleys). Leslie opened the throttle of each engine in turn. He looked at me. I looked at him: RPM, thumbs up, radiator shutters 'OPEN' oil pressure steady, thumbs up and so through the whole pre-take-off procedure, the ASI, the artificial horizon levelled up from its drunken position. There was an ever-present odour in the kite from 100-octane fuel, new rubber, exhaust

gasses and hot engine oil as well as the constant shaking, shuddering and engines roaring. A quick check of the boost gauges. Had the pitot head cover been removed? Damned if I could see. The NCO i/c ground crew thrust the Form 700 at the pilot to sign.

The green Aldis light went on for *G-George*. Leslie eased the throttles forward and set the elevator trim tabs. Stick forward; stick backward, left foot forward, right foot forward and a rap on the compass glass. My eyes flitted from gauge to gauge: boost pressure, fuel, oil temperature, oil pressure and air and hydraulic pressure. The gyros were spinning. All was now alive on *G-George*, which shuddered and rattled as if it would fall to pieces. A wave from the pilot signalled 'chocks away' to the ground crew outside. Les glanced at me and gave a wink and thumbs up. I returned thumbs up and the Skipper released the brakes. The throttles were gradually opened and the propeller pitch controls were at their selected positions. Leslie and I cast a steady glance over the instrument panels and the Lancaster rolled forward. Three of the squadron were already airborne and now we had left dispersal and were at the end of the runway ready for take-off. Again the green Aldis lamp for *G-George*, mutterings on the R/T and then the crescendo of our four Merlin engines deafening all other sounds as the Skipper selected through the gate for 'Take-off' on all four throttle levers. Leslie concentrated on his take-off procedures. Flaps were set and the propeller blades slapped at the cold night air as I firmly held the throttle levers at 'Take-off' position. 'Flaps set – wheels up.' I repeated each command in turn to the pilot. Each instrument danced to its respective tune: RPM, boost pressure, altimeter, compass – red lights went out, green lights came on. We were airborne, all 65,000lbs of us, including a little over 2,150 gallons of 100-octane fuel and four 5,000lb bombs. The fact that we were airborne brought sighs of relief!

The squadron headed for the coast to position ourselves with our contemporaries ready for the onslaught ahead of us. We had 'grouped up' and after a long incident free journey we were nearing our target area. It was a dark night. No moon and a little broken cloud at 1,000 feet below. R/T silence was being maintained with only our own aircraft R/T intercom 'ON'. Almost simultaneously Tom ('Piper') the mid-upper gunner and Les the pilot said, 'Path Finders ahead'. 'I looked forward and saw a pale orange glow in the sky. Nick, the rear gunner ('Tail-end Charlie') and Tom had fired off a few rounds previously to ensure satisfactory operation of the guns. We each in turn – Jim (bomb aimer, 'Bomber'), Fred (wireless operator, 'Nosy') and me now confirmed our readiness for action and positioned ourselves accordingly. At this stage of the proceedings my stomach was in knots. I felt terribly sick, long to be going home to base and found extreme difficulty in repeating 'The Lord's Prayer' to myself. The orange glow ahead had now turned red. Our Path Finders had done a wonderful job, as always and the target was well illuminated. The glow now pin-pointed other aircraft flying with us, aircraft which we knew were there but had been unable to see because of the darkness.

There was a sudden burst of gunfire from the rear guns. 'Bloody Hell!' 'Sorry Skip', I thought I saw a fighter.'

'Don't think, look! You'll have one of ours down in a minute.'

We moved ever nearer the target zone; the red glow changed in colour as the first Lancs in dropped their green flares to keep the target illuminated. I could see the flashes as the first 5,000 pounders fell in the target zone. Now things were livening up; searchlights were beginning to pierce the darkness; flash bolts were being hurled into the sky to illuminate our presence. The navigator, in a calm steady voice called, 'Three minutes to ETA', followed almost immediately by the bomb aimer, 'Keep her as she is skip – I have greens and reds straight ahead.'

We were now feeling the blast effect from the ack-ack shells. We were all at our respective tasks: the bomb aimer at his window, the navigator at his charts, complete with his shaded light and curtains drawn. The Skipper and myself were in almost total darkness apart from the occasional flash of moving searchlights. Les had his eyes fixed out to port, mine to starboard. Necessary adjustments were executed after sign language to each other. The pilot made various left and right deviations to our set course, as both searchlights and ack-ack shells became more numerous.

'Bomb doors open' came the bomb aimer's call and the whole aircraft seemed to want to fall apart as the Skipper operated the bomb doors lever with his left hand. I was now feeling pretty awful. I always felt sick over the target but this time I was in a cold sweat and felt very light-headed. The Skipper almost screamed at the bomb aimer. 'For Christ's sake Jim, hurry up. What in God's name are you doing?' There was a very pregnant pause, then a voice so calm and collected that I wanted to scream. Jim the bomb aimer said, 'Left, Left, Left, right a little, steady! Bombs gone!'

The aircraft seemed to take-off for a second time as the weight of the bombs was released. All of us looked in every possible direction outside the aircraft for fear of collision with another of the 300 air-craft out there in the dark. The bomb doors closed and the Skipper made a steep turn for home but we were now in the thick of a heavily defended area. The blast of shells rocked us continuously and tracer shells, bomb bursts and screaming shells were every-where. Five thousand pounders burst below us. It was Dante's Inferno! I was frozen in my seat. The Skipper completed his turn for the home run. This in itself was a major operation. The pilot was flying almost blind and was negotiating a manoeuvre with several dozen other aircraft making the same move. Something crashed through the perspex window behind me. It streamed past my head, buried itself in the cockpit floor and there was a sickly smell of burning and phosphorous. I released my harness, leapt from my seat and stamped and stamped on the object, finally using the cockpit fire extinguisher on it. The bomb aimer had, at this stage, been unable to leave his station due to the turn we were negotiating and various other manoeuvres. He suddenly screamed, 'Fire! For God's sake my suit's on fire!' Like anyone else in such a predicament in a confined space, he kicked and scrambled to get away from his window and then quite suddenly he crumpled up and was perfectly still.

There was suddenly a horrendous, blinding flash. The whole aircraft shook as if it was a fish in its final thrash of life. Something had passed clean through our forward perspex nose window, taking parts of the bomb aimer's equipment. I thought of all those famous last words, 'Keep calm; don't panic.' I wondered if the person who couched those words had ever been in such a position. I tried to struggle into the bomb aimer's station. The pressure from the ice cold blast now entering the nose section was immense. I put on my oxygen mask, not for oxygen but to help me to some state of normal breathing. The wind tore at my Irvin jacket. Debris was everywhere. Odd bits and pieces tore at my face. This was an impossible task. 'Skipper, I am on the R/T. This is bloody hopeless! I can't even stand up.'

There was another explosive crash somewhere aft in *G-George*. 'How is Jim?'

'I can't get near him but I think he's had it, Skip. He's bleeding from ears, nose and mouth.'

With the added assistance from the unbelievable force of the wind coming through the damaged nose, I returned to the cockpit to find chaos reigning supreme. The Skipper was as calm as always. He was a wonderful guy. There was glass, oil and various liquids everywhere. Several of the pilot's instruments were U/S but he just sat there as calm and collected as is humanly possible under the circumstances. For a moment our eyes met. Were we both thinking alike? Then one eye winked. I think there was a hint of a smile, perhaps of encouragement. 'Check the fuel levels, Den. I don't know what the situation is; you tell me.'

'I don't know if we have lost any. Poor old *George* is like a bloody sieve at the moment, holes everywhere.'

I hoped to God we'd got enough to get home. If we had lost any of our precious fuel, it was not much. I checked the levels of the tanks, opened the relevant bleed/transfer cocks and pumps and transferred the 100-octane fuel, as was the normal procedure. From here on I am not truly aware of what happened. I do recall the inferno below us at the target area. I remembered a Lanc' minus tail end with all four engines on fire hurtling to earth. From then on my mind was a blank. I was told many months later that I released the harness I had been wearing at my station, pulled off my helmet and started to walk aft. Apparently I was quite oblivious to frantic calls and abusive screams to sit down and I apparently failed to utter even one word or sound. I also failed to negotiate the main spar, which protrudes upward from the deck of the aircraft and fell to the deck remaining motionless. The navigator had apparently left his station to assist me but finding no visible wounds or blood and being unable to obtain any word from me, returned to his table and charts to plot the homeward journey. On landing it was confirmed that Jim was dead and I was taken from the kite by ambulance, which had been forewarned of our arrival by Les, our Skipper and I was taken to station sick quarters. With de-briefing, breakfast, etc., etc., the other lads on the crew lost touch with my treatment. After all, a mission such as we had endured, plus de-briefing, breakfast and a good sleep, they each had their own problems. All the lads came to pay their respects but regrettably I was never aware of their presence. I was in station sick quarters for approximately four days. I learned eventually that I was as much a problem to the crew on their visits as I was to station medical officers. I was diagnosed as having no wounds, no broken bones and no physical disabilities but I was apparently quite content to remain in bed oblivious of anything and everything. I could not stand or sit. I ate and drank nothing. I did not seem to understand any spoken word and, despite attempts by all medical staff, nothing would register in my mind. A civilian consultant psychiatrist from a nearby hospital was requested to attend the station sick bay. I only learned of this many months later, either by letters from my colleagues or from third or fourth hand word of mouth.

I was taken to an RAF psychiatric hospital at Matlock in Derby-shire (known to in-patients as 'Hatter's Castle', after the Mad Hatter in Alice's Adventures in Wonderland)[13] where air-crew types there were referred to by our RAF colleagues as 'A right load of nutters!' For many weeks my life was just a blank. A nurse accidentally knocked a steel dish of medical instruments from a trolley on to the floor and it seems I sprang to my feet, fell flat on the floor, because of my weak state and screamed, 'There's another poor sod going down, let's get the hell out of here. Look at the flares, look at the flares, shoot the Bastard down; they're coming closer. For God's sake shoot the Bastard down!' I then collapsed. I recall coming round. I was

adron Leader P Jousse DFC of Rhodesia, the Snaith station navigation officer, goes over a point
h Yorkshireman Flying Officer Harry Bowling on Flight Sergeant Geoff Brougham RAAF's
ifax crew on 51 Squadron prior to the crew's first operational flight on the 30/31 March 1944
iburg raid. Halifax LW544 and Brougham's crew were lost. Brougham and Bowling and three
ers were killed. Two men survived and were taken prisoner.

ng Commander R C Ayling briefs 51 Squadron crews at Snaith for the Nrnburg raid, 30/31 March
4. Group Captain N H Fresson the station commander sits in the front row. That night the
adron lost the highest proportion of aircraft dispatched on the raid. Twelve hours after this
otograph was taken thirty-five of these men were dead and seven were prisoners of war.

The duty Flying Control Officer in the control tower and the Snaith Station Commanding Officer, Group Captain N Fresson, on the balcony outside, anxiously await the return of 51 Squadron Halifax aircraft from Nrnburg on the night of 30/31 March 1944. (IWM)

The Snaith station CO, Group Captain N Fresson, and other officers wait on the balcony of the control tower for the return of 51 Squadron's Halifaxes from the disastrous raid of 30/31 March 1944. Five of the squadron's aircraft were lost and another crew killed in a crash on return.

eutnant Helmuth Schulte of 4./NJG5 who
~~~ed four bombers destroyed on the Nrnburg
~~o take his score to eleven victories.

Oberleutnant Martin 'Tino' Becker, *Staffelkapitn*
2./NJG6.

~~~aster III LM418 on 619 Squadron on 14 February 1944. This aircraft was wrecked a month later
~~/31 March on return from Nrnburg. Sergeant John Parker took off from Coningsby at
~~ hours and on return, crash-landed at Woodbridge. No one was hurt but the Lancaster was
~~med by fire. Parker and his crew were later killed on the operation to Kiel on 23/24 July 1944.

German *JLO* and *Spitter* girls.

crew of LL849 UM-B on 626 Squadron made a precautionary landing at Seething after being
k by lightning on the Nrnburg raid on the night of 30/31 March 1944. Allocated to
quadron at Ludford Magna, LL849 hit a tree at Lichfield, Staffs on the night of 31 July/1 August
during a training sortie. Flying Officer Cornelius and four of his crew were injured. Three other
members died.

Officer Freddie Watts on 630 Squadron at the controls of Lancaster III ND554 LE-C *Conquering*
at East Kirkby on 25 March 1944. Watts and his crew completed eleven operations
ary–March 1944, and after the 30/31 March Nrnburg raid they went to 617 Squadron at
dhall Spa for Special Duties. They did not want to lose *Conquering Cleo* so they took the aircraft
them and Watts and crew flew four ops on *Conquering Cleo* on 617 Squadron before it was
ned to 630 Squadron in mid-June 1944. The crew completed their tour on 29 October in
95/N, bombing the battleship *Tirpitz* in Troms Fiord with a 14,000lb *Tallboy* on their 37th trip.
and Flying Officer Robert Baines Knight RNZAF and crew were lost without trace on the
February 1945 raid on Plitz. (*Dennis Cooper*)

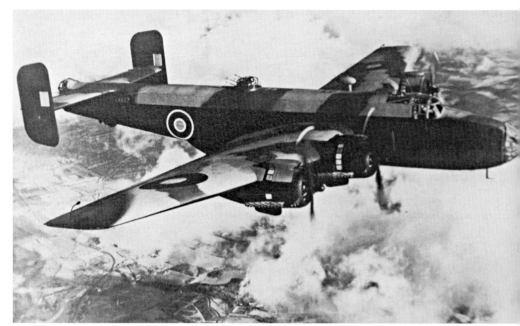

Halifax III LV857 on 51 Squadron, which was shot down on the Nrnburg raid, 30/31 March 1944 *Oberleutnant* Martin 'Tino' Becker, *Staffelkapitn* 2./NJG6. Sergeant Jack Percival George Binder, was from Moulton, Northants and his crew who were on only their third operation were killed.

A B-17 Flying Fortress crew in the 96th Bomb Group at Snetterton Heath, Norfolk, with a Lancaster crew of 622 Squadron at RAF Mildenhall in the spring of 1944. Note the unpainted *Window* chute beneath the nose of *F–Freddie*. (*IWM*)

ine-up of Merlin-engined Lancasters on 514 Squadron at Waterbeach April 1944, after they had
laced the squadron's original radial-engined Lancaster IIs. LM181 JI-E was one of four aircraft
t on the 20/21 July 1944 raid on the synthetic oil plant at Homberg. There were no survivors on
ing Officer Lamont Weir Q McLean RNZAF's crew. *(IWM)*

geant W Sinclair RAF and Flying Officer E H Giersch RAAF on 463 Squadron at Waddington,
their oxygen masks in the crew room before an operational sortie, April 1944. *(IWM)*

Lancaster I L7540 seen here in 83 Squadron markings (the letters OL-U freshly painted over the ol 44 Squadron codes on which squadron it served from January 1942) awaiting 4,000lb HC bombs. L7540 finished its career with 5 Lancaster Finishing School in 5 Group at Syerston and was SOC i April 1944.

Lancaster III ND787/F on 49 Squadron in a lovely spring setting at Fiskerton in the spring of 1944 This aircraft became operational on 49 Squadron on 5 April 1944 and flew forty-nine ops before it was replaced by a *Village Inn*-equipped Lancaster. (*Leslie Hay*)

(*left*) On the night of 10/11 April 1944 180 Lancasters of 5 Group bombed the St-Pierre-des-Corps railway marshalling yards at Tours in bright moonlight. One Lancaster was lost. The yards were seriously damaged although there are no reports of any French casualties. (*via 'Pat' Patfield*)

(*right*) *Hauptmann* Martin Drewes, *Kommandeur* III./NJG 1 who on the night of 3/4 May 1944 flying a 110G-4/U1 and fitted with the upward-firing *Schrge Musik,* shot down five Lancasters on what was his 113th operational sortie. Drewes, who was awarded the *Ritterkreuz* on 27 July 1944 and *enlaub* on 17 April 1945, ended the war with forty-three night and six day victories. (*Ab A. Jansen*)

Briefing for 460 Squadron RAAF at Waddington for the raid on Juvisy on 18 April 1944. Wing Commander Rollo Kingsford Smith, DSO DFC pilot, of Sydney who commanded 463 Squadron RAAF November 1943–June 1944 was a one of two nephews of the late Air Commodore Sir Charles Kingsford Smith, the great Australian flying pioneer. The other nephew, Flying Officer Peter Kingsford Smith DFC of Sydney reached Britain in May 1941 and carried out many bombing operations before he was taken prisoner on 20 February 1943. A third brother, Squadron Leader J W Kingsford Smith, pilot, had been in the RAAF since 1939. (*RAAF*)

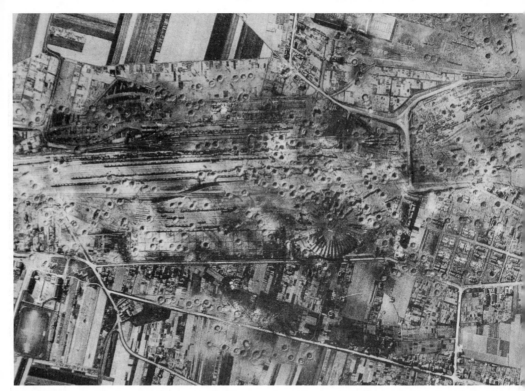

The St-Pierre-des-Corps railway marshalling yards at Tours virtually unusable after the raid by Lancasters of 5 Group on 10/11 April 1944. On the same night, railway yards at Ghent, Laon, Aulnoye and Terginier were attacked by aircraft of other groups. *(IWM)*

The scene in the control room at East Kirkby, Lincolnshire, on the evening of 20 April 1944. Aircr of 57 Squadron, based at the station, were involved in an operation against the railway yards at La Chapelle, just north of Paris. Typically for this period, it was just one of several operations tha

night, with separate forc of bombers raiding Cologne as well as othe French railway targets. addition, there was the staple fare of Mosquito nuisance raids, radio countermeasures sorties intruder missions and *Gardening* operations: al designed to keep the German defences busy. From a total of 1,155 sor flown, fifteen aircraft we lost, including two Lancasters from 57 Squadron.

Lancaster I W4783 AR-G *G–George* on 460 Squadron RAAF at Binbrook after completion of the
...h trip on 20/21 April 1944, when it was flown by Flying Officer J A Critchley's crew (pictured).
...is veteran Lancaster was subsequently presented to the Australian War Museum. (*IWM*)

...geant W Sinclair RAF and Flying Officer E H Giersch RAAF on 463 Squadron at Waddington,
...t their oxygen masks in the crew room before an operational sortie, April 1944. (*IWM*)

Bf 110G-4 C9+EN flown by Wilhelm Johnen of 3./NJG6 at Hagenau, who was forced to land at Zurich-Dbendorf in Switzerland on 28 April 1944 after shooting down Lancaster ND759 *R-Robert* flown by Warrant Officer Robert Peter on 35 Squadron, near Besancon, France on the operation on the Zeppelin sheds at Friedrichshafen. Peter ditched in the Bodensee.

Sea mines wait to be loaded aboard a Halifax V Series IA of 77 Squadron, probably at Full Sutton in Yorkshire, shortly after the airfield was opened in May 1944. The Halifax V was identical to the more common Mk.II version, except for its simplified Dowty undercarriage, which replaced the more complex – and slower to produce – Messier units fitted to the Mk.II. Both of these long-suffering early Halifax variants had been withdrawn from Main Force operations over Germany in February 1944 during the Battle of Berlin, but continued to fly *Gardening* sorties and less hazardous trips to France, now a routine part of Bomber Command's diversionary operations.

ot Officer R R Reed of 576 Squadron did a remarkable job of piloting and was awarded a well-
served DSO for bringing back Lancaster B.I ME703/UL-S^2 from the costly raid on Mailly-le-
mp. Enemy fire shattered the rear turret, killing the gunner and damaging the elevators and
lders, along with the oxygen and electrical systems. Because of the electrical failures the radiator
os were inoperative, causing engine overheating. The rear turret wreckage made control so
ficult that Reed had to have help from both the flight engineer and bomb-aimer in order to keep
essure on the control column and rudder pedals. (*IWM*)

is unusual night photograph was taken during a bomber attack on the tank and lorry depot at
illy-le-Camp, southeast of Rheims, on the night of 3/4 May 1944. The photograph shows a
ncaster flying just above the rising mushrooms of smoke. Forty-two Lancasters were lost.
t' Patfield)

Lancaster I LM429 VN-C on 50 Squadron at Skellingthorpe, which was lost with Pilot Officer Fran
Stuart McFarlin's crew on 10/11 May 1944 on the operation to Lille. All the crew were killed. (IWM

Lancaster LL744 VN-B on 50 Squadron at Skellingthorpe in January 1944. This aircraft was flown b
Michael Beetham, later to become Marshal of the Royal Air Force Sir Michael Beetham GCB CBE
DFC AFC ADC. LL744 was lost on 22/23 May 1944 on the operation to Brunswick. Flight Lieutena
George Charles 'Chas' Startin RAAF, an Australian from Tarbingar, Queensland, and his crew wer
killed.

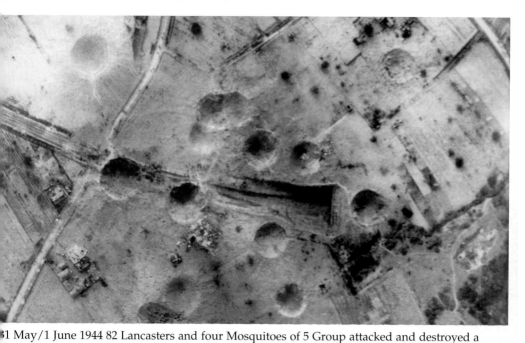

…1 May/1 June 1944 82 Lancasters and four Mosquitoes of 5 Group attacked and destroyed a …ay junction at Saumur, 125 miles north of the battle area in France, without loss. On 8/9 June …irst 12,000lb *Tallboy* bombs were used by 617 Squadron in a raid on a railway tunnel near …nur. The raid was conceived in great haste because a *Panzer* unit was expected to move by train …ugh the tunnel. The target was illuminated with flares by four Lancasters of 83 Squadron and …ked at low level by three Mosquitoes. Twenty-five Lancasters of 617 Squadron then dropped … *Tallboys* with great accuracy. The huge bombs exploded under the ground to create miniature …hquakes'. One actually pierced the roof of the tunnel and brought down a huge quantity of rock …soil. The tunnel was blocked for a considerable period and the Panzer unit was badly delayed. …ircraft were lost from the raid.

…Rhodesia) Squadron took …aster III LM625 KM-H *Sky* …ie on charge in June 1944. …employees of Shabani …es in Southern Rhodesia …ributed 1,255 and this was … for a petrol bowser. On …for the photograph are …ear-old Flying Officer …derleith who had …pleted thirty-four ops; …ear-old Flight Sergeant …Niekerk, who had flown …ty-six ops; and Corporal …son, a fitter; all these men …ng from Shabani. *Sky* …ie has seventy-eight …ping ops on the nose, the …s in white denoting …ght raids. In mid-1945 …25 was transferred to …quadron and after a spell …39 MU was scrapped in …ber 1945.

Lancaster III ED860 *N-Nan* on 61 Squadron with air and ground crews. *N-Nan* completed its 100th
on 27/28 June 1944 when Flying Officer B S Turner flew the aircraft on the operation to the Vitry
railway yards. ED860, here showing 118 ops on the nose, flew 130 operational sorties before bein
written off following a crash on take-off for Bergen on 28 October 1944, having flown almost
1,032 hours. Wing Commander R D Pexton the Squadron CO was so angry with the pilot, Flying
Officer Laurence A Pearce that he ordered the Australian to visit all the ground trade section hut
and apologise to the ground staff for this avoidable accident! (*IWM*)

(*Left*) In northern France the threat of *Panzer* reinforcements driving up from the south and east,
resulted, at very short notice, in Bomber Command being asked to launch two main attacks upon
the little town of Aunay-sur-Odon and Evrecy. The first strike was carried out on the morning of
Sunday, 11 June and was followed by a second the next morning by three waves of a dozen
bombers each. This photograph of the devastation at Aunay-Sur-Odon on 17 June 1944 was obta
with the vertical camera fitted to PRU Spitfire XI MD194 on 542 Squadron, flown by Flying Offic
H Reeves, who was briefed to carry out a reconnaissance from Benson and cover the Normandy
beaches, Aunay, Châtellerault, Rennes and the Lisieux area of north-west France.

(*Right*) On 27/28 June 1944, 214 Lancasters and nine Mosquitoes of 1, 5 and 8 Groups attacked
Vaires and Vitry railway yards. The 8 Group raid on the important railway yards at Vaires on th
outskirts of Paris was particularly accurate. Four Lancasters were lost – two from each raid. On
12 July, 153 Lancasters and six Mosquitoes of 1, 3 and 8 Groups visited the yards again. The targ
area was covered by cloud and the Master Bomber ordered the attack to be abandoned after two
Mosquitoes had marked and twelve Lancasters had bombed.

in bed with wonderful snow white sheets and beautiful soft white pillows. A nurse was seated at my bedside in a beautiful crisp, blue and white uniform. 'Doctor! Doctor! He's awake, please, doctor.' It was presumably the doctor who spoke to me. He was in white but his shoulders bore epaulettes bearing 'Air' rank.

'Well, laddie and how are we today?'

'A little bit confused, sir. No, very confused, hungry and feeling very weak thank you, sir.'

There followed a series of questions, from which I did not make an awful lot of sense. Instruments were inserted in my ears; instruments were put up my nose. He peered into my eyes from all angles, rubber mallets struck me here and there! For several weeks I was subjected to the most unbelievable set of tests. I do not recall all the details though I do recall 'ECT' (Electrical Convulsive Treatment) whose letters remain with me forever. The best part of this treatment was a super cup of strong tea 15 minutes after completion. The effects are not a suitable subject for print. In late 1944, still a patient at Matlock, my service life came to an abrupt end. I attended a RAF Discharge Medical Board and then a further medical board. I confirmed my name, rank and serial number but I had to admit that the previous years were a complete blank in my mind. I now find all this difficult to believe. There is no real end to this particular episode in my life. Even to this day the RAF remains prominent in my mind. I think of 'Skipper' and the 'boys' and of 'Hatter's Castle' with its abundance of broken lives.

At Waterbeach on Saturday 22 April, Ernest 'Sunny' Gledhill a WOp/ AG on 514 Squadron, discovered that he was 'on' that night. He would be on Flying Officer Maurice Morgan-Owen's crew for a second time and his ninth op overall. Sunny, who was from Odsal, in Bradford, West Yorkshire having been born in Halifax on 4 June 1921, was 5 feet 7½ inches tall, with brown hair, hazel eyes and a fresh complexion. He was a good-natured young man and the apple of his mother's eye. His older sister Margaret spent a lot of time looking after him after their father died when 'Sunny' was nine years old, which left their widowed mother to build the family pawnbroker's shop and keep them fed and clothed. He was an assistant in the business before volunteering for the RAF and joining up on 5 October 1941. Sunny's best friend had been Jim McGahey who was killed on the 30/31 March raid on Nuremberg.

Twenty-year-old Maurice Linden Morgan-Owen was from Wandsworth in London. He volunteered for the RAF on his 18th birthday and had trained to be a pilot in Canada, sending very spirited letters home to his family. Fun loving and liking a pint or two, he was a round faced and rather cheerful person having endured a long and snowy Canadian winter to obtain his pilot's wings on 16 April 1943. At one time he and his fellow pilots had to pitch in and shovel snow to rescue a snowbound locomotive from a nearby railway line. The crew's navigator was 23-year-old Flight Sergeant Alan William Green. Flying Officer George Alexander Jacobson the 27-year-old bomb aimer from Gunalda, Queensland was born on 25 March 1917, in Gympie. He enlisted on 5 April 1940 in Brisbane and embarked for England on 7 September 1942. Sergeant Alfred Douglas Tetley the 23-year-old rear gunner was one of three brothers. His family owned and ran a greengrocer's shop in Starbeck, an area of Harrogate, North Yorkshire. The mid upper gunner, 27-year-old Sergeant Herbert Stanley 'Bub' Hayward from Bishops Stortford, was one of five brothers and four sisters. Stanley's fiancée Mary lived at Hunstanton, Norfolk. Sergeant Henry Leo Sadler, known as Leo, the kindly, good humoured 25-year-old flight engineer, was born in Brighton on 21 October 1918. He had a younger brother and three sisters, two of whom were WAAFs. Leo's family had moved to Birmingham in 1922 and he joined the RAF in 1936. His mother was very proud that he was trained by Rolls Royce. Somehow Leo got himself into the Fleet Air Arm and served on the carrier *Eagle* in Crete and Ceylon. His family were not sure how or why he got into Bomber Command. In 1941 Leo married Joan from West Hartlepool at the Rosary Church, Saltley in Birmingham. They had a daughter who they named Maureen after one of Leo's sisters.

Morgan-Owen's crew were one of almost 600 aircraft detailed to raid Düsseldorf. That same night 238 Lancasters of 5 Group and 17 Mosquitoes and ten Lancaster 'active observers' of 1 Group were to attack Brunswick and another 181 aircraft were to bomb the locomotive sheds and marshalling yards at Laon in France. Morgan-Owen's Lancaster, *N-Nuts*, was bombed up with an 8,000lb bomb, 48 × 30lb bombs, 486 × 4lb bombs and 54 × 4lb incendiaries, and 1,360 gallons of petrol which allowed about 6½ hours' flying time. The anticipated duration of the flight was approximately 4 hours and 7 minutes. They took off at 22.58 and were supposed to return to Waterbeach at 03.00 on Sunday morning.

Included in the Brunswick force were 19 Lancasters on 617 Squadron and four aircraft of the Mosquito Marker Force. This was the first time that the 5 Group low-level marking method was used over a heavily defended German city. The raid was not successful. The initial marking by 617 Squadron Mosquitoes was accurate but many of the main force of Lancasters did not bomb these markers, partly because of a thin layer of cloud which hampered visibility and partly because of faulty communications between the various bomber controllers. Many bombs were dropped in the centre of the city but the remainder of the force bombed reserve H_2S-aimed TIs, which were well to the south. The first salvo of flares went down well SSW of the target and lured three Mosquitoes off to that area but Flight Lieutenant Gerry Fawke and his navigator Flying Officer 'Ben' Bennett pressed on to ETA target and were in prime position when the next salvo of flares fell across the city. 'Ben' Bennett recalled:

> The 'Market Square' aiming point was quickly identified and marked accurately, so much so that no backing-up was required and the bombing proceeded apace. Unfortunately, there had been a continuous example of poor VHF discipline among the Main Force crews, whilst a rogue *Wanganui* flare and a PFF Green TI five miles off the target attracted about 50 per cent of the bombs. It seemed that the crews inclined towards the more usual 'TI' than the HE and incendiary loads that the Lancasters of 617 unleashed on the red spot fires. Despite the disappointment felt at Woodhall Spa, very heavy damage was done to Brunswick that night.

The Brunswick force was largely ignored by the night fighters. Only four Lancasters failed to return. *N-Nuts* on 7 Squadron piloted by Flight Lieutenant MacGillivray, who a month earlier had crash-landed at Feltwell returning from Nürnburg, was shot down by a night fighter. The Canadian pilot and three of the crew bailed out and were taken prisoner. The three other crew members were killed.

At Düsseldorf 2,150 tons of bombs were dropped, mostly in the northern districts of the city, which caused widespread damage. This 'old style' heavy attack allowed the *Nachtjagd* to penetrate the bomber stream and 29 aircraft – 16 Halifaxes and 13 Lancasters were lost. Three of the missing Lancasters were on 514 Squadron. Two of them had collided and crashed at Ecke Rethel and all 14 men died. At 02.56 an SOS message was received giving *N-Nuts'* position as approximately 70 miles west of the Dutch coast. Nothing more was heard from the aircraft. All seven of Maurice Morgan-Owen's crew were posted missing. According to the acting Squadron Leader at the time, Barney Reid, at first light an ASR aircraft was dispatched to look for the crew. Reid personally took part in this. However, despite good visibility, nothing was found. Two of the crew were eventually washed ashore in the East Frisian Islands, off the northern coast of Germany. They were Leo Sadler, originally buried on the island of Nordeney and Alfred Tetley, originally buried on the island of Baltrum. They are now both buried in the Sage War Graves Cemetery in Germany. The other crew names were added to the Runnymede memorial.

Nine bombers – four Lancasters, two Halifaxes and three Stirlings – were lost on Laon. *P-Peter* a 635 Squadron Path Finder Lancaster at Downham Market flown by Pilot Officer D H Courtenay and carrying the Master Bomber, Wing Commander 'Pluto' Cousens,[14] orbited the target area for 20 minutes at an altitude of 4,000 feet until Cousens was satisfied with the attack. Courtney set course for home and took the Lancaster up to 10,000 feet. A night fighter attacked and the pilot threw the aircraft into a corkscrew, diving to port but Courtenay was blasted from the aircraft as it exploded. 'Everything suddenly went black,' recalled Courtenay, 'I was conscious but it was like being in a completely dark room and I was being thrown all over the place. I did not know if I was on my head or my heels.' Courtenay landed heavily near Vic-sur-Aisne. Unable to move, he was found by a farm labourer and on 24 April he was taken by train to Paris, where he received medical attention. He learned from the French that the wreckage of the aircraft was completely burned out and that it contained the five bodies and that two more were found a considerable distance away without parachutes. The nose turret was also found a long way from the main wreckage. It looked as if it had been cut off with a knife.[15]

The Canadian Halifax squadrons were hard hit this night with eight losses. *P-Peter* on 431 'Iroquois' Squadron RCAF at Croft flown by 1st Lieutenant E P Boyle USAAF was lost with all the crew. At Leeming there was no word from two Halifax IIIs on 429 'Bison' Squadron RCAF. *F-Freddie* was believed to have been hit by flak before crashing into a flooded area in Zuid-Holland on the island of Overflakkee. The pilot and two members of the crew were killed; four men were taken prisoner by the Germans. Three Halifax IIIs on 433 'Porcupine' Squadron RCAF at Skipton-on-Swale went missing in action. And three 514 Squadron Lancasters at Waterbeach were lost. One of them went down in the sea with the loss of all seven crew, and no-one survived aboard *C-Charlie*, which was hit by flak and collided with *D-Donald*, whose crew also died. *V-Victor* flown by Flying Officer E L Howland USAAF was attacked at 21,000 feet over Düsseldorf by a night fighter whose pilot made a beam attack on the Halifax, setting it on fire. Howland ordered the crew to bail out but he and two of his crew were the only survivors.

J-Johnny, a Halifax on 419 'Moose' Squadron RCAF at Middleton St. George was piloted by Flying Officer Chuck Thomas USAAF who was on only his second operation. His air bomber, the most experienced member of the crew, was flying his ninth sortie. On the bomb run Sergeant Arnold Greene RCAF the mid-upper gunner who was from Woodstock, Ontario reported a Ju 88 outlined against the flares at 100 yards range and 50 below. Sergeant Victor Alfred Knox the rear gunner shouted on intercom for the Skipper to corkscrew port. The Ju 88 closed to 50 yards, firing continuously, but Knox scored hits on the fighter's left engine and it caught fire. Their attacker was seen to go down and crash in flames but the Halifax too had been hit. Thomas cut the port inner engine but he was unable to feather the propeller. The American operated the extinguisher but it was no good. Bombs were jettisoned before another fighter attacked. A fire started amidships but the mid-upper gunner managed to kick it out with his flying boot. Greene heard bullets strike the fuselage and he saw a fire start in the under part of the starboard wing. Thomas, who received superficial wounds in the attack, ordered the crew to bail out as *J-Johnny* was down to 5,000 feet. He tried to put out the fires by diving and climbing for a couple of minutes but it was hopeless and the pilot finally left the aircraft at about 4,500 feet. Thomas saw the Halifax crash and it exploded at Couvron-et-Aumencourt in the Aisne, four miles north-east of Laon.

Greene bailed out in the target area and the raid continued for half an hour after he landed. Sergeant J L Thompson the flight engineer and Warrant Officer P J Murphy the wireless operator were captured. Knox was killed although it is not known if he left the aircraft. Thomas and Greene, Flying Officer John A Neal and Flight Sergeant P R Lindsay RCAF evaded capture. After three nights of walking in the general direction John Neal was discovered by a farmer who had connections in the local Resistance group and would have been escorted along the *Comete* line had not D-Day occurred before he could get started. While many of the members of the *Comete* line paid with their lives, and Dedee de Jongh, who started the line in 1941, was arrested in 1943 and put in Ravensbrück Concentration Camp for women, they were successful in escorting over 700 escapers to freedom. Chuck Thomas and Arnold Greene were success- ful in crossing the Pyrenees into Spain.[16]

M-Mother on 218 Squadron in 3 Group piloted by Squadron Leader Cecil Wardman Poulter MiD had taken off from Woolfox Lodge at 22.03. The airfield was situated along the side of the Great North Road opposite what was said to be a Henry VIII hunting lodge, a very impressive building with a large lake teeming with fish in front of it. Many fish were caught by the 'keen types' who seemed to spend the whole of their free time there. Poulter was a regular officer who had flown a number of ops in the early days of the war and had reached the rank of wing commander but reverted to squadron leader to allow him to return to operational flying. After successfully bombing the target, they were attacked by an enemy aircraft just after midnight. Both port inner and outer engines were ablaze and they lost altitude to about 10,000 feet. The order was given to bail out. Pilot Officer Harry Fisher, the WOp/AG, made his way to the forward escape hatch only to find it open and the navigator and bomb aimer gone. He looked at his pilot and received a tap on the shoulder indicating that it was time to go! Fisher jumped and naturally thought that Poulter would follow, but either he was too badly injured or lost control, as he went down with the aircraft. Flight Sergeant Fred Lambert, the injured mid-upper gunner, also died in the Stirling, which crashed at Hentefontaine in the Oisne. The five remaining airmen parachuted into France to meet different fates.[17]

On XV Squadron at Mildenhall ground crew anxiously awaited the return of *W-Willie* and Pilot Officer Oliver V Brooks' crew, who were on their 17th op. They had cheated death a month earlier on Nürnburg but at 01.10 hours on the morning of 23 April *W-Willie* was hit simultaneously by heavy flak and cannon fire from a Bf 109 at the precise moment that their bombs were released on Düsseldorf. Pilot Officer Alan Gerrard the Canadian bomb aimer, who was engaged to be married in another two weeks' time, suffered the most appalling injuries. He lived for another two or three minutes. Flight Sergeant Robert Barnes the wireless operator had sustained fatal chest injuries and had mercifully lost consciousness. It was found later that he had further very serious injuries to his lower body and shrapnel had almost severed one of his legs. He died before the Lancaster reached England. *Willie* limped home at 500 feet above the waves with the bomb doors stuck open and a fire-ravaged port inner engine. One starboard engine too gave very little power and the wing flaps were jammed down at 10°. An exhausted Brooks put the Lancaster down on its belly amid a shower of sparks, dirt, dust and debris at the emergency airfield at Woodbridge just inland from the Suffolk coast. When *Willie* slithered to a halt the bodies of Barnes and Gerrard were immediately removed from the crumpled fuselage while the surviving members were taken to the station sick bay to have their injuries attended to. *Willie* was unceremoniously hauled from the runway by the crash crew five minutes after the belly landing and scrapped.[18]

There were no Main Force operations on the night of 23/24 April and 114 aircraft – 70 of them Halifaxes – were detailed to sow mines in five areas of the Baltic. Four Halifaxes and two Stirlings failed to return. Two of the missing Halifax Vs were on 77 Squadron at Elvington. *L-London* was shot down by Bf 110s of NJG3 and crashed 500 metres north of the Traner Odde lighthouse on Als Island. Flight Lieutenant Edward Noel Thompson DFC and five of his crew were killed, one man surviving to be taken prisoner. Halifax *P-Peter* had also set a course for the coast of Denmark with four mines. While over Denmark they were attacked by *Focke-Wulf* 190s at 13,500 feet. The port engine and wing caught fire and they lost height rapidly. Flight Sergeant Paul Derrick Sykes gave the order to bail out of the crippled Halifax, which crashed at Hjaelm about six miles north-west of Nykobing. The parachute worn by Sergeant Glyn Jones, the flight engineer, failed to open and his body was found some distance from the crash, lying in a gravel pit at Sorup. The bodies of Sergeant William Henry Loverock the mid-upper gunner and Paul Sykes were recovered from the sea. The four surviving members on the crew evaded capture and escaped to Sweden. Bill Power the 25-year-old WOp/AG had completed 39 operations on 40 Squadron in the Middle East before joining 77 Squadron, and was on only his 7th op of his second tour. He owed his escape to a Doctor Hanson and numerous friends in the Danish underground movement who helped at great danger to their own lives. On 8 May the four RAF men were taken to Stockholm airport and flown home in four Mosquitoes of the British Overseas Airways Corporation. They were told to climb into the bomb bays of the

Mosquitoes and 'hold on'. Bill Power's aircraft was G-AGGC piloted by a Captain Brown. Just under three hours' later the Mosquitoes touched down at Leuchars in Scotland and they were taken to London for debriefing before being sent on leave for six weeks.[19]

On 24/25 April Oliver Brooks and his crew were on the Battle Order for the raid on Karlsruhe, which was the target for 637 aircraft. Wing Commander Watkins, the XV Squadron CO would be going along as the bomb aimer to see how they got on. A force of 234 Lancasters and 16 Mosquitoes were raiding Munich and 165 aircraft were detailed to fly a diversionary sweep over the North Sea.[20] Crews detailed for Munich hoped this would split the German night fighter force. Karlsruhe is about 30 miles south of Mannheim and roughly the same distance north-east of Stuttgart. What made crews uneasy was the knowledge that it was only 125 miles south-west of Nürnburg; about 18 minutes' flying time by a *Focke-Wulf* 190.

Joe Lennon's crew on Lancaster *K-Kitty* on 630 Squadron at East Kirkby were detailed for the Munich operation. They too were feeling uneasy. The New Zealander's flight engineer was Harry Parkins or 'Ackney 'Arry', as he was known because he was from Hackney and who, before the age of 20 had flown 36 operational raids on the Squadron. He recalls:

As air crew we received seven days' leave every six weeks because of the dangerous nature of our work. This was our fifth operation and we were very apprehensive because, if we survived, we were due seven days leave on our return. We were briefed that this raid would probably be one of the longest bombing trips a Lancaster would make. We had to trick the *Luftwaffe* night fighters by flying over the French Alps into Italy and then on to Munich, making a round trip of more than 2,000 miles. After our run-up to check the engines and pre-flight checks and owing to the limited amount of fuel we could carry we were to taxi to the runway take-off point, shut down our engines and receive a last-minute top-up of fuel before taking off. If we survived the raid, we would be running short of fuel by the time we arrived back in England so we were instructed to land in the south, which meant we would miss a day of our leave. Joe Lennon, who had worked on a dairy farm in New Zealand, did not take kindly to this and asked the rest of us what we thought.

The crew of *K-Kitty* were an incredible bunch. Bruce Reese our New Zealander navigator owned a racehorse. The rest of us were just ordinary guys. Our bomb aimer, Jim Hurman and the rear gunner Joe Pollard were from Australia; the mid upper gunner, Joe Malloy, came from Liverpool. I was the youngest. The Australian and New Zealander aircrew I flew with were all a bit crazy. We once upset a few officers at Skegness with our unconventional flying. In the early days at East Kirkby we used to fly out to sea and fire all our guns to test everything was working correctly. On this occasion we were flying below the level of Skegness pier. It was rather strange skimming along the surface and looking up to see the pier above us. There was one chap in a boat who leapt into the water when he saw us coming. On the way back we decided to take her over Butlins and the naval base where they were having a full military parade. We shot over their heads really low and they all ducked. Needless to say we were later taken into the group captain's office and given a good telling off. We heard later that the officer in charge of the parade had said the next time we tried it his men would open fire on us.

We all agreed that we should press on despite the risk and head back to East Kirkby in order to benefit from our full seven days' leave.

For Flight Sergeant Ron Storey, the wireless operator on Flying Officer John Cann's crew on 166 Squadron at Kirmington, Karlsruhe would be his second operation:

When the call came for briefing I was standing in the doorway of our Nissen hut when a fellow from Pilot Officer [David Reid] Tait's crew stood up at the end of his bed and calmly announced that a crew from this hut was 'going for a Burton' tonight. I gazed at him in astonishment when he confidently said 'It's OK mate; it won't be you.'

Cloud over the target at Karlsruhe and a strong wind that pushed the Path Finders too far north prevented accurate bombing. Only the northern part of the city was seriously damaged and most of the bombs dropped by the Main Force aircraft fell outside the target area, many in open countryside. About 100 bombers dropped their bombs on Mannheim, 30 miles to the north, and Darmstadt, Ludwigshafen and Heidelberg were also attacked by crews that were unable to find the main objective. Eleven Lancasters and eight Halifaxes were lost and two OTU Wellingtons went missing on the diversionary sweep over the North Sea. Ron Storey and the rest of John Cann's crew at Kirmington returned to their beds after a 'fairly uneventful' trip only to be awoken at 05.30 that morning when the door to the Nissen hut opened and in came the service police to pick up the other crew's personal belongings. Tait's crew had been the only 166 Squadron loss. There were no survivors.

The raid on Munich by 216 Lancasters of 5 Group and ten of 1 Group cost nine Lancasters. Luckily for Joe Lennon's crew on Lancaster *K-Kitty* on 630 Squadron the weather was good and they landed safely at East

Kirkby after ten hours and twenty-five minutes in the air. Harry Parkins recalls:

> As we started to taxi back to dispersal all the engines cut out. We had completely run out of fuel! We were towed in. They couldn't believe we had flown all the way back and risked our lives on a few drops of fuel just to get an extra day of leave! At our debriefing we were severely reprimanded by the Flight Commander for taking this risk. At this point the Group Captain walked in asking if that was an aircraft that had just landed. The Commander replied, 'Yes it was these fools from the Munich raid.' The Group Captain smiled and said 'Well done lads.' We received a good handshake all round for getting back in one piece. The rest of the squadron had kept to the rules and landed in southern England. Later we heard that this was the longest non-stop operation a Lancaster had flown during the war.

Six Lancasters on 617 Squadron flying ahead of the Munich force carried out a feint attack on Milan, dropping flares and target indicators, as if in preparation for a full-scale attack. No bombs were dropped but to support the illusion the crews talked 'tactically' on VHF. The 'Dam Busters' also supplied 18 Lancasters and four Marker Mosquitoes for the raid on Munich. Sir Arthur Harris had sanctioned the release of the Mosquitoes to 617 Squadron and insisted they could be retained only if Munich was hit heavily. 'Ben' Bennett recalls:

> Due to the limitation of their range by the non-availability of drop tanks, the four Mosquitoes had to position at Manston earlier in the day. All checks were carried out during the transit flight and the aircraft were then parked as close as possible to the duty runway. Their tanks were topped-up to the brim and they took-off on the operation without 'running-up' the engines. They had to fly the direct route from Manston to Munich and had the promise of a ten-minute fuel reserve on arrival back at Manston, providing they did not overstay their anticipated marking time at Munich. In the event, all four crews made it, with two crews being unsuccessfully attacked by a German intruder aircraft whilst making their landing approach at Manston.

The marking and controlling plan worked well and accurate bombing fell in the centre of the city. The intense flak and searchlight defences did not prevent the low-flying Mosquito markers from carrying out their task properly and none was seriously damaged.[21] While no award of the Victoria Cross was ever made for a Mosquito sortie, Wing Commander Leonard Cheshire's contribution to the success of the Munich operation, when he led four Mosquitoes of the Marking Force in 5 Group, was mentioned in his VC citation on 8 September 1944. In part it said:

> Cheshire's cold and calculated acceptance of risks is exemplified by his conduct in an attack on Munich in April 1944. This was an experimental attack to test out the new method of target marking at low level against a heavily defended target situated deep in enemy territory. He was obliged to follow, in bad weather, a direct route which took him over the defences of Augsburg and thereafter he was continuously under fire. As he reached the target, flares were being released by our high-flying aircraft and he was illuminated from above and below. All guns within range opened fire on him. Diving [from 12,000 to 3,000 feet and then flying repeatedly over the city at little more than 700 feet] he dropped his markers with great precision and began to climb away. So blinding were the searchlights that he almost lost control. He then flew over the city at 1,000 feet to assess the accuracy of his work and direct other aircraft. His own was badly hit by shell fragments but he continued to fly over the target area until he was satisfied that he had done all in his power to ensure success ... for a full 12 minutes after leaving the target area he was under withering fire but he came safely though ... What he did in the Munich operation was typical of the careful planning, brilliant execution and contempt for danger which has established for Wing Commander Cheshire a reputation second to none in Bomber Command.

Although pre-invasion targets were the main priority, Bomber Command continued its attacks on Germany. On the night of 26/27 April, Schweinfurt and Essen were the destinations for the heavies. There was a new moon and bombers heading for Schweinfurt would fly more than 130 miles on the long easterly leg, from Troyes south of Paris to Strasbourg, then into the target. The weather briefing predicted broken, medium stratocumulus cloud. During the forenoon Sergeant Roy Bradley, a Lancaster pilot on 106 Squadron in 5 Group at Metheringham was told by Squadron Leader Anthony O'Shea Murdoch, a New Zealander in the RAF, that he would be his co-pilot on *V-Victor*. His Flight Commander also suggested that the afternoon might be well spent 'in the pit'.

Another of the Squadron's Lancasters was *O-Orange*, which would be piloted by 22-year-old Pilot Officer Frederick Manuel Mifflin who was from Catalina, Newfoundland. The rear gunner was Flight Sergeant Hugh Johnson who had earlier been injured in a heavy landing. Off flying for two months he had flown several extra bombing trips with another crew to catch up with his own before returning to 'Miff's' crew. Just before take-off Flight Sergeant Norman Hugh 'Jacko' Jackson the flight engineer, who was flying his 31st op, having stood in for another crewmember one night, received the news of the birth of his son, his first child.

'Come evening and the very air was charged as only it can be when there was an ON,' recalls Roy Bradley. 'There were corny jokes and the nervous giggles and the haze and the maze of the briefing.' When he learned that it was to be Schweinfurt, Bradley thought, 'Funny that. I'd never heard of it before.' He could not even work up a feeling about the name. 'It hadn't the ring of the Essen's and the Frankfurt's but it wasn't far from Frankfurt' – 'a couple of loops of the River Main to the eastward.' There followed 'the studied confusion of getting the gear, the truck to the kite, the gathering dusk and in semi-silhouette, *V-Victor*', which to Bradley 'showed all the majesty of her breed.' Judging by the bombs painted on the nose he thought it could tell a lot of people's stories too. It seemed a 'nice kite' and he wished that he had a greater sentiment for it. Maybe if it were his own it would have been different. The crew he was flying with had had it for some time. 'Did somebody really say it was their 13th?' Bradley took another look at the outsize rabbit painted on the nose – hindquarter thumping and ears bristling in the defiant 'V'. He wondered who painted it. It was very well done he thought:

In what seemed no time at all, which happily cut down the time for wondering what the hell I was doing there, the engines were humming their harassed hymn of harnessed energy, the wheels were rolling and we were joining the line. We turned onto the runway and with their given freedom the engines sped us towards a shadowy horizon. I looked back and down. Could so much have really happened in these past few hours, down there within the scattered confines of what spells RAF Metheringham? Lying in the wispy band resting between a darkening earth and a paling sky was Lincoln and its cathedral identity.

It was a sight permanently etched in the mind of so many in 5 Group, which provided 206 Lancasters and 11 Mosquitoes (together with nine Lancasters of 1 Group) for the attack on Schweinfurt.

Another 493 Lancasters Halifaxes and Mosquitoes headed for Essen. It was an accurate attack thanks to good ground-marking by the Path Finder Force. Six Lancasters and a Halifax failed to return. *D-Dog* on 100 Squadron was hit by flak and exploded in mid-air and a 103 Squadron Lancaster was also downed by flak. The rear gunner on the 156 Squadron Lancaster that was shot down was 36 years of age; the American navigator and five Canadians died on *U-Uncle* on 408 'Goose' Squadron RCAF. Pilot Officer Everett Raymond Rognan was flying the Lancaster when it was hit. 1st Lieutenant F S Shove USAAF now rests in his home state of Connecticut.

Five Aussies died on *C-Charlie*, the 460 Squadron Lancaster at Binbrook that was lost.

At Schweinfurt the first spot fires fell south of the River Main and were followed by others still further off the mark. The master bomber made every effort to redeem the situation by instructing aircraft to overshoot the green markers but he was poorly received and the attack became concentrated to the south of the target area. The bombers found no cloud and high-level winds that were stronger than forecast, the delay *en route* resulting in the German night fighter force shooting down 21 Lancasters. Climbing and heading south for Schweinfurt Roy Bradley had noticed the sky filling up. He knew that by the time they were all *en route* it was going to be some 'mighty aerial brick of metal and men'. It was comforting to know that he was in company:

> Then it turned quite black. The others were still out there but it didn't give quite the same feeling of comfort now that I couldn't see them. It was quiet enough and not far to the Southeast turn point near Paris where there was a long, long leg coming up! On the long leg there was a fair old amount of flak. It was funny how it gave the feeling of a lot of little men down there flicking away at outsize cigarette lighters that wouldn't light. Then the flak stopped. I could see uncomfortably close glimpses of exhausts. Hell, there were a few being knocked down. I wondered how many, if any, got out. 'Now it was us! No. 4 was on fire. Then 3! Was this it? Then it came: 'Jump, jump, jump, jump!'

They had been attacked by 22-year-old *Experte Oberleutnant* Heinz-Wolfgang Schnaufer, and *V-Victor* was one of his two Lancaster victims that night. Roy Bradley put his parachute on and there was blackness: 'Is this what it was like to be dead?' he thought. 'Or was it all happening to somebody else?' He opened his eyes:

> The blackness had gone. If I had died, I didn't know about it. The sky beyond was a pale blue and then blackness again. Hell it was cold! My left leg looked a mess. I felt so stiff and sore all over. I couldn't stand! My flying boots had gone. Not surprising – those suede jobs were a pretty stupid design. Funny thing, it was the first time I'd worn them since early Flying School! This was real earth and above me was a real tree all right. Did I come through that? The chute was strung out around me. I tore a length for a bandage. Somehow or other, I hadn't 'bought it'. Were any of the others around I wondered? I called out. There was no response. The rising damp air carried my breath into the surrounding solitude. I buried my chute and crawled away, slowly, painfully and cursing the rough foliage which defied my progress.[22]

V-Victor was one of five missing aircraft on 106 Squadron. *J-Johnny*, flown by Pilot Officer Cyril Bishop, was attacked by *Hauptmann* Walter Bornschein a former bomber ace of KG2 and CO of that unit, who commanded 1 *Führerkurrierstaffel*, Hitler's personal transport unit. Bornschein had taken off from München-Riem, apparently on a whim, with two other pilots, and was flying a Ju 88. Sergeant Bill Stevens the Canadian rear-gunner, a former printer known on the Squadron as 'Eagle Eye', opened fire at the exact moment Bornschein fired. Both aircraft went down. The Ju 88 crashed near a flak battery on the edge of Schweinfurt and all three crew were killed. Only Flight Sergeant Bob Burns the navigator and Jack Pickstone the bomb aimer got out of the Lancaster and they were taken prisoner. Bishop, Stevens and the two other crew men were killed.

O-Orange too was shot down. Fred Mifflin was killed. So too was Flight Sergeant Hugh Johnson. For his actions on board the aircraft Sergeant Norman 'Jacko' Jackson was awarded the Victoria Cross, although this was not promulgated until after the war. His citation read:

> ... Bombs were dropped successfully and the aircraft was climbing out of the target area. Suddenly it was attacked by a fighter at about 20,000 feet. The captain took evading action at once but the enemy secured many hits. A fire started near a petrol tank on the upper surface of the starboard wing, between the fuselage and the inner engine. Sergeant Jackson was thrown to the floor during the engagement. Wounds which he received from shell splinters in the right leg and shoulder were probably sustained at that time. Recovering himself, he remarked that he could deal with the fire on the wing and obtained his captain's permission to try to put out the flames. Pushing a hand fire-extinguisher into the top of his life-saving jacket and clipping on his parachute pack, Jackson jettisoned the escape hatch above the pilot's head. He then started to climb out of the cockpit and back along the top of the fuselage to the starboard wing. Before he could leave the fuselage his parachute pack opened and the whole canopy and rigging lines spilled into the cockpit. Undeterred, Jackson continued. The pilot, bomb aimer [Flight Sergeant Maurice Toft] and navigator [Flight Sergeant Frank Higgins] gathered the parachute together and held on to the rigging lines, paying them out as the airman crawled aft. Eventually he slipped and, falling from the fuselage to the starboard wing, grasped an air intake on the leading edge of the wing. He succeeded in clinging on but lost the extinguisher, which was blown away.
>
> By this time, the fire had spread rapidly and Jackson was injured. His face, hands and clothing were severely burnt. Unable to retain his hold, he was swept through the flames and over the trailing edge of the wing, dragging his parachute behind. When last seen it was

only partly inflated and was burning in a number of places. Realising that the fire could not be controlled, the captain gave the order to abandon aircraft. Four of the remaining members of the crew landed safely. The captain and rear gunner have not been accounted for. Jackson was unable to control his descent and landed heavily. He sustained a broken ankle, his right eye was closed through burns and his hands were useless. These injuries, together with the wounds received earlier, reduced him to a pitiable state. At daybreak he crawled to the nearest village, where he was taken prisoner. He bore the intense pain and discomfort of the journey to *Dulag Luft* with magnificent fortitude. After ten months in hospital he made a good recovery, though his hands required further treatment and they were only of limited use. This airman's attempt to extinguish the fire and save the aircraft and crew from falling into enemy hands was an act of outstanding gallantry. To venture outside when travelling at 200mph, at a great height and in intense cold, was an almost incredible feat. Had he succeeded in subduing the flames, there was little or no prospect of his regaining the cockpit. The spilling of his parachute and the risk of grave damage to its canopy reduced his chances of survival to a minimum. By his ready willingness to face these dangers he set an example of self sacrifice which will ever be remembered.[23]

At Binbrook in April, Squadron Leader Jarman's Lancaster crew on 460 Squadron posed in their spare time for the expatriate, Official Australian War Artist Stella Bowen for her painting 'Bomber Crew' which resulted from her preliminary sketches and photos of the crew, six of whom were from all parts of Australia. Eric Gordon DeLancy Jarman had received the DFC and was from Yeppoon, north-east of Rockhampton in Queensland. Pilot Officer Thomas J Lynch the rear gunner, another Queenslander, was from Toowoomba. Flying Officers Hector Harrison the wireless operator and Francis Jackson DFC the bomb aimer were both from Lismore, 45 miles inland from Byron Bay in New South Wales. Flying Officer Ronald Neal the mid-upper gunner was from Grenfell, New South Wales. Flying Officer Marmion Carroll, DFC the navigator was from Ferntree Gully. Sergeant Douglas George Champkin the flight engineer was English.

Preoccupied with their flight preparations, the men expressed no particular interest in Stella Bowen's attempt to draw them. Her interest in group portraits stemmed from her discovery of the work of the Italian primitives and from her preference for the decorative portrait over the 'tedious realism' of the Royal Academy. She had left Australia in 1914, aged 20, never to return and was almost ready to give up any hope of making a career as a painter when she was offered a commission as an official war artist in 1943. She was given the honorary rank of captain and issued with an Australian Women's Army Service uniform to allow her greater access to restricted military areas. She had already become fascinated with painting the effects of war on civilian London and hoped to explore this further. However, her commission took her mainly into the world of the RAAF and later, the lives of returned prisoners of war. Although she found it extremely demanding, the war work had allowed her to resolve ideas about painting that she might otherwise not have pursued. It was a slow job though, with not much more than a frame-work completed by 27 April.

On the moonlit night of 27/28 April Jarman and his crew were one of 322 Lancaster crews detailed to bomb Friedrichshafen. Jarman took off at 21.27 hours. Various diversions and other factors confused the German controllers and the Lancasters reached the target area deep in southern Germany largely without being intercepted.[24] A total of 1,234 tons of bombs was dropped in an outstandingly successful attack, which wiped out a factory producing the engines and gear boxes for German tanks, damaged several others and destroyed 67 per cent of the town's built up area. However, while the raid was in progress 31 Bf 110s and three *Luftbeobachter* (air situation observer) Ju 88s were successfully guided into the bomber stream via radio beacon *Christa* and they wreaked havoc. Eighteen Lancasters were shot down and one more crashed on its return to England. Flying Officer Dan Cullen RAAF and his Lancaster crew on 460 Squadron RAAF were on their sixth operation and it was far from routine, as Warrant Officer D A Gray the flight engineer recalls:

We took off from Binbrook at 21.43 hours. Everything proceeded normally until we strayed off course and we were caught by heavy, predicted flak over Strasbourg. In spite of repeated corkscrews, we were hit in the starboard outer engine, in various parts of the airframe, and the hydraulics to the mid-upper turret were severed. I was hit in the right shoulder by shrapnel, which went right through and shattered the canopy above my head. Afterwards, assessing the angle the piece of metal took, it seemed impossible that it missed my head. My shoulder was numbed for a time but I managed to activate the fire extinguishers and then feather the engine. The Skipper asked for a damage report from the crew and it was decided to continue to the target, which we bombed all on our own at 02.19 hours; the target being seen to be burning fiercely over a large area. We were routed out over the Swiss border and encountered some neutral flak over Swiss territory. We were well behind the bomber stream by this time, struggling to maintain altitude and half-way up France and I decided to balance the petrol tanks. I asked the wireless operator to open the balance cock to feed the port engines off the starboard tanks and immediately the three remaining cut out and we dropped like a stone for 3,000 feet. As it was patently obvious that the fuel line was cut, I yelled to him to return the cock to the central position and after a lengthy quiet period, which seemed to last forever, the engines picked up and we resumed our course at around 8,000 feet. My shoulder was pretty sore by this time and there seemed to be a lot of blood on the aircraft floor but I decided, perhaps stupidly in hindsight, that we were in enough trouble and to say nothing. We passed to the west of Paris as dawn was breaking but our luck held and no fighters appeared. The Skipper then decided not to try and make base, as the port tanks were all but empty and we set course for Tangmere where we landed in daylight. My arm had stiffened up by this time and I asked the bomb aimer to come up and carry out the landing drill. The Skipper's language when he realised that I was wounded was frightful to hear![25]

Lancaster III ND759 *R-Robert* on 35 Squadron flown by Warrant Officer 'Bob' Peter RAAF who had set off from Graveley at 22.21 hours, was one of the Path Finder aircraft on the raid. The crew had been on Halifaxes on 51 Squadron and it was mainly due to the skill and accuracy of the Australian bomb aimer, Flight Sergeant Noel Davis, a former bank clerk of Sydney, that they were selected for Path Finder duties. *R-Robert* was hit in a head-on attack by a night fighter 50 miles from the target and a starboard engine caught fire. Peter feathered the propeller and in the evasive action that followed he lost 1,000 feet and approached Friedrichshafen at 16,000 feet. Davis dropped the bombs and they set course for home on three engines. A short while later *R-Robert* was attacked again, by a Bf 110G-4. This time the cockpit filled with smoke and the Lancaster failed to respond to the normal correcting action. Bob Peter gave the order to abandon the aircraft. Sergeant A S Brereton the flight engineer and Flight Sergeant Geoffrey Grant Foulkes RAAF the navigator jumped but the bomb aimer's parachute had fallen through the front escape hatch used by the two men when they bailed out. (Foulkes was later found dead on landing and he was buried in Switzerland at Vevey). Then the smoke began to clear. The two gunners, despite burns to their hands and face had managed to extinguish the flames and the wireless operator helped Peter with the controls. Finally he gave the one live starboard Merlin full throttle and cut back completely on the two port engines. It worked and the Lancaster, which was down to 3,000 feet, stopped spinning. With two crewmembers gone, the gunners out of action and their parachutes burnt and the bomb aimer without his chute, Peter put the ailing bomber down on Lake Constance. Friedrichshafen was an inferno and the fires cast their reflection on the lake and the surrounding mountains. Incredibly, Peter safely landed the stricken bomber on the lake and everyone escaped before the Lancaster sank. They were all interned by the Swiss. Bob Peter, who was repatriated in July 1944, received the DFC.[26]

Much damage was caused to the railway yards at Aulnoye where one Halifax went missing in action. At Montzen only one part of the railway yards was hit by the bombing. The bombing force, particularly the second of the two waves, was intercepted by night fighters, and 14 Halifaxes and a Lancaster flown by the Canadian deputy master bomber were shot down.[27] Three of the Halifaxes that were lost were on 51 Squadron at Snaith. Two of these crashed near Liège and *E-Easy* flown by Flight Lieutenant Lewis Rothwell DFC exploded over Maastricht. Rothwell and three of his crew were killed. Flight Sergeant 'Tony' Partridge the bomb-aimer was one of the three who survived. He recalled that when the crew arrived at Snaith they had an interview with the CO. He told them, 'Don't worry, we'll start you off on something easy.' Two nights later they were on Berlin and they went there five times in the next two weeks.[28]

Four of the Halifaxes that had failed to return were on 431 'Iroquois' Squadron RCAF at Croft. *N-Nan* flown by 1st Lieutenant John M Farman USAAF was set on fire by a night fighter, which attacked from the port quarter at 14,000 feet. The American pilot ordered the crew to bail out. Three who made it were taken prisoner but Farman and the others died in the aircraft, which crashed near Genk in Belgium. To complete the Canadian Group's night of misery, a 434 'Bluenose' Squadron RCAF Halifax V also failed to return to Croft and three crews on 432 'Leaside' Squadron RCAF at East Moor were among the other Halifax aircraft losses.

At Binbrook news was received that Dan Cullen had landed at Tangmere but there was no word from three other Lancasters, one of which was Squadron Leader Jarman's. All were posted 'missing'. The fate of *F-Freddie* and *B-Baker* was sealed: they had both crashed with no survivors. Stella Bowen had only made preliminary sketches when Jarman's crew were reported missing. She returned to her London studio to complete the painting, using her sketches and some photographs of the crew. She later wrote to her brother: 'It was terrible having to finish the picture after the men were lost; like painting ghosts.' Finally, in September came the first news of Jarman's crew. The parents of Flying Officer Tom Lynch received a small postcard from *Dulag Luft*. It was in the unmistakable handwriting of their son who was a prisoner of war. Eventually it was learned that he was the only survivor of a crash on 28 April in which he was badly injured. Their aircraft, he said, was shot down in the vicinity of Lahr, near the Swiss border. He was unable to remember whether or not he had jumped from the aircraft. In fact, he remained unconscious until 4 May, when he awoke as a patient in a German air force hospital at Baden-Baden. A German doctor answered his anxious inquiries concerning the fate of his comrades and told him that all had been killed. Lynch's right leg was amputated and he spent many weary weeks in various hospitals including Nemmingen near

Frankfurt, after which he was sent to Stalag IXC to await repatriation in the fifth exchange of prisoners arranged between the Allies and Germany. He arrived back in England on the *Arundel Castle*, which docked at Liverpool on 5 February 1945.[29]

Operations in support of the *D-Day* build up continued in May. On the first night Bomber Command sent six forces to bomb targets in France. At Chambly, about 22 miles north of Paris, the main railway stores and repair depot for the northern French system was the target for 82 Lancasters and 16 'G-H' equipped Stirlings on 218 Squadron at Woolfox Lodge. Eight *Oboe* Mosquitoes and 14 Lancasters of 8 Group marked the target, which was attacked in two waves. About 500 HE bombs fell inside the railway depot area and serious damage was caused to all departments and the depot was completely out of action for ten days. Three Lancasters and two Stirlings were lost.

Over 130 Lancasters of 5 Group attacked the aircraft assembly factory at Blagnac airfield at Toulouse where the marking was successful and the Lancasters severely damaged the factory. Other targets this night included the railway yards at St-Ghislain and Malines, which was attacked by 137 aircraft of 6 and 8 Groups and the *Société Berliet* motor vehicle works at Lyons, which was attacked by 75 Lancasters of 1 Group. The factory was badly damaged and railways and factories nearby were also hit. Forty-six Lancasters and four Mosquitoes of 5 Group also flattened the Usine Lictard engineering works outside Tours, which was being used as aircraft repair workshops.

On Wednesday 3 May Bomber Command were detailed that night to attack a *Panzer* depot and training centre at Mailly-le-Camp almost half-way between Troyes and Châlons-sur-Marne, about 50 miles south of Rheims, which was reported to house up to 10,000 *Wehrmacht* troops.[30] Up until 1940 Mailly had been a French Army artillery training area. The whole complex covered about 55 square miles but the barracks, workshops and garages were concentrated into about 400 acres at the northwest corner, next to the village of Mailly. The area was known to be defended by two six-gun batteries of radar-controlled 88mm heavy anti-aircraft guns and about twenty-eight 37mm and 20mm light guns. Nineteen *Airborne Cigar* Lancasters on 101 Squadron at Ludford Magna would jam night fighter communications. 100 Group would provide six *Serrate* Mosquitoes and three ECM Halifaxes on 192 Squadron to carry out Special Duty patrols in the target area. Other operations, including a raid on Montdidier airfield by 84 Lancasters and eight Mosquitoes of 8 Group would hopefully disperse the German night fighter force in the area. 1 and 5 Groups provided the Main Force and were to attack Mailly in two phases. Some 173 aircraft of 5 Group would go in first and aim their bombs at a point near the southeast end of the barracks area. This would be followed by another 173 Lancasters of 1 Group, most of which would attack the northwest end of the barracks while 30 aircraft were to concentrate on a special point near the workshops. Wing Commander Lawrence Deane or his deputy, Squadron Leader Neville Sparks, both of 83 Squadron, would orchestrate the attack. The weather forecast was for mostly clear skies and good visibility in all areas and there was nearly a full moon.

At Elsham Wolds Pilot Officer Roy Whalley's crew on 576 Squadron prepared to fly their 30th and final op of their tour. They shared a Nissen hut with Pilot Officer Bodger's crew, who had completed their tour but had agreed to wait until Whalley's crew returned and they would all travel down to London where his parents owned a pub in Islington and they would have a big party to celebrate. Both crews had been together on 101 Squadron and had become good friends and rivalry was intense, but it was a good-humoured rivalry, which, on occasion could get out of hand. At the 'Oswald' in Scunthorpe one night the two crews had challenged each other. Whalley's crew were to take the barometer from the pub while Bodger and his crew were to take the bell from the base at Elsham Wolds. The pub landlord at the 'Oswald' found out who had taken his barometer but said that if it was returned, then no more would be said about it. Unfortunately, Whalley's crew could not remember where they had buried it so Whalley had been taken to court and fined £5. Wing Commander G T B Clayton the 576 Squadron CO said since he had a good idea who had taken the bell, if it was back in place by lunch time, nothing more would be said. Otherwise, everyone on the station would be confined to camp. The bell was back in place by 12.00.

Jimmy Graham was the rear gunner on the crew of *Q-Queenie* on 576 Squadron. He had been in a reserved occupation when war broke out, working in a local iron foundry, but he had watched his pals go off one by one to join up and he knew the excitement of war. When he and a close friend decided to volunteer it had seemed like a good idea at the time. The crew Jimmy belonged to were a mixed bag of people who had come to rely very heavily on each other on their last dozen operations. Now they lazed the morning away waiting for the afternoon briefing. There would be the usual anticipation of the string drawing out the route to the target but nothing special was anticipated. It never was. If it were a short string it would look like it was another 'easy' operation. It was a short string but by the time the Intelligence Officer had introduced the reality and that Mailly had to be destroyed – it was essential – the penny dropped. 'It was just another raid but this one really mattered' he recalled.

Jack Spark DFM, the wireless operator on Fred Browning's crew at Elsham Wolds, recalled:

There was always a sense of tension – a tightness – when there was going to be a raid, which was quite different to the days when no

raid had been announced. Then there would be a rush to get ready
for a night on the town. There wasn't the usual tension on 3 May. We
didn't expect any trouble. We were told that it would be 'a piece of
cake'. And we believed it.

At Waddington Pilot Officer Colin Dickson RAAF and the crew of
Naughty Nan on 467 Squadron got ready for the raid. He and his four
fellow Aussies – Flight Sergeants S D Jolly, Robert I Hunter, Oscar Skelton
Furniss and Hilton Hardcastle Forden – and Sergeants Philip Weaver
and Horace Skellorn, the two English air gunners, had their own song.

We are the crew of Naughty Nan
and though we do the best we can
We always seem in trouble's way
with gremlins at the wicked play
the engines stop, electrics fail
we'd do much better with a sail
the turrets always seem to tire
of going round and never fire
So it's out to The Wash and drop the load
to scare the fish in their abode
another target, failed to 'prang'
another bloody boomerang.

At Ludford Magna, Gordon Wallace, a tail gunner on 101 Squadron, had
never heard of Mailly-le-Camp but he recalled that 'we all gave a sigh
of relief as French targets were supposed to be easy.' At Kirmington in
1 Group, Flight Sergeant Ron Storey on 166 Squadron was detailed to do
an air test for a wireless operator who was late back off leave. Storey
hated flying with a crew other than his own. However, he did it and
briefing time came. There was a model of the Mailly-le-Camp area for
them to study and the squadron's task was to bomb the ablution block. 'It
will be "a piece of cake chaps," ' Wing Commander D A Garner the CO
told his Lancaster crews, 'just like falling off a log. Tonight there will be
no night fighters, very little ack-ack; just go in and wipe it off the map
and come home.'

The Squadron were to bomb from 8,000 feet. On reaching the assembly
point they were to circle the avenue of flames and await the instructions
from the master bomber who would then give the go-ahead for them to
bomb precisely on the markers. To Storey 'it all sounded so simple and
we were in such good spirits.' He met the wireless operator for whom
he had air tested and let him know that he was not very pleased with
him. 'He replied that he'd had a rotten leave; he had fallen out with his
girlfriend, didn't like tonight's operation as it was out of *Gee* range
and without it his navigator was "useless". His final words were, "this

operation; we've had it." We had a good laugh and parted.' Three of the crews at the briefing would not be coming home. Among those killed would be the wireless operator for whom Storey had air tested.

At around 21.30 hours the 346 Lancasters and 14 Mosquitoes of 1 and 5 Groups began taking off for Mailly. All were airborne by 22.25 hours and heading south via Reading and Beachy Head to make landfall ten miles north of Dieppe on the French coast. It was a bright moonlit night, so bright that crews could clearly see the countryside below. Châlons was to be the first assembly point before approaching Mailly from the north. Red flares had been dropped 20 miles from Mailly to tell crews that they were on the right route.

At Woodhall Spa two Path Finder Mosquitoes of 617 Squadron, one flown by Wing Commander Leonard Cheshire, the 'Marker Leader', were dispatched. Flight Lieutenant 'Benny' Goodman DFC[31], a Mosquito B.IV pilot on 627 Squadron at Oakington in 5 Group, who with his navigator, Flight Lieutenant 'Bill' Hickox DFC flew on the operation, recalls:

Cheshire was to lead the low-level marker aircraft, and eight Mosquitoes on 627 Squadron were to be at a slightly higher level and were to dive bomb the light flak positions which were known to be around this depot. The raid was timed to begin at 00.01 hours, when all good troops should be in bed. The Mosquito force arrived over Mailly, five minutes before zero hour as briefed. Although the target was marked accurately and Cheshire passed the order to bomb, confusion occurred. The first wave did not receive instructions and began to orbit the target. This was fatal and the German night fighters moved in and began to shoot down the Lancasters. Eventually the situation was sorted out and bombs began to crash down unto the depot. From our worm's eye view, Bill and I could see bomber after bomber coming down in flames towards us. We had a scary time as we dived on the light flak batteries, dropped our bombs singly on them, avoided light flak and burning Lancasters and contrived to keep ourselves out of harm's way. When our fourth bomb had gone I called Marker Leader and was told to go home. Bill gave me a course to steer for the French coast and I should have climbed to 25,000 feet but because of the mayhem in the target area I stayed at low level. All went well for a few minutes and then a searchlight shone directly on us, followed immediately by two or three more. Light flak batteries opened up and the pretty blue, red, green and white tracery associated with light AA fire came shooting up the beams and exploded all around us.

We were at 500 feet and I did not dare to lose height, not could I climb because this would have been a 'gift' to the German gunners. With Bill's exhortation 'watch your instruments' ringing in my ears I turned steeply to port through 30°, levelled out for a few seconds,

then rolled into a steep turn to starboard and repeated the performance. Although we were in searchlights and flak for quite a long
time, we were not being held by any one light or being shot at by any
one gun for very long; and we zigzagged our way steadily towards
the coast. It was a tense time for us and we did not speak; we could
hear the explosions around us from light AA shells but incredibly,
were not hit. Deliverance came eventually as we breasted a low hill
and ahead of us lay the sea. Now we were treated to a rare sight. The
final group of searchlights was shining through the trees on top of
the hill we had just passed and the beams were actually above us
and lighting us on our way. We roared along a river estuary, below
the level of the lighthouse at Le Treport and then were away over the
'drink' and climbing to safety, home and bed.

The Mosquito crew had been lucky. For the heavies it was a different
story. The control of the raid in the target area failed to go according
to plan. The initial Mosquito low level Red Spot Fires were accurate
but were soon lost to sight. Flight Lieutenants Gerry Fawke and 'Terry'
Kearns both dived to within 3,000 feet of the ground and released their
Red Spot Fires on the western end of the camp. Both pilots courageously
flew across the target amid light flak while Lancasters continued to bomb.
One of the reserve Lancaster marker aircraft was now called in to place
its markers on the western edge of the fires with a slight undershoot.
Flying Officer Hubert Edwards on 97 Squadron flew in and his bomb
aimer, Flying Officer Jack Skingley released the ten Red Spot Fires at the
right place.[32] Cheshire ordered the Main Force, which was orbiting at
a holding pattern to the north, to come in and bomb. However, Wing
Commander Laurence Deane the 'Main Force Controller' could not
transmit the order because his VHF radio was being drowned by an
American forces broadcast and his w/t was 30 kilocycles off frequency.
Nachtjagd fighters arrived during the delay with deadly results. A RAF
pilot wrote:

I switched on for the Main Controller's commentary and was
surprised to hear him ordering the Main Force to wait, as the target
had not yet been marked. The air was really blue with a succession
of replies from the Main Force. I had never before heard R/T in-
discipline and this was really the measure of the panic and fear
that was abroad that night. We heard brief snatches of R/T, on one
occasion someone said, 'For Christ's sake! I am on fire!' A wing
commander came up on the R/T, identified himself and said, 'This
has got to stop. Cut your R/T and wait for instructions to bomb.
This was quite enough for me – I had no intention of joining the
crowd round those death-trap markers, so we turned east towards
the darker sky ...

Jack Spark heard Fred Browning say on intercom 'To hell with this. It's like moths caught in a candle' and he flew on and started circling 30 miles away. A tail gunner recalled:

> We circled and circled for what seemed an eternity without receiving any instructions. During this time the German fighter activity became more intense. There was tracer everywhere and aircraft were going down in flames all around us but still no instructions. One could sense the bombing force getting restless, like a herd ready to stampede.

Gordon Wallace felt as though they were circling for hours but it was probably only minutes. He heard 'Kit' Carson who had a distinctive Canadian accent ask the same question and get the same reply, 'No do not bomb, continue circling.' Carson replied, 'Fuck the RAF; we're coming in'.

Suddenly the R/T on Jimmy Graham's aircraft was broken by a strong Australian voice. It was his pilot. 'The hell with this; let's go before we're picked off' he said. And go they did. He lined them up for a clear run in and the bomb aimer dropped his bombs right on target and they made a bee line for home without further incident but 'going like hell.' Another Australian pilot obviously under fighter attack and who could not hear his gunners' evasive action instructions because of those that were breaking R/T silence, called out for those shouting abuse to 'shut up and give my gunners a chance.' Gordon Wallace also heard one man with what sounded like an English voice, screaming, calling out for his mother and crying:

> 'We're going to die; we're going to die.' A rough Australian voice answered, 'Be quiet. Turn off your R/T. If you're going to die, die like a man.' Everything went quiet. I heard one of the Pathfinders say, 'I've been hit. I've got to go down' in such a matter-of-fact way as if he was saying he was going out for a walk.

Warrant Officer J M Knox, a Canadian bomb aimer on 550 Squadron recalled that, 'When the order to bomb was finally given the rush was like the starting gate at the Derby.' 'We were called in to bomb at 12.32 hours' recalled Jack Spark. 'We should have bombed at 12.15. Those extra minutes were disastrous for so many crews. The fighters were waiting for us when we returned.'

The main attack eventually began when the 5 Group Deputy Controller, Squadron Leader Neville Sparks, who was on his 21st operation, took over. Between five and ten minutes after zero hour Deane ordered Sparks to release all of his ten red spot fires. As the bombing had been in progress for some time and was falling towards the south-east end of the target Sparks gave the message to bomb the opposite end of the camp, 300 yards 10 o'clock from the concentration of spot fires. This message was received by 5 Group and immediately re-broadcast. Squadron Leader Sparks continues:

At about zero plus 40, i.e. after circling the target for three-quarters of an hour, I called up the controller on VHF and suggested that it was time to set course for base. He answered, 'OK. Let's go.' Considering that my aircraft was at the extreme end of the bomber stream, I now decided to set a direct course back to England instead of the long route south of Paris. As we left the target area at 4,000 feet my rear gunner, Warrant Officer 'Tiger' Teague, reported four fighters on our tail. I immediately started a corkscrew intending to lose height rapidly from 3,000 feet to return as near ground level as possible and I took a straight line from Mailly towards England. During our second steep bank to the left I saw another fighter directly beneath us, perhaps 1,000 feet below. I pressed on with the corkscrew but this chap somehow put perhaps a dozen cannon shells into my starboard wing fuel tanks. We had no nitrogen suppression and in a short time the top skin of the wing had burnt through with a mass of flame. I had seen so many Lancasters with burning wings that I knew my aircraft had at most two minutes before the main spar failed with a consequent uncontrollable spin. I had considerable difficulty in controlling the aircraft, which was vibrating strongly. No report was received from the gunners after the attack although the intercom was working satisfactorily. I heard a groan on the intercom just after feathering the engine but had no chance to ascertain whence it came as at the same time the whole wing from fuselage to starboard outer engine went up in flames. I gave the order to bail out in my No. 2 method, which was unofficial but known and practised by my crew. This method was that the crew were to get up and get out without delay and any intercom. This they did. The visual air bomber jettisoned the front hatch and jumped directly after this. He was followed by the flight engineer, H_2S operator, navigator and wireless operator. I was sitting there keeping an eye on the burning wing and calling up all crew positions to check that no one was left on board. There was no response and as I was calling the last position, the wing folded up and I immediately made a turning dive through the front hatch. The Lancaster was then in an uncontrollable turn to starboard, with three engines running, height unknown. I came down and landed in a tree about 25 miles from the target area. My parachute had only been fastened on the left side.[33]

Fred Browning's Lancaster had hardly got into position on the bombing run when the bomb aimer in another Lancaster 20 feet above them, pressed the bomb release. 'Our gunner', says Jack Spark 'shouted out, "For God's sake, duck!" It all happened too quickly for us to realize what a lucky escape we had had. As we turned for home another plane exploded in the air. It was mayhem.'

While awaiting the order to bomb, Flight Sergeant J A Sanderson RNZAF on 166 Squadron at Kirmington called the crew on intercom that their Lancaster had been hit by flak and that the port inner engine was on fire. The New Zealander feathered the engine and Sergeant W T Viollet the wireless operator went to the astrodome and peered out, his face illuminated by the flames coming from the engine. Then the fire went out. The Lancaster completed its bombing run and 30 minutes after midnight, Sanderson set course for home. Ten minutes later they were attacked by a night fighter. Sanderson corkscrewed violently but cannon shells tore into the fuselage and set the hydraulic system on fire. Sergeant John Thomas Cockburn the mid-upper gunner left his turret and was trapped by fire which stretched right across the fuselage immediately behind the turret. One by one the crew began bailing out. Viollet landed in a small ploughed field surrounded by woods north of Troyes. As he made his escape through the woods he saw the wrecks of three Lancasters. He could not distinguish any identity marks but in one he saw the dead body of the rear gunner. Viollet was able to evade capture and return to England. Sanderson was badly burnt but was found and helped by local people and taken to Madame Duquesne at Troyes where he stayed for a short while before being taken to Loines aux Bois where he was sheltered by Madame Patris. Sanderson was discovered by the Germans and both he and Madame Patris were arrested. She was sent to a concentration camp but died on the train *en route* for the camp on 2 July.[34] Sanderson and three of the crew were taken into captivity. Cockburn was killed and Jack Bodsworth the rear gunner who had bailed out with his parachute on fire, died also.

Approximately 1,500 tons of bombs were dropped on the target[35] and the only French civilian casualties in the village of Mailly nearby occurred when a Lancaster crashed into a house. Fourteen Lancasters of 5 Group, which provided nearly all the marker aircraft and the entire first wave, were lost. Twenty-eight bombers of 1 Group, which was subjected to the greatest delay at Mailly, were lost.

One of four *Airborne Cigar* Lancasters lost was Z-Zebra flown by Flight Lieutenant John Alexander Keard, which exploded over the village of Aubeterre near Voué, 30 miles south of Châlons. When the crew were told to bail out 19-year-old Sergeant Jack Worsford the rear gunner opened his turret doors and was about to get his parachute when he saw the flames all down the fuselage. He quickly shut the doors and the next instant he seemed to be in a haze. While he knew that he was falling he was not frightened. It seemed to be happening to someone else. He thought of home. Then there was a jolt and remembered waking up in the tail section of the Lancaster in woods. The only thing that he could think about was the pain in his leg. It was almost unbearable. Worsford hid until morning and then he set out across fields towards a village to find help. He met a group of people who were amazed because they had seen the aircraft explode in the air and thought that there could not possibly be any survivors. They had not bothered to go and look and had only come to look at the wreckage of the aircraft to satisfy their curiosity. (The rest of the crew were killed when the Lancaster had broken up into three distinct sections). The pain in his leg was so bad that he could hardly think. He was found and given first aid by Monsieur Noel and his 18-year-old daughter Nellie and taken to the village *Mairie* (town hall) suffering from a broken thigh and a bullet wound in the neck. He was laid on the conference table and a doctor was summoned. He bandaged Worsford's leg but the doctor said that there was nothing further that he could do. Worsford needed hospital treatment. The Germans were informed and he was taken to a hospital in Troyes. Later the rear gunner was moved to hospital in Paris and when he was well enough, he was taken into captivity. Worsford had been lucky because the tail section had spiralled down and had caught on some overhead cables and trees, which had slowed its descent.[36]

Aircraft had been roaring over the village of Courboin for a quarter of an hour when a teacher in the village saw a torch of flame falling out of the sky. There was a terrific explosion and he ran towards it. He had not had time to put on his shoes. What a sight met his eyes. A tangled mass of metal was burning on the ground and in the forest there were a dozen more fires. The heat was intense. Black oily smoke rose in the sky and a pungent smell filled the air. Later a French woman handed the teacher an identity disc bearing the name 'H Brady RAF'. Sergeant Henry George Brady DFM was the wireless operator on the crew of Pilot Officer Douglas Wadsworth DFC who flew *G-George*, a 619 Squadron Lancaster at Dunholme Lodge that they called *Dirty Gertie*. Later, a local policeman painstakingly collected the body parts of all the eight crew. The village wheel-right made the coffin. They only needed one. On 5 May the coffin was placed in the chancel of the local church. It soon disappeared under a mountain of flowers. Next day more than 400 people filled the church for the funeral service.

FW 190s without radar but using searchlight and moonlight and the bombers' marker flares destroyed six bombers. Flight Sergeant 'Lizzie' Lissette RNZAF, pilot of *F-Freddie*, a Lancaster III on 207 Squadron, who was on his fourth operation, was attacked by a FW 190. The 26-year-old pilot's girlfriend had been a nurse on a hospital ship bombed off Crete and was believed lost but 'Lizzie' a tough, powerfully built New Zealander, who had been a teamster with four horses hauling logs out of the mountains near Napier, never spoke much about it. A third attack soon finished off the bomber. Tracer hit the port wing, blowing off the dinghy hatch. The dinghy began to inflate and then shot back over the tail plane like a big hoopla ring. Lissette could see down through the wing to the ground. The port undercarriage was partially down. A little later the rear gunner reported a fighter coming in port quarter down. They were hit again in the bomb bay and a small fire started. Lissette, who remained at the controls to the end, was critically injured and he died later in a French hospital.[37] Leslie Harry Lissette and Sergeant Ronald Ellis the 25-year-old rear gunner shared a joint grave in Chaintreaux Communal Cemetery.

Many aircraft were fortunate to make it back. Flight Lieutenant Charles Owen on 97 PFF Squadron in 8 Group went in to the target at 8,000 feet but circled outside the target at 4,000 feet while waiting for the order to bomb. He saw several fighters but was not attacked until on the bombing run at 5,000 feet. Owen wrote:

Luckily, he was a rotten shot and we were able to carry on and drop our markers. We were attacked again coming out of the target and he shot away our mid-upper turret and made a few holes elsewhere. The mid-upper gunner, miraculously, was only slightly wounded but had to leave what was left of his turret. The fighter came in again but the rear gunner drove him off and claimed him as 'damaged'. I came home to Bourn at nought feet.[38]

Fred Browning and his crew got their Lancaster back to Elsham Wolds where they were one of the last aircraft to return. Although the ground crew were pleased to see them there was a subdued air on the station. A badly shot up Lancaster on 576 Squadron had crashed on the runway with the rear gunner dead in his turret from a fighter attack. Another Lancaster had to be chased down the runway by the fire crews because its brakes had failed. One of the fire crew remarked that 'they got out OK but the crew must have set a record with the speed that they got out.' And there was no sign of Roy Whalley's crew. Bodger's crew waited until long after the last Lancaster had landed. It was then that they heard that they had been shot down. Bodger's crew decided to go to London to the pub in Islington. They had the sad task of telling Roy's parents. Even then they did not think they had been killed. Ken Watkins the WOp/AG on Bodger's crew recalled: 'They had been so much alive when they had set out on the raid. We told his mother that he had probably had to land at another airfield or they would have parachuted out. You didn't think of death; not even when you had to face it so often but I think that we knew in our hearts that we wouldn't see them again. Life was there to be lived and we lived it.'[39]

One rear gunner who made it home hardly had enough strength left to climb out of the aircraft. He was absolutely exhausted. Reaction had set in. He and the crew looked around the Lancaster. It had been knocked about and it would need to be patched up before it flew again. The crew was subdued when they went to the de-briefing. They took their coffee to the de-briefing table. It had a tot of rum in it. The rear gunner did not like rum. What the hell. They had got home and they were alive. It tasted good.

When the 101 Squadron Lancaster with Gordon Wallace in the rear turret arrived back at Ludford Magna 12 minutes after the previous aircraft they were the last of their squadron to return. They had already been chalked up as lost but their aircraft they were flying that night was slow. The crew disconnected themselves and clambered out of the aircraft. The crew bus took them to debriefing where they told the Intelligence Officer what they had seen and what they had heard. After de-briefing Wallace went to the Sergeants' Mess and had a meal of egg and chips and then went to bed. So too did Flying Officer Don Street's crew on 61 Squadron at Skellingthorpe, once they had been debriefed. It was only the next morning that they discovered how many aircraft and men had been lost. Sergeant Geoff Gilbert the rear gunner recalled. 'Our Squadron was lucky. They all returned but 50 Squadron lost four of their Lancasters.'[40] One of these was piloted by Flight Lieutenant Thomas H Blackham DFC who lost five of his crew. Blackham was unable to shake off a fighter, which followed them soon after leaving the target area. Luckily he was wearing a seat type parachute when the aircraft exploded. He and Flight Sergeant Stewart James Godfrey evaded capture but Blackham was picked up and later incarcerated in Buchenwald concentration camp. Godfrey was assisted by Madame Deguilly of Romilly-sur-Seine before being passed to a Resistance group but on 24 June he was killed when the *Wehrmacht* attacked their camp. Flight Sergeant Godfrey has no known grave.

At Wickenby 12 Squadron had also lost four crews.[41] At Binbrook, where 17 Lancasters on 460 Squadron RAAF had been dispatched, no word had been received from six of the crews. *Fox Squared* flown by Pilot Officer Norman David K Lloyd RAAF crashed at Avant-les-Marcilly in the Aube with the loss of all seven men. Sergeant Brian Wootton-Woolley had taken the place of Sergeant Riddell a Canadian who was unwell. At first the crew were posted as 'missing'. The parents of Flight Sergeant Richard 'Ginger' Johnson the crew's rear gunner, were not informed until two years later that he had been killed.

E-Edward piloted by Flight Sergeant H J G Fry RAAF crashed at Mariguy-le-Grand again with no one surviving. *J-Johnny* crashed at Donmartin-Lettree killing Pilot Officer F W Baker and his crew. *G-George* flown by Warrant Officer J W Smart RAAF crashed at Chapelle-Vallon in the Aube with the loss of all seven men and Flight Lieutenant W E Hull's crew were lost, their Lancaster crashing at St-Remy-sous-Barbuise. *R-Robert* flown by Flight Sergeant G K Gritty RAAF crashed at Châlons-sur-Marne. Sergeant Bryan Morgan the rear gunner recalls:

I could see aircraft going down all around me. We were shot down about midnight. Suddenly our fuel tanks were hit and I could see a mass of flames, my mid-upper gunner in his turret in flames, there was no chance for him. I knew our communications had failed though the aircraft was still flying but losing height. There was no point waiting for an order to bail out so I opened the door, got my parachute and clipped it on. I turned the turret manually and jumped out. I pulled the cord and remember looking back at the aircraft and seeing it disintegrate. I later discovered we had been shot down by a *Focke-Wulf* 190. Four of our crew died; three got out. My pilot died along with my wireless operator, mid-upper gunner and engineer. I later met up with the bomb aimer. The navigator got out and was hidden in a nearby village but we never met up. I landed in Châlons-sur-Marne on a bridge. There were Germans in the distance walking away, watching the sky and they didn't see me. I jumped into the Marne and came up near a barge which was low in the water. I spent a few hours on it under a tarpaulin then in the early hours I walked down the river bank and hid for the day. I could see a farm in the distance and remembered from the Escape & Evasion lectures that we should look for an arable farm, as the Germans regularly visited dairy farms for supplies. My hands were swollen, especially the knuckles, but I knocked on the door late in the evening. There was a party taking place inside but immediately there was silence then the door opened slightly by a Madame Castagne. I managed to say *Je suis aviator Anglais*. Apparently I then fainted and the next thing I remember is sitting in a chair in a dressing gown. A girl was breastfeeding her baby. I was 19 and had never seen such a thing before and must have looked surprised as they all laughed at me! I had a bandage on my burnt face and I'd also torn the skin on one leg. I hadn't adjusted the parachute harness as you never think anything will happen, so my shoulders were in a bad way. I must have been in shock as I don't remember feeling any pain. They put me to bed where I stayed for two days. A man who spoke English visited me but said there was nothing he could do for my shoulder but it looked OK. After about a week I could move it more easily. There was always a cauldron full of chicken and rabbit cooking on the stove because if it was being cooked it couldn't be stolen by the Germans! The farm belonged to Monsieur Champenois who was wounded in WWI and had contacts with the local *Maquis*. He contacted a local Basque man, André Etchegoimbery, who ran a 'safe house' in a small village.

After about a week I was taken by car and joined the *Maquis* Group *Melpomène* which was led by Jacques Degrandcourt. Others in the group were Jacques Songy, Roger Romagny and Gino Zappola. As an air gunner I was made very welcome, as they needed help with their armaments. I slept either in the woods or in a barn on a farm owned by the Jeanson family in Le Fresne, not far from Châlons. The *Maquis* group had hand grenades, guns and ammunition, much of which had been dropped by the British but some of the instructions were in English and some of the explosives had not been stored properly. They had opened the metal containers, resealed some of them and buried them in a line several feet apart. The plastic explosive had been buried separately and had become damp and some exploded later. It made a large hole and the Germans had come and investigated but didn't return. The Germans didn't like going into the woods, they probably suspected the *Maquis* were there but didn't know how many. We were a very big group but never all together at the same time. Several of them were charcoal burners and woodsmen and we would have got lost without them. There was also a Russian, Maxime (known as *le petit Russe*), who had been captured at the Russian Front but escaped and managed to walk across Germany. He was our expert in trapping and shooting hare, rabbit and deer. He also knew all the edible plants in the forest. He dug with wooden tools and found all sorts of root vegetables we never knew were there. We had a car equipped with a machine gun and the post of machine gunner was occupied by Maxime. I wasn't allowed to go with them on active patrols but was told their most common target was German vehicles, which used to be accompanied by out-riders. I used to check the villages and try to ascertain where the Germans were, as no-one would recognise me. I had been given an identity card as Marcel Julien Bernad, which said I was *sourd-muet*, a deaf mute. I stayed with the partisans from May until August by which time I was very weak and malnourished so they took me back to the Jeanson's farm to be looked after. General Patton's 3rd Army was coming through and, aided by the *Maquis*, I managed to get a note to them. They came to get me in a Red Cross jeep driven by Private Clura H Long and carried me back through the front line to a field hospital where I stayed a few weeks and I'm sure the Americans saved my life. I was flown back to England on 3rd September.

I later discovered that Jacques Songy and Roger Romagny had been sent to Natzweiler-Struthof and then transferred to Dachau where they both survived. Jacques Degrandcourt was caught in July 1944 and deported to Germany where he perished in 1945 in Vaihingen, a sub-camp of Natzweiler. I owe my life to those brave people in the

Resistance. If they had been caught they would undoubtedly have been shot whereas I would have ended up in a PoW camp.

Only three out of the 42 men on the squadron who went missing that night, survived. All three evaded capture.[42] Of the 346 bombers despatched to Mailly-le-Camp 42 Lancasters were lost.[43] Only 58 of the 315 men lost survived: 24 were taken prisoner of war and 34 evaded.

At Waddington two Lancasters were missing. *G-George* on 463 Squadron was lost with all seven men on Pilot Officer Graham Fryer RAAF's crew when it went down on the approach to the AP. On 467 Squadron, who shared 'Waddo' with 463, *Naughty Nan* too was missing. *Nan* had crashed 25 kilometres NNW of Troyes shortly after bombing. Colin Dickson and four other crew members were killed. Flight Sergeant Jolly managed to bail out safely and Robert Hunter, having tried to bail out via the forward escape hatch was forced to go back to the rear door with the aircraft well ablaze. He then fell through the floor but was suspended by his parachute on his back, completely surrounded by flames. After considerable effort he was able to open the door in the rear and jump. By this time he was badly burned on his face and different parts of his body. He managed to land without further injury though nearly unconscious and was unable to remember much of what happened thereafter. Jolly owed his initial freedom to Mme Berque who risked her life getting him onto a train for Paris where he was assisted by Bernard Monin.[44]

At Dunholme Lodge, Stephen Rew, a fitter who in his youth had fallen in love with aeroplanes but had been rejected as a fighter pilot, waited in vain for the return of *Dirty Gertie* and Douglas Wadsworth's crew:

The Lancs started coming back. The sergeant went through their letters. *C-Charlie, M-Mother, F-Freddie.* Gradually silence fell as, one after the other, boys returned with their torches and snag sheets, said goodnight and cycled off to supper and bed. Still no news of *George.* The Sergeant rang Woodbridge, which had a long runway. We reckoned 2 o'clock would be the end of her fuel. Never had the hands of a clock moved so slowly, the seconds ticking away reluctantly, like water dripping from a leaky tap. The hands crawled to half-past two. Finally it was reported that *George* was officially missing. There was no use hanging about the office. On my way back to the billet I felt an unreasoning hatred for every damned aeroplane I saw. Why couldn't it have been that one, or that one? Why *George*?

The next morning Rew received confirmation that his beloved Lancaster had gone down over Mailly-le-Camp.

At Kirmington during the debriefing Wing Commander Garner went over to a group of crewmembers and demanded to know what had gone wrong. A flight sergeant who was on his third tour with about 90 ops, including trips to Berlin, turned on the CO and told him to fuck off: 'And don't you talk to me about falling off a log; give me Berlin any time.' The CO quickly disappeared.[45]

After Mailly large numbers of aircraft no longer attacked a single target in a concentrated stream. Because of the risk to civilians, targets in France and Belgium now required greater accuracy from smaller formations of heavy bombers but it was not always so. On the night of 6/7 May when 149 aircraft attacked railway installations at Mantes-La-Jolie, a suburb of Gassicourt, for the loss of two Lancasters and one Halifax, over 860 houses were destroyed and 54 civilians were killed in the western part of the town. Lancasters and Mosquitoes of 5 Group raided an ammunition dump at Sable-sur-Sarthe without loss. Another 52 Lancasters of 1 Group destroyed an ammunition dump at Aubigne, 25 miles south of Le Mans and about 120 miles inland of the Normandy coast.[46] A 576 Squadron Lancaster at Elsham Wolds was the only aircraft that was missing from this raid. Air Commodore Ronald 'Chaps' Ivelaw-Chapman, whose staff duties at Group included accessing details of the coming invasion, had gone along for the experience. During the past three to four months 'Chaps' had done what he could to appear at briefings, debriefings, intelligence rooms, dispersal, hangars and workshops at each of his three stations as frequently as possible, apart from coping with the inevitable administration work at Base HQ. Nevertheless, he felt that he was not really being much use as a base commander and was not likely to be until he had at least one operational sortie under his belt. High Wycombe had said that sorties to French targets were easier than those to Germany and should count only one-third of an 'op' towards a man's tour. Ivelaw-Chapman shared the view that sorties to France should count towards a tour of 30 operations and it crossed his mind that it might help things along if he 'signed on' for one of these sorties as an extra aircrew. He had been given permission by his Group commander to fly the operation. At 00.15 hours 'Chaps' had taken off from Elsham Wolds in the Lancaster flown by Flight Lieutenant James Maxwell Shearer RNZAF. Now that the aircraft was missing the fear was that if the World War One veteran pilot had survived the operation and was handed over to the *Gestapo* for 'questioning' then D-Day might be compromised.

'Chaps' Ivelaw-Chapman recalls:

Shearer took us out there with no untoward event at 18,000 to 20,000 feet in a three-quarter moon and with no cloud cover. As we neared the target I crouched alongside Sergeant Ford of the Royal Australian Air Force in the bomb aimer's cubbyhole as a ringside spectator. On the appointed dot the marker flares went down. I was amazed at the accuracy and the skill with which these marker chaps had found this depot, which later I discovered to be a nondescript wood with no prominent or lead-in features nearby and stuck well out into the countryside. How they did it astounded me. Half a dozen of the stream may have bombed before us and by the time we were running in to the target it was well alight and the conflagration, with its periodic vast explosions, was a sight I shall never forget. Even Sergeant Ford, with his long tally of ops behind him, said he had never seen anything like it before. By the time we left the target it was not so much a 'Brocks' benefit as a burning fiery furnace.

We had settled down on the first leg of our homeward run for about five minutes when our rear gunner suddenly opened up, shouting down the intercom to his Skipper, 'Corkscrew!' which Shearer promptly did. Within seconds there was a flash from a night fighter flare and cannon shot riddled our Lanc all down its fuselage, followed by the acrid smell of burning. Then came the first sign of flames in the middle of the fuselage and almost immediately our captain's order to 'bail'. Sergeant Ford snatched his 'brolly' and was away. Mine was strapped to the side of the fuselage just below the second pilot's seat. I remember grabbing it and making for the bomb aimer's exit but at that moment an explosion occurred in one of the petrol tanks and I found myself in the air suspended by a parachute to which, in my panic, I had only managed to get myself attached by one buckle instead of the more orthodox two. By moonlight from 15,000 feet or so I could see the flat countryside of Normandy below me. Our poor ill-fated Lanc' with all its crew save Sergeant Ford and myself had become a ball of flame and I saw the wreckage hit the earth at least a minute before the trees on the edge of the forest loomed up alarmingly close below me. I landed with a bump, badly shaken but otherwise all in one piece. For the next ten minutes, mindful of the briefing I had been given at Elsham six hours earlier, I dug like a beaver and buried my parachute as best I could and was making for such cover as the locality offered.

With help from the Resistance Sergeant J A Ford and Ivelaw-Chapman were able to evade capture for a month but finally 'Chaps' did fall into the hands of the *Gestapo*, who fortunately, did not appreciate the importance of their prisoner, and the man who became the most senior RAF officer to be captured flying on operations was sent to a PoW camp in the normal manner.[47]

On 7/8 May, 471 sorties were flown to France to bomb five airfields and ammunition dumps and a coastal gun position. Twelve aircraft including seven on the raid on an ammunition dump at Salbris by over 60 Lancasters and Mosquitoes of 5 Group, failed to return. The following night, rail yards, an airfield and seaplane base and gun battery positions in France were bombed in 452 sorties and once again twelve aircraft were lost; seven of them Halifaxes and four, Lancasters. The largest operation of the night was an attack by 123 aircraft on rail yards at Haine-St-Pierre, which cost six Halifaxes and three Lancasters. The Canadian Halifax and Lancaster squadrons bore the brunt of the losses with 431 'Iroquois' and 432 'Leaside' Squadrons RCAF each losing two Halifax IIIs while 405 'Vancouver' Squadron RCAF at Gransden Lodge were missing two Lancaster IIIs. *A-Apple* a Halifax III on 425 'Alouette' Squadron RCAF at Tholthorpe piloted by Flying Officer Larry White USAAF did not return. The American pilot was killed – six of the seven crew bailed out and two subsequently evaded. A second American pilot who died this night was 1st Lieutenant John K Smith DFC AM*** PH who piloted Halifax *J-Johnny* on 426 Squadron at Linton-on-Ouse. Only his flight engineer survived to be taken prisoner. A third American pilot who died was Flight Lieutenant Robert Frazer Mead RCAF from Detroit, who was piloting Halifax *X-X-Ray* on 431 Squadron at Croft. The bomber, which was attacked by a night fighter flown by *Leutnant* Georg Fengler of IV./NJG1 who finished the war with 16 victories, crashed 26 kilometres south-east of Mons. There were no survivors on the crew, which included an Australian and four Canadians. Sergeant Joseph Victor Jacques Gravel RCAF was 18 and Sergeant Derek Vernon Guttridge the flight engineer, just a year older.

Attacks on coastal batteries continued on the night of the 9th/10th and heavy bomber raids were made by 5 Group Lancasters and Mosquitoes on the *Gnome et Rhône Ateliers Industriels de l'Air* factory and another factory nearby, at Gennevilliers and a small ball bearing factory at Annecy. Bomber Command claimed to have hit the Gnome et Rhône factories but 24 French people were killed and 107 were injured. The weather en route to Annecy was very bad and only two Mosquito marker aircraft reached the target but the ball-bearing factory was bombed and all the aircraft returned safely. Five Lancasters failed to return. On the night of 10/11 May Bomber Command went out in force when just over 500 aircraft were dispatched to bomb rail targets at Courtrai, Dieppe, Ghent, Lens and Lille. At Ghent, 48 Belgian civilians were killed and 58 were injured. One Lancaster was lost on the raid on Dieppe. Twelve Lancasters were missing from the 5 Group attack by 89 Lancasters on Lille where a prolonged delay in the midst of the raid occurred when the TIs were blown out and the target had to be remarked. The losses ended all talk of sorties to French targets counting only one-third of an 'op' towards a tour.

On 11/12 May, just over 420 bombers and 22 Mosquitoes of the Main Force carried out attacks on Bourg-Leopold in north-east Belgium, the railway yards at Hasselt and at Louvain in Belgium. Furthermore, just over 230 heavies and 20 Mosquitoes in three forces attacked the railway yards at Boulogne and Trouville and a gun position at Colline Beaumont. At Hasselt the target was marked and 39 aircraft bombed but all missed the railway yards because of thick haze and the Master Bomber ordered the bombing to stop, as Flight Sergeant Brian Soper recalls:

> This was controlled by a Master of Ceremonies who specified by radioed instructions where the bombs should be dropped. However, over the target he was unable to accurately find the centre point and the raid was abandoned. Unfortunately, flying into the target area we were attacked head-on by an enemy fighter believed to be an FW 190. Both gunners replied when it came round for a second attempt; we could see the tracer in both directions. It finally turned over and disappeared towards the ground. We were then fired at by some very accurate light flak which we had to corkscrew violently to starboard to avoid. Fortunately there was no damage to our aircraft.

Five Lancasters were lost on the raid. Four others failed to return from the raid on Louvain where the railway workshops and nearby storage buildings were hit. Two Halifaxes that failed to return from the attack on Boulogne are thought to have collided southwest of the entrance to Boulogne-sur-Mer harbour. There were no survivors on *G-George* on 432 'Leaside' Squadron RCAF at East Moor or *S-Sugar* on 427 'Lion' Squadron RCAF at Leeming, which was piloted by Flight Lieutenant Davis Hamilton Perry RCAF. Perry's crew included four other Canadians and American navigator, 1st Lieutenant R E Stevens USAAF who was from Oregon.[48]

The target for the 190 Lancasters and eight Mosquitoes of 5 Group with three Mosquitoes of 8 Group was the former Belgian *Gendarmerie* barracks at Leopoldsburg (Flemish)/Bourg-Leopold (French), which was being used to accommodate 10,000 SS *Panzer* troops who awaited the Allied invasion forces. One of the Lancasters taking part was *S-Sugar* on 467 Squadron RAAF flown by Pilot Officer T N Scholefield who was from Cryon, New South Wales. If *Sugar* returned to Waddington it would be considered this famous Lancaster's 100th completed operation. There was intense excitement on the station and its ground crew and those of many of the other Lancasters at Waddington waited up until the early hours of the morning to welcome *Sugar* home again. The weather was bad with low cloud and poor visibility and a serious error was made with the broadcast winds.[49] As a result, the aircraft were late over the target area and consequently flare-dropping was scattered and provided no adequate illumination. An *Oboe* Mosquito flown by Flight Lieutenants Burt and Curtis on 109 Squadron dropped a yellow marker. The Mosquito marking force on 627 Squadron arrived late over the target with the result that the *Oboe* proximity marker was seen by only one of the marking aircraft and the proximity marker, unfortunately, seemed to burn out very quickly. Flare dropping was scattered and did not provide adequate illumination of the target. Haze and up to 3/10th cloud conditions hampered the marking of the target. The Marking Leader then asked the Master Bomber (Squadron Leader Mitchell of 83 Squadron), if he could drop Red Spot Fires as a guide for the flare force. The Master Bomber agreed and 'RSFs' went down at 00.24 hours in the estimated vicinity of the target. Unfortunately, the Main Force started to bomb this red spot fire immediately it went down and half of the main force bombed this. The result of this was the five Mosquitoes on 627 Squadron returned to Oakington with their bombs and were unable to mark the target. Immediately Mitchell ordered 'Stop Bombing', as he realized it was impossible to identify the target but VHF was very poor, particularly on Channel 'B' and the Germans had jammed Channel 'A'. Only half the main force received the instruction and 94 Lancasters bombed the target. Unfortunately, the village of Beverlo was very badly hit and 84 people were killed with many more seriously injured. At 00.34 hours a wireless message, 'Return to base' was sent out to all crews. Five Lancasters were lost taking the night's losses to 16 heavies, all except one being claimed by the *Nachtjäger*. Among the dead were Group Captain John Raeburn 'Sam' Balmer OBE DFC RAAF flying a 467 Squadron Lancaster, and South African Wing Commander Hubert Reginal Goodman ROYAL HELLENIC AF AFC on 103 Squadron.

At Waddington, where everyone was waiting for the return of *Sugar* there was no sign of Scholefield and his Lancaster. Having received the signal to return to base he was attacked by a night fighter. Scholefield jettisoned his 4,000lb bomb in order to gain height quickly and he intended to drop the rest of the bomb load into the sea but he could not get his bomb doors open. Once over land he ordered all of the crew except for the flight engineer to bail out and they jumped over Coleby.[50] Eventually, Scholefield landed safely at Waddington where, at 01.22 hours *S-Sugar* had touched down to a hero's welcome, having made a century. Later on, after the crew had rested, *Sugar* was welcomed back officially and was drawn up outside the watch office and the members of the crew stood on a trestle placed by the nose, while the rest of the station, including the station commander, gathered round in a circle. Glasses were raised and as an airman painted the 100th bomb on the fuselage, the gathered personnel gave three hearty cheers.

Sugar's 100th operation proved to be one of the most exciting operations of its long career. Leaving the area two Ju 88 night fighters picked them up. The enemy fighters attacked for 9½ minutes but with some excellent co-operation between pilot, gunners and the wireless operator on *Monica*, the nine or ten attacks were all successfully forestalled, in spite of the handicap of a full bomb load. *Sugar* was at 16,000 feet when first attacked but was down to 9,000 feet when the fighters gave up. The bomb load was jettisoned over the North Sea. After landing back at base, the rear gunner Flight Sergeant K E Stewart of Sydney described the incident to the waiting reporters:

> We still had our bombs on board and therefore old *Sugar* wasn't as easy to handle as usual. The two fighters didn't attack at the same time but came in at us alternately, first from one side, then from the other, they seemed determined that we shouldn't escape. Sometimes they closed in to about 300 yards. Both the mid-upper gunner and I opened up at them and we feel pretty sure that we downed one of the enemy. It was a long, grim struggle. They attacked us seven times in ten minutes and it was only the grand co-operation between the members of the crew which enabled us to escape. During the fight I got in one long burst of fire. After that I kept on taking squirts at the enemy. Old *Sugar* went beautifully and never faltered for a moment. She's a grand old bus.

The flight engineer, Sergeant R H C Burgess, of Chester, said '*Sugar* flew up to her usual standard ... and that is a very high standard indeed.' 'I like old *Sugar*,' he added, 'she's got good engines and you can trust them. The ground crew are like mothers to her; they check everything a second time before she takes-off.'[51]

S-Sugar would fly 69 sorties on 467 Squadron RAAF and would finish the war having flown 137 sorties.

On the night of 19/20 May, Bomber Command resumed operations with raids by 900 aircraft on five separate rail targets (all of which lay within a radius of 150 miles of Caen), coastal gun positions at Le Clipon and Merville and a radar station at Mont Couple, on the Picardy and Normandy coasts.[52] At Longueau southeast of Amiens the Master Bomber cancelled the attack on the railway yards by over 120 Lancasters and Mosquitoes of 5 and 8 Groups because they were cloud covered. One Lancaster which failed to return is believed to have been shot down by a night fighter north of Poix. A second aircraft crashed near its base at Dunholme Lodge on returning to England when it hit a tree. Of the other four rail targets that were attacked, three (Le Mans, Orléans-Les Aubrais and Tours-St Pierre de Corps) were severely damaged. Boulogne's yards were damaged by 143 aircraft of 4 Group. The raid on the marshalling yards and repair shops situated on the south side of Le Mans by 112 Lancasters and four Mosquitoes of 3 and 8 Groups claimed three Lancasters. This included the 7 Squadron aircraft with Wing Commander John Barron DSO DFC DFM the Master Bomber and that of his deputy, Squadron Leader John Mervyn Dennis DSO DFC, which collided over the target. Barron, who was on his 79th operational sortie, and Dennis, who had successfully controlled the Main Force at Chambly three weeks earlier and their crews were killed.[53] The third aircraft almost certainly was shot down by light anti-aircraft guns whilst pulling away from the target. The attack led to much re-routing of German troop trains from the south of France and to delays during the early part of the Normandy Campaign.

Some 113 Lancasters and nine Mosquitoes of 5 and 8 Groups took off from their Lincolnshire stations for Tours. At Waddington 463 and 467 Australian Squadrons were seen off by John Curtin, the Australian Prime Minister, who had been dining in the Officers' Mess during a visit to the station. At the target Wing Commander Willy Tait the Master Bomber had problems with his VHF radio and he handed over control to his deputy, Wing Commander Jeudwine. The initial marking by 627 Squadron's Mosquitoes was accurate and from start to finish the attack lasted 26 minutes, during which time 107 aircraft had dropped 477 tons of HE from an average height of 8,000 feet. One Lancaster, which was diverted to Benson, hit the corner of a barn on the approach and the pilot and two crew were killed.

At Orléans-Les Aubrais four *Oboe* Mosquitoes dropped red and green TIs and they were followed by illuminating and marking by Lancasters of 635 (PFF) Squadron at Downham Market. Wing Commander W T Brooks the Master Bomber and his deputy, Flight Lieutenant Smith, directed the attack by 118 Lancasters of 1 Group, which dropped almost 1,500 bombs or 615 tons of HE which left 200 craters in the marshalling sidings and destroyed a large number of goods wagons. One Lancaster failed to return, having fallen victim to a night fighter south-west of Paris. On returning, 1 Group's squadrons found that mist was forming on the Lincolnshire Wolds and a number of Lancasters were diverted to airfields further to the south. One aircraft was so badly damaged by flak that it had to be written off. A further six aircraft received varying degrees of damage as a result of enemy action and five were damaged in minor incidents, including a collision over the target at Boulogne.

There were no Main Force operations on the night of 20/21 May but Bomber Command directed its might against German targets once again on 21/22 May, when 532 aircraft raided Duisburg. The target was covered by cloud but the *Oboe* sky-marking was accurate and much damage was caused in the southern areas of the city. Twenty-nine Lancasters were lost on the operation and three more were lost on mine-laying operations off enemy coasts. *Tame Boar* crews claimed 26 bombers shot down, most of them over the southern provinces of the Netherlands. First Lieutenant Max Dowden on 625 Squadron, who had crash-landed in a field near the Duke of Bedford's estate returning from the Nürnburg raid two months earlier, went down near Antwerp. The American and pilot and Sergeant Frank Moody the engineer went down with the aircraft with their arms around the control column pulling as hard as they could to keep the aircraft reasonably straight to enable everyone else to get out. Three men were captured but Sergeant Russell Margerison the mid-upper gunner and Dick Reeves the wireless operator were in the care of the Resistance for several weeks. Eventually they were in a group of evaders who were betrayed and they were put in the hands of German military intelligence in Antwerp before being taken into captivity.

Among the victory claimants were *Hauptmann* Martin Drewes who shot down a Lancaster, which crashed into the sea, for his 40th victory, and *Oberleutnant* Fritz Lau of 4./NJG1 who destroyed a Lancaster west-north-west of Rotterdam for his seventh victory. Lau recalled: 'I saw one of the crew bail-out over the sea and I believed it to be my absolute duty to worry about his fate so I notified the rescue service immediately after I landed. I gave the rescue services the position and time of the shoot-down so that they could get the search and rescue operation under way as quickly as possible.'[54]

Dortmund was attacked by over 370 Lancasters and Mosquitoes the next night. A second stream of 225 Lancasters and ten Mosquitoes mean-while headed for Brunswick. At Skellingthorpe, Flight Lieutenant 'Chas' Startin and his Lancaster crew, who had beaten the odds and returned from Nürnburg in *H-Harry* on 30/31 March, boarded *B-Baker* for the trip to Brunswick. Sergeant Ernest D Rowlinson the 22-year-old wireless-operator was sick so his place was taken by another crew member. He never saw his crew again. *B-Baker* was one of 13 Lancasters that failed to return and was presumed to have been lost over the North Sea on the return. Flight Sergeant 'Ben' Lawrence the 22-year-old bomb aimer, Sergeant Ernest McIlwine the 'short and stocky' Irish mid-upper gunner and Sergeant Eric Hopkinson the rear gunner, who had both survived Nürnburg, were killed. McIlwine's body and that of Warrant Officer Frank M Linton RCAF, who was American, were found washed up on the shoes of the Dutch coast. Startin, Sergeant Daniel Patrick Duggan, an Irishman from Ballydehob in County Cork in the Irish Republic and Sergeant George Reid, a Scot from Kirkcaldy have no known grave.

The Lancaster flown by Cliff Chatten on 97 Squadron at Coningsby was attacked and badly damaged by a night fighter while coned over the target. (It was cloud covered and the raid was a failure.) Despite the loss of his instruments Chatten got the bomber back to England and he circled the Wash until it was light enough for a crash-landing. Everyone walked away. Chatten, who the previous August had been shot down over Norfolk by an Intruder returning from Berlin, was awarded an immediate DSO. He decided that he no longer wished to remain teetotal.

Most of the bombs that were dropped on Dortmund fell in residential areas, mainly in the south-eastern districts of the city. Eighteen Lancasters, including *H-Harry* piloted by Wing Commander David Sinclair Jacobs DFC RCAF, commanding 408 'Goose' Squadron RCAF, which was shot down by a night fighter, were lost. Jacobs, a graduate of McGill University in Toronto, and his eight crew members were killed.

On the night of 24/25 May Bomber Command mounted four main raids. At Eindhoven bad weather prevented bombing of the Philips factory by a force of almost 60 Lancasters, who returned without loss. Raids on French coastal batteries by over 200 Halifaxes and Lancasters and 16 Mosquitoes, and another by 44 Lancasters and seven Mosquitoes on the Ford motor factory at Antwerp were all without loss. It was a different story for the force of over 440 aircraft of all groups, whose targets were the railway yards at Aachen-West (which was well hit) and Rothe Erde (which escaped serious damage). Before the bomber stream reached Aachen, the 'Night Ghost of St-Trond' – *Oberleutnant* Heinz-Wolfgang Schnaufer – claimed five Halifaxes destroyed in 14 minutes. Seven Lancasters and 18 Halifaxes failed to return from the operation on Aachen. One was *T-Tommy* on 51 Squadron, which was one of three Halifax IIIs that failed to return to Snaith that night. Flying Officer C McQuiston USAAF, the American pilot who was from Kansas, was killed. His two air gunners also died, while two crewmembers were taken prisoner and two others managed to evade capture with the help of the Dutch Underground.

In all, *Nachtjäger* claimed 32 kills on the night of 24/25 May. Adolf Galland commented:

There was no shortage of night fighter aircraft. From the middle of 1944 onwards we could even speak of a surplus. The decrease of the German night fighter successes in this period was mainly due to interference, shortage of fuel and the activities of 100 Group. The task of this specialist unit was to mislead our fighters and to befog our conception of the air situation by clever deceptive manoeuvres. This specialist unit finally solved its task so well that it was hardly ever absent from any of the British night operations and it can claim to have set really difficult problems for the German night fighter command. The British increased their raids at the end of 1944 from month to month, with decreasing losses.

After a night of minor operations on 26/27 May, Main Force crews of Bomber Command steeled themselves for raids on Aachen, Nantes, Rennes and coastal batteries on the French coast and Bourg-Leopold, where the raid had ended in disaster a few nights earlier. It is little wonder that some were apprehensive. Sergeant George Burton, flight engineer in Pilot Officer William Kalle's crew in Halifax *G-George* on 420 'Snowy Owl' Squadron RCAF at Tholthorpe, Yorkshire recalls:

27th May 1944 was a day in my life I would never forget. After waking at 07.30 hours and shaving (in cold water) etc we made our way half a mile to the Sergeant's Mess for breakfast Then walked another half a mile to the group section on the main 'drome. At approximately 11am we heard that ops were on that night. We then spent the rest of the day preparing our aircraft. In the late afternoon we attended briefing and heard that our target was the military camp of Bourg-Leopold in Belgium. We were hoping to catch a *Panzer* division there. We then marshalled our aircraft around the perimeter track, one side for 420 'Snowy Owl' Squadron RCAF the other for 425 'Alouette' Squadron RCAF. Then back to the Sergeant's mess for our supper of bacon and eggs.

This time the Force would consist of 150 Halifaxes of 4 Group and 32 Lancasters and 117 Halifaxes of 6 Group, while 1 Group would provide ten *ABC*-equipped Lancasters of 101 Squadron, and 8 Group, 14 Lancasters and eight Mosquitoes. At Skipton-on-Swale, Yorkshire where 424 'Tiger' Squadron RCAF was stationed, Flight Lieutenant B L Eric Mallett RCAF, pilot of Halifax III QB-B *Blonde Bomber* prepared for the difficult trip. 'After leaving the briefing room I mentioned to the crew [all of whom were Canadian except for the flight engineer] that we were being sent on a mission for the sole purpose of killing people. We carried 14,000lbs of anti-personnel bombs and the aiming point was to be the officers' quarters. This mission did not sit well with the crew. We had already been through some tough missions against industrial targets but this mission made us uneasy.'

His bomb aimer, Warrant Officer 2 Ken Sweatman thought that the raid would be 'a piece of cake': 'Located in the NE corner of Belgium it was little more than two-hour flight from Skipton-on-Swale. I remember the Wing Commander's caution however. "The target is a rectangle image of lines dividing it diagonally. Our prisoners are on the close side and to your left. Don't undershoot." '

Sergeant George Burton meanwhile was *en route* to Bourg-Leopold, having taken off at 00.11 hours, climbing on course, 5,000 feet over England then down to 1,000 feet over the North Sea. They hoped that this would be below the German radar. Over the enemy coast they climbed up to 9,000 feet, on track to the target and made their turning into their bomb aiming run. Burton recalls:

At 9,000 feet flying straight and level, bomb doors open and bombs primed live, Bill Haliburton, the bomb aimer, was giving our Skipper instructions: 'Left, left, steady.' Our position was over the village of Oostham five miles due west of the target. Sergeant Metcalfe our rear gunner yelled, 'Corkscrew port: go!' A FW 190 was on our tail but Metcalfe had the satisfaction of hitting the enemy fighter, see it slowly turn over, burst into flames and crash. The next thing the fuselage was on fire and full of cordite. I got the fire extinguisher from my position and went back to fight the fire and was pleased that this soon went out. Then back beside the pilot, only the starboard inner engine and wing were on fire! I pressed the circuit breaker 'inner engine' and 'Graviner fire system button' to extinguish the fire but after a few minutes it was still burning. Consulting the Skipper we decided that the only alternative was to try to blow it out and we dived to 350 feet. Kalle gave the order to prepare to abandon the aircraft. I got his parachute and made sure that it was clipped on properly. Then I got my own. The three crewmembers in the front of the aircraft stood by the escape hatch waiting for the words 'Jump; Jump!' I looked out onto the wing: the fire had blown itself out! I shouted, 'Pull her out Skipper – the fire's out!' After a few moments he ordered us back to our positions. The wireless was unserviceable so Sergeant Cusack the WOp/AG was unable to send a Mayday call and he went aft to man the mid-upper turret. Then a roll call but there was no reply from the mid-upper, Sergeant John Elsliger. Our Skipper ordered me to go and see what happened to him. I found Elsliger's helmet plugged into the intercom and blood on his helmet and then noticed that the rear escape hatch was open so he must have bailed out.[55]

Then once again it was 'Corkscrew starboard go!' and we evaded another fighter. Our three engines were OK but now it was time for another tank change. Back to the rest position and I looked so see what damage had been done. As luck would have it, the only tank controls not damaged on the starboard side were the ones I wanted to change. Once more another corkscrew to evade trouble. When I went back to check for bomb hang-up I found damage in the bomb bay and the floor of the Halifax and we still had seven 500lb bombs on board! They were all mixed up and one bomb had its fins off. I tried to jettison the bombs but the bomb-doors would not operate.

At last we had the pleasure of seeing the Norfolk coast line. It was a wonderful feeling. After flying inland for a few miles the Skipper said he wanted us to bail out and he would fly the plane back towards the coast and bail out at the last minute so that the Halifax would crash into the sea. But we said we had come so far together we would stick it out. Sergeant Magson the navigator gave a course to Tholthorpe but I saw a light on port side and said, 'It looks like a drome' [North Pickenham, an American B-24 base]. I fired a red distress flare and then the colours of the day and after a few minutes the airfield put the landing lights on. I lowered the undercarriage and with great relief the green light came on saying it was locked down. On the final approach I lowered the flaps then the Skipper ordered me to go at rest position with the others on the crew. Kalle made a wonderful landing, if rather bumpy as the starboard tyre was soft. We got a great reception from the personnel of the 491st Bomb Group. The following morning we were taken out to see the extent of the damage to our Halifax. The undercarriage fairings from the starboard engine had come off and hit the rudder and elevator. There was a hole behind the starboard engine that you could have put a jeep in. The aircraft was like a pepper pot with hundreds of shrapnel holes. The main floor under the mid-upper was like tissue paper and you had to be careful where you walked or you would have fallen through the bomb bay. A piece of shrapnel had made a hole in the astrodome where I had been standing during the attack. A senior American officer came to have a look and commented that 'aerodynamically it was impossible for this kite to fly!' Later that day we were flown to Tholthorpe in a Lancaster.[56]

Sergeant Ernest Turtle, flight engineer on Halifax LW873 on 76 Squadron flown by Pilot Officer N F Conway RAAF recalls:

We were airborne from our base at Holme-on-Spalding Moor at 00.13 hours with a 9,000lb bomb load. Our Flight to the target was uneventful and we attacked the primary flares at 02.16 hours from 10,000 feet and bombed on the Master Bomber's instruction. The target was hazy but the Path Finder Markers very clear. We saw many bomb bursts on and around the target indicators. We well remember the journey home due, principally, to the three fighter attacks from the target area to England. We were 'Corkscrewing' all the way with the occasional Fighter Flare being dropped overhead. We can still see one of these fighters going down in flames as a direct result of accurate defensive gunfire from our rear and mid-upper gun turrets. We were continually attacked until well over the English coast. We landed back at base at 04.08 hours, well after most other aircraft. This was our sixth operational trip and one that we were thankful to survive.[57]

E-Easy, better known as Expensive Babe, a 51 Squadron Halifax III, was attacked by a Bf 109 when leaving the target. Flight Sergeant K H McKnight RAAF, the pilot, recalled: 'The bomb load carried by our aircraft when we left Snaith consisted of 16 × 500lb HEs, which were released at 02.14 hours from a height of 11,000 feet. The target indicators were very scattered in a circle and smoke had obscured the red target indicators when we bombed.'[58]

All 24 aircraft on the squadron attacked Leopoldsburg successfully and all crews returned safe to base, although Flight Sergeant Skinner and his crew had a narrow escape:

We had the same bomb load as the rest of the squadron but had to release it 1½ minutes short of the target at 02.07 hours from a height of 13,000 feet. The reason the bomb load was released short was because our aircraft was damaged by an enemy fighter at 02.06 hours. A big hole was made in the starboard fin, damage sustained to starboard wing elevator and hydraulics, the aircraft became difficult to handle, particularly with a full bomb load and so bomb load was jettisoned on the run in. We made a safe landing at Snaith at 04.45 hours.

Eighteen crews on 427 'Lion' Squadron RCAF were detailed to carry out the raid to Leopoldsburg. Two aircraft and crews on this operation were lost. One of the crews who made it back was that of Warrant Officer A E 'Rex' Clibbery DFM RCAF and the crew of *V- Victor* a Halifax that left Leeming in North Yorkshire at 23.25 hours with a bomb load of sixteen 500-pounders. Sergeant Len Pratt the flight engineer recalls:

LW161, call sign 'Hold Tight', was a new aircraft replacing LV986 (also ZL-V) which we had written off on 10 May at Woodbridge and this after a raid to Ghent, Belgium. Leopoldsburg was to be the first trip of many operational trips that LW161 was to complete and but for Sergeant Bill 'Shorty' Martin the rear gunner, Clibbery and crew went on to complete their operational tours using this aircraft. Martin was screened 12 trips after the rest of the crew on 420 'Snowy Owl' Squadron RCAF at Tholthorpe. We were a crew of eight. The other members of the crew were navigator Flight Officer Morrison USAAF, bomb aimer Flying Officer Atkins, wireless operator Warrant Officer Jim Jardine and mid-upper gunner, Sergeant Dick Qualle DFM. Flight Lieutenant Clarke flew with us on this trip. We did not expect it to be a particularly eventful trip but on approaching the target area we saw tracer exchange and what looked to be light 'flak'. There was obviously some fighter activity and we were attacked at 02.08 hours from 10,000 feet. We bombed on a Yellow target indicator and bombs were seen bursting on and around the yellow target indicator. There was also a great deal of smoke and small fires were seen in the target area. As we made our bombing run I saw a single-engine fighter aircraft approach on a directly head-on course but above. It did not attack and passed overhead. The target picture, which I saw later, indicated a good strike on the aiming point, a large rectangular building block was in the picture. After bombing and clearing the target and because of the fighter activity in the area, Rex Clibbery asked the navigator for a dog leg course at low altitude. We descended rapidly near to the ground and eventually crossed the English coast. Because of fog and bad visibility at Leeming, we were diverted to Charter Hall, Scotland.

Flight Sergeant Lounsbury the tail gunner on Flying Officer Friedman's Halifax crew on 432 'Leaside' Squadron RCAF recalls:

> We took off at East Moor at 23.51 hours. Our target was the 'barracks' in the camp. We were told that this was a very large rest camp. The night was very clear of cloud over the target area and the markers from the Path Finders made a vivid and clear picture in my memory. We attacked from 12,000 feet at 02.06 hours. The markers were in the bomb sight at moment of release. The Master of Ceremonies was very helpful. We were bombing from a lower than normal altitude. From the rear turret the view was magnificent. I saw a stick of bombs go through the centre of a cluster of buildings. This scene remained with me for many years and the older I got the more it bothered my mind. What was once a joyous feeling became one of sadness because of the destruction. I was pleased to hear that the people of the area accepted the episode as a necessary evil and do not regard us as cruel and ruthless. Base was reached without incident. We landed at 04.17 hours.[59]

Nine Halifaxes and one Lancaster were lost on the Bourg-Leopold raid. In all probability they were all shot down by prowling *Nachtjäger* over Belgium.[60] One Halifax that was lost was *N-Natch* on 432 'Leaside' Squadron RCAF flown by *Natch's* regular Skipper, Pilot Officer Howard J Menzies of Vancouver. The flight across the Channel to the Belgian coast had been uneventful, then the Sky markers led them to Bourg-Leopold. In the nose, Flying Officer Don Rutherford, an Ontarian, huddled over the bombsight like a priest before his altar, lining the plane up with the sparkling target indicators dropped by the Path Finders. Busy with his charts, Pilot Officer Jack Gouinlock the navigator, who was on his tenth operation, heard Rutherford sing out, 'Bombs gone'. Now it was his job to plot their course home. He gave the pilot a heading and the aircraft swung around. They were just south of Eindhoven when they 'bought it'. Tail gunner Flight Sergeant Tom McClay, an Irishman, sounded the first and only warning, 'Fighter coming in – 6 o'clock low.' The sound of his guns was all but lost in the roar of the engines as the pilot gave *'Natch'* additional boost for some violent evasive action. Then the Halifax shuddered under the impact of cannon shells and both port engines burst into flame.

'She's going down,' Menzies shouted over the intercom. 'Bail out.'

Menzies was killed in the crash. McClay and the mid-upper gunner, Warrant Officer Herb Rogers of Vancouver, who was making his 24th trip, and Flight Sergeant John Clark the English flight engineer, have no known grave. WOp/AG W S 'Jock' Rowan from Edinburgh and Sergeant R S Hall, riding in the co-pilot's seat and an American serving in the RCAF, from a small Illinois town with the improbable name of Normal, both survived. They were both taken into captivity. Jack Gouinlock and Don Rutherford evaded and after being moved to Liège in July they awaited the liberation by the American army. On 6 September German soldiers rounded up forty hostages as a reprisal for the killing of two soldiers that same morning. Among them was Jack Gouinlock. That night the hostages were locked in a barn and the next morning they were given spades and ordered to dig their own graves. An officer gave the order to fire and two of the hostages who had already been beaten up were shot. The officer then turned to the remaining 38 hostages and incredibly he told them they were all free to go. Gouinlock and Rutherford were liberated when the American army arrived later in the day.[61]

Flight Lieutenant Eric Mallett RCAF on 424 'Tiger' Squadron RCAF arrived at the target after weaving *Blonde Bomber* around flak stations and avoiding getting coned by searchlights. A lone Mosquito bomber had already dropped a yellow flare on the target and it was backed up by a Path Finder Force dropping flares. In all, five *Oboe* Mosquitoes dropped TIs and the third and most accurate salvo fell 320 yards of the aiming point. The early visual markers were wide to the south but a salvo of 'whites' went down 250 yards southwest. Wing Commander 'Pat' Daniels, the Master Bomber, saw early bombs fall among the camp buildings and the aiming point soon became obscured by smoke. Daniels reported:

Our load for the trip to Leopoldsburg was 4 × 7 hooded flares, 6 TIs yellow. 5 TI yellow, one 4,000lb 'cookie'. The weather over the target was no cloud and the vertical visibility good. The target was identified visually, aided by a red TI and flares. On approach to the target at 01.59 hours two Red TIs seen on aiming point. I broadcast from 02.01 hours to 02.13 hours. Our own yellow target indicator was dropped on the NW end of the red TI. I instructed the Main Force to bomb on the yellow target indicators. White TIs were well backing up yellows. I instructed the Main Force during the last three minutes to bomb on whites to port and this with one-second overshoot. The Main Force bombing was good. One large explosion from the centre of target, rising well above ground with minor explosions in the air was seen at 02.07 hours.

The target began to look like a 'bulls-eye' to the crew of *Blonde Bomber* by the time the first wave of bombers began their bomb run. Ken Sweatman the bomb aimer was about to put the fusing switches down when he reported an enemy aircraft passing below from port ahead. Sergeant Vic 'Pop' Poppa the Canadian rear gunner saw him too:

The aircraft lurched upwards as if struck by a gigantic hammer. Flames ran down our left side. A few seconds later there was the clatter of machine gun bullets and cannon shells slamming through the plane. The Plexiglas nose was shot out and I could hear the patter as they came close. Our bombs did not explode. Inside the fuselage it was cherry red. There were fires from the front to the rear.' Mallett reported, 'Port inner engine on fire'. Then Mallett's voice, very faint, said, 'Abandon aircraft! Jump! Jump!' I gave the order 'abandon aircraft' immediately, as I knew from past experience that we only had seconds before the flames reached the tanks and the 100-octane gasoline would blow. (Strange as it may seem we were not able to drop our load. Just a few seconds prior to being hit I had an urge to take evasive action but I didn't want to spoil the bomb aimer's sighting, as there was no indication of the attack.) The whole crew was supposed to go out of the top forward escape hatch in the navigator's position so that I would know when all were out. However, Flight Lieutenant Bob Irwin, our navigator couldn't open the hatch [which had melted together where an incendiary bullet had passed through the door-jamb]. The second pilot [Flying Officer W J Elliott, who was along for his first trip to gain experience as a pilot] and flight engineer Sergeant M Muir [the only Englishman on the crew] took off and went out of the rear entrance hatch. I went forward to see how our navigator was doing and by good fortune he was beginning to have some luck so I went back to my seat and straightened out the aircraft.

Vic Poppa called on the intercom but there was only static:

I pulled my flying helmet off, opened my turret doors and snapped my parachute onto my chest but I stayed in my position until I saw another parachute open. Then I swung my turret 50° to the fuselage but I could not get out because of the fire and wind. Twice I tried but to no avail. By this time the ground appeared quite close. Reaching the aft fuselage exit would have entailed too much time and by then it would be too late anyway so I sat there awaiting my end. The aircraft went into a flat spin, my turret rotated free and the brute force flung me out. My left leg came free. I was falling flat on my back. I looked on my chest for my parachute. It was not there! The parachute had been pulled away from my chest by the wind force and was now three feet from my face and above. I pulled on the harness and brought the parachute down close enough so I could grab the 'D' ring and pulled. It opened with a sharp snap. A pain knifed through my groin.

Ken Sweatman and Bob Irwin between them managed to force the escape hatch open and Warrant Officer Wilf Wakely the WOp/AG went first followed by Irwin and Eric Mallett. Sweatman could remember little of the bail out. He assumed that he had gone out feet first facing forward but when his chute cracked open the casing must have hit him under the jaw and he landed unconscious, taking quite a beating. His ankle hurt as someone ripped the leggings off his escape boots and Mallett and someone with him said, 'Oh, good, it's Ken.' Sweatman had no idea who Ken was and what was more, he 'didn't give a damn.'

Vic Poppa hit and collapsed to the ground with his parachute falling on top of him. He was sure the chute had opened at less than 100 feet and the aircraft had been at 11,900 feet when they were first hit by flak and then shot up by the Junkers 88. Poppa was soon apprehended and three days' later he was placed in the back of a truck with four caskets. A German NCO pointed to one and said, *Kamerad Irwin*. Poppa again gave a negative response. The NCO then pointed to another casket and said, *Kamerad Wakely*. Again Poppa gave a negative response. Poppa was not questioned about the third casket, which must have contained the body of his close friend, Sergeant George Freeman, the mid-upper gunner. The fourth was empty, as Poppa had moved it with his foot. The Belgian underground found Mallett and Sweatman and hid them in a forest for ten days. After this began a series of moves that eventually led to them being liberated by American troops not long after D-Day, 6 June 1944.[62]

Flight Sergeant Louis Wooldridge DFC, who had flown a first tour on 51 Squadron, was now a second tour man in Sergeant Jim Allen's crew on 578 Squadron[63] and they also flew the 27/28 May Bourg-Leopold raid:

We arrived at the target with no difficulties. We attacked with 18 500lb GP bombs at 02.13½ hours from 10,000 feet. Smoke obliterated ground detail but bombs were seen to burst among the markers. There was moderate to heavy flak over the target. After attacking the target area without incident, course was set for the return to base. Due to bad weather conditions in Yorkshire at that time, wireless signals sent to the squadron aircraft on the return leg instructed everyone to divert to the RAF Silverstone, Northamptonshire where we landed at 04.34 hours the next morning. The next day all the squadron aircraft left Silverstone to return to base.

In Belgium after the raid Marcel Heselmans (a resistance fighter code-named *Sixtus* whose brother Leon was also in the resistance) cycled to see the damage to Bourg-Leopold so that he could transmit information to England.[64] According to *Sixtus* 7,000 German soldiers were killed or missing and 218 German women, who arrived on 26 May to receive nursing training, were killed also. He added that the spirit of the German soldiers at Leopoldsburg was totally destroyed. Many were still absent and hiding in the surrounding woods and had deserted. Civilian casualties were 22 killed. All the buildings 'including the big messes' had been destroyed. The 'Cavalry Camp', which held many Belgian political prisoners, survived the attack. The guards had closed the doors and ran away leaving the prisoners locked up unattended. Marcel, together with other members of his team, was taken prisoner a few weeks later and was shot on 15 July 1944 as he tried to escape when he was transported from the interrogation office to the prison of Hasselt.

Another facet of the operations in support of the forthcoming invasion was the bombing of batteries on the French Channel coast. As part of the cover plan, for every bomb dropped west of Le Havre, two were dropped on batteries to the north. On 31 May/1 June, 219 aircraft[65] attacked the railway marshalling yards at Trappes in two waves and other forces targeted a coastal wireless transmitting station at Au Fèvre, a radio jamming station at Mont Couple and the railway yards at Tergnier, while two 5 Group formations of Lancasters attacked the railway junction at Saumur and attempted to bomb a coastal gun battery at Maisy. No aircraft were lost on the raids at Au Fèvre and Mont Couple, which was 'rendered completely unserviceable' and none were lost at Saumur but at Tergnier two Lancasters were shot down. 'This raid was illuminated with flares and red/yellow TIs,' recalls Flight Sergeant Brian Soper on 626 Squadron 'and was again directed by an MC and was very accurately carried out.'

At Maisy the Lancaster crews found their target covered by cloud and only six of the 68 aircraft bombed. Two Lancasters on 44 Squadron at Dunholme Lodge that turned back due to the cloud obscuring the aiming point crash landed at Westcott and at Oakley airfields in Buckingham-shire. None of the crew members on Q-Queenie was injured but at Westcott V-Victor, its bomb load intact, ran off the runway and across the main A41 road and was wrecked. At 03.30 hours, with the crew unhurt and well clear of the aircraft, the bombs exploded, killing a Flying Control Officer at the scene of the crash.

For Flight Sergeant Louis Patrick Wooldridge DFC the mid-upper gunner on Halifax III D-Dog on 578 Squadron, Trappes was to be his crew's last operation before a seven-day period of leave:

The purpose of the operation, carried out in brilliant moonlight, was to disrupt German troop movements and war materials from eastern France, central Germany and the occupied countries. As we approached the target area, flying high above the almost 10/10ths low lying cumulus cloud I observed a Ju 88 night fighter about 7,000 feet below, streaking away at an angle of about 45° in the direction of our starboard quarter. It was soon several miles away and posed no danger to us but the target area was apparently full of night fighters. The Master Bomber called for assistance but the anguished reply from the Deputy Master Bomber was, 'I bloody can't. I've been hit', whether by one of the numerous bursts of heavy flak in the target area at that time or enemy fighter activity. On the whole enemy fighter activity was considered intense in the target area. Presumed to be a relatively easy target, Trappes apparently lived up to its name and had become an operational aircraft trap.

It may have seemed from the intensity of the battle that several aircraft had gone down but just four Lancasters, all of which were shot down by NJG4 and NJG5, failed to return. One of these was *H-Harry* on 622 Squadron at Mildenhall that was flown by 1st Lieutenant J E Braithwaite USAAF. Four of the seven crew bailed out safely, the American pilot and one of his crew being taken prisoner and the two others evading. The three other crew members went down in the Lancaster, which crashed in wooded countryside near Poigny-la-Fôret. *D-Dog* and Flight Lieutenant Frank Randall's crew on the same squadron were shot down during a sustained attack by a Ju 88 night fighter and exploded. Flight Lieutenant L F Berry, who was thrown out of his rear turret, was the only man to survive. *C-Charlie*, a XV Squadron Lancaster that failed to return to Mildenhall, was also shot down by a night fighter, all the crew going down with the aircraft, which crashed at Lormaison. The presence of 14 Bomber Support RCM aircraft and 16 *Serrate* and nine *Intruder* Mosquitoes may have helped keep the loss rate down.[66]

Their tour completed, Arthur Rew's crew received fourteen days' leave. Most of them, Soper included, were awarded the DFM:

Arthur Rew had been commissioned by this time and qualified for the DFC. 'Wild Bill' Redding (who wasn't at all wild) was the only one to be chosen to receive his medal at Buckingham Palace. The rest of us got them in the post. At the start of our 14 days' leave I was going around the station on Bill's motor bike on the pillion. We had got out clearance chits all signed up and were about to leave when a Lanc crash landed on the runway followed by the crash trucks. We didn't know if it was returning from a raid or if it had a bomb load on but we decided to make our departure, having done our thirty. I never found out the outcome of that interlude.

Now Brian Soper could at last telephone his fiancée Mary in Battersea to arrange marriage as they agreed they would once the young flight engineer had got through his tour of 'ops': 'The crew split up after leaving Wickenby although most of them came to my wedding with Mary on 10 June. We had quite a problem sorting out arrangements, since all travelling was restricted because of D Day.'

Notes

1. See *Legend of the Lancasters* by Martin W Bowman (P&S 2009).
2. Eight men on *Might of the Eighth* a B-24J in the 389th Bomb Group at Hethel were killed and only two men survived from B-24H 41-29485 in the 392nd Bomb Group from Wendling. The seven men in the forward fuselage of the

389th Liberator were killed instantly when five 500lb bombs and the full fuel load exploded. The forward section disintegrated and wreckage flew through the air. In all, three bombs, which failed to explode, fell near the bomb dump at RAF Foulsham. Captain John Driscoll, the 389th Bomb Group Gunnery Officer and two others were trapped in the still intact tail section of *Might of the Eighth,* which spiralled down like a falling leaf. The three men grabbed their chest packs and tried to escape through the hatches but the tail gunner failed to open his hatch and he was killed in the crash. Driscoll opened his hatch with some difficulty and bailed out at 1,000 feet, pulling his parachute shroud as he drifted to avoid hitting the now burning tail section. Although there was no fuel in the tail section, a combination of hydraulic fluid and oxygen from the bottles quickly started a fire. Driscoll landed in the back garden of Bailey's Farm near Foulsham. *Fields of Little America* by Martin W Bowman (Wensum Books 1977, 1983, PSL 1988, GMS).

3. Middlebrook and Everitt.
4. Operating from Juvincourt Hauptmann Gerhard Friedrich, Staffelkapitän, 1./NJG6, a former transport pilot who had joined the *Nachtjagd* in 1942, claimed two Halifaxes in the Montdidier area. (One was possibly Halifax LV880 on 51 Squadron, which went down near Montdidier after a most unusual head-on attack by a night fighter).
5. *Point Blank and Beyond* by Lionel Lacey-Johnson (Airlife Classic 1991).
6. See *No Need To Die: American Flyers in RAF Bomber Command* by Gordon Thorburn (Haynes Publishing 2009).
7. *Pathfinders At War* by Chaz Bowyer (Ian Allan 1977). He joined 15 Squadron as a sergeant pilot on Stirlings. After a tour of 42 ops he was rested and became an instructor. Less than four months later he returned to operations with 7 Squadron and flew a second tour. On 14 February 1943 Barron completed his second tour and he returned to instructing, this time for over a year. He again volunteered to return to operational flying and on 28 April 1944 he was given command of 7 Squadron, now flying Lancasters.
8. *Point Blank and Beyond* by Lionel Lacey-Johnson (Airlife Classic 1991).
9. Two Stirlings and a Halifax failed to return from the minelaying operation taking overall losses to 14 for the night, which had seen a new record for Bomber Command with 1,125 sorties being dispatched.
10. *Intruders over Britain: The Luftwaffe Night Fighter Offensive 1940 to 1945* by Simon W Parry (ARP 2003). During March to July 1944 KG51 destroyed 40 Allied aircraft for the loss of 12 crews.
11. 175 aircraft of 6 and 8 Groups to Lens, with 14 Stirlings attacking a rail depot at Chambly. Also, 196 aircraft of 4 and 8 Group attacked rail yards at Ottignies in Belgium, without loss. Five Fortresses of 214 Squadron, including one captained by the CO, W/C Desmond J. McGlinn DFC flew their first jamming operation this night. The Squadron's role was to jam the night fighter controllers on the ground and the German night fighters in the air. Among other countermeasures, they also jammed the FuG 216 *Neptun* tail warning system. Two Mosquito NF.IIs that provided Bomber Support for the Cologne raid and the attacks on rail targets FTR.
12. During 1940–1941 Lofty Wiltshire served as Engine Fitter IIE on 82 Squadron on Blenheims at Watton before he was posted overseas. In 1943 he remustered to flying duties and during training in Canada he survived a bad crash and

remained in the wreck of the aircraft in sub-zero temperatures for two days before being rescued. He then spent 2 months in hospital recovering from frostbite and snow blindness. He recovered and became a Flight Engineer on Lancasters, being posted to 90 Squadron at Tuddenham.

13. This institution with twin turrets, high on a hill overlooking the town had been the Rockside Hydro, a 160-bed spa hotel before the war.

14. W/C Alan George S Cousens DSO DFC MC (Czech).

15. With the help of the French Resistance Courtenay made it across the Pyrenees and he and the rest of a group of evaders were well inside Spanish territory when they were apprehended by two German soldiers and escorted back to France. Courtenay was incarcerated in St. Michel prison in Toulouse and there he remained until 19 August when they were liberated by French irregular forces. See *RAF Evaders: The Comprehensive Story of Thousands of Escapers and their Escape Lines, Western Europe, 1940–1945* by Oliver Clutton-Brock (Grub Street 2009).

16. Dedee's father Frederick took over for six months before he was arrested and executed. Dedee survived Ravensbrück and became a nurse in Ethiopia after the war. John Neal later wrote about his experiences in *The Lucky Pigeon*.

17. The navigator and bomb aimer both made it across the Pyrenees into Spain and finally England. The others were hidden in France by the Resistance until the liberation. After evading capture until 5 June 1944 when he was captured by the Germans, Harry Fisher finally escaped on 19 August 1944. 218 Gold Coast Squadron Association Newsletters No. 17 & No. 58, edited by Margery Griffiths.

18. See *Bomber Squadron: Men Who Flew with XV* by Martyn R Ford-Jones (William Kimber 1987) and *Legend of the Lancasters* by Martin W Bowman (Pen & Sword 2009). F/L Oliver Brooks flew his last operation on 21 June. At Mildenhall on 5 July he received the DFC from HM King George VI. F/Sgt Ken Pincott was awarded the DFM. F/L John Fabian, the Squadron navigation leader, who on 23/24 April flew as the H_2S operator, received a bar to his DFC. For a man who initially had no great ambition to fly, Brooks' record was impressive. After a period of instructing at 1651 CU at Wratting Common he finished the war on 156 PFF Squadron at Upwood. He remained in the RAF post-war and flew at least 17 different types of aircraft, including helicopters before transferring to the Fighter Control Branch. He finally retired in 1972.

19. In August Bill Power was posted to 24 Squadron at Hendon for VIP duties, flying in Avro Anson, Flamingo, Dominie and Dakotas as a Wireless Operator. In October 1945, 24 Squadron ferried VIPs to and from the Nürnburg Trials. One of Bill's more famous trips was Operation *Argonaut* in January 1945 when he escorted 'The Big Three' (Churchill, Roosevelt and Stalin) on Dakota FL584 for their conference at Satchi in Russia.

20. 100 Group flew 11 RCM, 21 *Serrate* and eight Intruder Bomber Support sorties in support of the operation on Munich.

21. The *Bomber Command War Diaries: An Operational reference book 1939–1945.* Martin Middlebrook and Chris Everitt (Midland Publishing 1985). One 617 Lancaster, DV394 KC-M flown by F/L J L Cooper DFC (FTR). Six of the crew became PoWs; the bomb aimer F/O George Harden died in the crash near Tigerfeld.

22. Roy Bradley was the only survivor and he was later taken into captivity. His own crew was subsequently posted to 619 Squadron at Dunholme Lodge where they received a new pilot, F/O Lawrence Ambrose Hall. On 9/10 August 1944 on Lancaster I ME866, this crew went on operations and were involved in a collision with Lancaster LM435 flown by F/O Derek Wilfred Best on 50 Squadron over Châtellerault near Poitiers. Only F/O H J Cleland in Hall's crew survived and he evaded. No-one on the 50 Squadron Lancaster survived.

23. Sgt Norman Cyril Jackson, 106 Squadron, Lancaster ME669; awarded for action 26/27 April 1944, *London Gazette*, 26 October 1945. Toft, Higgins, F/Sgt E 'Sandy' Sandelands the wireless operator and Sgt W Smith the mid-upper gunner had all bailed out safely. The award of the DFC to Mifflin, recommended earlier, came through after he was reported missing.

24. 159 OTU aircraft on a diversionary sweep over the North Sea, 24 Mosquitoes on a diversion raid to Stuttgart, 11 RCM sorties, 19 *Serrate* and six Intruder patrols, 8 Halifaxes mine laying off Brest and Cherbourg. Some 223 bombers of 4, 6 and 8 Groups headed for the railway yards at Aulnoye and the objective for another 144 aircraft of 4, 6 and 8 Groups was the railway yards at Montzen in Belgium. At Aulnoye bombing was concentrated and much damage was caused to the railway yards. One Halifax FTR. At Montzen only part of the railway yards was hit. Fourteen Halifaxes and one Lancaster were shot down. *The Bomber Command War Diaries: An Operational reference book 1939–1945.* Martin Middlebrook and Chris Everitt (Midland Publishing 1985).

25. Bomber Command Association Newsletter October 1993. Gray was hospitalised for a month or so and did not rejoin his crew until the middle of June, finishing his 32 operation tour with 10 trips as a spare 'bod'. Cullen was awarded the DFC and Gray the DFM. Lancaster JA683 D2 was issued to 300 Squadron in May 1944 and was lost on 13 June.

26. *R for Robert* had been shot down by Wilhelm Johnen of 8./NJG6 who after experiencing engine problems landed his Bf 110G at Dübendorf airfield in Switzerland after claiming the 'Halifax' near Strasbourg as his 17th victory. The German authorities fearing that he had defected immediately ordered the arrest of his family but Johnen had simply made an emergency landing after being hit by return fire from a second bomber intercepted over the Swiss-German border. He was soon repatriated and a German agent was permitted to blow up his Bf 110 and destroy the radar equipment. The Swiss Government received a *Staffel* of Bf 109E fighters as reward! Johnen was awarded the *Ritterkreuz* in October 1944 and he took his score to 34 victories. He survived the war as *Gruppenkommandeur* of III./NJG6.

27. LQ-S *S-Sugar*, piloted by the deputy master bomber 24-year-old S/L Edward Wyman Blenkinsop DFC cdeG (Belgium) RCAF on 405 'Vancouver' Squadron RCAF at Gransden Lodge. Blenkinsop evaded capture but the other seven other members of his crew died when the aircraft exploded. He was taken in by a Belgian Resistance Group and remained with them until December 1944 when he was en route with White Army irregulars to try to blow up a *Gestapo*-occupied house, but they ran into 200 *Gestapo* men and they were captured. S/L Blenkinsop was kept a virtual prisoner by a Belgian who wanted to produce the Canadian airman to the British when they liberated his village but he was captured by Belgian fascists acting under German orders. He and 72 other men and three women were taken to *Gestapo* HQ at

Louvain and then to the central prison there. A few days later he arrived at the infamous St-Gilles prison in Brussels. An American in the next cell heard him tapping out a message in Morse saying that he had been condemned to death. However, Blenkinsop was taken to Neuengamme concentration camp 20 kilometres from Hamburg and put to work as a forced labourer working in the shipyards. Officially he died of 'heart failure' on 23 January 1945 but by this time he was at Bergen-Belsen and had developed TB and he died sometime between 28 January and 3 February 1945. He has no known grave. *See* Chorley and Middlebrook and See *RAF Evaders: The Comprehensive Story of Thousands of Escapers and their Escape Lines, Western Europe, 1940–1945* by Oliver Clutton-Brock (Grub Street 2009).

28. See *Bombers: The Aircrew Experience* by Philip Kaplan (Aurum Press 2000).

29. After the war ended, Stella Bowen sought repatriation to Australia. Sadly, in 1947 she found she had cancer; too frail to make the journey home, she died in London, having never returned to her homeland. She was only 54 years old.

30. Mailly actually accommodated a *Panzer* regiment HQ, 3 *Panzer* battalions belonging to regiments on the Eastern Front and elements of 2 more as well as the permanent training school staff.

31. Later Group Captain DFC* AFC AE.

32. F/Os Hubert William Joseph Edwards and Jack Skingley DFC and the rest of the crew were killed on the raid on Courtrai on 20/21 October 1944.

33. Sparks and five others in his crew evaded after bailing out of Lancaster III JB402 OL-R. The French Resistance found Sparks and told him that his rear gunner (W/O W G 'Tiger' Teague DFM who was one who evaded) had shot down one of the German fighters. The two others in the crew were taken prisoner. Whilst evading, Sparks heard that bodies were still being dug out of wreckage at the target area 14 days following the raid. Sparks was back with 83 Squadron at Coningsby seven weeks later. On the night of 29/30 August on the raid on Königsberg he was shot down again. This time he was captured and sent to a PoW camp.

34. *Not Just Another Milk Run: The Mailly-Le-Camp Raid* by Molly Burke and Geoff Gilbert (Barny Books 2004).

35. 114 barrack buildings, 47 transport sheds and workshops and some ammunition stores were hit; 218 Germans were killed or missing and 156 were wounded. 102 vehicles were destroyed, including 37 tanks. Damage to the buildings was German assessed as '80% destroyed, 20% worth repairing'.

36. *Not Just Another Milk Run: The Mailly-Le-Camp Raid* by Molly Burke and Geoff Gilbert (Barny Books 2004).

37. Lancaster III ND556 went down at Chaintreaux in Seine-et-Marne, 12 km SE of Nemours. Four of Lissette's crew evaded. 1 PoW. 1 KIA.

38. Hastings.

39. Ken Watkins, writing in *Not Just Another Milk Run: The Mailly-Le-Camp Raid* by Molly Burkett and Geoff Gilbert. (Barny Books 2004). P/O Whalley DFC and four of his crew were KIA. F/Sgts Vandervelde and Ward had bailed out, hidden in a wood and then taken in by the Mayor of Oeuilly; they were then taken to Spain by members of the French Resistance and returned to England. Ron Whalley and his crew were buried in the little village churchyard at Oeuilly.

40. *Not Just Another Milk Run: The Mailly-le-Camp Bomber Raid* by Molly Burkett & Geoff Gilbert (Barny Books 2004).
41. A Halifax of 192 Squadron at Foulsham in 100 Group on Bomber Support FTR. Six of the nine man crew were taken into captivity. Two crew members evaded. One KIA. One Mosquito *Intruder* was also shot down.
42. P/O Norman David Livingstone Lloyd KIA. His Lancaster (AR-F2) crashed at Avant-les-Mailly (Aube) at 21.47 hours. *RAF Bomber Command Losses of the Second World War. Vol 9. Roll of Honour 1939–47.* W R Chorley (Midland 2007).
43. Or 11.6%. Two more were so badly damaged that they had to be written off.
44. *RAF Bomber Command Losses of the Second World War. Vol 5. 1944*, by W R Chorley (Midland Publishing 1997). Robert Hunter made his way to les Grandes-Chapelles (Aube) and asked for help. Most people were too frightened and turned him away but one woman took him in. Despite his burns and his dizzy state a member of the FFI arrived and took him to their camp about two hours away. Moved to Troyes later that day, 4 May, Hunter received the first medical treatment for his burns. The French doctor who attended him said that he would have to go to 'the Hôpital de Dieu (l'hôtel-Dieu Saint-Nicolas) and have his hands amputated as gangrene had set in and the blood had practically stopped circulating. That evening a Frenchman and his wife took him to the hospital and the Germans were notified. Operated on, on 5 May, Hunter remained unconscious for the next two weeks but the good news was that doctors had managed to save his hands. The *Gestapo* tried to get him to talk but using his burnt and badly swollen lips as an excuse, he pretended he was unable to do so. When the time to evacuate the hospital came on 22 August, the Australian was ignored and left in isolation. Just in case, the French doctor injected him to raise his temperature and he was sent to another hospital as a 'fever case'. He was liberated on 27/28 August by the US 3rd Army. *RAF Evaders: The Comprehensive Story of Thousands of Escapers and their Escape Lines, Western Europe, 1940–1945* by Oliver Clutton-Brock (Grub Street 2009).
45. Ron Storey. Four Lancasters failed to return from the raid on Montdidier. Two of them were on 582 Squadron at Little Staughton. Everyone on *O-Orange* was killed and only one man survived on *F-Freddie* flown by W/O2 Charles James Erskine O'Nel RCAF. 23-year-old Sgt Frank Holmes, a six footer, who normally flew as the crew's rear gunner, was finding that the rear turret was giving him cramp so he had changed places with F/O J B Armstrong RCAF the mid-upper gunner, who was the only man who survived. Holmes' hobby was poaching. His parents ran the newspaper shop in Barnetby near Elsham and Frank poached chiefly on the estate of the neighbouring Earl of Yarborough whose gamekeeper had once confiscated his guns. The Earl had returned them and said that Frank was free to shoot on his land whenever he wished. Before joining 582 Squadron Holmes had flown on Sgt Geoff Maddern's crew on 103 Squadron at Elsham near the Wolds he loved so much. See *No Moon Tonight* by Don Charlwood (Penguin 1988).
46. Mosquitoes were out in force too, with 28 of them attacking Ludwigshafen and others, including five to Leverkusen, making 'nuisance' raids on German targets.
47. See *The Bomber Command War Diaries: An Operational reference book 1939–1945*. Martin Middlebrook and Chris Everitt. (Midland 1985).

48. Mostly the bombers missed their targets at Boulogne, Hasselt and Trouville and the heavies had to return to these targets before the week was out. The following night the bombers returned to Louvain, where the bombing was more accurate on this occasion and Hasselt where most of the bombs that were dropped fell in open fields and only a few hit the railway yards.

49. Result of wind speeds and wind directions worked out by selected aircraft in the Main Force and transmitted to England. It was analysed and the mean average broadcast to all bombers in the stream. It thus ensured that all would arrive on the same wind and keep concentration intact.

50. See *Point Blank and Beyond* by Lionel Lacey-Johnson (Airlife Classic 1991).

51. Adapted from an article by the late Stuart Howe. *S-Sugar*, which completed its 137th and final operational bombing sortie on 23 April 1945 to Flensburg, is now on permanent display at the RAF Museum, Hendon, London.

52. Mosquitoes also raided Cologne and Halifaxes and Stirlings dropped mines off the French coast.

53. John Fraser Barron did not live to receive the award of a Bar to his DSO which was promulgated after his death.

54. *The Bombing of Nürnburg* by James Campbell (Futura 1973). Ward was taken prisoner.

55. Elsliger, thinking that the aircraft was out of control had jumped for his life. He came down with his parachute on fire and with a wounded wrist. He hid his parachute and took care of his wound and made contact with the local resistance who took him to Overpelt where Mr Bergh, a policeman, and his family hid him for 18 days and he received medical treatment from Dr Poelmans. On 16 June Elsinger moved to the home of Van der Feeten and he and another RAF member were moved to Antwerp. He had to follow a man with ginger hair and was told that after a few days he would leave for Spain but the man handed him over to the Germans and he was put into jail at Antwerp. Elsliger was wearing civilian clothes and had a false ID card. He travelled back and forward to Brussels for interrogation and twice he was put in front of a firing squad. At last he was recognized as a PoW and was sent to *Stalag Luft VII* at Bankau. Elsliger survived a long march to Berlin at the end of the war and was liberated by the Russians.

56. Halifax LW432 *G-George* was scrapped. P/O Kalle was awarded the DFC, Sgt George Burton the DFM. On 30 July 1944, a new *G-George* took off to attack Amye-sur-Seulles. The target was successfully attacked but one bomb hung up. Back over England the pilot was forced to make a crash landing at the Air Transport Auxiliary airfield at White Waltham. Kalle overshot the short landing run and ran into a railway cutting. The 500lb bomb exploded. All the crew were badly burned and injured. John Elsinger's replacement, F/Sgt Charles Cusack later died of his injuries. Burton injured an arm and became one of Sir Archibald McIndoe's patients at East Grinstead.

57. The crew completed 40 operational trips in September 1944.

58. *Expensive Babe* was one of the few Halifaxes that flew more than 100 operations during WWII. It made its 100th operational sortie on the 6/7 December 1944 on an attack on Osnabrück.

59. After his tour on 432 'Leaside' Squadron RCAF, F/Sgt Lounsbury was posted to 405 'Vancouver' Squadron RCAF, the Canadian Path Finder squadron.

60. In all, 1,111 sorties in 17 separate operations were flown this night for the loss of 28 aircraft. 12 Lancasters were lost on the raid on the Rothe Erde railway yards at Aachen, 45 miles southeast of Bourg-Leopold; 1 Lancaster FTR from the attack on a railway junction at Nantes and 1 Lancaster and a Mosquito were lost on the raids on coastal batteries on the French coast.

61. See *RAF Evaders: The Comprehensive Story of Thousands of Escapers and their Escape Lines, Western Europe, 1940–1945* by Oliver Clutton-Brock (Grub Street 2009).

62. F/O W J Elliott RCAF and Sgt M Muir also evaded.

63. Halifax LW675 LK-B.

64. A photo reconnaissance revealed that 150 personnel huts and all the main barrack blocks had been destroyed or badly damaged. Shelter trenches had been partly obliterated by bomb craters. Considerable damage was also caused to the town of Leopoldsburg, including a school and 20 houses. Civilian casualties were listed as 22 killed and a few wounded.

65. 125 Lancasters, 86 Halifaxes and 8 Mosquitoes.

66. A Mosquito Intruder, 1 Stirling minelayer and 2 Halifaxes and a Hudson, which were on Resistance operations, FTR.

CHAPTER 4

Overlord

Overlord must now presumably be regarded as an inescapable commit-
ment ... It is clear that the best and indeed the only efficient support which
Bomber Command can give to Overlord is the intensification of attacks on
suitable industrial centres in Germany. If we attempt to substitute for this
process attacks on gun emplacements, beach defences, communications or
dumps in occupied territories, we shall commit the irremediable error of
diverting our best weapon from the military function for which it has been
equipped and trained to tasks which it cannot effectively carry out. Though
this might give a specious appearance of 'supporting' the Army, in reality it
would be the greatest disservice we could do to them. It would lead directly
to disaster.

Air Marshal Sir Arthur Harris to Sir Charles Portal,
13 January 1944

At Woodhall Spa in Lincolnshire on 5 June 1944 everyone on 617 Dam
Busters Squadron was confined to camp. One of the pilots was Flight
Lieutenant Hubert C 'Nick' Knilans. The American, who had flown a first
tour on 619 and who would finish the war with both the DSO and DFC,
had joined 617 Squadron at Woodhall on 14 January. On 1 June, when
Avro experts had installed new automatic pilots in sixteen Lancasters
for the *D-Day* operation, Knilans at last found out why his much-cursed
R-Roger flew like a lump of lead and had so often frightened his crew.
The elevators had been put on upside down at the factory and *Roger*
needed longer elevator cables than the other Lancasters on the station.
Knilans had been flying the aircraft for months like that and, as Wing
Commander Leonard Cheshire VC DSO** DFC said 'only you and God,
Nicky, know how you stayed up.'

'Not me, sirrrr,' Knilans drawled ... 'only God. I didn't know.'[1]

At dusk, with guards on the doors of the briefing room, Cheshire told
his assembled crews that the invasion was about to start. Most everyone
had known for several weeks that the invasion was imminent but only

146

the Chiefs of Staff knew when and where. Postponed by 24 hours because of bad weather the *D-Day* invasion finally began with thousands of ships and aircraft setting out for five beach landing areas on the Normandy coast. Cheshire outlined the operation that the Dam Busters would be required to fly. He explained that the object of Operation *Taxable* was to induce the German crews manning the radar installations on a part of the French coast, designedly left intact for the purpose, to believe that a large convoy was proceeding at seven knots on a 14-mile front across the narrowest part of the Channel between Dover and Cap d'Antifer and heading straight for them. The necessary reaction on the radar screen was to be reproduced by the 16 Lancasters and by 18 small ships, of which some towed balloons fitted with reflectors to simulate echoes given off by a large ship. The Lancasters, flying at 3,000 feet, in a series of elliptical courses, were to circle these ships again and again, at the same time releasing *Window* cut to a special length and pattern to produce a response similar to that created by an aircraft or a ship. Intense rehearsals, in which the crews of the Lancasters flew 50 hours, were exacting enough. 'The tactics' Cheshire explained later, 'were to use two formations of aircraft with the rear formation seven miles behind the leaders, each aircraft being separated laterally by two miles. Individual aircraft flew a straight course of seven miles, turned round and flew on the reciprocal one mile away. On completion of the second leg it returned to its former course and repeated the procedure over again, advancing far enough to keep in line with the convoy's speed of seven knots'.

The first wave of eight aircraft would take off at about 23.00 hours with 12 men in each aircraft: an extra pilot, extra navigator and three men to drop the bundles of *Window* out. At around 3am the second wave of eight aircraft would take over. The task set the navigators was one of extreme difficulty. A ship cannot suddenly alter its position on the sea but an aircraft, flying at three miles a minute or more has only to maintain its course for ten seconds too long for it to be seen much too far forward on the screen and thereby to ruin the deception. *Window* had to be discharged with the same accuracy and 24 bundles were to be thrown overboard on every circuit at 12 second intervals. It would take an error of only four seconds in timing to make the convoy suspiciously change position on the German radar.

Operation *Taxable* began soon after dusk and 'went steadily and mercilessly on through the night'. With curtains drawn and nothing but instruments to guide the navigators, the Lancasters moved round and round their orbits. At the same time, in order still further to heighten the illusion, the German radar was jammed but not too heavily. A similar operation (*Glimmer*) was carried out by eight Stirlings on 218 Squadron, off Boulogne, while Halifaxes and Stirlings on 138, 149 and 161 Squadrons dropped dummy parachutists, rifle fire simulators and other devices such as squibs and fireworks, which produced the sound of gunfire.

Taxable successfully created the impression that an airborne landing near the village of Yvetot in northwest France was taking place. Hour after hour the Lancasters flew in the blackness over the Channel, turning on stop-watches up and down on reversed courses while the *Window* was tossed out at four-second intervals. Right on cue at about 3am the second wave of eight aircraft took over. This was the trickiest part of all because they had to come in directly behind with split-second timing to carry on. They saw nothing of the invasion. Seven miles off the French coast they broke away just before dawn, before the light was good enough for the Germans to see from the shore that they had been tricked. Crews had their reward as they turned for home; the German coastal batteries opened up ... not the flak but the big guns, aiming 12-inch shells by radar prediction at the ghost armada. Enemy *E-boats* came out from Calais and Boulogne but they would have needed aerial torpedoes to do any damage.[2]

Nineteen-year-old Phil Stonehouse was an instructor in an Aircrew School (3 Group) where they revised navigators before they went on their second or third tours:

> The call came through at our roll call at 8am on 5th June when we were called for volunteers for a 'job' that night. Twenty men were asked for and two of my navigators were accepted. The next day [D-Day] we found out that our boys had been sent on a trip over the Calais area dropping *Window*. Neither of my boys came back and I, with an officer, had to go to their bunks and retrieve their personal belongings. It was the most distressing period in my whole life in the forces. To pick up their pictures of their wives or girlfriends was very heart-breaking. We then had to sit together, read all their letters received and destroy any that in our opinion would cause distress. I had to remove bodies, sometimes burnt, from crashed aircraft, strapped them on to stretchers and carried them to where an ambulance could receive them, but that was nothing compared to removing things belonging to absent aircrew.[3]

Overhead, massive aerial support was given before dawn to the Normandy landings.[4] Flight Lieutenant Charles Owen of 97 Squadron wrote: 'The Army had pulled its finger out at last and D-Day was on. We bombed at 05.00 hours just as it was getting light and had a grandstand view of the Americans running in on the beach.'[5] Allied intelligence had pinpointed 73 fixed coastal gun batteries that could menace the invasion. In Operation *Flashlamp* just over 940 aircraft dropped more than 5,000 tons of bombs on ten coastal batteries in the Bay of the Seine along the fringes of the Normandy landing beaches. It was the greatest tonnage in one night so far in the war. Only two of the batteries were free of cloud, at La Pernelle on the Pointe de Barfleur and at Ouistreham; all other bombing being carried out on *Oboe* marking. The attacks opened at 23.31 hours on 5 June when 92 Lancasters of 1 Group, with two *Oboe* Mosquitoes, began dropping bombs on the guns at Fontenay-Crisbecq, which covered *Utah* beach on the east side of the Cherbourg Peninsula. C-47s carrying the 82nd and 101st US Airborne Divisions were due over the area an hour later, so it was essential that 8 (PFF) Group aircraft marked on time using *Musical Parramatta*. In the ensuing ten minutes, 1 Group's Lancasters, bombing through solid cloud and rain, dropped 534 tons of high explosives, mainly 1,000-pounders. Ten minutes later, a further 94 Lancasters of 1 Group dropped 547 tons of bombs onto the casemates of the St-Martin-de-Varreville battery a few miles further south, between the beaches and the 101st US Airborne Division's dropping zone. The target had been well marked by five Mosquitoes. American paratroopers who captured the battery positions soon afterwards reported that, although the bombing had been accurate, the guns had seemingly been moved prior to the raid. Low cloud obscured the Merville battery, which lay very close to the area chosen for landing the British 6th Airborne Division. Out of a total force of 104 aircraft, 83 Halifaxes and 10 Lancasters of 6 Group attacked at 00.25 hours. Three of the five Mosquitoes dispatched were able to release their markers, which were rather scattered and appeared as indistinct glows beneath the cloud. Nearly all the 4,000lb bombs dropped missed the target.

There then followed a lull in Main Force operations until 03.14 hours on 6 June when the positions at Maisy was the first of the remaining seven batteries attacked, by 101 of the 110 Halifaxes of 4 Group. A 77 Squadron Halifax lost an engine on take-off at Full Sutton and crash-landed six minutes later, injuring everyone on board. Although silenced during the actual seaborne assault, most of the bombs fell east of the target, which had been bombed already on the night of 4/5 June and the gun crews recovered to fire and be fired on by the US Navy. This went on until 10 June. The six-gun battery at La Pernelle, which commanded the approaches to the American beaches, was the target for 1,000lb bombs of 108 aircraft of 5 Group, which dropped 600 tons between 03.31 and 04.44 hours. The attack opened with marking by four *Oboe* Mosquitoes of 8 Group followed by four Mosquitoes of 5 Group dropping ground markers. The battery was silenced during the initial assault but at 05.25 hours guns from two of the batteries fired on Allied minesweepers. The battery was only finally silenced when overrun by the Americans in the last week of June. When it was captured it was discovered that only one casemate had been damaged, probably by naval gunfire. At Houlgate 102 Halifaxes of 6 Group dropped mostly 500lb bombs on the battery but the gun crews were not silenced permanently and it remained a thorn in the side of the Allies until 19 June when the battery was temporarily put out of action, again by naval gunfire. The guns were still intact when it was captured in August. No aircraft were lost on the raid but a

426 'Thunderbird' Squadron Halifax at Linton-on-Ouse crashed and exploded near Bircham Newton killing all the crew.

During the next hour and a quarter the remaining four batteries were bombed. At Longues the battery survived intact after the raid by Lancasters and was still operational after another attack at dawn by American bombers and a bombardment by the naval forces off shore. The Lancaster piloted by Squadron Leader Arthur William Raybould DSO DFM on 582 Squadron was lost in the attack. A 578 Squadron Halifax, which crashed into the sea near the Cherbourg Peninsula and a 76 Squadron Halifax failed to return from the 4 Group raid by 101 aircraft on the battery at Mont Fleury, which was believed to contain several Russian 122mm guns. In fact there was only one such gun. Despite some damage it continued firing until the casement was captured later by ground forces. At Pointe-du-Hoc (St-Pierre-du-Mont), 3.7 miles west of Vierville, a six-gun battery (thought to be 155mm, with a range of 25,000 yards) was emplaced at the top of a cliff rising 100 feet high from a very rocky beach and could engage ships at sea and fire directly onto *Utah* and *Omaha* beaches. The gun positions, which were considered to be the most dangerous battery of all, were bombed throughout May, with a heavier than average attack by both day and night three days before D-Day and it now received the heaviest and most concentrated attack of the night with 637 tons being dropped on it by 108 Lancasters of 5 Group.

One Lancaster on 50 Squadron at Skellingthorpe was lost. The only crewmember who survived managed to evade capture. One of two Lancasters on 97 Squadron that were lost was flown by the CO, Wing Commander Edward James 'Jimmy' Carter DFC who was shot down by a Ju 88. Carter's crew, which included Squadron Leader Martin Bryan-Smith DFC* MID, the squadron gunnery leader, and Flight Lieutenant Albert Chambers DFC, the signals leader, was lost without trace. The other Lancaster was flown by Lieutenant Finn Yarde Jespersen DFC. The Norwegian pilot and his crew also perished.

At 06.30 three companies (225 men) of the US 2nd Ranger Battalion, using rocket propelled grapple hooks attached to climbing ropes and portable extension ladders, scaled the cliffs within ten minutes after landing and captured the position. To everyone's surprise the six guns had long since been relocated to a well-camouflaged but unguarded emplacement in an orchard 2½ miles further inland, pointed at *Utah* Beach and with ammunition piled up neatly. Ranger Alban Meccia recalled: 'There wasn't one bomb crater near them.'[6]

Ouistreham was the last target to be attacked, between 05.02 and 05.15 hours. All but one of 106 Lancasters of 3 Group dropped their 1,000lb bombs onto the 8 Group markers. Although they destroyed service buildings, the casemates remained intact and the guns appeared intact when captured late on D-Day. In all RAF Bomber Command flew 1,211 sorties: a new record.

On 6/7 June, 1,065 RAF four engine bombers and Mosquitoes dropped 3,488 tons of bombs on nine choke points including bridges and road and rail centres behind the Normandy battle area. Important road and railway bridges at Coutances were badly damaged by five squadrons of Halifaxes of 6 Group who bombed visually onto red and green TIs dropped by two Lancasters and three Mosquitoes of 8 Group. But much of the town was hit and set on fire and 312 civilians were killed. Two Lancasters were lost and a Halifax III on 426 'Thunderbird' Squadron, which was hit by a bomb while over the aiming point, was later abandoned over Slapton Sands off the south coast of Devon and crashed near Torquay. A 408 'Goose' Squadron Halifax landed damaged at Melbourne. Four Lancasters were lost on the 5 Group attack on Caen where the Main Force of bombers had to wait for the target to be properly marked and then fly over an area teeming with German units and guns at bombing heights below 3,000 feet. At Dunholme Lodge two Lancasters were missing: one on 44 Squadron with the entire crew and one on 619 Squadron, whose pilot Flight Lieutenant Kimberley Roberts DFC RAAF and four of the crew were killed. Two men who survived were taken into captivity. There were only four survivors on the two other missing Lancasters: *Q-Queenie* on 630 Squadron at East Kirkby and *B-Baker* on 83 Squadron at Coningsby. Among the dead was 1st Lieutenant C J Van Horn USAAF, the navigator on *B-Baker* flown by Flying Officer George Mervyn Kennedy RNZAF who also died.

The centre of Caen was left in flames, the river barrage over the Orne was destroyed, four other bridges were destroyed or had their approaches blocked and the main roads from the town to Falaise and Bayeux were badly cratered. At Vire two of the three Lancasters lost were shot down by enemy fighters, the other to flak. The attack, by 1 Group, was over in about five minutes, during which time the bombers hit all the choke points and partly destroyed the railway station. The centre of the town was in ruins with rubble blocking the roads. The last of the initial raids was on the rail centre at St-Lô by 103 Halifaxes of 4 Group without loss. Wing Commander 'Pat' Daniels, the Master Bomber on 35 Squadron, controlled the attack well. Having dropped his markers from 4,000 feet, just below the cloud, he was able to observe some good, concentrated bombing on the town and railway yards. The locomotive depot was partly destroyed.

Argentan, Conde and Lisieux were next. 5 Group's Lancasters attacked Argentan with more than 100 aircraft and everything appeared to go well. But at 02.28 hours, *A-Apple* and 23-year-old Flight Sergeant Cliff King's crew on 9 Squadron at Bardney contacted Waddington direction finding (DF), believed to be asking for a weather report. Due to the weak signal, Waddington reported back the message and at 02.42 hours sent a weather report. Neither message was acknowledged. Later it was learned that *A-Apple* had collided with trees and crashed near Belvoir Castle in the Leicestershire Wolds not far from Grantham. Only the rear gunner survived. King, whose commission had come through the day before and who had a wife in Boscombe, died at the controls of the Lancaster. The other five men on his crew, which included the navigator, 20-year-old Flight Sergeant James Morton Stevenson RCAF, were killed. Stevenson's parents had emigrated from Scotland to the USA and had gone to live in Parkchester in the Bronx district of New York. Their son had completed his first trip on 28 May when the squadron flew a feint towards the German battery at St-Martin-de-Varreville at Cherbourg. He too would not get to wear his Pilot Officer rings on his sleeves or enjoy the modest increase in pay, still way short by USAAF standards, but it went without saying that few if any of the American volunteer airmen in the RAF were in it for pounds, shillings and pence.

About 100 aircraft each of 3 and 6 Groups attacked Lisieux and Conde. The Canadian Group suffered no losses but at Lisieux a 115 Squadron Lancaster was lost. At Châteaudun in clear conditions 100 Halifaxes in 4 Group were directed by the Master Bomber, Squadron Leader E L Chidgey of 35 Squadron. It took five attempts to mark the rail junction using *Oboe* and Chidgey could see that his back-up markers had landed some way from the Aim Point, so he ordered the Main Force to bomb on those dropped by his deputy, Flight Lieutenant Lambert. A 578 Squadron Halifax which was hit by flak failed to return. To the east, at Achères near Paris, about half of the 97 Lancasters of 1 Group did not bomb. Thick cloud covered the target and the markers that were dropped could not be seen. A few of the crews took it upon themselves to drop below the cloud and start bombing but Squadron Leader G W Godfrey the Master Bomber decided that the risk to French civilians was too great and ordered the raid to be abandoned. A Lancaster which failed to return crashed at Eragny with the loss of all seven crew. More than 1,060 aircraft had attacked and dropped 11,500 tons of bombs.

Raids on the communications targets continued on the night of 7/8 June when 337 aircraft were dispatched to bomb railway targets near Paris at Achères, Juvisy, Chevreusse and Versailles-Matelet and an important road and rail junction at Massy-Palaiseau, about 14 miles south of Paris. This target was very well marked with red and green TIs, and bomb bursts were concentrated amongst them. The railway track could be seen in the light of explosions. Crews bombed from 6,000 feet and at this height they encountered intense light flak. On the leg into the target they also met considerable fighter opposition and eight bombers failed to return. Twenty-eight Lancasters and Halifaxes were lost on the raids on the road and rail targets. At Mildenhall, where 25 Lancasters had been dispatched for the operation on Massy, no word was received from three of the four missing Lancasters on XV Squadron and the two on 622 Squadron. The Lancaster piloted by Flight Lieutenant W J Bell DFC on XV Squadron was badly shot up by a Me 410 and the navigator, Sergeant

tropolitan-Vickers built Lancaster I ME701 JO-F *Whoa Bessie* of 463 Squadron, which was
naged beyond repair on 2 July 1944.

t) On 30 June 1944, 266 aircraft of 3, 4 and 8 Groups carried out a daylight raid on a road
ction at Villers-Bocage. Tanks of two German *Panzer* divisions, the 2nd *SS Das Reich*, which was
ouluse, and the 9th *Panzer*, were believed to be *en route* to Normandy and would have to pass
ugh the junction in order to carry out a planned attack on the Allied armies in the battle area.
raid was orchestrated by the Master Bomber, who ordered the bombing force to drop down to
0 feet in order to be sure of seeing the markers in the smoke and dust of the exploding bombs.
ll, 1,100 tons of bombs were dropped with great accuracy on the road junction and the planned
man attack was called off.

ht) Halifax over a V-1 site on the night of 5/6 July 1944. (*AWM*)

On the night of 5/6 July 1944 Halifax III MZ657 on 431 'Iroquois' Squadron RCAF piloted by Flying
Officer A H Phillips RCAF swung on take-off and crashed, caught fire and then exploded.

(*Left*) Warrant Officer Robert John Hooker RCAF (pictured), the 36-year old American wireless
operator, and Flight Sergeant J Content RCAF, the mid-upper-gunner, helped the crew get out of
Halifax MZ657 before it exploded. Flying Officer Gordon Dumville RCAF, bomb aimer, died of his
injuries.

(*Right*) On 7 July 1944, 467 Lancasters and Halifaxes were dispatched to help the Canadian 1st and
British 2nd Armies held up by a series of fortified village strong-points north of the Caen. The Main
Force dropped 2,500 tons of bombs onto aim points situated more in the city centre rather than on
the German positions on the northern outskirts. After some fierce fighting, the Allied troops finally
gained the centre of the city, only to be delayed by rubble. The city was in ruins; some of the French
inhabitants who had ignored the warnings to evacuate stayed in their cellars or wandered around in
a dazed condition amongst the piles of rubble that had been their homes.

...oyal visit to Mildenhall on 6 July 1944, when crews on 15 and 622 Squadrons operated from the ...on. (*IWM*)

...ht crew on Lancaster III JB370 on 57 Squadron at East Kirkby. The aircraft and Pilot Officer Max ...e RAAF and crew were lost on the operation on the flying bomb storage site at Ste-Leu-...sserent on 7/8 July 1944. Rose was killed, but four of the crew evaded and two were captured.

A Royal visit to a Pathfinder Squadron on 6 July 1944. (*IWM*)

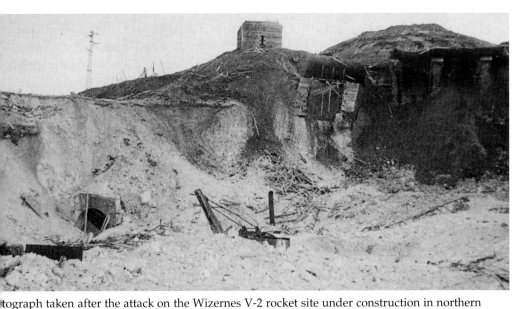

...tograph taken after the attack on the Wizernes V-2 rocket site under construction in northern ...ce on 17 July 1944 by 16 Lancasters of 617 Squadron, with a Mosquito and a Mustang as marker ...raft. The 'Dam Busters' aimed 12,000lb *Tallboy* earthquake bombs with 11-second delay on the ...e concrete dome, 20-feet thick, which lay on the edge of a chalk quarry, protecting rocket stores ...launching tunnels that led out of the face of the quarry pointing towards London. One *Tallboy* ...apparently burst at the side of the dome exploded beneath it, knocking it askew. Another ...sed part of the chalk cliff to collapse, undermining the dome, with part of the resulting landslide ...blocking four tunnel entrances, including the two that were intended for the erected V-2s. ...ugh the construction was not hit, the surrounding area was so badly 'churned up' that it was ...pproachable and the bunker jeopardised from underneath. The site was abandoned and the V-2s ...e pulled back to The Hague in Holland where, in September, the Germans began firing them ...n mobile launchers. (*IWM*)

...caster I LL779 SR-V and its unidentified crew of 101 Squadron at Ludford Magna, Lincolnshire, ...ebruary 1944. From October 1943, 101 Squadron was equipped for radio countermeasures using ...orne Cigar (ABC) equipment. As well as a normal bomb load the Lancasters carried extra radio ...ipment and a German-speaking 'special operator', whose job was to tune into enemy air-to-...und R/T communications and jam them using a powerful transmitter. This aircraft was one of ...on the squadron which FTR from a costly operation to the synthetic oil plant at Homberg on ...21 July 1944, when night-fighters claimed a total of twenty Lancasters. Flying Officer Jack Arthur ...vey RCAF and crew were killed. (*IWM*)

(*Left*) On 25 July 1944, ninety-four Lancasters and six Mosquitoes of 5 Group bombed an airfield and signal depot at St-Cyr. Bombing was accurate and one Lancaster was lost. This followed an earlier raid on 10/11 April 1944 by seventeen Lancasters and a Mosquito on 617 Squadron. (*via 'Pat' Patfield*)
(*Right*) The airfield and signal depot at St-Cyr from 10,500 feet on 25 July 1944. (*via 'Pat' Patfield*)

Lancaster II *Fanny Firkin II* DS842 which operated on 514 Squadron December 1943–July 1944, photographed during a visit to the 8th Air Force B-17 base at Deenthorpe in 1944. DS842 operated on 1668 HCU at Bottesford before being SOC in March 1945. (*USAF*)

...d from 15,000 feet on 23/24 July 1944, when 629 aircraft carried out the first major raid on a ...man city for two months. Only four aircraft, all Lancasters, were lost. (*via 'Pat' Patfield*)

...caster II LL734 JL-O on 514 Squadron flown by Flying Officer C B Sandland on the aircraft's ...d sortie during the attack on the V-1 site at Les Catelliers on 27 July 1944. Twelve Lancasters of ... Squadron dropped eighteen 500-pound bombs on *Oboe* marking. Five V-1 sites were attacked ... day by seventy-one aircraft, thirty-six of them Lancasters. All targets were cloud-covered and ...st of the bombing was 'confused and scattered'.

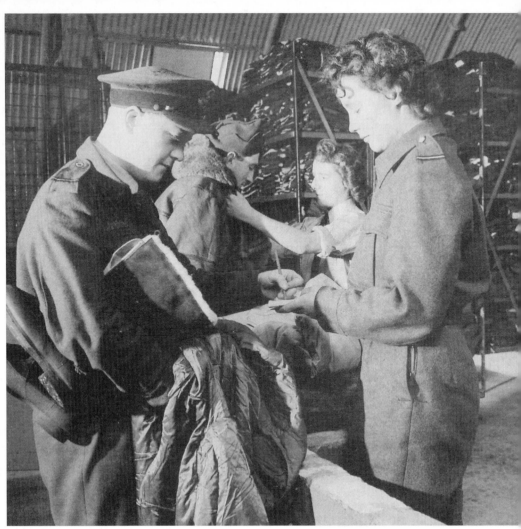

In the clothing store at a bomber station in August 1944 a WAAF section officer and her assistant issue new items of flying kit to two aircrew. (*IWM*)

...caster II LL634 on 426 Squadron at Linton-on-Ouse in the summer of 1944. This aircraft went to ...3 HCU at Bottesford in August and was SOC in March 1945.

...ancaster flying over the oil storage depot of Bec-d'Ambes near Bordeaux on 4 August 1944, ...en 288 Lancasters of 1, 3 and 8 Groups attacked Bec-d'Ambes and Pauillac in clear conditions without loss.

On 4 August 1944, 288 Lancasters of 1, 3 and 8 Groups attacked Bec-d'Ambes and Pauillac (pictured) in clear conditions and without loss. Twenty-seven *Serrate* Mosquitoes were used as escorts to the bombers. Pauillac was one of three oil storage depots on the River Gironde attacked the next day by 306 Lancasters of 1, 3 and 8 Groups. Blaye and Bordeaux were the other two targets. One Lancaster was lost from the Pauillac raid. Thirty Mosquitoes of 100 Group escorted these for without loss. (*via 'Pat' Patfield*)

Lancaster ND465 OL-L on 83 Squadron which crashed at Coningsby returning from the raid on Givors on 11/12 August 1944. There were no injuries to Flight Lieutenant A J Saunders RAAF and his crew. The crew were later shot down in the target area on the operation on I'Isle-Adam on 18 August 1944. Saunders and the two gunners evaded capture. The four other crew members were captured.

adron Leader Jim Verran DFC, now on his third tour, on 83 Pathfinder Squadron with his crew
 ground crew. (*Verran via Ian Frimston*)

 yards at Douai on 11 August 1944. (*via 'Pat' Patfield*)

The devastated town of Darmstadt, an important centre of the German chemical industry and a trunk railway junction, after the Bomber Command attack on 11/12 September 1944. (*IWM*).

Volkel airfield in Holland on 15 August 1944 taken from 15,000 feet. (*via 'Pat' Patfield*)

...dow over Gelsenkirchen on 12 September 1944. *(IWM)*

...caster I PD217 EM-Z on 207 Squadron in the hangar at Spilsby after being involved in a collision ...h a 57 Squadron Lancaster in the bomber stream on the operation on Stuttgart on the night of 13 September 1944.

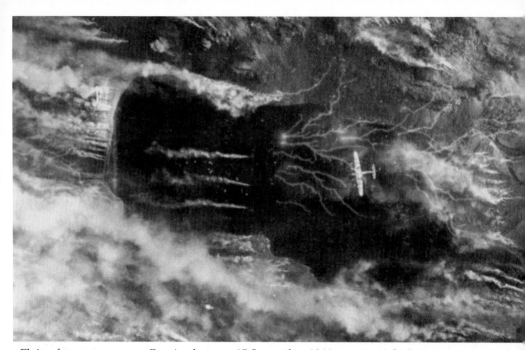

Flying from a temporary Russian base on 15 September 1944, twenty-eight Lancasters on 9 and 617 Squadrons, twenty of which were carrying *Tallboys* and six or seven others, twelve 500lb *John Walker* oscillating mines, caused considerable damage to the *Tirpitz* in Kaa Fjord in northern Norway. The enemy smokescreen failed to prevent the bombing and the battleship was hit by one thirteen *Tallboys* that were dropped. Subsequent reconnaissance revealed that although badly damaged, the *Tirpitz* was still afloat (albeit beyond practical repair, although this was not known the time). The Norwegian resistance stated that the ship left for Troms Fjord, where it was to be used as a heavy artillery battery. (*IWM*)

Safely back at Skellingthorpe, Lincolnshire, this 50 Squadron crew, commanded by Flying Officer J Lees RCAF (standing left) in front of their battle-scarred Lancaster III, ED470 *O-Orange*, after returning from Leipzig on 4 December 1943. The Lancaster had been raked by fire from a night-fighter, which knocked out the flaps, damaged both gun turrets and shot part of the tail-plane aw Undaunted, Lees and his crew bombed the target and then brought their aircraft home to base. N the holes in the fuselage, made by the night-fighter's 20mm cannon shells. ED470 went MIA on 61 Squadron on 23/24 September 1944 when it crashed into the Waal on the raid on Mnster. Flyir Officer Albert Keith Hornibrook RAAF and crew were killed. (*IWM*)

German 'Fortress' of Boulogne was attacked on the morning of 17 September 1944 by
aircraft of Nos 5 and 8 Groups, 370 of them Lancasters, in preparation for an assault by Allied
nd forces. More than 3,000 tons of bombs were dropped in and around the city.

photograph shows the concentration of bomb bursts and TIs with a Lancaster on 61 Squadron
head. One Halifax and one Lancaster were lost. The German garrison surrendered five days
. (*IWM*)

The attack on Cap Gris Nez on 26 September 1944 when 722 aircraft carried out two separate raids; 531 aircraft being dispatched to four targets at Cap Gris Nez and 191 aircraft to three targets near Calais. Two Lancasters FTR. (*IWM*)

Pilot Officer Hubert Clarence 'Nick' Knilans DSO DFC, an American who joined the RCAF and later became a Lancaster pilot on 619 Squadron and later 617 Squadron.

Charlie Kirk, was killed by a cannon shell. Bell crash-landed at Friston on Beachy Head where the aircraft immediately burst into flames but the remaining crew all escaped with minor injuries.

On the raid on Chevreusse, 115 Squadron at Witchford lost six Lancasters, one of which exploded over Paris. On the raid on Juvisy 78 Squadron at Breighton lost three Halifax IIIs and a fourth crashed at West Malling. The raid on Achères resulted in the loss of three Halifaxes, and a fourth, piloted by Squadron Leader William Brodie Anderson DFC RCAF on 429 'Bison' Squadron RCAF was hit by flak as the Halifax passed Dieppe and would not make it back to Leeming. Anderson was mortally wounded and while still conscious, ordered his crew to bail out. Three did so over enemy territory. At this point Flight Sergeants John Mangione, the mid-upper gunner, and Gordon Ritchie, the rear gunner, dragged Anderson to the rear escape hatch, attached a static line to the pilot's parachute and pushed him out. Sergeant G E J Steere the flight engineer had taken over the controls and he managed to fly the Halifax back across the Channel to reach the Oxfordshire area where he and the rest of the crew abandoned the aircraft before it crashed near Benson. The gunners' efforts were in vain and Anderson died. Mangione and Ritchie were awarded the DFM and Steere received a CGM.

In another attack, which was requested by the US 1st Army, 112 Lancasters and ten Mosquitoes of 1, 5 and 8 Groups carried out a raid on an important six-way road junction in the Fôret de Cerisy, half way between Bayeux and St-Lô. The area was believed to contain fuel dumps and German tank units preparing to attack 1st Army units. The bombing was not successful however, as the Main Force bombed on a stray marker, which had been dropped in error six miles from the target. A Lancaster on 101 Squadron failed to return.

The night following, 483 aircraft attacked rail targets at Alençon, Fougères, Mayenne, Pontabault and Rennes to prevent German reinforcements from the south reaching the Normandy battle area. Three Lancasters and a Mosquito failed to return. The raids created so much devastation that much of the German 3rd Paratroop Division, which had arrived in Rennes from its bases around Brest on twelve trains before the attack closed the station, was soon bogged down; the approach road to St-Lô, the final destination, was cratered heavily over its last 20 miles. By the evening of 9 June, most of the 3rd Paratroop Division had got only as far as Brecey, east of Avranches. At Fougères the leading train transporting the 265th Infantry Division from Vannes and Quimper on the Brest Peninsula was bombed and cut in two, and the rear half, which contained the Division's horses, rolled back down the line for four miles. When the wagons came finally to rest, the French released the horses and a 'Wild West'-type of round-up followed in which the German soldiers wasted much time acting as cowboys![7]

The first 12,030lb 'Tallboy' bombs developed by Dr. Barnes Wallis had been tested successfully at Ashley Walk range in the New Forest and on the night of 8/9 June these fearsome weapons were used operationally for the first time. The target for the 25 Lancasters of 617 Squadron was the Saumur railway tunnel near Tours, which had to be destroyed to prevent the 17th (SS) *Panzer Grenadier* Division's move from south of the River Loire to the Normandy front by train. The *Panzer* unit had begun leaving the Poitiers area on 7 June. French Resistance attacks had started before they reached the Loire bridges, some of which had already been destroyed on 7 and 8 June. Heavy attacks by Bomber Command during the ensuing three nights on all the rail centres in both eastern Brittany and the Cotentin caused general chaos on those railways, which were being used by the 17th (SS) *Panzer Grenadier* Division. The Saumur tunnel area was devoid of features that would assist the H_2S sets of the four aircraft from 83 Squadron that were to act as the flare force. Their flares were laid too far south and too far east, with only the last two or three flares in each stick being useful to the three Mosquitoes. Leonard Cheshire found the tunnel mouth and laid his spot flares perfectly on the aiming point. During the latter part of the attack Flight Lieutenant Gerry Fawke and his navigator Flying Officer 'Ben' Bennett were to mark the other end of the tunnel where it emerged on to a bridge across the Loire and some Lancasters were to drop 'Tallboys' on these markers, while two other Lancasters with full loads of 1,000lb bombs would attack the bridge. As Fawke's Mosquito came round to assess Cheshire's spot flares 'Ben' Bennett felt that they could not have been positioned more accurately than if they had 'been wheeled there in a barrow!'

Bennett recalled:

Cheshire gave the order to begin bombing and the 21-foot-long weapons encased in blue-black steel were dropped from 13,000 feet. The first 'Tallboy' was so near the markers that the glow of the spot fires was vividly reflected in the debris thrown up. Another pierced the hill through which the tunnel ran and exploded on the track. Other 'Tallboys' were effectively grouped around the aiming point. The bridge was demolished along much of its length. [The blocking of the tunnel came just at the wrong time for five of the trains, which, unable to proceed any further, disgorged their troops with orders to land-march.] Rail access to Normandy was denied to the *Wehrmacht* and their forces arrived piecemeal on the Normandy battlefield, failing to make the impact that their compact arrival might have achieved. The indefatigable Germans set to work to clear the line and this work was completed, only to be abandoned through the rapid advance of Allied forces in strength into the area. The line was not brought into full use until four years after the end of the war.[8]

On the night of 10/11 June, 432 aircraft attacked rail targets in France. Fifteen Lancasters and three Halifaxes were lost.[9] Raids on flying bomb sites and communications targets in France and synthetic oil targets in Germany were high on the Bomber Command target list. On 12/13 June, 671 aircraft attacked communications targets, mostly railways in France, and a stream of 286 Lancasters and 17 Mosquitoes headed for Gelsen-kirchen. Seventeen Halifaxes and six Lancasters failed to return from the communications raids and 17 Lancasters were brought down on the Gelsenkirchen raid by the German defences.

It was in the small hours of 13 June, when the Germans launched the first of 30,000 V-weapons against Britain, that a Lancaster on 75 Squadron RNZAF, its pilot, Pilot Officer G McCardle RNZAF unconscious, was flown from France and put down safely by an Australian bomb aimer who had never before been alone at an aircraft's controls. This achievement resulted in a CGM for the temporary pilot, Warrant Officer Alec Hurse RAAF. The target that night was the railway centre of Nantes at the head of the Loire estuary in western France. The Lancaster took off in the starlight about midnight and all was quiet as it flew in over France, coming down from 7,000 feet to 2,000 feet to get below the cloud to bomb. Then, over the target, after it had bombed, six searchlights picked up the aircraft. McCardle corkscrewed and during this manoeuvre the bomber was hit simultaneously three times – twice in the port wing and once in the cockpit. McCardle was wounded in the neck, leg and side. He was just able to say on the intercom: 'I'm hit; I'm hit – get out!' The navigator, Flying Officer A H R Zillwood RNZAF, who was awarded the DFC for his part in the night's ordeal, called Hurse up forward to see the pilot. Hurse found him clutching the stick to his chest, just conscious but unable to see because of his injuries. The aircraft was going almost vertically up through the cloud and out of the searchlights' glare. Hurse took the control column from the pilot and levelled up while Zillwood got McCardle out of his seat and laid him beside the bed. Hurse had never had any training as a pilot, except that he had had a little dual instruction in a Stirling bomber but there was no one else on the crew who could take the controls and he felt confident he could get the aircraft back to base – but not so sure he could land it. On the way back the wireless operator received a message to land on a grass airfield about 400 miles from Nantes. There the Lancaster, with Hurse at the controls, arrived at 4.50am. White flares were sent up to guide it in. Hurse circled twice while he asked whether anyone wanted to bail out but all said 'No' and Hurse brought the Lancaster down to a 'definitely unprofessional' landing. It bounced four times, swung to port and stopped.

The railway yards at Cambrai were one of the communications targets detailed for 671 aircraft on the night of 12/13 June. One of the 285 Lancasters that took part was *A-Apple* on 419 'Moose' Squadron RCAF flown by Pilot Officer Arthur de Breyne RCAF. A Ju 88 attacked from below and astern and set both port engines on fire. The area between the mid-upper turret and the rear turret, as well as in the port wing, were also set alight. The flames soon became fierce and 'Art' de Breyne ordered the crew to abandon the aircraft. Sergeant Jack Friday RCAF, the bomb aimer, was knocked unconscious as he opened the front escape hatch and was bundled through by others of his crew as one of them pulled the ripcord of his parachute. Pilot Officer Andrew Mynarski, the mid-upper gunner left his turret and went towards the escape hatch. He then saw that Flying Officer George P Brophy RCAF, his friend and rear gunner, was still in his turret and apparently unable to leave it. The turret was, in fact, immovable, since the hydraulic gear had been put out of action when the port engines failed, and the manual gear had been broken by Brophy in his attempts to escape. Without hesitation, Mynarski made his way through the flames in an endeavour to reach the rear turret and release Brophy. Whilst so doing, his parachute and his clothing, up to the waist, were set on fire. All his efforts to move the turret and free the gunner were in vain. Eventually Brophy clearly indicated to him that there was nothing more he could do and that he should try to save his own life. Mynarski reluctantly went back through the flames to the escape hatch. There, as a last gesture to the trapped gunner, he turned towards him, stood to attention in his flaming clothing and saluted, before he jumped out of the aircraft. Mynarski's descent was seen by French people on the ground. Both his parachute and clothing were on fire. He was found eventually by the French but was so severely burnt that he died from his injuries. George Brophy, thrown clear of the wreckage when the Lancaster crashed had a miraculous escape. He subsequently testified that, had Mynarski not attempted to save his life, he could have safely left the aircraft. Mynarski must have been fully aware that in trying to free the rear gunner he was almost certain to lose his own life. He was awarded a posthumous VC for his most conspicuous act of heroism, which called for valour of the highest order.[10]

On 14 June more than 220 Lancasters and 13 Mosquitoes of 1, 3, 5 and 8 Groups carried out two separate raids on Le Havre where 15 *E-boats* and light naval forces were a threat to Allied shipping off the Normandy beach heads just 30 miles away. The raid took place in two waves, one during the evening and the second at dusk. Most of the aircraft in the first wave were from 1 Group and the second from 3 Group, both waves being escorted by 123 Spitfires of 11 Group. In all, 1,230 tons of bombs were dropped on the pens. Just before the first wave bombed, 22 Lancasters of 617 Squadron released their 'Tallboys' on red spot fires dropped by three Mosquitoes, including one flown by Wing Commander Cheshire. They marked the *E-boat* pens in the eastern area of the port and eleven Lancasters attacked this aiming point. The attack was timed for 22.30 hours to catch the *E-boat* fleet fully armed and manned for the night sortie, just before they put to sea. The concrete-covered *E-boat* pens suffered hits and several near misses. One 'Tallboy' blasted a 16 foot-diameter hole in the north-west corner of the blast pens. The total shipping destroyed was 53 boats of various kinds.[11] When Barnes Wallis saw the PR photos that confirmed that the pens had collapsed along much of their length he commented that the best use of 'Tallboys' against such structures was a deliberate near miss. 'Their earthquake effect undermines the foundations and thus their massive roof weight then becomes a tremendous liability!' The light flak was 'tremendous' but only the one Lancaster failed to return and a 617 Squadron Lancaster had to be written off after returning. Sergeant Alf 'Bing' Crosby, 'Nicky' Knilans' mid-upper gunner suffered a leg wound. The Nôtre-Dame district near the port was devastated but fortunately the inhabitants had been evacuated long before the raid. Other districts were also hit and 700 houses were destroyed; 76 civilians were killed and 150 injured.[12]

That night over 330 aircraft bombed the vital road centre at Aunay-sur-Odon and German troop positions at Évrecy near Caen. At Aunay at least 31 civilians had died two days earlier in the daylight bombing and another 165 civilians were killed. While no Germans were present the town's six medium-class and four minor roads was considered by Allied commanders as being vital for German reinforcements arriving in the area.[13] All the bombers returned without loss. Another 330 aircraft took off for railway targets at Cambrai, Douai and St-Pol but all were either partially cloud covered or affected by haze and the bombing was not completely concentrated or accurate. Two Canadian Halifaxes were lost on the operation to Cambrai with all the crew of *X-X-Ray* on 424 'Tiger' Squadron RCAF surviving and either being taken prisoner or evading capture. All the crew on *P-Peter* on 433 'Porcupine' Squadron at Skipton-on-Swale, including Flight Sergeant Russell Lyle Porter the pilot and three fellow Canadians and also Flying Officer Charles H. Ramsdell USAAF were killed. A Halifax and a Lancaster carrying the Master Bomber failed to return from the operation on Douai.

Railway yards at Lens and Valenciennes and an ammunition and a fuel dump at Fouillard and Châtellerault were bombed on the night of the 15th/16th by just over 450 aircraft for the loss of 11 Lancasters. On 15 June the French resistance reported that all rail traffic in south Brittany had come to a halt except for one single-tracked line running from Nantes to Rennes. On the night of 16/17 June, 405 aircraft of Bomber Command began a new campaign against V-1 flying-bomb launching sites in the Pas-de-Calais, with raids on four targets accurately marked by *Oboe* Mosquitoes. No aircraft were lost on the raids in Northern France but 321 Halifaxes, Lancasters and Mosquitoes of 1, 4, 6 and 8 Groups that went to bomb the synthetic oil plant at Sterkrade/Holten were hit hard. The route the bomber stream took passed near a German night fighter beacon at Bocholt just 30 miles from Sterkrade and the *Jägerleitoffizier*

(*JLO*, or GCI-controller) had chosen this beacon as the holding point for his night fighters. Twenty-two of the 31 bombers that failed to return were Halifaxes, including seven out of 23 despatched by 77 Squadron from Full Sutton near York. On 19 June, after standing by for three days waiting for cloud over the Pas-de-Calais to clear, 18 Lancasters and two Mosquitoes of 617 Squadron, with nine Mosquitoes of 8 Group providing preliminary marking, set out to attack the *Blockhaus* flying bomb store in the Fôret d'Eperlecques, a mile from the village of Watten. The conditions proved too difficult for accurate marking and the nearest 'Tallboys' to the main building were 75 feet and 100 feet away from it.

On 20 June 17 Lancasters and three Mosquitoes of 617 Squadron, with escort, were dispatched to the V-2 launching and storage bunker in a quarry near Wizernes with 'Tallboys' but they were recalled just before reaching the French coast because of 10/10ths cloud at the target. The Lancasters were intended to return on the 21st but this raid was cancelled an hour before take-off, probably because of bad weather.[14]

At Dunholme Lodge, four miles north of Lincoln, on Wednesday 21 June were two Lancaster squadrons – 44 and 619. The Rhodesia Squadron would suffer the heaviest overall losses in 5 Group and the heaviest Lancaster losses and highest percentage Lancaster losses both in 5 Group and in Bomber Command. But, they had been operating Lancasters longer than anyone else and they were the only squadron with continuous service in 5 Group.[15] On the other hand 619 had been flying Lancasters for just over a year. *C-Charlie*'s crew on 619 Squadron was captained by 20-year-old Pilot Officer Mark Anthony Hamilton 'Dave' Davis RAFVR from Birmingham. He was the fifth and youngest child of John and Martha Davis, and his brother, Dudley Hamilton Davis had been shot down four years before flying a Hampden and had parachuted out at 50 feet and survived to be taken prisoner.[16] Flight Sergeant Peter Edmund Knox RAAF, 20 years old, the only son of Brigadier Sir Errol and Lady Knox from Sydney Australia, was the bomb aimer. Educated at Xavier College at Melbourne University and Newman College, Knox then trained at No. 2 Air Observers School at Mount Gambier and at Port Pirie in South Australia and Nhill, Victoria before sailing for San Francisco on the Matson liner on 5 May 1943. After further training at Camp Myles Standish, Massachusetts, he sailed to the UK on the *Queen Mary* troop ship on 30 June–1 July and completed further training at Penrhos, Turweston, Silverstone, Scampton, Winthorpe and Syderstone.

Pilot Officer John Ernest Ralph 'Porky' Bowering RCAF from Kingston, Ontario and Sergeant George Harry Moggridge RAFVR from Mile End in London manned the mid upper and rear gun turrets respectively. Harry's father worked in the London Docks. As a boy he loved anything to do with aircraft and flying. It was said that 'He always had a model aeroplane in his hands.' He was also a keen member of the Boy Scouts. At family 'sing songs' around the piano the scouting song *Riding Along on the Crest of a Wave* was his favourite. Not surprisingly as a much-loved son, his parents George Percy and Clara called him 'Sonny'. Sergeant Thomas Alfred Newberry, 21 years old from Chadwell Heath, Dagenham, was the wireless operator. His father was a railway line keeper. Having joined the RAF Tom Newberry was part of a crew that trained on Short Stirlings on 1661 Heavy Conversion Unit at Winthorpe before being posted to 619 Squadron at Dunholme Lodge. Flight Sergeant Leslie Edwin James 'Tag' Taylor the 21-year-old navigator was from Cheltenham, Gloucestershire. He joined the RAF as a volunteer after his elder brother, Norman, was killed in a Blenheim on 114 Squadron returning from a shipping patrol in the North Sea on 28 April 1941. Sergeant W Dennis 'Geordie' Belshaw the 20-year-old flight engineer was born and brought up in Ladysmith Terrace, Ushaw Moor, Durham, the only son of Dorothy and Arthur Belshaw. 'Geordie' had an older sister, Dorothy, who sadly died at the age of eight when he was six, and a younger sister, Vera, who was born not long after Dorothy's death. His father died when he was eight years old and the family moved to Bearpark. 'Geordie' left school at 14 and was a delivery boy for a local shop, until starting work in the store at 16 with a view to eventually training as a manager but he joined the RAF in 1941 at the age of 18 and passed out in 1943.

At Fiskerton, five miles east of Lincoln, BBC correspondent Kent Stevenson, a Canadian from Winnipeg, Manitoba hoped to record a broadcast of a raid that night for 'War Report'. He probably was wondering which crew he would fly with. Stevenson had joined the BBC in March 1941 and was one of the announcers in the North American Service before freelancing special programmes in connection with American troops in Britain. He transferred to the War Reporting Unit when it was established in 1943 and in April 1944 read out a series of his own talks under the title 'What War Means To Me' on the Home Service. Like his fellow correspondents Stevenson underwent rigorous training in military survival techniques and how to work in battle conditions. The war correspondents were issued with revolutionary new lightweight recording devices known as 'midget disc recorders', which had been specially developed by BBC engineers. Because the correspondents recorded their despatches straight onto disc, they had to learn the art of 'instant censorship'.

The weather, as with previous days, remained dull and the slight northerly wind kept temperatures a little chilly. On this, the shortest night of the year, for crews at Fiskerton and on 44 and 619 at Dunholme Lodge and on 57 and 630 at East Kirkby and at all the other Lancaster stations in 5 Group, their date with destiny was a synthetic oil plant at Wesseling, nine miles south of Cologne. At Fiskerton just after lunch a small crowd had gathered as an airman pinned up the Battle Order: 20 crews were detailed for the main briefing at 20.00 hours. For those crews listed, the usual pre-operational routine began, then later, after a noisy meal in the Sergeants' Mess and with coffee flasks filled, crews walked or were ferried over to the main site for specialist briefings and then the main briefing. The tape on the wall map showed a route ending just below the Ruhr near Gelsenkirchen . . . Germany for a change. Crews were immediately aware that this meant one thing: fighters! One hundred and thirty Lancasters would be accompanied by five crews in 1 Group and six Mosquitoes would mark the target using the *Newhaven* method. Another 123 Lancasters and nine Mosquitoes of 1, 5 and 8 Groups would attack a synthetic oil plant at Scholven/Buer. Plans were to bomb both targets simultaneously.

One by one the various specialists gave their talks, with 27-year-old Wing Commander Malcolm Crocker DFC*, the American CO of 49 Squadron, concluding the briefing by stating that he too would be operating and would be taking along Mr Kent Stevenson, on *T-Tommy*. Also flying this night would be 49's two flight commanders. The CO's second tour crew would be flying their eighth operation. Pilot Officer Leslie Benson, the 24-year-old recently commissioned navigator from Harrogate in Yorkshire, had just received news that his award of the DFC had just been gazetted. He had been awarded the coveted medal on 25 January while a flight sergeant, after having flown 28 ops. The citation said that 'His ability, courage and determination have often been of the greatest help to the captain in carrying out a difficult task. He has always been keen to help the new man and has never hesitated to carry out the last detail to any duty assigned to him.'

Benson was educated at Harrogate Grammar school and before enlisting worked in the Harrogate Borough Council's Treasurer's Office. Pilot Officer David Carr the rear gunner was also a recipient of the DFM. Flight Lieutenant Albert Matthews, the 30-year-old flight engineer, and the WOp/AG, Flying Officer James Worthington, also 30, who was from Southport, Lancashire had each been awarded the DFC; as had Pilot Officer Allan Creighton, the 26-year-old mid-upper gunner from Vancouver, British Columbia, who had recently arrived from 619 Squadron. The seventh member of the crew was Flying Officer Kenneth Dutton.

Clear weather conditions were expected at both target areas but as the midnight hour approached the weather deteriorated and both targets were covered by 10/10ths cloud, so at Wesseling H_2S was used and at Scholven/Buer Path Finder aircraft provided *Oboe*-based sky-marking instead. Only slight damage was reported at Wesseling though the plant suffered a 40 per cent loss in production for a while after this attack and Scholven/Buer suffered a 20 per cent loss in production following the raid. Eight Lancasters were shot down and a 61 Squadron aircraft, which landed at Woodbridge was wrecked when it was hit by a Flying Fortress on 214 Squadron that was badly damaged on a special operation.

More than fifty *Abschüsse* were claimed by *Nachtjagd* as the result of an effective Tame Boar operation against the Wesseling force, I./NJG1 being credited with 16 victories by eight He 219 Uhu ('Owl') crews. In fact 37 Lancasters were lost on the Wesseling operation. At 03.32 hours combat exhausted 49 Squadron crews began landing back at Fiskerton. Their opening remarks gave the first hints of the disaster that had befallen the aircrew of 5 Group. Meanwhile, outside the intensity of the operations block, in another world, dawn was just breaking over the Lincolnshire Wolds, heralding the start of a fine new day. A corporal removed the blackouts from the windows, letting shafts of bright sunlight penetrate the stuffy smoke-filled room; the sun's rays played upon the operations board, where, written in large chalk white capital letters against the names of six aircraft captains were those three impassive words ... 'MISSING WITHOUT TRACE'. The Station Commander, having just returned from his long vigil at the Watch Office, scanned the ops board in silence, still numbed by the realisation that in just one very short evening, 49 Squadron had lost 42 good men, including its Commanding Officer, Wing Commander Malcolm Crocker. He and his second tour crew were blown out of the sky outbound near Jülich-Mersch by a night fighter. The intrepid Kent Stevenson's broadcast now would never be heard.

Five crews on 207 Squadron at Spilsby and three on the two Lancaster squadrons at Waddington were also lost, and at East Kirkby six Lancasters on 57 Squadron and five on 630 Squadron were missing. At Dunholme Lodge 44 and 619 Squadrons had each lost six Lancasters. Among the missing was C-Charlie flown by 'Dave' Davis, which at 01.20 BST was hit by ground fire over Bladel Woods near Postel in Belgium and the starboard engine was set on fire. Davis said in a calm, clipped voice, 'Abandon aircraft – emergency jump jump'. He must have known his fate. In the face of death he made the greatest of all sacrifices; he kept the Lancaster steady so that his crew could bail out. His body was never recovered. 'Porky' Bowering and George Moggridge also died. Peter Knox, Charlie's bomb aimer wrote:

We each had to confirm over the intercom that we were jumping. As I had to lift up the escape hatch I responded first. 'Air-bomber jumping'. There was no shouting, no calls for help. In a numbed state, I moved into the escape routine. All this time the pilot was holding the plane steady. This was an environment for which there had been no rehearsal. I was no longer responding like a robot to in-built commands. The disaster which had hit us struck me. Then I recollect thanking God I had escaped and rather desperately willing that my mother and father should somehow know I was alive. Within a very short space of time I saw the explosion as our plane plummeted into the ground. I wondered if the others had got out and I shouted out the name of 'George' (Moggridge). My voice seemed to be lost in the vast dark space around me and I realised there was no possibility of making any form of human contact. It took 15 minutes to reach the ground. I passed through some clouds and hit the ground on the fringe of a pine forest. My parachute was snagged on a small tree. Luck was on my side. I was unhurt. The weather was fine. It was dark and I was in an isolated area.

After initially receiving help from the Resistance, 'Geordie' Belshaw was captured and became a prisoner in *Stalag Luft III* where he was joined by 'Tag' Taylor and Tom Newberry, who is believed to have been the last person to bail out of the crashing aircraft. He landed in a tree, possibly damaging his arm before he was captured by the Germans.[17] Peter Knox evaded capture and within a week of being shot down was accepted as a valid RAF escaper. On 26 June he was brought into direct contact with the Balen resistance group and was sheltered by Frans and Maria Clementina Sterckx and their young family and friends at their farmhouse at Hoge Hof in Geel. Knox was also delighted to find out that there was another RAF man being held on the farm. He was a flight sergeant navigator, Reg Brookes, also aged about 20, who had been shot down on 22/23 April returning from a raid on Düsseldorf. The farm was to be their base for the whole of July and the first part of August while the great battles around Normandy were being waged. The escape route for airmen through France was blocked and there was little the underground movement could do except to put them in a safe haven until the Allied forces liberated the occupied territories. Jeanne Leemans, a central figure in the underground movement who helped Knox and the others, was arrested in the summer of 1944 and sent to a prison camp.[18]

Telegrams were sent to the next of kin of all those lost on Scholven/Buer and Wesseling, informing loved ones that their sons were 'missing, presumed killed' or when Red Cross confirmation was received that that they were prisoners of war. The letter announcing Wing Commander Crocker's death arrived at his parent's house in Boston, Massachusetts. The parents of Technical Sergeant Albert E Martin USAAF, one of four men killed on *S-Sugar* on 44 Squadron flown by Pilot Officer Russell Wood RNZAF, received word that he had been killed in action. Three of the crew were taken prisoner. In Calgary, Canada, Lucy McMurchy received a letter informing her that her husband Flying Officer Lorne Sinclair McMurchy, pilot of Lancaster *B-Baker* on 9 Squadron that was lost on Scholven/Buer was dead. It must have been equally heartbreaking for relatives in Lethbridge, Alberta when they were notified that Sergeant Donald A H Redshaw RCAF the 18-year-old rear gunner had been killed.

On 23 June when 97 Squadron flew a formation flying practice two Lancasters were involved in a mid-air collision. Flight Lieutenant Henry Van Raalte, the tough Australian pilot, drifted into the slipstream of another Lancaster in front of him and Van Raalte's aircraft was blown wildly into Flight Lieutenant Edward Leslie John Perkins' aircraft. Earlier that morning the tiny Fiat car owned by Perkins had been hauled onto the top of a large air raid shelter at Coningsby by 50 pairs of arms and left there. Crews were still laughing when they took off. Both Lancasters broke up as they went down. All eight crew including the visual air bomber aboard Van Raalte's Lancaster, which crashed at Cloor House Farm on Deeping Fen, were killed. Only Sergeant Coman, the wireless operator on Perkins' aircraft, who had no idea how he managed to get out of the aircraft when it broke in two at 1,000 feet, bailed out and miraculously survived. Perkins' two wild Canadian gunners had been sent to the 'Aircrew Refresher Centre' at Sheffield in punishment for smashing up the sergeant's mess one night and thus missed the crash that killed their pilot. At Coningsby Perkins' little Fiat was quietly removed from the top of the air raid shelter by the chastened young crews. Six weeks after the collision another crew took Coman on another training flight. He landed shaking, was later diagnosed as a tuberculosis case and never flew again.

On the night of 23/24 June 390 heavies and 22 Mosquitoes carried out attacks on four V-1 sites in the Pas-de-Calais Area and 203 Lancasters and four Mosquitoes of 1 and 5 Groups set out for rail yards at Limoges and Saintes. All four flying-bomb sites were hit and the rail yards were bombed with great accuracy. Two Lancasters were missing from the raid on Saintes and four failed to return from the raid on the flying bomb site at Coubronne. A fifth was lost on the operation on l'Hey.

Next day, 24 June, 321 aircraft including 200 Halifaxes and 106 Lancasters of 1, 4, 6 and 8 Groups attacked three V-1 sites in the clear in the Pas-de-Calais. All targets were accurately bombed and no aircraft were lost. Sixteen Lancasters and two Mosquitoes of 617 Squadron returned to the flying-bomb site at Wizernes escorted by 11 squadrons of Spitfires. This time the target was clear and Leonard Cheshire dived to mark the huge dome with spot fires but his stores hung up and he called in Gerry Fawke, who dropped his smoke bombs as an area marker instead. His Mosquito was hit several times by flak, as were four Lancasters but he accurately marked on the lip of the dome. The bombing was excellent and well-grouped. A hit at the top had caused a big landslide while others bombs had destroyed secondary installations and work at Wizernes continued.[19] The heavy anti-aircraft defence was very accurate and the long, steady and sustained run-up that the Stabilised Automatic Bomb-Sight demanded for its superb performance resulted in more damage than usual being sustained by the Lancasters. *G-George*, captained by Flight Lieutenant John Andrew Edward DFC suffered a direct hit and crashed near the village of Leulinghem. Flight Sergeant Gerry Hobbs the wireless operator was the only survivor from the eight man crew. He was badly injured after bailing out and was taken into captivity when his injuries had been treated.

A few hours later, 739 aircraft of all groups attacked seven V-1 sites. It was a clear, moonlit night and 22 Lancasters were lost, mostly to night fighters. An exception was Wing Commander D R Donaldson RAAF and crew on 463 Squadron RAAF which attacked the V-1 site at Prouville in northern France. They arrived a little early and Donaldson decided to go round again. A burst of flak exploded at their height of 12,000 feet and set fire to the port inner engine. In feathering the port inner the flight engineer feathered the port outer as well and owing to a failure of the accumulators was unable to un-feather the port outer. Donaldson gave the order to jettison the bombs and for the crew to bail out. He was one of four to evade capture while the other three were taken into captivity.

Another of the missing aircraft was flown by Flight Lieutenant W M Walton DFC on 97 Squadron who also bailed out safely and evaded capture. Tony Aveline a navigator on another 97 Squadron Lancaster could smell the stink of the bomb-aimer's vomit as the pilot hurled their Lancaster into a corkscrew during an attack by a night fighter.[20]

Next day, Sunday 25 June, at Melbourne Arthur C Smith was awoken at 03.45 hours along with his pilot Flight Sergeant Charles 'Wag' Winter and the five other members of the crew, to go on their first operational raid. Some 323 aircraft of 1, 4, 6 and 8 Groups were detailed to three more V-1 sites. After breakfast, briefing and all the other pre-flight preparations Winter's crew took off at 07:45 in Halifax H-Harry with 20 other aircraft on 10 Squadron, part of a force of 100 Halifax bombers detailed to attack the flying bomb base at Montorgueil near the northern coast of France. Arthur Smith recalled that 'the bomber force was an impressive sight on the way out, in bright sunlight against a clear blue sky.' From his bomb aimer's station in the perspex nose he counted nearly 80 aircraft in a loose gaggle to port. As they climbed to 13,000 feet, Ron Day the rear gunner on Flying Officer Alan Bruce's crew, who were on their 20th op and second daylight, passed close to Day's home between Bishop's Stortford and Stansted. The bombers were leaving contrails as they passed over the Thames estuary. There was a little heavy flak bursting just below as Winter's crew crossed the French coast and some more in front at their height of 16,000 feet. H-Harry was near the back of the stream of bombers as they approached the target, which was almost obscured by a mass of smoke from bursting bombs with target indicators just showing through. The weather was clear as at 18,000 feet Alan Bruce's crew in Z-Zebra approached the target and began their bombing run. From his tail turret Ron Day could see many aircraft above and below and one directly astern with bomb doors open. One by one each Halifax dropped its deadly cargo of fifteen 500lb bombs. Day glanced to port for a split second and then as his eyes came round to the aircraft astern at the same level and quite close, it disintegrated. 'The air filled with pieces and an aircraft below seemed to have been hit by falling wreckage ... bombs were falling all around ... There was an aircraft directly above us: I reported it to my Skipper and Tom Bidley the navigator called back that he could see we were directly beneath it but we were on the bombing run and could not move. Having witnessed the sudden explosion only seconds before, I was alarmed to say the least but the aircraft drifted slightly to starboard and his bombs fell between our starboard wing and the tail area.'

H-Harry was on its final bombing run when Arthur Smith suddenly saw the Halifax in front and slightly above blow up with a vivid orange flash. It disintegrated into fragments of burning wreckage and a huge pall of black smoke, through which *Harry* flew before dropping its bombs. Anthony Bebb a flight engineer on 77 Squadron at Full Sutton, who was on his 17th operation and first daylight op, had seen a 500lb bomb fall into the wing root of the port wing, breaking the wing off and almost immediately afterwards a great explosion and the Halifax was no more. He saw a parachute floating down but there was no one with it. The flight engineer on this aircraft had borrowed a penknife off Bebb before leaving. It was the type carried in a flying boot.

Flight Lieutenant Bill Rodney, pilot of *S-Sugar* on 78 Squadron at Breighton, who was well into the bombing run, could see the bomb doors of the aircraft in front and above open and after a brief interval, the bombs starting to fall away. He saw a 500 pounder smash through the inboard section of the starboard wing of the Halifax that was ahead and slightly below them:

Immediately the stricken aircraft nosed up and to its right in a violent barrel roll, while the wing struck by the falling bomb tore away from the fuselage. Simultaneously, a cloud of vapour streamed from the wing root area as the fuel tanks and lines ruptured. The next moment the damaged Halifax, by then on its back, exploded in a blinding orange flash. My aircraft, then virtually above the doomed aeroplane, was hurled upwards and almost thrown over on its back by the force of the detonation, forcing me to dive and half roll in order to bring it back to a level keel and more or less on track. Fortunately, our bomb load had dropped away only moments before. Not surprisingly, we didn't get a picture of the target. Our photograph showed nothing but sky but at the time that was the least of our worries. Fortunately, *S-Sugar* was unaffected structurally by the blast of the unexpected strains to which she had been subjected and the return flight was uneventful.[21]

The bombs that brought the Halifax down had been dropped from another one on 10 Squadron flown by Flying Officer Ray Rosen. Jock McKinnon, the rear gunner sitting in the tail watched as the Halifax immediately broke up; the wing hit another aircraft, which exploded. The fuselage of the first one twisted and turned below him and he saw two or three parachutes open. At that time he did not know that it was their bombs that did the damage. The Halifax that had been struck was *N-Nan*, a 77 Squadron Halifax flown by Flight Sergeant Donald McGonigill Steven. Hit by the falling wing of this aircraft, *M-Mother*, the Halifax flown by Squadron Leader Guy Benjamin Treasure on 102 Squadron went down also, both aircraft falling at Fontaine l'Etalon in the Pas-de-Calais. There were no survivors on either aircraft. *K-King* on 102 Squadron overshot the runway at Pocklington on return and was wrecked. There were no injuries to the crew.

It is believed that all three raids on the V-1 sites were accurate. Early in the morning, 17 Lancasters each carrying a 'Tallboy', and two Mosquitoes were dispatched to a flying-bomb launching bunker under construction at Siracourt, three miles WSW of St-Pol-sur-Ternoise in the Pas-de-Calais. Wing Commander Cheshire accompanied them in a P-51 Mustang[22] with the purpose of using it as a low level marker aircraft in the early morning attack. Cheshire, who had not flown a single-engined aircraft for three years, took off an hour after the rest of the aircraft and caught them up on the way. He dived the Mustang from 7,000 feet to 500 feet through accurate heavy flak to drop his two under-wing red spot fires and was followed by Squadron Leader Dave Shannon in one of the two Mosquito marker aircraft carrying four smoke bombs and two red spot fires each. They were so accurate that the second Mosquito did not need to mark. The Aiming Point was easily identified and twelve 'Tallboys' burst close to the AP; four of them very close. When the smoke cleared there appeared to have been one direct hit on the concrete bunker. The 'Tallboy' had penetrated the 16-foot-thick supposedly bomb-proof roof and had caused a massive explosion. Other bombs had fallen on the east and west sides of the building. Cheshire landed safely back at Woodhall Spa at 10.18 hours.[23]

On 27 June, 104 Halifaxes of 4 Group with five Mosquitoes and two Lancasters of the Path Finders attacked the V-weapon site at Mimoyecques where fantastic gun-barrels, designed to fire 600 tons of explosive daily into London, were sunk 500 feet into the ground. This target was only 30 by 20 yards square from above. There were no losses, bombing conditions were good and two large explosions were seen. That night over 720 aircraft attacked railway targets at Vaires and Vitry. While the yards at Vitry were hit only at the western end the attack on Vaires was particularly accurate. Four Lancasters failed to return from the raids.

On 28/29 June 230 bombers hit the railway yards at Blainville and Metz for the loss of 18 Halifaxes and two Lancasters.[24] Eleven of the Halifaxes including *S-Sugar* on 76 Squadron piloted by Pilot Officer I Weir RNZAF were lost on Blainville. Weir ordered the crew out, the flight engineer handing the pilot his parachute as he went past. The New

Zealander clipped it on, upside down in his haste but the aircraft exploded before he could get out through the escape hatch. He recovered in time to open his parachute at 4,000 feet after he finally found the D-ring. The Halifax on 433 'Porcupine' Squadron RCAF flown by Warrant Officer H McVeigh was attacked four times by a night fighter and he evaded the first three but was hit on the fourth attack when he performed a corkscrew turn. The starboard fin and rudder were shot away, the starboard elevator damaged and the flap, aileron and wing tip of the starboard wing were smashed. The Halifax went into a tight spin at 13,000 feet and McVeigh ordered the crew to bail out. Two of the crew managed to get out of the aircraft before he regained control and levelled off at 6,000 feet. Shortly after setting course for home the port engine failed but McVeigh made it to Woodbridge, where he landed the crippled Halifax at 155 mph in order to keep the damaged wing up.[25]

On 30 June two German *Panzer* divisions, the 2nd *SS 'Das Reich'* in Toulouse and the 9th *SS* were believed to be en route to Normandy and would have to pass through a road junction at Villers-Bocage in order to carry out a planned attack on the Allied armies in the battle area. Some 258 aircraft dropped 1,176 tons of bombs on the junction. The Master Bomber ordered the bombing force to drop down to 4,000 feet in order to be sure of seeing the markers in the smoke and dust of the exploding bombs. Two aircraft were lost. One eye-witness reported that he had seen the remains of a German tank strewing the top of a two-storey building. The planned German attack was called off.

During the prelude to the invasion of Normandy, Bomber Command had been controlled by the Supreme Allied Commander and *Nachtjagd* was given a brief respite as the RAF heavies and American bombers were switched to bombing targets in France. Although the *Nachtjagd* had little reaction time to counter these shallow penetration raids, these ops were no picnic for bomber crewmen. Navigator-bomb aimer Bob Hilliard, a Melburnian born on Anzac Day 1923 and with a soldier of the 1914–18 war for a father had lost his original pilot, Flight Sergeant 'Merv' Fettell, who was killed on an OTU flight. Hilliard and the four other survivors, who earned the right to wear the Caterpillar badge, were required to fly again before being given seven day's leave. Crewed up with another pilot, Hilliard went to 466 Squadron RAAF at Leconfield and completed 11 ops, seven on Wellingtons and four on Halifaxes. He recalls:

When we were posted to 35 Squadron PFF we were feeling reasonably confident with just over a third of a 30-op tour completed. We suddenly found ourselves back behind the starting line with another 34 trips needed for a 45-op PFF tour (the trips on 466 still counted). In April 1944 when French rail targets became common prior to

D-Day with a noticeable decline in the loss rate, our masters decreed that ops to France, Belgium and Holland only rated as a third of an 'op' so many totals shrunk as the new rule was retrospective. French 'ops' didn't stay 'easy': sometimes casualty rates equalled those of German targets. In July the masters relented to the extent of allocating three points for French targets and five points for Germany. A Main Force tour became 150 points and a PFF 225 and this applied for the rest of the war. In my own case it took 55 ops to reach a final tally of 228 points. A tour at the beginning of the war was 200 hours operational flying and then a 'normal' tour became 30 operations. A PFF tour was 45. At some time a normal tour was increased to 35 or 40 operations. Towards the end of the war some trips were classed as only a third of an operation.

July began with a series of heavy raids on V-1 flying bomb sites in France save for an attack by 467 aircraft on 7 July when they were dispatched to help relieve the situation at Caen. On 4 July, 328 bombers – mostly Halifaxes – attacked V-1 flying bomb sites in northern France without loss. That night 282 Lancasters and five Mosquitoes of 1, 6 and 8 Groups attacked railway yards at Orléans and Villeneuve. Fourteen Lancasters were lost. Over 230 Lancasters and five Mosquitoes of 5 Group were given a special target, a flying bomb site in limestone caves at St-Leu-d'Esserent near Creil, 30 miles north of the centre of Paris. The French originally used these caves for mushroom growing but the Germans had commandeered them for the storage of their V-1 weapons. The roof was about 25 feet thick, consisting of a 10 feet layer of soft clay surmounting 15 feet of limestone. It was to be hit first by 17 Lancasters of 617 Squadron supported by a Mustang and a Mosquito and then immediately after by the rest of 5 Group carrying full loads of 1,000lb bombs, with some Path Finders. The markers were accurately laid and the bombing was very concentrated, although six of the 617 Lancasters brought their 'Tallboys' back as smoke obliterated the red spot fires before they were able to bomb. One of the 'Tallboys' scored a direct hit on a cave entrance, causing a large subsidence. A near miss had also helped to render this entrance useless and the railway line had been destroyed.[26]

The following night, Wednesday 5 July, was clear and there was a bright moon when the Main Force flew two bombing operations to France again. Some 542 aircraft of four groups were detailed to bomb flying-bomb sites and 154 Lancasters of 1 Group, the main railway area at Dijon. At Croft, Halifax III aircraft on 431 'Iroquois' Squadron RCAF were detailed to bomb a flying-bomb site at Biennais. At take off time at 01.24, *K-King* piloted by Flying Officer R W Harrison RCAF crashed and caught fire due to loss of control. An explosion followed, completely wrecking the aircraft. Warrant Officer (later Pilot Officer) Robert John

Hooker, the 36-year-old American WOp/AG, saw movement in front of the aircraft as he was leaving the wreckage. He went forward and, finding the flight engineer wounded and unconscious, dragged him from the burning aircraft and left him some distance away. Hooker, who was born in Rolla, North Dakota and had enlisted in Regina, Canada in June 1941, then returned to the wreckage and extricated the bomb aimer who was also wounded and unconscious. He then dragged both airmen further away from the crash. While returning to the scene a third time in order to determine whether all members of the crew were accounted for, one of the bombs in the aircraft exploded and Hooker was thrown to the ground. By his prompt action and total disregard of danger he saved the lives of two members of the crew. He was later awarded the George Medal. One other member of the crew, Flight Sergeant J M Content RCAF was awarded a Mention in Despatches for bravery in the same incident. Flying Officer Gordon Dumville RCAF died later in the day from his injuries. The rest of the crew were admitted to Friarage Hospital.

All flying-bomb targets were hit. Three Lancasters were lost without trace and another was brought down by flak in the bombing of Wizernes. Eighty-one Lancasters dropped mixed loads of eleven 1,000lb American-made semi-armour piercing bombs and four 500 pounders from 8,000 feet after marking by five Mosquitoes. At Dijon the main railway area was heavily bombed and all aircraft returned safely.

On Thursday 6 July 551 aircraft attacked five V-Weapon sites. A 424 Squadron Halifax was shot down by flak attacking the Siracourt flying bomb storage facility. All the crew were killed. Three other Halifaxes attacking Croixdale flying-bomb site crashed on return to their bases. Everyone on *U-Uncle* on 578 Squadron at Burn was killed when the Halifax III crashed 12 miles NNE of Nottingham. *L-London* on 12 Squadron at Wickenby lost its starboard fin and rudder after the aircraft was hit by a bomb from another aircraft in the attack on the modified V-1 launch site at Fôret-du-Croc. Flight Lieutenant H I Gray had retained control but was unable to prevent it crashing during approach to Faldingworth. Two men died and Flight Sergeant Tony Silverman, who was critically injured, finally succumbed on 18 July.

On 6 July also, Wing Commander Leonard Cheshire accompanied 17 Lancasters and two Mosquitoes of 617 Squadron in an afternoon raid on the uncompleted V-3 long-range gun site at Marquise/Mimoyecques, nine miles northeast of Boulogne and 95 miles from London, when he piloted a Mustang marker aircraft. The damage was later assessed as one direct hit against a corner of an 18 feet thick slab of concrete that had been cast to cover three of the five gun shafts on the hilltop, blasting a crater 35 feet across and 100 feet in diameter. It was later found that this bomb had also blown a cavity beneath the slab, causing part of it to collapse inwards. Up to three thousand Germans and other workers were entombed when the water table was breached and flooded the lower workings. Another four 'Tallboys' were within 60 yards of the AP, one being a near miss at the north end of the slab. All this led to the collapse of one of the gun shafts and some of the upper level of tunnels.

Upon his return Cheshire was ordered to leave the squadron and rest. He had completed four tours and had flown at least 100 operations. On 12 July he was replaced as CO of 617 Squadron by Wing Commander James 'Willy' Tait DSO* DFC, a taciturn 26-year-old Welshman who it was said that when he opened his mouth it was usually to stick a large pipe into it.[27] James Tait was educated at Wellingborough School and decided at the age of twelve that he was going to be a pilot after seeing one of Sir Alan Cobham's air displays in 1928. He graduated as a Pilot Officer from RAF College Cranwell in August 1936 and joined 51 Squadron flying Whitley bombers. He had previously served with 4 Group and like Cheshire he had also completed 100 operations.

Meanwhile, on 7 July at dusk, 467 Lancasters and Halifaxes of 1, 4 and 6 Groups and 14 Mosquitoes of 8 (PFF) Group were dispatched to help the Canadian 1st and British 2nd Armies held up by a series of fortified village strong-points north of the Normandy city of Caen, which General Montgomery had hoped and planned to capture by the evening of D-Day.[28] Watched by cheering troops of the 3rd and 59th Infantry Divisions and those of the Canadian 3rd Infantry Division, in clear weather conditions the Main Force dropped 2,500 tons of bombs onto well laid markers. Caution had dictated that the bomb line should be well ahead of the British forward positions so the Aim Points were situated more in the city centre rather than on the German positions on the northern outskirts. Smoke and dust soon obscured the markers but the Master Bomber Wing Commander 'Pat' Daniels of 35 (PFF) Squadron returned the bombing to the target area. There was little German defence in Caen itself and because of a six-hour delay between the end of the bombing and the ground attack only newly arrived troops of the 16th *Luftwaffe* Field Division were affected by the bombing (the 12th *SS Panzer* Division had recovered before the Allied troops attacked). After some fierce fighting, the Allied troops finally gained the centre of the city, only to be delayed by rubble.[29] During the air attack, intensive flak from the south of the city was encountered but only two Lancasters were shot down. A 550 Squadron Lancaster crash-landed at Manston on return.

That night 123 Lancasters and five Mosquitoes of 1 and 8 Groups accurately bombed the railway yards at Vaires without loss and 208 Lancasters and 13 Mosquitoes, mainly from 5 Group but with some Path Finder aircraft, attacked the flying bomb site at St-Leu-d'Esserent again. Bombs destroyed the mouths of the tunnels and the approach roads and the enemy was no longer able to use the flying bomb site. Its stores and the weapons were transferred to the Nucourt caves, the entrances to which were attacked on Monday 10 July and again on Saturday afternoon, 15 July. The closure of St-Leu-d'Esserent came at a price; 32 Lancasters were shot down by night fighters though one was believed shot down by another Lancaster. Five out of 16 Lancasters dispatched by 106 Squadron at Metheringham were lost. Losses at East Kirkby totalled four with loss of three Lancasters on 57 Squadron and the demise of *R-Robert* of 630 Squadron flown by the South African CO, Wing Commander William Inglis 'Bill' Deas DSO DFC*, who was flying his 69th operation. Only one man on the crew survived.

By the middle of July when they could be identified and marked, railway targets in France were being bombed on a regular basis. On the 12/13th 378 Lancasters and seven Mosquitoes of 1, 5 and 8 Groups sought marshalling yards at Culmont, Revigny near Nancy and Tours. Culmont and Tours were accurately bombed but cloud interfered with the all 1 Group raid at Revigny. Half of the force brought their bombs home and those that had dropped them did little damage to the railways. Two nights' later 242 Lancasters and 11 Mosquitoes returned to Revigny and also to the railway yards at Villeneuve. At Villeneuve the railways were hit though much of the bombing fell to the east of the target. The raid on Revigny was abandoned because the railway yards could not be identified. Seven Lancasters failed to return from the raid.

Flight Lieutenant John Alec Bulcraig DFM's Lancaster crew on 57 Squadron at East Kirkby flew their first op on the night of 15/16 July, when 222 Lancasters and seven Mosquitoes attacked railway yards at Châlons-sur-Marne and Nevers, neither attack being successful. Three days later Bulcraig's crew took part in the attack by 1,032 bombers on five fortified targets south and east of Caen that were still holding up the Canadian 1st and British 2nd Armies. The raids, in support of Operation *Goodwood*, the imminent armoured attack by British Second Army, took place at dawn in clear conditions.[30] Bulcraig's 19-year-old air gunner, Sergeant Len Manning, had a 'grandstand' view from the rear turret as they turned for home after dropping their bombs. 'The whole area was covered in smoke and dust to about 5,000 feet. It was also an amazing sight to see so many planes in the sky at one time.'

At Grimsby a 100 Squadron Lancaster crashed and exploded on take-off on the operation to Sannerville, killing all but the rear gunner who bailed out. Four of the targets were marked by 8 Group Mosquitoes and Lancasters and at the target, where *Oboe* failed, the Master Bomber, Squadron Leader Keith Creswell of 35 Squadron, and other Path Finder crews, used visual methods. At Colombelles, 126 Lancasters of 5 Group and 64 Halifaxes and 33 Lancasters, all in 6 Group, flew in at altitudes of 6,000–9,000 feet, dropping mostly 1,000lb bombs onto prepared positions of the 16th *Luftwaffe* Field Division. Almost simultaneously 1 and 4 Groups, each with more than 100 aircraft, attacked the area around Sannerville. The three remaining targets were attacked between 06.00 and 06.25 hours. Mondeville was attacked by 3, 5 and 6 Groups; 1, 3 and 4 Group attacked Mannerville; and 3 and 8 Groups attacked Cagny. In all, it was one of the greatest air bombardments of troops ever seen. Bomber Command dropped more than 5,000 tons and American heavy and medium bombers, 6,800 tons. In one orchard, near the village of Guillerville, 15 tanks and nearly all the motor vehicles of a company from 21st *Panzer* Division were destroyed, some of them being thrown into the air to land on their backs 'like struggling beetles'.[31] Despite heavy flak around Caen, only six aircraft – five Halifaxes and a Lancaster – were lost and four more bombers were lost on their return over England. Coming home from the attack on Emieville, Lancaster *J-Johnny* on 115 Squadron crashed on to a farm at Great Offley in Hertfordshire, killing Pilot Officer Sydney Albert Letts and his crew and Mrs. Alice Handley and her two daughters, one of whom was on leave from the ATS.[32]

One by one the Lancasters returned to East Kirkby past the familiar windmill at Old Bolingbroke and brushing its sails with their prop wash. Bulcraig's crew had taken off at 4am and on their return they were told that they were 'on' again that night. The 5 Group target was a railway junction at Revigny in northern France.[33]

Two Lancasters were lost on the raid on the Aulnoye railway junction, which formed part of the attack on Revigny, by a total of 253 Lancasters and 10 Mosquitoes of 1, 3, 5 and 8 Groups. At Revigny the illuminating flares went down over the 'brilliantly lighted target' but no target indicators followed. The crews could hear the Master Bomber and his deputy talking but a German night fighter hit the Master Bomber's Lancaster and the marker flares 'went down all right'. James Campbell wrote a graphic account of the Master Bomber going down:

Over France the stars shone big and bright above the main force from a slow moving endless conveyor belt of black velvet. Scanning the vast panorama of needle-sharp pointers [the navigator] found Vega and Altair. High on his starboard Polaris burned above Dubhe. He stretched himself leisurely along the bombing mat and watched the flak snake round the bombers ahead. He watched it with detachment, for there was nothing he could do about it. It was fascinating to glimpse the varied hues of the light flak, fear chilling, when he remembered the lethal powers of the garish arcs of fast moving light. The glaring white flashes of the camera flares burst ahead and around them, illuminating for seconds the black trails left by the heavier shells. Listlessly they floated past, mute reminders to him of their once deadly bursts. Clear, crisp and unruffled the voice of the Master Bomber came over the R/T from somewhere far below them, down amongst that fiery volcano of light and heavy flak.

'Sentinel One to Reapers! Bomb the Greens! Sentinel One to Reapers! Ignore that cluster of Reds. They are off the aiming point! Bomb the Greens!'

'Sentinel One to Reapers! Undershoot that last cluster of Greens by two seconds! Do not bomb the Reds on any account! Sentinel One to Reapers, rep——.' The voice broke off abruptly...

'Sentinel Two calling Reapers! Sentinel Two calling Reapers! Concentrate on the Greens! Ignore all Reds! Sentinel Two to Reapers. Let 'em go on the Greens!'

So they had got the Master Bomber, wheeling round the target thousands of feet below them – an aerial policeman directing the jammed traffic above, making sure that their loads went where they were intended.[34]

A few crews bombed the flares in the burning aircraft but they were not in the railway yards. Fighter flares were then dropped, air battles broke out and 24 Lancasters went down in flames. 619 Squadron at Dunholme Lodge lost five of its 13 aircraft taking part in the raid. The deputy Master Bomber called to abandon the attack. By the end of the night 'trains were still running through Revigny.'[35]

Sergeant Len Manning on John Bulcraig's crew recalls:

After crossing the French coast we were picked up by searchlights. During our evasive action we lost the protection of the stream and became vulnerable to attack by fighters. Having lost the searchlights we set a new course for the target. Shortly after this there was an enormous explosion in the port wing. We had been hit by cannon fire. Immediately flames were streaming past my turret, which had stopped working as the pumps for the drive supply for the hydraulic motor were powered by the port engine. I centralised the turret by hand and opened the doors into the fuselage and climbed in. Fred Taylor our mid-upper gunner was already out of his turret and was clipping his chute on to his harness. He struggled to open the rear door and jumped out into the night. By this time the fuselage was a mass of flame and molten metal and the aircraft was in a steep dive. My chute, which was stowed on the port side, had started to smoulder. I pulled it from its stowage and struggled to clip it on to my harness. This was difficult due to the force of 'G'. I managed to fix it to one of the clips but the other was impossible. With every-thing burning thought 'It's now or never' and leapt through the door into the night. As I fell I pulled the rip-cord and hoped that the chute would open. It did but I was hanging to one side. I felt something brush my face. It was my intercom lead, which was attached to my helmet and it had been whipped off when the chute opened. The lead had become entangled in the silk shrouds. I grabbed it and hung on. This probably saved my life as it helped to take my weight. My helmet should have been removed before I jumped. I looked up and saw that the chute was burning and I hoped that I would get down before it fell apart. On the way down there was a terrific explosion when the Lancaster hit the ground with the full bomb load still aboard.[36]

On 20/21 July 30 Lancasters and seven Halifaxes failed to return from Main Force raids.[37] Three nights later over 620 bombers were detailed to hit Kiel in the first major raid on the city in two months. Attacks by other forces on an oil refinery and storage depot at Donges near the mouth of the River Loire and flying-bomb sites in France were also ordered. One Halifax failed to return from the raids on the V-1 sites and all returned safely from the raid on Donges. The leading edge of the starboard wing of Lancaster *S-Sugar* on 408 'Goose' Squadron RCAF at Linton-on-Ouse opened six minutes after taking off for Kiel and with its bomb load intact, Flying Officer J A Brown RCAF landed at Marston Moor airfield, Yorkshire. Seconds later it skidded off the runway and caught fire. None of the crew was badly injured. At the target no contact could be made with the Master Bomber and his deputy took over. Marking was by H_2S and considered accurate, although bombing was rather scattered in the early stages of the attack. Both marking and bombing appeared to become more concentrated towards the end of the raid and many explosions and fires were seen. In a raid lasting only 25 minutes, 612 aircraft got their bombs away on the glow of green and red TIs and skymarking flares, green with red stars, as seen through the 10/10ths cloud that covered the target. Severe damage was caused to the north-east portion of the *Deutsche Werke* shipyards, and hangars at Holtenau airfield were partially destroyed. A considerable amount of damage was done to the facilities and barrack area near the torpedo boat harbour and moderate damage to a torpedo components and electrical signalling works. Sixteen medium-sized buildings in the Marine Artillery Depot were partially destroyed.

Four Lancasters, one of them an all-Polish crew on 300 'Masovian' Squadron, another on 625 Squadron who were all lost without trace, were shot down on the operation without a single survivor among them. Flying Officer Raymond Alexander Rember RCAF, an American pilot on 582 Squadron from Cincinnati, Ohio and his crew were buried in Kiel War Cemetery. Lancaster *A-Apple* on 166 Squadron returned to Kirmington and was destroyed following the collapse of the undercarriage on touch-down. The pilot was the only one injured. Lancaster *U-Uncle* on 582 Squadron at Little Staughton ran short of fuel on the return and the pilot, Lieutenant Edwin 'Ted' Swales SAAF attempted an emergency landing at the Handley Page facility at Radlett in Hertfordshire.[38] Swales, born in Inanda, Natal, enlisted in the South African Army in June 1935 and when war broke out in 1939 had fought in Ethiopia and later through the North African desert campaigns as a Warrant Officer. After the victory at El Alamein he returned to his native land and transferred to the SAAF. In August 1943 he was seconded to the RAF. The South African was injured in the crash at Radlett that resulted but he was not seriously hurt and his crew suffered nothing more than bumps and bruises.

The oil refinery and storage depot at Donges was attacked again on Monday night 24/25 July by just over 100 Lancasters of 5 Group. Another 461 Lancasters and more than 150 Halifaxes were dispatched to Stuttgart in the first of three heavy raids on the German city in five nights. Flight Sergeant Jack Stephens, a 'WAG' or wireless air gunner on 463 Squadron RAAF flew his fourth 'op', on Donges. He had volunteered for the RAAF from Sydney University and trained in Australia, mainly at Parkes NSW where he gained his radio skills, before crossing the Pacific to complete his training in America. From there he crossed the Atlantic aboard the *Queen Mary* to his European posting. Stephens would write up each and every raid in his diary:

> It was a 5¼ hour trip, bombing at 02.00 at 8,000 feet. We carried 11 × 1,000lb plus 2 × 500lb. We hit a big oil dump and were one of the first to bomb, getting away before most of the flak started. There was a bit of heavy flak around. I saw the red tracer from it; also bomb bursts and TI's going down. We were trailed by a single engined fighter soon after we left the target until near the coast. It stayed near us through five corkscrews but was shaken off by others. It was very dark; gunners couldn't see most of the time.

Three aircraft were lost on the raid on Donges and 21 aircraft – 17 of them Lancasters – failed to return from the attack on Stuttgart. Two of the missing Lancasters were on 166 Squadron at Kirmington and all fourteen crew members on *Y-Yorker* and *U-Uncle* died. The dead included Flying Officer W G Shearer USAAF the American pilot of *U-Uncle*. *D-Dog* and *P-Peter*, two Halifax IIIs on 466 Squadron RAAF, failed to return to Driffield. *D-Dog* went down with the crew, which included five Australians, one of them Pilot Officer Henry Blonin Shaw the pilot. Fifteen minutes' earlier *P- Peter*, which was being flown by Flying Officer Ronald James Walsh DFC RAAF, was hit fatally. Flight Sergeant Keith Campbell RAAF the wireless operator, recalled:

> I was just about to unclip the chute when there was what seemed to be a heavy, dull explosion behind me and someone saying 'Bloody hell'. The next thing I knew I was in mid-air, floating down on one strap of my harness! The explosion, stray flak, which scored a direct hit on 'Peter' blew me straight out through the nose and just blew the kite to hell. It took a long time to come down and it was a fantastic experience. I could see the last of the raid; all the flak and searchlights at the target, the fires in the city, PFF flares burning out and strings of bombs bursting. It looked like fairyland somehow; everything seemed so unreal. At first I mistook the cloud for the

ground and made several 'perfect book landings' only to find that I went right through the 'ground'. Finally, I came to earth. I was sprawled out in a wheat field.

Campbell was the crew's only survivor. *P-Peter* and the rest of the crew went down in a thickly wooded area 14 kilometres south of Stuttgart.

Overall, the losses might possibly have been higher but for the usual support operations, which on this night numbered over 100 aircraft of training units on the diversionary sweep and over 80 Mosquitoes flying to several targets while a handful of Halifax aircraft laid mines off Brest. Over 100 other aircraft headed for a flying-bomb site at Ferfay but the Master Bomber allowed only 73 aircraft to bomb. One Halifax failed to return.

There followed a raid next day on aircraft assembly depots and wireless/telegraphy stores at St-Cyr on the outskirts of Paris by 100 Lancasters and Mosquitoes of 5 Group. Jack Stephens on 463 Squadron, which lost the only Lancaster on the entire operation, wrote:

The close concentration of Lancs was escorted by twelve squadrons of Spitfires. I saw a Jerry fighter shot down by Spits. Flak – light and heavy predicted – was moderate but deadly accurate all the way in and back. Hardly a kite returned without a few holes. We had one small hole in the starboard wing and a big lump of Perspex out of Geoff's turret. He was stunned momentarily but not hurt. I saw dozens of bomb loads go down together – one × 4,000, 2 × 1,000 and 14 × 500. One great billow of smoke marked the target. I saw five parachutes from Lanc JO-Y. The whole starboard inner engine caught fire and the Lanc went in.[39] All the rest got back OK. One brought back his bombs. He had duff (failed) hydraulics, bounced his 'cookie' up the runway and the kite finished up at the end of it with a broken back. The crew were OK.

Another Main Force raid took place that night on Stuttgart again with two other forces going to the Krupp *benzol* plant at Wanne-Eickel and to three flying-bomb sites in France. The eight Lancasters and four Halifaxes that failed to return were all lost on the raid on Stuttgart. Near Orléans while outbound, *M-Mother* on 300 'Masovian' Squadron at Faldingworth was involved in a collision with an American aircraft. Flight Sergeant Jan Danieluk, the pilot, and four of the crew died and only two of the Poles were able to bail out before the aircraft crashed. Flight Sergeant F Witrylak quickly made contact with the local *Maquis* and he arrived back in England on 20 August 1944. The rear gunner managed to evade capture also. Lancaster *V-Victor* on 428 'Ghost' Squadron RCAF at Middleton St. George collided in the air with another aircraft over France and was wrecked when the pilot attempted a landing at the emergency airfield at

Woodbridge in Suffolk. None of the largely Canadian air crew was injured. UL-V^2, a 576 Squadron Lancaster III at Elsham Wolds flown by Flying Officer Robert J Sarvis USAAF was abandoned by six of the crew. Two men evaded and four landed behind friendly lines in the battle area. Sarvis died at the controls of his aircraft, which crashed near Liesville ten miles north-west of Carentan. Fellow Americans Flying Officer W Adams USAAF and Technical Sergeant J Keisow USAAF, pilot and mid-upper gunner respectively on *Y-Yorker* on 630 Squadron, failed to return to East Kirkby. Adams and three of his crew evaded capture. Both air-gunners were killed.

Again 166 Squadron lost two Lancasters. One of these was *Z-Zebra* flown by Pilot Officer John Cann who took off from Kirmington at 21.20 hours. It was their 29th operation. As they climbed away into the night sky he and Flight Sergeant Ron Storey, his wireless operator, and the others on the crew were thinking that after tonight, they had only one more trip to do.

They were about an hour from the target when Reg Feveyear the rear gunner noticed a series of small fires burning on the ground. They were spaced at fairly regular intervals on either side of their track. It suddenly dawned on him that they must be 'fighter flares' marking the flight path of the bomber stream to guide the enemy night fighters onto the bombers. He reached up to switch on his microphone to warn the pilot and out of the night sky, cannon and machine gun tracer came streaming at him from dead astern. In the flashes from the fighter's guns, he could see the radial engine of a FW 190. The tracers streamed passed his turret striking the aircraft further forward. Reg instinctively lined up his sights on the fighter and opened fire with his four machine guns. His tracers indicated that some of his fire was going into the FW 190's radial engine. The fighter sheared off and Reg raked his underside with another burst of fire. He then switched on his microphone to warn the pilot. His mike was dead, but he could hear the rest of the crew discussing the damage and speculating on how he had fared.

The damage was quite extensive. One engine was on fire; the under-carriage had dropped down on one side making the aircraft completely unstable. They could not open the bomb doors to jettison the bombs. The flames were streaming back down the full length of the fuselage and they knew that the aircraft could not remain in the air for much longer. Cann gave the order to bail out. Bob Drongeson the flight engineer, Bernard Taylor the bomb aimer, Warrant Officer Nik Zuk, navigator, Ron Storey and Hugh Hill the mid-upper gunner left by the front escape hatch. Feveyear climbed out of his rear turret, clipped on his parachute pack and tried to open the rear door, but it would not budge. As he turned, he noticed to his horror that bright green smoke was pouring from the flare chute. The photoflash, which was still in the chute, was being baked by the flames from the burning wing and at any moment could explode.

It did not occur to him that the bombs in the bomb bay must have also been getting quite hot too. Feveyear made his way forward. Cann looked down and pointed to the front escape hatch. Feveyear dropped down into the nose, sat on the edge of the opening with his feet in space and rolled forward out of the aircraft. He does not remember pulling his ripcord but there was a sudden jerk as the parachute canopy opened.

It was a moonlit night so Feveyear could see the ground long before he reached it. He drifted over some trees and then made an almost perfect landing in a field. As he rolled forward his parachute canopy collapsed in front of him. He bundled up his parachute and Mae West and hid them in a ditch and then made his way to a small wood about two miles away. The time was 00.30 hours. He concealed himself in the under-growth and went to sleep. It was daylight when he awoke, so he made his way to some houses, which turned out to be the village of Lainsecq. On the way he met a farmer who took him to his house and gave him some bread and wine. Later a priest took him to meet Hugh Hill, who was hiding in a house nearby. He returned to the farmhouse and later that evening, a captain of *Maquis* came and took them both to a *Maquis* camp near Etais where they met up with John Cann, Bob Drongeson and Ron Storey.

John Cann, who was the last to bail out, landed in a field two miles north of Thury unharmed, though he had lost his flying boots on the way down. He hid his parachute and Mae West and started walking north but his feet soon became very sore so he lay down under a hedge and slept until daybreak. He then began to walk in a southeasterly direction. In the afternoon, a man on a bicycle came up to him and asked him if he was RAF. He told him to wait as he cycled off. Soon, he returned with a *Maquis* officer who took him on his bicycle to their camp in the forest near Etais where later he met up with four members of his crew.

Bernard Taylor had landed in a field near Etais. He hid his parachute, Mae West and flying suit under a thick hedge and started walking in a southerly direction till dawn. He then hid in a small wood and at dusk set off again, still heading south. The following day he again hid in a wood walking at night keeping to forest tracks. To quell pangs of hunger, he ate berries from the trees and food from his escape kit. He continued like this for another day and a night, making no contacts. On 29 July he was able to establish his position as 8kms west of Varzy. The following day Taylor passed west of Champlemy. On 1 August he called at a farmhouse where he received food and drink. That evening he continued south. The next day at 17.00 hours when crossing the Route National from Premery to Nevers Taylor was approached by five FFI men who took him to their camp near Nolay. Later he was taken to another camp north of Chateau Chinion and then a *Maquis* officer drove him to the 1st SAS camp at Ouroux. Finally, the SAS took Taylor to their HQ at Chalaux where he met up with the rest of the crew.

Nik Zuk had landed in a field South of St-Sauveur. He hid his parachute and Mae West in a stook of corn and headed off in a westerly direction. He walked all that day, except between dawn and noon when he hid and slept. When he woke up, he noticed two men working in the field close by and now as he was feeling very hungry, he decided to approach the two men. They turned out to be the farmer and son. Nik explained who he was with the help of his phrase list and was taken to the farmhouse and given a good meal. They also filled his escape kit water bottle with wine. At 21.00 hours he set off again and then hid in a wood and slept until dawn. He walked again until 15.00 hours when northeast of Lavau he met a Frenchman sitting on the river bank fishing. At 18.00 hours a man and a woman arrived in a horse and buggy to collect the fisherman. After some discussion, it was decided that it would be safer for Zuk to change clothes with the fisherman and travel back to the village of Bonny in the buggy and the fisherman would cycle back by the back lanes. The French couple fed and hid Zuk for the night. They sent a message to the local *Maquis*, who the following morning took him to their camp near Lavau. He stayed until 3 August when he was taken to the SAS HQ at Chalaux and was reunited with the rest of the crew.

Bob Drongeson landed in a field near the village of Lainsecq. He hid his parachute and Mae West in a wood where he hid till the next night. When it became dark he started to walk towards the village. For the rest of that night and the following day he hid in a barn. As darkness fell, he set off in the direction of St-Sauveur. It started to rain so he took shelter in a wood until the following morning when he set off again. About midday he stopped a boy on a bicycle, explained who he was and asked for help. The boy took him to a house in St-Sauveur where he was given food. Later a man called to tell him that Cann, Storey, Hill and Feveyear were safe in a *Maquis* camp. Next morning Drongeson was given some civilian clothes and taken by car to the camp to join them.

Hugh Hill had landed in a field behind a farmhouse at Lainsecq. During the attack he had been hit in the face by flying splinters and although the wounds were superficial they were bleeding quite profusely, so he lost no time in asking for help from the farmer. After they had bathed and dressed his wounds, the farmer took him back to the field to collect his parachute and Mae West, which he had hidden under a hedge. The farmer and his wife put him to bed and later that night the *Maquis* captain brought Reg Feveyear to see him and then he took them to the camp in the forest.

Ron Storey had landed in a cornfield north of the village of Thury. After hiding his parachute in a hedgerow, he set off in a south-westerly direction. He had not walked very far when he saw a barn. It was unlocked so he bedded down and slept till dawn. Escape and Evasion lectures had said that most French farmers were willing to help shot down Allied airmen, so he went across the yard to the farmhouse and knocked on the door. When he explained who he was the farmer took him in and gave him food and drink. The local *Maquis* were contacted and Storey was taken to another farm and in turn, to the camp at Etais where he was united with four members of the crew. Captain Guthrie of the SAS suggested that they join him at the 1st SAS camp. Arms were given to them in case they encountered any German patrols and shortly after dark on 30 July a car came to take them to Chalaux. They were overjoyed to meet up with Nik Zuk and Bernard Taylor. On Friday 8 September all seven crew, accompanied by the members of the 1st SAS who were returning to England, were flown from Orléans to RAF Middle Wallop. This must have been a record; that a bomber crew could be shot down, evade capture and return to England 45 days later. Of course, none of this would have been possible without the unselfish help of the extraordinary courageous French people who faced certain death if caught helping an Allied airman to evade capture. Their innate bravery is beyond comprehension.[40]

On the night of 26/27 July, 178 Lancasters and nine Mosquitoes of 5 Group attacked rail yards at Givors near Lyons. Jack Stephens on 463 Squadron RAAF wrote:

> The kite – 'D' – came out of the hangar (with a new bit of perspex in Geoff's turret) and was bombed up just in time – $8 \times 100 + 4 \times 500$ and 2,000 gallons of fuel; a maximum load. We went all the way at 8,000 to 10,000 feet. Over the target we struck a big thunderstorm; violent bumps and lightning and blue sparks lighting up all the aerials, edges, props and everywhere. The whole kite was alight with dancing blue flame. All the hundreds of kites over the target put their navigation lights on while in the thunderstorm. I saw bomb bursts, lightning, etc. All the villages and towns around that part were blazing with light, which they didn't even put out during the raid. There was no blackout. There was no opposition – flak or fighters – at all, all the way. There was only the odd fighter flare. The bombing wasn't too bad. We were five hours over enemy territory, 9 hours 20 minutes in the air. We took off and landed in daylight and got back with practically empty tanks.

Four Lancasters and two Mosquitoes failed to return. Two of the Lancasters were claimed by *Leutnant* Otto Huchler of 2./NJG2 for his first two victories. A Mosquito on 627 Squadron, one of the 30 in the LNSF that went to Hamburg, was also lost.

After raids on V-1 flying bomb sites on the 27th and 28th, the Main Force attacked Stuttgart and Hamburg on the night of the 28/29th. The force of 187 Halifaxes, 106 Lancasters and 14 Mosquitoes that raided Hamburg was attacked by Tame Boars on the bombers' homeward flight and 18 Halifaxes and four Lancasters were shot down. Among those lost were a Halifax and three Lancasters on 408 'Goose' Squadron RCAF at Linton-on-Ouse; the Canadians beginning their second spell equipped with Halifaxes, taking delivery of the Mk. VII, though for the time being the Squadron would continue to operate Lancaster IIs. The missing Halifax was flown by Squadron Leader Gerald Bennett Latimer RCAF who was lost with all his crew who included four fellow Canadians and an American, 2nd Lieutenant Alfred Hauzenberger. At Croft five Halifaxes and crews on 431 'Iroquois' Squadron RCAF including *H-Harry* piloted by Flying Officer Joe Collver, who was just 19 years of age, were missing.

Nachtjagd units intercepted the stream heading for Stuttgart, and aided by the bright moonlight, shot down 39 Lancasters. Three of the losses were on 514 Squadron at Waterbeach. *C-Charlie* piloted by Flying Officer Robert Jones was shot down by *Hauptmann* Heinz Rökker of I./NJG2. The Lancaster began to plunge earthwards and then it exploded. Sergeant Tom Harvell the flight engineer, and the navigator, Sergeant George Robinson were the only survivors. Harvell evaded capture. Robinson was captured. The Lancaster flown by Flight Lieutenant E A Campbell RCAF carried a crew of seven and a pilot on his first flight as second dickey. The aircraft was hit by gunfire from a night fighter and burst into flames. Campbell ordered the crew to bail out. The second dickey panicked and began screaming while trying to grab the controls. Sergeant William Donaldson, the flight engineer, jumped on him but was thrown off. In the struggle that followed the second dickey pulled the ripcord of his parachute, filling the aircraft with billowing silk. Then he pulled the ripcord on Donaldson's 'chute. The front gunner had by now joined the struggle and he managed to subdue the second pilot. He and Donaldson gathered up the parachute shroud and shoved the terrified pilot out of the escape hatch. His chute opened and he landed safely. Donaldson, Campbell and four others on the crew successfully evaded capture. One other man was taken prisoner and one died in the aircraft, which crashed near the village of St-Cloud-En-Dunois, eight kilometres south-southeast of Châteaudun.

V-Victor, a Lancaster on 463 Squadron RAAF piloted by Flight Lieutenant John Anthony Howard Wilkinson RAAF, which failed to return to Waddington carried the Gunnery Leader, Flight Lieutenant Brian Moorhead DFC, who had survived four years of war on operations. Stuttgart was his last op. So it was for the rest of the crew. There were no survivors. Telegrams were duly sent to next of kin. Brian Moorhead's mother was first to receive the news that her son was missing in action. As soon as she got the telegram she rang her daughter Lorraine, who recalls:

My mother said Brian was missing. She did not say any more. I went home and my mother was unconscious on the floor. The whole time Brian was flying it was constant tension. You have to go through it to know what it was like. Always you were reading about people getting killed. Brian was MIA for a year and my mother always thought that he was alive and a prisoner of war but I knew that he wasn't. The letter was really frightful: 'Dear Mrs Moorhead, It is with the most heartfelt grief that I now confirm the tragic news that your son, Flight Lieutenant Moorhead ...'

On Sunday 30 July almost 700 aircraft, 462 of them Lancasters, were dispatched to bomb six German tank concentrations in front of a mainly American ground attack in the Villers Bocage–Caumont area. At Waddington Jack Stephens on 463 Squadron RAAF was up at 2am. The squadron was briefed to bomb German tank concentrations south of the Cherbourg Peninsular at Cahanges. Stephens wrote:

The cloud base was at 20 feet at take off and cloud was 10/10 (complete cloud cover) to 10,000 feet. We left contrails (condensation trails) on the runway. We were carrying 18 × 500 GP (general purpose bombs) aboard. Cloud was still 9/10 at 3,000 to 6,000 feet over the target, so after 15 minutes orbiting and arguing over the R/T (radio telegraph), the bombing was scrubbed due to the proximity of Allied troops. After leaving the target we saw a bit of the Cherbourg Peninsula through the gaps in the clouds. Fields and beaches and harbours and wharves and ships were all very peaceful as far as we could see. Further inland we saw a bit of smoke from the artillery and some bombs and shell craters. The rest of the view was just hundreds of Lancasters, some Mustangs and Spitfires, a Mossie fighter-bomber and endless cloud, which looked wizard in the morning sun. We did a cross country on the way back via Pershore, Squires Gate and Hawarden to base to wait for the weather to clear and to empty the tanks a bit. Cloud was down to about 400 feet on return. We ran off the runway into the grass on landing and bounced beautifully with our full bomb load but it stayed in place and so did we.[41]

On 31 July we got nine day's leave and I went to Scarborough. It took four hours from camp to Scarborough, about 90 miles, including about one hour on the Humber Ferry at Hull. I did quite a lot of motor biking around Scarborough, including the Yorkshire Moors and Forge Valley. I went for one swim in the sea and came out after half a minute to thaw out. There were two days cloudless out of nine, the sun being just warm enough to be warm. This constituted a heat wave. I spent most of the time sleeping and eating raspberries. I started out for camp on Wednesday afternoon and the bike went well to Hull. Then the clutch cable broke and we just got it fixed in time to catch the ferry. It then went well for about 20 miles and then started to go phut again, finally seizing up about half a mile north of Scampton where we left it and got back to camp by bus.

While Jack Stephens was on leave the next raids on rail targets in France were carried out by Lancasters, with Mosquito markers by 1, 5 and 8 Groups. Just over 120 Lancasters bombed the railway yards at Joigny-la-Roche on Monday 31 July. The raid was accurate and one Lancaster was lost. At Le Havre just over 50 Lancasters of 1 Group bombed the port area. One of the Lancasters failed to return. Sixteen Lancasters and two Mosquitoes on 617 Squadron and 97 Lancasters and six Mosquitoes of 5 and 8 Groups attacked the railway tunnel at Rilly-la-Montagne seven miles south of Rheims, which was being used as a V-1 store. They were escorted by 102 Spitfires. Wing Commander Willy Tait and a second Mosquito marked for 617 Squadron flying at 12,000 feet despite the Main Force being detailed to arrive at 18,000 feet. The marking points and APs were the north and south entrances to it and 617 would bomb both of them with 'Tallboys'. Six Lancasters on 83 Squadron were detailed to destroy enemy communications and storage installations. The formation met its escort at the French coast and flew to the target without incident and Mosquitoes marked the target, so well in fact, that the two 617 Squadron Mosquitoes were not required. The formation achieved a good bombing concentration, attacking both ends of the tunnel with what was considered equal success. Main Force bombs cut the track on both sides of the tunnel while those 'Tallboys' that fell, apparently caved in the entrances.

Flight Lieutenant Bill Reid vc dropped his 'Tallboy' and was about to turn away when his bomb aimer, Pilot Officer 'Les' Rolton DFC asked him to hold his course for another 28 seconds until their aiming point photo had been taken. Rolton had been Reid's bomb aimer on the Düsseldorf operation when their Lancaster had been shot to pieces by fighter attacks, and for which Reid was awarded the VC. Rolton had accompanied his Skipper when Reid had recovered from his wounds and went back on ops in January 1944. The Scot had also invited Cyril Baldwin to join him on 617 Squadron but the 5 feet 4½ mid-upper-gunner had declined, saying he had only a few more ops to complete his tour. And also, his brother-in-law, an engine fitter on 617, had warned him that the Dam Busters' squadron was full of 'bloody lunatics'.

Now, as Reid held his course a 1,000-pounder dropped from above hit *S-Sugar*. Reid wore a harness with chest clips. As his flight engineer handed his chute to him, another bomb struck them, the two hits causing damage to one of the port engines as well as the fuselage. *Sugar* began to spin down in two pieces. As Reid unstrapped himself and struggled to open the crash exit overhead, the nose seemed to break away, leaving him to tumble through empty air. He pulled his ripcord but kept a tight grip on the lines, being uncertain as to whether he had properly locked the chute to his harness. Landing in a tree, he slid down it, with injuries to his face and one hand. Reid applied his field dressing to his cut face and then he headed south towards Paris, 30 miles away. He carried a silk escape map and he was confident of his ability to speak French but his attempt at evasion was cut short when three German soldiers challenged him. Reid was taken to a flak site and attended to by a doctor, where he met up with Flying Officer Dave Luker, his wireless-operator, who had also been thrown out of the Lancaster when the nose of the plane broke off as it spun down. The other five crew members were killed.[42] Reid and Luker spent ten months in *Stalag Luft III* Sagan and *Stalag Luft IV* Bellaria.

A 9 Squadron Lancaster crashed at Puisieulx near Rheims with the loss of all the crew.

The Main Force now reverted to tactical targets, assisting the Army against the Wehrmacht, and in operations against the 'V' bomb weapon sites. In consequence, operations, both by day and by night, were carried out against such places as Thiverny, Bois de Cassan near Paris, Forêt de Nieppe, Forêt de Mormal and Hazebrouck. In all, 1,114 aircraft – 601 Lancasters, 492 Halifaxes and 21 Mosquitoes – made bombing attacks on these targets and Trossy-St-Maxim flying bomb stores in northern France on 3 August.

At Kirmington, Sidney Witham, a 22-year-old six foot two flight engineer was on the Pay Parade when the paying officer said 'All operational crew report to briefing immediately'. Witham was born at Old Whittington, Chesterfield on 22 April 1922 and lived with his parents, Ada and Fred Witham, and siblings Ada, Fred, Lillian and Ernest, on Holland Road. After leaving school he had worked as a welder for Sheepbridge Coal and Iron Company. He joined the RAF at Sheffield, trained in Wales and 'crewed up' in the time-honoured tradition:

> The rest of my crew consisted of Hugh 'Wagg' Wagner the pilot, two gunners – 'Lou' and 'Buzz' – a bomb aimer (a little snooty to the rest of us), a Canadian navigator and lastly our wireless operator, Joe Buckler. On 166, I found a mixture of working boys like me and also university graduates, but we all rolled along together. At the briefing we were told we were going to Northern France on a bombing raid, we were to leave at a quarter to two in the afternoon. This was unusual in itself as the Lancaster bombers were night bombers. The raid should have been carried out by the Americans. As usual, the padre gave us two Wakey-Wakey pills to keep us awake and said, 'May you live long and die happy but may you be in heaven ten days before the devil knows you are there. God Bless you.'
>
> When we got to France we manoeuvred our planes into a line to start bombing, I said to 'Wagg', 'Look at this lot up here'. There were

some of our aircraft positioned above us and they should have not been there. Next to us was a 625 Squadron Lancaster flown by Flight Lieutenant Jobson. Our bomb doors were open and the order was given to drop our bombs. The bomber above us dropped his bombs, one knocked our wing and engine off and hit Jobson's aircraft on the middle upper gunner; they flew for another ten minutes and then crash landed in France. Five of the crew survived and they were taken prisoner by the Germans. Back in our aircraft Wagg was in trouble; the control column had jammed and we couldn't move, 'Wagg' was fast in and couldn't get out so I went down to the bomb aimer's compartment and opened the escape hatch. A terrific wind came in and he shouted 'I am free' and came running down the steps. He bailed out and I followed him to the ground. Even with a parachute the ground was coming up pretty fast. We were met in the air by enemy gunshot and the other five crew members unfortunately did not make it.[43]

Down on the ground 'Wagg' was in quite a bad way. His parachute was torn to shreds but I was aware that the Germans would be hot on our heels so I decided to make a run for it. The Germans came along and took him into captivity. It was tough being in a strange country without any supplies; we had landed in a large forest not far from Paris and I walked for four days without water or food. I eventually came out of the forest and saw a teenage girl mowing a field; I whistled to her and got out my phrase book which was issued to soldiers in such an event. After some difficulty, she eventually indicated that she understood and would go and fetch help. Sometime later she returned with two men and two women, they told me to strip off all of my clothes so that I could not be recognized as an English airman. They brought me some old clothes and a pair of old shoes. Being six foot two you can imagine how ridiculous I looked in clothes meant for a much smaller Frenchman, the trousers were almost up to my knees and the shoes crippled my feet. I was taken to a safe house in the forest and was given water to drink. The next day I went to Chantilly to another safe house, I was to follow a teenage girl from one safe house to the other, although at a short distance. She walked in front of me flaunting herself, moving in and out of doorways until we reached our destination which was a bungalow owned by a lovely lady called Yvonne Fournier. Yvonne looked after me very well; I was given food and drink and very relieved to be there. The French Resistance arrived and said they were sending me to Switzerland. Later that same day another bloke came who spoke perfect English, I said 'what tribe do you come from' but all he said was 'you are not going to Switzerland, a guide will take you over the Pyrenees to Spain and a representative will meet you there.'[44]

In all five Lancasters were lost on the operation on Trossy and a Lancaster on 514 Squadron at Waterbeach failed to return from the Bois de Cassan raid. Flying at about 16,000 feet the Lancaster, which was flown by Flying Officer J B Topham, received a direct hit from an anti aircraft shell and the bomb load erupted in a huge pall of dense black smoke centred by bright reddish orange flames. Several minutes later, when the dense black smoke began to disperse and thin out, a vacant space could be observed where the Lancaster had been. Amazingly all eight men – Sergeant F W Dennehy was carried as a mid-under air gunner – managed to bail out safely.[45] Topham and Dennehy evaded and the others were taken into captivity.

A Halifax on 78 Squadron that returned was damaged beyond repair.

Flying bomb sites were attacked again on 4 August and the next day. On the 4th oil storage depots too were hit and 27 Lancasters, two Mosquitoes and a Mustang of 617 Squadron attacked a railway bridge at Etaples. Some hits were scored but the 1,000lb bombs failed to destroy the bridge.

At bomber bases the pace was relentless. Sergeant Malcolm Crapper aged 19 from Sheffield, flight engineer on Flight Lieutenant 'Stan' Scutt's Lancaster crew on 57 Squadron, recalls:

The summer of 1944 was a very busy time at East Kirkby. We were doing flying training, attending briefings, flying ops – and sleeping. In the week between 18 July (our first op.) and 25 July, when we went on leave, we did five ops and two training flights. In the ten days after our leave, we flew eight ops and two training flights. The weather was pretty good and I don't recall any delays or postponements.

I really wanted to join the air force. On my way home from Sunday school (almost 18 years old and still going to Sunday school I ask you!) we saw 617 [Squadron] Lancs low flying over the Derwent Dam. We didn't know what they were up to. No-one did; not until after the Dams raid that is. Anyway, those big, dark aeroplanes and their noise really got to me. I knew then what I wanted to do.

The others on the crew were around the same age although 'Stan' Scutt was 30-years old and had previously served as a flying instructor. Scutt hailed from Chichester. The navigator was Flying Officer Arthur Stienstra from Canada, aged 21. The bomb aimer, Flying Officer R E Trindall from Yorkshire, was aged 25. The wireless operator, Pilot Officer Jack Farnhill, from Lancashire, was aged 23. Flight Sergeant J Shields the 24-year-old mid-upper gunner was from Australia. Sergeant Clifford Alfred Harris the 21-year-old rear gunner was from Essex.

'On returning from leave on 6 August we discovered that the pace hadn't relented' continues Malcolm. 'The Lanc we flew our first op in,

DX-F PD212, had gone missing and we took Lancaster LM582, DX-B for a daylight raid on a V-1 storage site at Bois de Cassan, just outside Paris.'

Shortly before noon on 6 August every German fighter unit in the Paris area, including 26 Third *Gruppe* Bf 109s of JG 26, was scrambled to intercept a formation of heavy bombers. Word was that these were American and they were reported to have little or no escort. In fact over 220 aircraft that set out to attack the flying bomb supply sites at Bois de Cassan and Fôret de Nieppe once more were RAF Halifaxes and Lancasters. Bombing was scattered and was no more successful at Hazebrouck where just over 60 aircraft, mostly Halifaxes, attempted to bomb the railway centre. Four Lancasters failed to return from the operation on Bois de Cassan, which proved eventful for 'Stan' Scutt's crew, as Malcolm Crapper recalled:

> We were caught by two Bf 109s whilst on our bomb run – the worst possible time – not that any time was a good time to be in a British bomber in daylight, bounced by a couple of Jerries. The Skipper ordered me to the front turret as the bomb aimer was prone working his bombsight. I can't remember if I fired a few rounds in anger or not. It happened so quickly. As soon as it started, the attack seemed to finish and I slid out of the nose turret, avoided trampling our bomb aimer and made my way back to the Skipper's right hand. After a few seconds, he caught my eye and tilted his head at the port wing. I knew that the Lanc's wings flexed in flight – I had seen it so often that I no longer noticed – but this was different. The movement was not only more obvious, but far more pronounced than I had ever seen. I drew breath to speak, at which point the Skipper held up his forefinger to his pursed lips in a semi-theatrical 'Shhh!' mime. I got the message and remained silent. The trip home was largely uneventful and we landed OK.

The Commanding Officer of 57 Squadron, Wing Commander Humphries, was also attacked by a pair of Bf 109s. He and his crew survived, Humphries being awarded an immediate DFC for his actions.

One Halifax and its crew on 51 Squadron at Snaith were lost on the raid on Hazebrouck. I/JG1 arrived at the bomber stream first, but were driven off by a single squadron of Spitfires. III/JG26 and III/JG54 next hit separate parts of the formation and used up all their ammunition on the bombers without seeing an Allied fighter. III/JG1 was last on the scene and were prevented from making a decisive attack on the cripples by the Spitfires of 332 (Norwegian) Squadron, which shot down the two 109s providing high cover for the Gruppe and then dived on the main German formation, dispersing it. Third *Gruppe* pilots claimed four Halifaxes and three Lancasters. *Unteroffizier* Heinz Gehrke's element leader, *Feldwebel* Karl Laub, picked out a straggling and damaged Lancaster at 10,000 feet. The tail gunner was slumped over, dead in his wrecked turret and Gehrke and Laub were able to attack from the rear, entirely unmolested. The bomber crew could only retaliate by throwing out bundles of *Window* but Gehrke hit the left outboard engine and the Lancaster dived away, smoking. As the bomber had previously been damaged, Gehrke was not awarded a full victory credit, but rather one for a 'final destruction' but it was added to his victory total. His story matches that of the surviving crew of a 207 Squadron aircraft in most details; this Lancaster was one which reached England and was then scrapped.[46]

That evening a dozen Lancasters and three Mosquitoes of 617 Squadron and 16 Lancasters of 106 Squadron, escorted by 17 Spitfires, set out to bomb the *U-boat* pens at Lorient, which was due to be attacked by the US 4th Armored Division the next day. Heavy flak hit four of 617's Lancasters and several of 106 Squadron but there were no losses. Three 'Tallboys' hit the roofs of the pens without penetrating them. The bombs dropped by 106 Squadron, which were timed to explode between 6 to 36 hours after the attack appeared to have fallen east of the pens. Despite being surrounded by the Americans the German defenders in Lorient refused to capitulate and they only finally surrendered shortly after VE Day.[47]

Next day at dispersal at East Kirkby 'Stan' Scutt's crew were told a cannon shell had hit the spar between No. 1 and No. 2 fuel tanks. Malcolm Crapper recalls:

> Fortunately the spar had not failed. Equally fortunate was the fact that neither tank had received the shell. However, further investigation revealed an even less welcome surprise in the form of an unexploded 20mm cannon shell embedded in the main spar. Had that one exploded … The only time, as far as I remember, that I visited any of the hangars in my time at EK, was to see the unexploded shell in the main spar. All routine servicing took place on the dispersals, regardless of the weather. And, of course, I only saw the summer cycle. How they [ground crew] coped in the ice and snow and screaming winds coming in from the North Sea is beyond me. We were grateful that the Americans had significantly reduced the effectiveness and expertise of the Luftwaffe fighters. I am quite sure more experienced pilots would not have let us off.

An hour before midnight on 7 August, 1,019 heavy bombers set out to blast the Normandy battle area again. Five aiming points on German defences protecting the approaches to Falaise were marked for air bombardment, which was joined by 720 artillery pieces delivering high explosive and flares. The targets were in front of Allied ground troops 16 miles from Falaise so bombing was carefully controlled and only 660 aircraft bombed before 600 Canadian tanks attacked, followed by infantry in armoured personnel carriers. By dawn of 8 August the Canadians had penetrated the German defences for three miles. Ten heavies were victims of *Nachtjäger* and one to flak. *Oberleutnant* Heinz Rökker claimed three Lancasters north-east of Le Havre for his 39–41st victories.

The night following, 170 Lancasters and ten Mosquitoes of 1, 3 and 8 Groups attacked oil depots and storage facilities at Aire-sur-Lys and the Fôret de Lucheux in France for one Lancaster lost. On 9 August, 12 Lancasters of 617 Squadron and 17 Lancasters of 9 Squadron escorted by a dozen Mustangs and 44 Spitfires bombed the *U-boat* pens at La Pallice. Six 'Tallboys' hit the 20 feet thick pen roof, one blasting a crater 5 feet deep and another penetrating one of the pens to 9 feet before exploding. Damage was not decisive and 617 returned to La Pallice on Friday 11 August with 2,000lb armour-piercing bombs because of the shortage of 'Tallboys'.

Next morning 10 Lancasters of 617 Squadron led by Willy Tait and 68 Lancasters of 1 Group were dispatched to bomb the *U-boat* pens at Brest. Tait's 'Tallboy' hit close to the centre of the pens and all others were on target except for one which fell about 100 yards from the front of the pens. The tidal wave sank a tanker and damaged a *U-boat* while a second tanker capsized and blocked the harbour. Later the same day 117 bombers attacked fuel dumps in the Fôret de Montrichard and blasted U-boat pens at La Pallice and Bordeaux. Eight Mosquitoes of 100 Group provided a fighter escort for the bombers attacking the French Atlantic coast and no bombers were lost during the day's operations. Lancasters of 617 and 9 Squadrons and others carried out further attacks on the *U-boat* pens at Brest, La Pallice and Ijmuiden during August.[48]

Squadrons in 1, 3, 4 and 8 Groups meanwhile, attacked three railway yards and a bridge on the 11th and that night 179 Lancasters and ten Mosquitoes of 1 and 8 Groups attacked the railway yards at Givors near Lyons again. Jack Stephens on 463 Squadron RAAF wrote in his diary:

> The weather was excellent this time. Another dusk to dawn trip. Very quiet trip, no fighters, the only flak was from the Channel Isles which were a long way off. There were bags of our rockets around which looked like shooting stars, but none came near us. We were over the Allied beach head as far as the River Loire. Had an excellent view of the target, bright red fires, bomb bursts and runs of explosions, also green TIs. No aircraft were lost.

Jack Stephens' next raid was on Saturday 12 August when a force of 297 attacked the Opel factory at Rüsselsheim, just south west of Frankfurt-am-Main, which was believed to be contributing to V-1 production:

> A 2,000lb and J type clusters. Went out over East Anglia and in through Belgium, dog legging (zigzagging) to the target where we

were amongst the first and highest and the way to be. Attacked red and green TIs on the Opel factory which was making flying bombs and pranged it pretty well. Plenty of fighters all around, combats, kites going down and scarecrows (combination incendiaries fired from the ground to simulate burning RAF aircraft and to lower morale) all the way. Plenty of search lights around the target but I didn't see anything. Bombed at 19,750 feet at 00.16B. West winds. Only two fighters came anywhere near us (Messerschmidts [sic] probably) but we didn't have time to finish a corkscrew before they went away. Otherwise we were untouched. Got back about 3 am. 5½ hours. 9,000lb of bombs, 18,000 gals of fuel.

Most of the bombs fell in the surrounding countryside. Thirteen Lancasters and seven Halifaxes failed to return, *Nachtjagd* claiming all of these. *Schwerterträger Hauptmann* Heinz-Wolfgang Schnaufer, *Kommandeur* IV./ NJG1 was credited with the destruction of four Lancasters, which took his score to 93 victories that night.

Altogether on 12/13 August, Bomber Command mounted 1,167 sorties, 297 of them on Rüsselsheim. Another force of 379 bombers attacked Brunswick and 144 aircraft attacked German troop concentrations at Falaise. Forty Halifaxes and 12 Mosquitoes bombed two flying-bomb sites and a storage depot in France. Brunswick, flanked 30 miles to the east by Hannover, 120 miles to the west by Berlin, with Magdeburg almost half-way between was 'an area' wrote James Campbell 'ringed by heavy-calibre guns and fast-winged night fighters'. This was an experimental raid. No Pathfinder aircraft took part and there was no marking. The intention was to discover how successfully a force of aircraft could carry out a raid with each crew bombing on the indications of its own H_2S set.[49] The bombers, crews had been told at briefing, would fly past Brunswick, then wheel in a slow deliberate formation and start the time run from east of the city: On the approach, the bomb-aimers would pick up on the H_2S the huge factory owned, according to Intelligence, by *Reichmarschall* Herman Goering. From the factory, they would begin the bomb run on Brunswick.

As James Campbell's pilot turned the Halifax on to the approach heading, the navigator checked the Air Speed, Height and Course on his duplicate panel and pulled out his stop-watch. Campbell wrote:

An extra length of cable had been attached to the bomb-tit' to cover the stretch from the nose to the bomb-aimer's position beside the H_2S set. The bomb aimer eased himself round from the Mark 14 bomb-sight head, knelt down beside the bombing computer box and checked that the pre-flight settings had been correctly fed in. He set on a new wind-speed and a new wind direction which the navigator had given him a few minutes earlier. He switched on the Bombing

Master Switch, selected and fused the bombs. Then he set the 'Mickey Mouse'; a device for automatically releasing the cans of incendiaries carried in the wings with correct time lag. The bomb aimer rose and gazed speculatively through the perspex of the nose. What he saw sent his limbs jerking convulsively. Brunswick's concerto of murderous fire hosed through the cloud layer below to leave a closely interwoven pattern of grimy pock marks in the clear sky ahead-a sky brilliantly illuminated in the bursting camera flares and exploding shells. The frantic, feverish race by the German ground-gunners to fill the aerial box ahead of the bombers and keep it filled with HE was on. And he knew they must fly through that box barrage. No point in weaving, even if they could take evasive action. More than likely they would corkscrew into a burst. Pure luck from now on. Skill didn't come into it any more. A faulty fuse setting by a German gunner could be just as effective as a carefully predicted shell. Christ, how he hated the run in on a target with the bomb doors wide open, revealing the unprotected bomb-racks.

'Herman coming up ... Left! Left! ... Steady! ... Right! ... Steady now! Steady!' His tone was sharp, imperative ... 'Hold it!' The tiny blob of light was creeping up the dimmed screen. 'Bomb doors open! Marker coming up!' 'On Marker!' he corrected. He stabbed the button of his stop-watch and began to count: 'Nine-eight-seven-six-five ...' The seconds seemed long, desperately drawn-out hours. God, this was worse than straight, visual bombing. And for what? Probably their load would only make craters in some farmer's field. They could see nothing. The set was their eyes, impartial, remote and unfeeling. '... Four-three-two-one.' The bomb aimer's voice was toneless. He saw the longer, jagged blip that was the city beneath them crawl over the bearing ring and the bone in his right thumb gleamed white, then pink. The Halifax reared and her lethal load spewed earthwards. The bomb aimer slipped through the black-out curtain and shoved the jettison bars over. Through the perspex nose his mind photographed a fragment of the night sky – a night splashed and sprayed with the bright marigold flashes of heavy AA shells. Pieces of spent shrapnel tip-tapped along the black belly of the bomber like skeletons dancing jerkily on an empty oil drum. Always the sound made him shudder. A dull red glow was spreading in a great infectious rash through the white vapour beneath them. Brunswick was burning.[50]

The raid on Brunswick was not successful and there was no concentration of bombing, with bombs falling in the central and Stadpark areas while other towns up to 20 miles away were bombed by mistake. The German defences destroyed 17 Lancasters and 10 Halifaxes.

On Monday 14 August, over 800 aircraft – 411 Lancasters, 352 Halifaxes and 42 Mosquitoes – attacked German troop positions facing the 3rd Canadian Division, which was advancing on Falaise. A careful plan was prepared with *Oboe* and visual marking and with a Master Bomber and a deputy at each of seven targets. Jack Stephens wrote:

> Daylight on Falaise bottleneck. Target was German troop concentrations at Quesnay on the Caen-Falaise Road. Flew in loose formation at 7,000 feet out over Brighton. There was very little cloud and bright sunshine. The Channel was full of all kinds of boats and convoys with balloons up and the beaches were just masses and masses of ships unloading. Also plenty of patrol boats. The whole trip there were hordes of Lancs with and passing the other way in a continuous stream. By the time we bombed, about midday, there was one great cloud of dust and smoke about 3,000 feet high and stretching for miles. Target was 2,000 yards in front of the Canadian troops who were waiting to advance to close up the gap and encircle a large proportion of the German army when we finished. I saw the whole attack. It was fairly open country with neat orchards and woods (one of which was our target). On the way back we saw the beaches again and the east side of the Cherbourg Peninsular. Also stooged around Oxford a bit. (Other groups got some of our own troops and a conference of high officers.)'

Most of the bombing was accurate and effective but about half-way through the raids some aircraft started to bomb a quarry in which parts of the 12th Canadian Field Regiment were positioned. This error may have been caused by the yellow identification flares which were ignited by the Canadians. It was unfortunate that the target indicators being used by the Pathfinders were also yellow. Bomber crews claimed that the Canadians used the yellow flares before any bombs fell in the quarry; the Canadians said that the bombs fell first. The Master Bombers tried in vain to prevent further bombing in the wrong area but about 70 aircraft bombed the quarry and other Allied positions nearby over a 70-minute period. Thirteen Canadians were killed and 53 were injured and a large number of vehicles and guns were hit.[51] Two Lancasters were lost.

Another 155 Lancasters and four Mosquitoes of 5 Group made two separate attacks on the harbour at Brest. Since Cherbourg remained the only major port in American possession the harbour facilities were needed so that supplies and reinforcements for the land battle could be unloaded from ships sailing directly from the US. Brest itself was defended by about 38,000 German troops. The bombers hit the *Clémenceau* and the cruiser *Gueydon* and left them slowly sinking. Two Lancasters were shot down by flak and a 9 Squadron Lancaster piloted by Bill Scott was hit. A piece of shrapnel fatally struck Sergeant Henry John Tollast, the 18-year-old wireless operator from Thames Ditton. Jim Brookbank the bomb aimer had teamed up with him at OTU at Bruntingthorpe in Leicestershire four months' earlier. 'He was young, flamboyant and extrovert combined with a brash self-assurance, which he wore as a cloak to conceal the uncertainty of his adolescence.' Brookbank wrote a poem, 'Johnny Comes Marching Home', in his memory.

When the Germans in Brest capitulated on 18 September the Americans found that everything had been totally destroyed by the pounding from land, sea and air, and the Germans had wrecked anything remotely useful. Not until November when Antwerp was finally opened to sea transport would the Allies solve their problem of having enough ports of entry into the Continent.

In August, mass raids on targets in the Normandy battle area and further afield continued. On Tuesday the 15th, 1,004 aircraft attacked night fighter airfields in Holland and Belgium in preparation for a renewed night offensive against Germany. A force of 110 Lancasters and four Mosquitoes heavily cratered Volkel and put both runways out of action. Jack Stephens on 463 Squadron RAAF, whose Lancaster was among those who were detailed to bomb Gilze Rijin airfield in Holland, wrote:

> We went in, in loose formation, over Rotterdam. The only opposition was moderate to heavy flak, some of which was pretty close. One piece came in through the starboard side of the fuselage, just behind Taffy. No Jerry fighters were up. Not in one piece anyway. About four bomb loads dropped within 50 yards of us on the bombing run. There were $10 \times 1,000$lb + 6×500 GPG and we all planted them square on the runways. The bombing was, if anything, too concentrated. Saw plenty of reclaimed land, great low lying flats, green fields, dykes etc, flak and bombs jettisoned. A squadron of Fortresses (aircraft of the US Army Air Corps) a couple of miles away were in perfect formation in striking contrast to the gaggles and straggles (loose formation) of Lancs but there were so many of us that it was one big mass. The visibility was perfect: at least 60 miles from 15,000 feet with negligible cloud and you could see France, Holland, Belgium and England all at once at one stage.[52]

On Wednesday 16 August the RAF bomber airfield at East Kirkby in East Lincolnshire received the usual morning notification by teleprinter that 57 and 630 Squadrons would be operating that night. By the time Sergeant Malcolm Crapper joined 57 Squadron, the practice of specialist briefings was in place. All operating and stand-by flight engineers would be briefed before an op by Flight Lieutenant Blanchard, 57 Squadron Engineer Leader. Bomb aimers, navigators, wireless ops and gunners all had their own specialist briefings by their respective leaders, as did pilots. Final briefings included all crewmembers scheduled to operate or be on stand-by. Stettin would be the target for sixteen crews at East Kirkby, but another six crews would sow mines off the port of Swinemunde. Blanchard recalls that the abnormally low dropping altitude (300 feet) caused considerable concern amongst the crews obliged to operate at that height. All 89 aircrews mining off Swinemünde in the Baltic and Kiel Bay (four more would plant them in the River Gironde) came from 5 Group. Low flying over water at night in virtually no moonlight – the new moon was only two days off – was a potentially hazardous operation. Light coastal and ship-mounted flak and roaming night fighters could surprise and inflict terrible punishment on the minelayers. Blanchard wrote: 'Our Station Commander was present at the briefing. I shall always remember him standing there, chipping in with "there will be ships there, big ships – and flak." Not exactly confidence building!' The port of Stettin was to be bombed by 461 Lancasters from high level at approximately the same time as the mining was to take place. Another 348 aircraft were detailed for a heavy raid on Kiel.

Desmond Evans was part of the ground crew which looked after Lancasters on 97 Squadron at Coningsby:

There was a very close relationship between aircrews and the ground crews who serviced their aircraft. During my time on 97 Squadron I lost three aircrews and each time it was devastating. The loneliness of waiting for your particular Lanc to return was awful and when yours didn't return on time there was that awful half an hour to an hour wait until you knew their fuel reserves would have run out and there was no chance they were coming back. Later of course someone would come to your dispersal where the aircraft would be normally parked and tell you, 'Sorry lads – they've had it.' Our dispersal point would be empty for a few days and we would probably help out on another aircraft until our replacement Lancaster would arrive. We would then check the engines and probably later in the day a new aircrew would arrive. In most cases very young and very raw with no operational experience. We would get introduced to the pilot and crew and the whole sequence would start over again. You would look at them, mostly no older than 22 years of age, and wonder how long they would be with us.

An operational unit was unique in the closeness between ranks. My particular Skipper was Wing Commander Porter and he and his crew were all officers and yet this lovely man and his crew would take my pal and me, just ordinary LACs, out with them for drinks to the local pubs as though we were their buddies. Porter was the Leader of the first Berlin raids [he had commanded 9 Squadron throughout the Battle of Berlin] and was decorated with the DFC and Bar. We all went on leave at the beginning of August. The Wing

Commander came back two days early from his. One pilot due to fly on ops was taken ill, so Porter said he would fly in his place.

Before they left for the Swinemünde Canal the 97 Squadron crews had long consultations with Wing Commander Guy Gibson, drawing on his experience gained while dam-busting. Gibson had recommended that the three marking aircraft make one low-level run down the canal before turning to drop their flame-float markers. Noel 'Ed' Parker, an Australian pilot who was near the end of his second tour, was Master Bomber with a scratch crew. He would mark the middle of the canal, Wing Commander Edward Leach Porter DFC* the south end and Squadron Leader Harry Locke DFC, another Australian, the north.

At East Kirkby after final briefing Flight Lieutenant 'Stan' Scutt's crew wanted to get to their dispersal as quickly as possible to go through the pre-flight checks. Malcolm Crapper recalls:

Stan Scutt was an extremely conscientious pilot who insisted on strict intercom discipline. We had great faith in him and he was very much the gentleman. We took pride in the fact that we were a daylight formation leader. There was no obvious apprehension amongst the crew because this would be our thirteenth op. Like virtually every wartime crew, we were superstitious, but there was a strong feeling that 'it couldn't happen to us'.

At Chedburgh, 21-year-old John Field, formerly a trainee groundsman for a famous London football club, was one of the Lancaster pilots on 218 Squadron who was 'on' that night. His crew (he was the only officer) – six NCOs all older than himself – was the usual mixed bag. The navigator was formerly a captain in the Salvation Army in Glasgow, the bomb aimer had been a blacksmith at a coal mine, the Aussie W/Op had sold insurance in Sydney, the mid-upper gunner, as Welsh as a leek, had formerly working for a camera company in Cheltenham. The rear gunner was born in Canada but had returned to old England just before the war. The flight engineer was formerly a baker in a village near Cambridge. This was their 14th trip.

When the curtains covering the end wall of the Briefing Room were drawn back, showing maps covering Britain and most of Western Europe, there was a sharp intake of breath and a general murmuring from the assembled crews who were 'On' for this particular operation. The red tapes showing the route into and return from the target were marked quite clearly by a label at their Eastern point 'Stettin'!

'All right, settle down, you've been there before,' said the Squadron Commander. 'It's a long haul, but at least you don't have to overfly the Ruhr.'

'True' Field thought. 'We do have a daylight take-off – what a mad business night flying was. Even the birds don't fly at night!'

The Squadron Commanding Officer got into his usual stride, telling what and what not to expect, the recognition signals to use, codes, colours of the various navigation marker beacons and areas to watch out for and then the parade of the various section leaders began. Lastly the 'Met Man' forecast good weather! Whatever they said this was NOT going to be a 'picnic' even though they were routed over North Holland and Denmark. Field told his crew that he would be first in the queue for the toilet after this briefing. He thought and felt panic. It always crossed your mind that this could be your last briefing. OK once you got started, but the hanging around waiting for it all to happen.

Bernard Aves was equally philosophical 'Once your name was on the Battle Order you just went; no picking or choosing, you accepted that it was your duty and hoped you would come back safely.' He had survived many ops on Stirlings before flying his first op on Lancs, a short 3 hour ten minute sortie on 17 July to Mont Candon. 'No ops were carried out by Stirlings into Germany after mid-1943 as it was found that losses were very high and Lancasters were coming into their own. It really could not be said to have been enjoyable (can anything be enjoyable in a war?) but it was an interesting experience with not too much stress involved.'

'Stan' Scutt's crew made their way to the dispersal where Lancaster III PB384 *F-Fox* awaited them. This was an almost brand new aircraft, the previous DX-F [PD212] having been lost whilst the Scutt crew was on leave. PD212's flying career had totalled just 58 hours, and it was in that aircraft that they had flown their first operation. With ground checks completed, the aircraft fuelled, the six Mk 14 sea mines loaded in the capacious 33 feet-long bomb bay, guns armed and crew provisions stored; the pre-flight checks proceeded; engines could be started to check oil pressures, engine temperatures, compressors, hydraulic systems, generators and magnetos. At 21:17 *F-Fox* took off and headed east over the famous Clock Tower at Skegness. Malcolm Crapper recalled the low level flight across the North Sea:

> It was a dank and misty evening. Not at all pleasant. We kept hitting the slipstreams of aircraft in front of us, but never actually saw one. There were short moments when it was possible to relax amid the noise and vibration of a heavily loaded bomber, after it had clawed its way upward. Comfortable that engine and oil temperatures were OK and all pressures were right. Check the fuel tanks ... fine. A crackle on the headphones and the all too brief overture of an intake of breath preceded 'Enemy Coast ahead!' Aaah! The eternal bomb aimer's cliché! Very soon, we knew, lay The Baltic.

Jack Stephens, *en route* to Stettin, wrote:

> Out over the North Sea at 2,000 feet, climbing the other side to 21,000
> feet over Denmark and down over the Baltic to the target, which we
> bombed with 1,000lbs. Half the force used J type incendiaries. A
> good prang; lit up the cloud for miles. Very little flak, but a few AI
> fighters (aircraft interceptors) with red lights in their noses. Only
> one bothered us, but they didn't stay. A pretty quiet trip all around.
> Landed at dawn. 8 hours.

Bernard Aves recalls:

> Stettin was about ten hours and we began to appreciate how nice it
> had been on Stirlings. It was all nice and quiet across the North Sea
> but Sweden didn't seem to like us going across their country and
> gave us all they had and quite a bit more. We were only at 10,000 feet
> so shelling was fairly accurate. Talk about 'All this and heaven too' –
> well it nearly was! Once we had escaped from Sweden things were
> fairly quiet; the odd bit of flak now and again but over the target
> there was nothing – did we get to the right place? Anyway we
> dropped our bombs and came home.[53]

At Stettin much damage was meted out to the port and industrial areas
with 29 factories destroyed and over 1,500 houses destroyed and another
1,000 homes damaged. Around 1,500 bodies were recovered from the
ruins and over 1,600 people were injured. Five ships were sunk at their
moorings and eight other vessels were seriously damaged. Two of the
four Lancasters lost went down in the Baltic and a fifth Lanc crashed in
Sweden, killing the pilot. The rest of the crew were interned. John Field's
crew aborted after the port outer engine lost power half-way to the
target. The flight engineer had then feathered both the port outer and
the port inner by mistake. As soon as they were clear of the Danish coast
they jettisoned the bomb load in the North Sea and they returned safely
to Chedburgh.

The raid on Kiel was only partially successful. Four Halifax aircraft
and two Lancasters were lost on Kiel docks, another Halifax crew ditched
off Scarborough and a sixth crashed in England. Three Halifaxes mine-
laying in Kiel Bay also failed to return.

The mining force had climbed to altitude before crossing the Danish
coast with the Main Force at 20,000 feet. Malcolm Crapper describes the
next phase of the operation:

> We descended to 200 feet over the Baltic and northern Germany. We
> circled an inland lake that at our briefing was identified as our hold-
> ing point whilst the mining area was marked by Pathfinder Lancs of

97 Squadron using flame floats. Light flak was encountered, but we were not hit. Our gunners fired back although they almost certainly knew they weren't going to do much harm but maybe make a few heads duck. Wing Commander Porter, the Master Bomber on 97 Squadron who was coned by searchlights over the canal, called up Squadron Leader Parkes, one of the deputies, on the VHF that he had been hit by flak and that his aircraft was on fire. I clearly remember Porter saying 'I'm afraid we have had it. I shall have to leave you now. Bailing out; Good luck everybody.' And with that, they were gone. You don't easily forget something like that.

The demise of the Master Bomber was witnessed by Flight Lieutenant Blanchard:

One could see the light and medium flak firing at the marking force. Suddenly the Master Bomber was hit. A minute later, a W/T message was received from the wing commander's aircraft for the main force to go in and drop their mines over the flame floats. I think he went in to the hills east of the channel.

It is believed that his crew had every chance to bail out successfully but they were too low for parachutes and all eight men died.

Squadron Leader Harry Locke's Lancaster, with four other Australians in the crew, was first to place a precision marker at the northern entrance to the channel then drop mines as far north in the channel as possible. Locke's aircraft lost *Gee* on the outward run but approached the canal dead on time at 300 feet on his preliminary run to find the five flak ships moored by the side of the channel already hosing up fire. The bay was ringed by the horizontal beams of searchlights but Locke put both markers and mines in exactly the allotted area on their second run. Their flame floats had just fallen away when they were engaged by a flak ship mounting cannon, machine guns and searchlights and they plunged towards the water. 'Pull out' yelled the wireless operator, Tony Boultbee, as he glanced from his window to see the water rushing up at them. Locke climbed away and turned for home. By then both gun turrets and all the hydraulic system of the aircraft were useless and there was a bad petrol leak, but through superb calculations by Squadron Leader H Makepeace the navigator, Locke found a gap in the coast and by crossing Denmark at 6,000 feet and dropping down to fly below trees was able to dodge the searchlights and successive defensive positions. Despite the leaking hydraulic fluid swamping the H_2S and the lack of almost all navigational aids, dead reckoning by the navigator brought the Lancaster back to England where Locke belly-landed at Coningsby and the crew all walked away.[54]

Blanchard's Lancaster was called in to bomb by one of the deputies. 'The Skipper held the a/c steady for the drop and all six mines went away. The bomb doors were closed and we increased revs and prepared to climb to miss the high ground at Swinemünde. At that moment another aircraft was on fire and going in – right in front of us.' That aircraft was Stan Scutt's.

Malcolm Crapper recalls:

One of the deputies called us in and we started our mining run. The light flak intensified and appeared to be coming from all angles. As we flew straight and level at 300 feet we took hits. It turned out we were hit very badly by light flak from dead ahead. Stan Scutt called for a bail out as he tried to climb from our 300 feet mining altitude. We knew that the aircraft was fatally damaged and we were already on our way out. Our bomb aimer kicked out the hatch under the nose and went through; I followed him. The aircraft was not even at 500 feet altitude. In those short few seconds since the kite was first hit, she was burning quite fiercely. Without hesitation I yanked the ripcord. Despite my fear, I still had the presence of mind to recognise that counting to ten before pulling the handle was not a good idea. It seemed that I fell out of the burning Lanc and into the sea in one movement. One crystal clear memory of those few fleeting seconds was seeing the reflection of our Lanc's flames in the sea below as I jumped. Our aircraft evacuation training must have been pretty good. On hitting the water I hit my parachute release button to avoid being dragged under by the rapidly saturating canopy. Only then did I recall that swimming was not one of my strong points.

Not content with sweeping the water with searchlights, the Germans started machine-gunning what they thought were aircrew struggling in the water. Every time a searchlight swung my way I tried to duck under the water. Whether my four crew mates who lost their lives died when the plane hit the water or were shot struggling in the sea, I don't know. Somehow I made the shore. It was then that I realised I had lost one of my baggy flying boots. It was the one in which I stowed my revolver. My other boot, in which was secreted the 0.38 ammunition, was still there. What use were bullets without a bloody gun? Bugger! Edging up the shore I came to a sign planted in the sand. It was too dark to read and anyway it would be in German. I guessed, bearing in mind the nature of the English coast since 1939, that it would almost certainly read *ACHTUNG! MINEN!* On this premise I agreed that discretion was indeed the better part of valour.

Moving back a few yards towards the sea, I found a shallow depression in the sand that would shelter me from the sea breeze and I tried to get some rest, preferably sleep. I must have dropped off. When I woke daylight was breaking and the sign, which had troubled me a few hours earlier, now taunted me. It read *'Baden'* (Bathing) and underneath hung a vivid red and white lifebuoy! 'Idiot!' I thought.

Unknown to Malcolm at this time, Flying Officer R E Trindall, the bomb aimer, who bailed out immediately in front of Malcolm, landed close to Flight Sergeant J Shields the mid-upper gunner who somehow had struggled free from his turret and leapt from the fuselage door. He broke his pelvis on hitting a tree on his way down and medical treatment became an absolute priority. Stan Scutt and Cliff Harris, Jack Farnhill and Arthur Stienstra had been killed.

Malcolm Crapper now made his way inland into nearby woodland, struggling through the undergrowth for what seemed an age. Eventually he emerged into a clearing that opened up in front of him. Relief turned to shock and alarm:

Oh Christ! There was a light flak battery at the opposite edge of the clearing. Had they seen me? Do I turn and run? What do I do? What? I didn't want to risk a bullet in my back if I turned and legged it, so I raised my hands. The buggers had not seen me! But by then it was too late. Some young squaddies ran over to me and roughed me up a bit. An older Sergeant appeared from nowhere and barked an order. From the tone of his voice, I guessed the NCO was giving the youngsters (they were probably only 17 or 18 years old) a right royal bollocking. I was helped to my feet, taken to the flak battery and basic interrogation took place.

'Your name?'
'Crapper.'
'Initials?'
'M.'
'Rank?'
'Sergeant.'
'Serial number?'
'1591526.'

None of the phoney Red Cross forms and whatnot we had been repeatedly warned about. Coffee and bread were offered. The coffee, or whatever it was, tasted awful but it was hot. The bread, black bread, was inedible but I took it and saved it for later. Later I was put in the sergeant's bed. It had blue and white gingham sheets. Now that detail I have absolutely no doubt about whatsoever. We were supposed to be winning the war and the Germans were supposed to be suffering unbelievable privations. So how come this was the first

time in months – no, the first time in years – that I had enjoyed sleep
in 'proper' bedclothes?

Even in the drama that had unfolded at Swinemünde, moments of
humour emerged. Blanchard's Lancaster mined at the prescribed 300 feet
but 30° of flap proved necessary to provide extra lift at the relatively low
mine-dropping airspeed. On the return journey over Denmark at around
12,000 feet, the pilot remarked about the aircraft's sluggishness and
poor airspeed. Only then did the penny drop that they had struggled
westward across the Baltic, still with 30° of flap on!

At Coningsby LAC Evans was distraught:

It is hard to describe how you feel about the loss of a whole crew.
One minute you are chatting and having a smoke before they take
off and four or five hours later, they have gone – just a memory.
They took off at 21.40 and at 01.33 a radio message came in: 'We
are hit – burning, burning abandoning ...' That was all they had
time to transmit. One [Sergeant Terence Michael Twomey DFM the
rear gunner] is buried on the Island of Bornholm [in Pederskirke
churchyard]; four including Wing Commander Porter are buried at
Poznan Polish War Cemetery – three were never found. Anyone
who says they were full of fun before they went on a raid and that
they hadn't a care in the world, are fools. These young men knew
exactly what lay before them; they were tensed up and nervous and
that's what made them brave – they still went and did what they had
.to do.

Notes

1. *The Dam Busters* by Paul Brickhill. On 4/5 June, 259 aircraft of all groups
bombed four of the gun batteries, three of which were deception targets in the
Pas de Calais. But the fourth battery at Maissy, which was covered by cloud
and could only be marked by *Oboe* sky-markers before being bombed by
52 Lancasters of 5 Group, was in Normandy between what would soon be
known as *Omaha* and *Utah* beaches.
2. At 19.30 hours on 6 June a message was received from the AOC HQ 3 Group:
'I have received the following message from C-in-C for aircrews – begins – you
did famously last night in the face of no mean difficulties, fire from the coastal
batteries, which were your targets, have been reported virtually negligible.' A
further message from C-in-C Bomber Command to OC 218 Squadron. 'It is
already established that the operations on which you were engaged on the
night 5/6th June were very successful and it may well be that when the full
facts are known it will be found that you achieved results of even greater
importance than can be known at present. This can only have been brought
about by intensive training and attention to details, as a result of which crews
concerned, acquitted themselves admirably. The Naval Commanders have

expressed their great appreciation of the support of 218 and 617 Squadrons and it is now disclosed that this and the patrol carried out by 101 and 214 Squadrons succeeded together in delaying the enemy's appreciation as to the actual point of the assault thereby assisting the measure of tactical surprise gained for our main assault forces.'

3. 218 Gold Coast Squadron Newsletter No. 57 January 2010. The two Stirlings with nine man crews were on 149 Squadron at Methwold on *D-Day* Support. One complete crew was lost without trace and only three survived on the other aircraft.

4. 110 aircraft of 100 Group carried out extensive bomber-support operations. 24 *ABC*-equipped Lancasters on 101 Squadron patrolled all known night fighter approaches. Two Intruders were lost and 1 *ABC* Lancaster ditched off Beachy Head. 58 aircraft of 3 and 5 Groups flew diversion operations.

5. An outstanding operational captain, Owen was a squadron leader by 1944 and he ended the war as a Master Bomber with a string of decorations. See Hastings.

6. *Remembering D-Day; Personal Histories of Everyday Heroes* by Martin W Bowman (Harper Collins 2004).

7. See *Point Blank and Beyond* by Lionel Lacey-Johnson (Airlife Classic 1991).

8. *Panzer* units moving by rail to Normandy used the main line Toulouse–Limoges–Chateauroux–Tours. Up to 14 June a single track bridge at Port-Boulet near Saumur was used to traverse the Loire but on its destruction the division had to use the only other bridge available, that at Tours-la-Riche. To do so the railway waggons had to be pushed over it one by one, for the bridge had been too heavily damaged to support the weight of a locomotive. The last elements of the division had not arrived in or near the lodgement area until 23 June, having taken 17 days to travel about 450 miles. Had no air assault been made, the movement would have taken about five days. *The Fight Is Won: Royal Air Force 1939–45 Vol. 3* by Hilary St. George Saunders (HMSO 1975).

9. *Nachtjagd* claimed 21 Lancasters and Halifaxes, *Hauptmann* Paul Zorner, *Gruppenkommandeur* of III./NJG5, being credited with three Halifaxes and a Lancaster in the Dreux area to take his score to 52. *Leutnant* Walter Briegleb of 10./NJG3 was credited with four Lancasters to take his score to eight confirmed victories.

10. P/O Andrew Charles Mynarski RCAF, 419 'Moose' Squadron RCAF, Lancaster KB726; awarded for action 12/13 June 1944, *London Gazette*, 11 October 1946. George Brophy, 'Art' de Breyne, F/O Robert Body RCAF the navigator and W/O W J 'Jim' Kelly RCAF all evaded capture. Jack Friday and Sgt R E Vigars the flight engineer became PoWs. Altogether, 23 aircraft, 17 of them Halifaxes and six Lancasters were lost on the raids on communication targets this night and 17 Lancasters failed to return from the operation to the Nordstern synthetic-oil plant at Gelsenkirchen by just over 300 aircraft.

11. *Cheshire VC* by Russell Braddon (Arrow Books 1966).

12. The following evening a similar operation was mounted against the *E-boat* pens in Boulogne harbour when 297 aircraft of 1, 4, 5, 6 and 8 Groups were dispatched. 1 Group Lancasters bombed their targets but cloud over the assembly area of the port prevented 10 of 617 Squadron's 22 Lancasters from bombing. Even so, according to one account, over 130 *E-boats* were sunk along with 13 other vessels wrecked or badly damaged, as at Le Havre by a

tidal wave. One Halifax FTR. This and the operation to Le Havre forced the remnants of the *E-boat* flotillas to a new base at Ijmuiden in Holland, which was bombed by 617 Squadron on 24 August.

13. Middlebrook and Everitt.
14. Watten was bombed again on 25 July by 16 Lancasters of 617 Squadron, with a Mosquito and a Mustang marking the target. The Germans ordered that Watten be abandoned.
15. *The Bomber Command War Diaries: An Operational reference book 1939–1945.* Martin Middlebrook and Chris Everitt. (Midland 1985).
16. See *Into the Silk* by Ian Mackersey. P/O D H Davis was flying a Hampden on 61 Squadron on a *Gardening* sortie on the night of 20/21 July 1940 when he was shot down.
17. Tom Newbery died aged just 26 on 5 July 1950 of Hodgkin's disease. He left a widow, Jean Spears, who was aged 19 when they married on 17 August 1946.
18. Peter Knox married Monica Newcombe an English WREN on 17 November 1945 at Newman College Chapel, Melbourne University. They later had nine children. Peter Knox died on 21 May 1998 in Kent.
19. 617 Squadron returned to Wizernes on 17 July and again on the night of 20/21 July with 1 Group, after which the site was abandoned by the Germans.
20. *Bomber Command* by Max Hastings (Pan 1979).
21. *Raider–The Halifax and its Flyers* by Geoffrey P. Jones (William Kimber, London 1978).
22. Either HB825 or HB837.
23. Four B-24 Liberator Groups in the 2nd Bomb Division, 8th Air Force tried to hit the bunker with GP bombs on 31 July but most of the 112 tons dropped fell in fields around the north side of the building. *Barnes Wallis' Bombs: Tallboy, Dambuster & Grand Slam* by Stephen Flower. Tempus 2002).
24. The combined loss rate was 8.7%. Thirteen Tame Boar crews were credited with 21 *Viermot* kills. 33 Mosquitoes of the LNSF (Light Night Striking Force) went to Saarbrücken and another ten were despatched to drop 4,000lb 'Cookies' from 32,000 feet on the Scholven/Buer oil plant in the Ruhr. All the Mosquitoes returned without loss.
25. *Handley Page Halifax; From Hell to Victory and Beyond* by K A Merrick (Chevron Publishing 2009).
26. *Barnes Wallis' Bombs: Tallboy, Dambuster & Grand Slam* by Stephen Flower. Tempus 2002).
27. *Barnes Wallis' Bombs: Tallboy, Dambuster & Grand Slam* by Stephen Flower (Tempus 2002). Cheshire then resumed his previous rank of group captain and was awarded the VC two months later.
28. After 7 June two attempts at encirclement followed, the first, on 13 June, which involved a drive towards Villers-Bocage but the heavy bombers were to become involved in the V-1 campaign and were not used. Consequently, the ground attack failed. A second attempt began on 25 June, having been delayed by the great storm over the Channel between 19 and 23 June. However, the heavy bombers were grounded by residual bad weather in England, cancelling again the preliminary aerial bombardment. The British troops came up against units of the 1st *SS Panzer* Corps and very little progress was made. Early on 30 June, 266 aircraft of Bomber Command bombed German tanks, which had been concentrating for a counter-attack;

two aircraft were lost and the German attack failed. See *Point Blank and Beyond* by Lionel Lacey-Johnson (Airlife Classic 1991).

29. The city was in ruins; some of the French inhabitants who had ignored the warnings to evacuate stayed in their cellars or wandered around in a dazed condition amongst the piles of rubble that had been their homes. By the time the British troops had gained the River Orne they found that all the bridges had been blown up and that there was some very stiff opposition on the far bank. See *Point Blank and Beyond*.

30. The operations to break out from the Normandy beach-head were planned to take place in the latter half of July. The British attack in the Caen sector, known as Operation *Goodwood*, was designed to draw German armour away from the American sector so that their Operation *Cobra* could strike swiftly south from the north of the Cherbourg Peninsula, which was by then in Allied hands.

31. *Point Blank and Beyond*.

32. *Point Blank and Beyond* by Lionel Lacey-Johnson (Airlife Classic 1991). A 51 Squadron Halifax crashed at Snaith on return and a 158 Squadron Halifax crashed in Bridlington Bay killing all the crew, to take the Squadron's total losses to three. A 578 Squadron Halifax crashed near Bisham, Berkshire and all the crew perished. Three Halifaxes, including a 466 Squadron Halifax that was abandoned near Dungeness, Kent failed to return from the raid by 110 aircraft on the railway yards at Vaires.

33. In all, 972 sorties were flown that night, the two biggest raids being oil plants in Germany by 1, 6 and 8 Groups. Five heavies were lost on the raids on the oil plants.

34. *Maximum Effort* (Futura 1957).

35. See *Chased By the Sun*.

36. Bomber Command Association Newsletter October 1983. Lancaster JB318 had been hit in the port wing by *Schräge Musik* cannon fire from a Bf 110 night fighter flown by *Oberleutnant* Herbert Altner of 8./NJG5 at Laon-Athies. Within 30 minutes Altner shot down another four bombers for his 18–21st victories. JB318 crashed in flames and exploded with its full bomb load at La Boue, Bassevelle, killing four of the crew. F/O E H Ruston, navigator survived and was taken prisoner and Sgt F J D Taylor and Leonard E S 'Len' Manning, who was in great pain from burns to his face and arms, evaded. Manning was taken in by the French Resistance and his wounds treated by a doctor before he was taken across country by a member of the Resistance called *Lulu*. They eventually arrived at a small cafe in the village of La Tretois, which was owned by two elderly ladies, 59 year-old Madam Lousette Beaujard and her mother. Although they did not speak English they made him very welcome and he was given a room in their hotel across the courtyard. Len Manning remained in their care until the liberation. Lousette Beaujard was later awarded the *Legion d' Honore* for her work in the Resistance.

37. 971 sorties were flown on 20/21 July for the loss of 38 aircraft. 87 heavies bombed V-weapon sites at Ardouval and Wizernes and 302 Lancasters and 15 Mosquitoes of 1, 5 and 8 Groups bombed rail targets at Courtrai. 153 heavies and 13 Mosquitoes of 4 and 8 Groups attacked the synthetic oil refinery at Bottrop while another 147 Lancasters and 11 Mosquitoes of 1, 3 and 8 Groups

attacked an oil plant at Homberg. 106 aircraft from training units made a diversionary sweep over the North Sea while Lancasters and Mosquitoes made a spoof raid to Alost. More Mosquitoes raided Hamburg and RCM aircraft and Stirlings made other sorties to further stretch the resources of the *Nachtjagd*. Nine Lancasters were lost on the Courtrai raid (2 of which were destroyed on their way back by *Oberstleutnant* Lent, *Kommodore* NJG3, within sight of the British coast off Dover for his 106th and 107th victories). 21 Lancasters and 7 Halifaxes FTR from the Bottrop/Homberg raid. 75 Squadron RNZAF at Mepal lost 7 of its 25 aircraft.

38. Chorley.
39. This Lancaster, which crashed at Omerville, was flown by Sgt P O Wadsworth who was killed. One other crew member was killed also; the rest either evaded or were taken prisoner.
40. *Lancaster Down* by PO John Cann via Andy Bird.
41. Only 377 aircraft were able to bomb, on to *Oboe* markers because of cloud and only two of the targets were effectively hit. Four Lancasters failed to return. Middlebrook and Everitt.
42. See *Barnes Wallis' Bombs: Tallboy, Dambuster & Grand Slam* by Stephen Flower. Tempus 2002) and *Legend of the Lancasters* by Martin W Bowman (Pen & Sword 2009).
43. Sergeants Lewis John 'Lou' Arthur, Francis James 'Buzz' Graham, Henry Charles Joseph Buckler and John Richard Davies and F/O William Samuel Richards RCAF.
44. 'I made the long and arduous journey into Spain and as I got to Salou we got word that the war had ended. I made my way back to Chantilly and up pulled a Yank in a jeep and I asked him to take me to Paris to his HQ. He gave me some wonderful food and drink and said 'hang on a minute I will just ring up the airport' he came back and said 'we can't get you back to England as someone has sabotaged the landing lights'. He took me to Limoges Airport. Whilst I was walking outside an English soldier came up to me and said 'can you help me? I have been in a PoW camp at St-Denis for the last 5 years and need to get home' I said 'I need help myself but if I can't help you no one can.' We both travelled back to England together on the same plane. The pilot came and introduced himself. The soldier said 'who is flying the plane?' and the pilot replied 'George'. The worried soldier replied 'well I can't see George so can you go back and fly the plane please?' When we got back we went to the Air Ministry. They sent me to Ennersley Gardens Hotel which was run by the RAF. When I got there a WAAF corporal said 'you look scruffy' and I suppose I did as I had not had a bath for months. An officer came out of his room and played hell with her he said 'have you just come out?' and I said 'just'. I borrowed some money off another bloke and rang Wragg's Coal Merchants on Holland Road a few doors from my parents' house. Cissie Wragg the daughter answered the telephone and I said that it was Sid Witham and that I was all right and to let my family, including my wife Kathleen with our young son John know that I was OK. She replied 'Sorry but Sid is missing in action' and put the phone down! Nevertheless I did manage to get the message through eventually and finally after many months return home.'

45. The Frazer-Nash FN 64, armed with two 0.303 in machine guns was normally fitted into the rear of the bulged bomb bay doors. However, it was not popular with some units and in many cases it was removed, as with 1 and 5 Groups. *Avro Lancaster The Definitive Record* by Harry Holmes (Airlife 2001).
46. *The JG 26 War Diary Vol. 2 1943–1945* by Donald L Caldwell (Grub Street, London 1998). Laub was KIA on 14.12.44.
47. See *Barnes Wallis' Bombs: Tallboy, Dambuster & Grand Slam* by Stephen Flower. Tempus 2002).
48. See *Barnes Wallis' Bombs: Tallboy, Dambuster & Grand Slam* by Stephen Flower. (Tempus 2002).
49. *The Bomber Command War Diaries: An Operational reference book 1939–1945.* Martin Middlebrook and Chris Everitt. (Midland 1985).
50. Adapted from *Maximum Effort* by James Campbell.
51. *The Bomber Command War Diaries: An Operational reference book 1939–1945.* Martin Middlebrook and Chris Everitt. (Midland 1985).
52. Three Lancasters FTR.
53. 218 Gold Coast Squadron Assoc Newsletter No. 50 March 2008.
54. Locke, Wing Commander Porter and Squadron Leader Parkes were awarded immediate DSOs, and message of congratulations from the AOC followed.

CHAPTER 5

The Daylights

The Night is long,
That never finds the Day...

Macbeth IV.3

At quarter to one on the morning of Saturday 19 August, Jack Stephens was hauled out of bed at Waddington for briefing and another dusk to dawn trip, after just two hours sleep following a raid on a flying bomb supply depot just north of Paris. The weather had been beautiful and the sky, as usual, was full of Lancasters in formation and in waves with one or two Mosquitoes playing around all the way. His Lancaster had thirteen 1,000-pounders on and flew at 12,000 feet in the 'gaggle' formation. Eleven of the Mosquito low-level markers flew in and marked the target at L'Isle-d'Adam but a large chunk of cloud got in the way at the critical moment and the target could not be identified, though some of the 158 Lancasters of 5 Group dropped their bomb loads into cloud. Two Lancasters were lost and another failed to return from the raid on Bordeaux.

Throughout that night fleets of bombers followed with a devastating raid on Bremen and an attack on the synthetic oil plant at Sterkrade. More heavies and Mosquitoes of 6 and 8 Groups and 1 and 8 Groups attacked a railway station and yards at Connantre, 70 miles east of Paris, and an oil depot and fuel storage depot at Ertvelde Rieme.

The attack on Connantre marked the end of the long series of attacks on the French and Belgian railway networks. In 1,069 sorties four aircraft had been lost.

At briefings at the 5 Group stations in the early hours of Saturday morning bleary-eyed crews learned that the target later in the day was a submarine oil storage dump at La Pallice on an island in the Bay of Biscay. Jack Stephens' diary entry on 19 August read thus:

We took off at 05.00. There were 50 kites down from Waddington and Skellingthorpe with no fighter cover. There was thick patchy cumulus cloud all the way (12,000 feet). Flew in the usual gaggle formation. Cloud over target, but dropped the bombs somewhere near it we hope. Intense flak was expected but only 2 or 3 guns fired at us. Besides the usual black bursts some were dirty green. Came back over St-Nazaire, St-Malo and Cherbourg Peninsula and had a pretty good view of them. On return, cloud was down to the deck in patches but our diversion was mixed up and we landed OK. One flak hole above the Elsan [chemical toilet in the rear of the aircraft]. We think one burst against the bombs on the run up with bomb doors open.

No aircraft were lost. When Halifaxes of 4 Group and Lancasters of 5 Group attacked ports and E-boat bases on the French coast on the 24th all aircraft again returned safely. Next day 161 aircraft attacked five V-1 launching sites in the Pas-de-Calais. Two Halifaxes were lost in the attack on Watten and a Lancaster was shot down in the raid on Vincly. One of the Lancasters was Q-Queenie on 218 Squadron at Methwold flown by Flight Lieutenant Douglas Charles Haggis, which was possibly hit by flak near St-Omer. Haggis was lost from sight and subsequently crashed in the sea off Felixstowe. All the crew were killed and their bodies recovered from the sea. A Lancaster on 514 Squadron that returned to Waterbeach was so badly damaged by flak that it had to be written off. O-Orange, a 158 Squadron Halifax III at Lissett, which bombed Watten from 12,500 feet, was hit by flak, which wounded the pilot, Pilot Officer J A Fletcher and two members of the crew. Homebound the port inner engine seized, followed by a loss of power from the two starboard engines and Fletcher landed at Woodbridge in emergency. The three wounded crew members were taken to the East Suffolk and Ipswich Hospital. Their Halifax was deemed beyond repair.[1]

Attacks on Rüsselsheim and Darmstadt on the night of the 25/26th resulted in 22 Lancasters being shot down and they included the two deputy Master Bombers.[2] Len Gillies RAAF, pilot of C-Charlie on 218 Squadron, recalling the raid on Russelsheim, says:

We were at 18,000 feet stooging along minding our own business and watching the spasmodic flak bursts in the vicinity. Suddenly there was a 'loud bang and a twang!' and a strong smell of cordite. I anxiously enquired of the crew if they were OK and all was well. Nobody was hurt and nothing was leaking or burning. All engines and gauges were functioning as they were supposed to do. We went on to drop our bombs and made an uneventful journey home. We left C-Charlie at its dispersal, went to debriefing, had a meal and then into bed and slept soundly until about 01.00. After breakfast we went to the flight office to see what was going on when Flight Sergeant 'Chiefy' Edwards came in and gave me a nod and said

'Come with me'. Away we went to the dispersal where *C-Charlie* was getting a check up and refuel etc. 'Chiefy' found a ladder and pointed up to the nose and said 'See that hole?' I could see it all right; you could put your hand in it ... he then told me to climb up the ladder and sight through the hole and towards the rear of the aircraft. Whatever had come in the front had gone between my legs while I sat at the controls and out the rear without doing any major damage! A little higher and I would have lost my interest in girls and WAAFs and not be able to start a family. Fortunately a little luck is worth a ton of judgement![3]

On Saturday night, 26 August, 372 Lancasters and ten Mosquitoes of 1, 3 and 8 Groups visited Kiel and 174 Lancasters of 5 Group went to Königsberg, an important supply port for the German Eastern Front and the capital of East Prussia. Jack Stephens wrote:

Off at 20.30, low over the North Sea. Receiver broke down but came on again after a bit of bashing and stayed the trip. Up to 9,000 feet over Denmark, which including Copenhagen and then Sweden were all were brilliantly lit up; over Sweden they filled the sky above us with Bofors flak, which was pretty, but they were careful not to shoot near us. Then over the Baltic to the target, just 100 miles from Uncle Joe's (Stalin) war and 1,000 miles from base. PFF dropped their flares and then we dropped our J type clusters and a 2,000lb. The whole city and docks were an intense reddish white with fire. The flak was light and spasmodic and there were about 200+ searchlights. One swept over us. On the way back Sweden looked just as good, but only a couple of guns going. Diverted to Wigtown in Scotland on return and kept out of the rain. We returned to base in time for late tea.

At Kiel the Path Finder marking was hampered by smoke-screens but heavy bombing was reported in the centre of the town and the resulting fires were fanned by a strong wind. Henry Baskerville, a pilot newly arrived on 460 Squadron at Binbrook, with only 16 hours flying experience on Lancasters, 10 of them being solo, did a day and a night cross-country and a fighter affiliation exercise before he flew on the operation as a 2nd dickey, as he recalls:

Every pilot had to do their 'second dickey' where they stand as a passenger behind an experienced pilot and watch what happened on a real operation. Mine was with Flying Officer Arch Campbell DFC. I stood close to him throughout the trip trying not to get in the way of the flight engineer. We had to fly out over the North Sea under 500 feet to avoid the German radar and then climb quickly to cross the Dutch Coast at a reasonable height so as to avoid the light flak. It was quite exciting to see all these planes low down over the water some lower than others, as the evening closed in. We lost sight of them once darkness fell by which time we were at height and saw them not again till we were over the target. Then, in the light of the searchlights, the fires and the exploding photo-flashes, they were all there, above, below and around, a milling throng all vectoring in on to the aiming point marked out by pathfinder flares on the Naval base below. How there were no collisions or planes destroyed by bombs dropping from above one never knows; the fact is that, on every raid, these factors would have accounted for some losses but few survived to tell the tale. Suffice it to say that, on this occasion, we got through and dropped our bombs on Kiel without incident and got safely back to base. Now I, as the pilot and captain of my own crew, knew something of what it was about and that experience was supposed to stand me in good stead. David Sandell, a good friend of mine, was posted to 467 Squadron at Waddington in 5 Group just weeks before I arrived at Binbrook. One of his earliest trips, his first as captain with his own crew, was to Königsberg in East Prussia on 30 August – a target, at extreme range for a Lancaster, which was covered by low cloud when they got there which caused a twenty minute delay in opening the master bomber-controlled attack. One hundred and eighty-nine planes circling the target while German night fighters sought them out. What a trip on which to send a new crew! Fifteen planes were lost and David's was one of them. Later in my tour I took two other new captains on their 'second dickey' trips. Neither of them survived their subsequent tour of operations.

Seventeen Lancasters were lost on Kiel, all of which were probably shot down by Tame Boars. The eastern part of Königsberg was bombed and four Lancasters failed to return. One of these was a Path Finder Lancaster on 83 Squadron piloted by Jim Verran DFC, now a Squadron Leader on his third tour. Verran was heading for home crossing from the Baltic to Jutland on the Danish coast at 12,000 feet when his Lancaster was raked from underneath by 20mm shells fired by *Major* Höfele of III./NJG1 who was flying a Bf 110 night fighter. Verran recalled:

Our rear gunner, Keith Tenant caught a glimpse of the 110 and managed to shoot it down but sadly died of his injuries just minutes later. Incendiary bullets from the night fighter ripped into the hydraulic header tank near the navigator, causing blazing fluid to fall into the cockpit area and the bomb doors to open and the undercarriage to drop. I tried to call the crew members but got no reply. Having trimmed the aircraft I got out of my seat, the fighter having killed five of my crew. My bomb aimer, Warrant Officer Raymond Page had left through the nose hatch. I left by this exit and was swept up into the rear of the bomb bay. Burning hydraulic fuel was falling through holes, up which the bombs were winched. The aircraft was wallowing and eventually I fell free. I could not feel the D-ring of my parachute, so prising open one burnt eyelid was able to make out the cable floating in front of me. I grabbed the ring and pulled the cord. Having escaped from the Lancaster my luck still held because I landed in a ploughed field, just yards from the edge of a Fjord near the village of Hogsholt. In the half light I could make out a white farmhouse so I walked to it and knocked on the door. It was not until I saw myself in a mirror that I realised just how badly burnt I was. An open boat was quickly acquired with the intention of taking me across to Sweden. However, the farmer realised just how bad my state was and called an ambulance. The two ambulance men were superb, for we were shot at twice by Germans troops. I made a point of returning after the war and thanking them. Initially I was treated in a local cottage hospital at Vejle but the burns being so severe, was transferred to a hospital at Frederica [where *Major* Höfele refused to speak to him], which was being used to treat casualties from the Eastern Front. I was treated equally, even to the extent of receiving the same cigarette ration as the Germans. Being a non smoker, I sold the cigarettes.

A German doctor saved Verran's life, carrying out skin grafts without an anaesthetic due to the shortage of drugs and with only paper bandages. The Germans had buried Verran's five crew members in a mass grave and the local people later exhumed the bodies and gave each one a Christian burial.[4] Verran was taken on a journey to *Stalag IXC*, on a stretcher. While in Hamburg railway station there was an air raid:

> I was taken down into the cellar on the station and there were numbers of little German girls with fair hair plaited down their backs playing 'Ring a ring of Roses'. When you saw that you realised that they were the kind of people you were bombing. You didn't have a very good feeling I must admit but when you were actually flying, you were only concentrating on the target you were bombing and that was all. If you are going to win a total war there is no way that you can do that job without killing civilians. If they were in the area it was just bad luck.[5]

On 27 August, 243 aircraft were detailed to bomb the Rhein-Preussen synthetic oil refinery at Meerbeck near Homberg in daylight. This historic raid was the first major operation by Bomber Command to Germany in daylight since 12 August 194?, when 54 Blenheims had attacked power stations at Knapsack near Cologne for the loss of 10 aircraft. At Homberg the bombing was based on *Oboe* marking but 5–8/10ths cloud produced difficult conditions, though some accurate bombing was claimed through gaps in the cloud.[6] Bernard Aves called Homberg 'that hostile little town' where the flak was so accurate that 'we got more than one hole in us but fortunately none serious.' There was intense flak over the target as Aves feared but no bombers were lost.[7]

On Tuesday night 29 August, 402 Lancasters and one Mosquito of 1, 3 and 6 and 8 Groups attacked parts of Stettin that had escaped damage in previous attacks and 189 Lancasters of 5 Group carried out one of their most successful attacks of the war when the target was Königsberg again. Jack Stephens, who went to Königsberg, wrote:

> Route was via Northern Denmark and Sweden. Spasmodic Bofors flak over there, not so far from us. There was thin cloud over Sweden but we saw the towns lit up as before. Koenigsberg was waiting for us with plenty of fighters and all the searchlights and flak they could muster. Had to orbit for 25 minutes during which time we were held for 5 minutes and had a piece of flak through the bomb doors in line with my leg but it didn't penetrate the floor. We bombed on a timed run from red TIs with J types and a 2,000lb. Attacked at the end of the bombing run by a Do 217 or a Me 410, which put a 20 mm cannon shell through the back of our fuselage. Johnny let him have it and he disappeared into cloud, crashing into the sea. The searchlights were pretty good and flak cascaded up. We reckoned we'd rather go to Berlin. Bombed from 8,000 feet.

Four separate aiming points were selected but 'H-13' (thirteen minutes before H-hour) was delayed for 20 more minutes by low cloud over the city. The attack only commenced after the 627 Squadron Marker Mosquito found a break in the cloud and Wing Commander John Woodroffe, probably 5 Group's most skilled Master Bomber, ordered the Flare Force to begin illuminating the aiming points. As usual this was begun by two high-flying Lancasters from either 83 or 97 Squadron, which dropped half a dozen or so green Target Indicators which would burn for about five or six minutes. At 'H-11' another flight of Path Finder Lancasters passing over the target area and also using H_2S dropped a wave of parachute flares which floated slowly to the ground, lighting up the whole area. Two minutes later at 'H-9' a second flare wave was dropped by a third flight of Lancasters, thus creating an environment that literally turned the night into day so that the low flying Mosquitoes could sight and properly mark the target with their TIs. From 'H-13' radio silence could be broken by the Master Bomber if he felt that the weather conditions warranted it, calling the Marker Leader in normal plain language to ask if he could see the green TIs going down. Inevitably, the deployment of the green TIs was the signal for the enemy defences to open up on the Lancasters with their anti aircraft guns and illuminating searchlights, although, once the flares had been dropped, the search-lights were, in effect, neutralised and posed no further threat. On the other hand the Mosquito markers, flying by this time at no more than 4,000 feet became the targets of the more numerous light ack-ack batteries.

'To see hundreds of fiery-red tracer shells 'hose-piping' around our aircraft was a salutary experience for even the most sanguine amongst us,' remarked one Mosquito pilot. 'From "H-9" the Marking Team had just nine minutes in which to find and identify the Marking Point, mark it, assess the accuracy, get another four aircraft to drop their TIs to back it up and then get away from the target area before the Main Force bombs began to drop.'[8]

Only 480 tons of bombs could be carried by the Main Force because of the distance from England but severe damage was caused to the city and thousands of people were 'de-housed' in a single night. There was heavy fighter opposition in the target area and 15 Lancasters failed to return. Included in this total were three aircraft on 50 Squadron, including ED588 G-George, which was being flown by Flying Officer Anthony Hugh Carver on George's 128th op. Carver and his crew perished in Sweden after attacking Königsberg. Over the previous year ED588 had been a very lucky aircraft for many of the Squadron's aircrew at Skellingthorpe where it had been the third Lancaster on the station to reach a century, on 4 July.

Jack Stephens concluded: 'Had a quiet trip back and landed at 07.20. 10 hours 40 minutes. Signals and bombing leaders were lost in two kites from our squadron. 467 lost 3 and Skellingthorpe 5. Losses, including Stettin were 41, the worst for a long time.'

At Stettin over 1,500 houses and more than 30 industrial premises were destroyed and almost 600 more houses and premises were badly damaged. Just over a thousand people were killed and another 1,034 people were injured. A 2,000 ton vessel was sunk and seven other ships were damaged. Twenty-three Lancasters failed to return, two of them 460 Squadron RAAF aircraft.

One of these was flown by Flying Officer P N Aldred RAAF. Over Stettin the Lancaster gave a sudden lurch and the crew heard the pilot give a scream over the intercom. Flight engineer Sergeant Rodney Allcott scrambled from his position into the cockpit to see what was wrong, to be confronted by an awful sight. A stick of incendiaries dropped by a bomber higher up had crashed through the cockpit cover. Working with the front gunner Allcott managed to throw the incendiaries out of the aircraft but not before Aldred had sustained severe burns to his legs. Allcott cut away Hood's trousers to apply dressings and then gave him a shot of morphia to dull the pain. The navigator set a course over the

Baltic to Sweden, while Allcott stayed in the cockpit to help Aldred fly the bomber. After some minutes Aldred passed out, so Allcott dragged him from the seat and took over the piloting completely. When the Lancaster reached Svensköp, Allcott admitted that he was not confident about landing the damaged bomber in the dark and asked the navigator to come to help him. However, Aldred had recovered his senses by this time and despite his wounds crawled back to the cockpit, where he supervised Allcott's landing. All the crew were interned.

The other 460 Squadron Lancaster III that failed to return was *Fox 2* piloted by Flying Officer K W Humphries RAAF which at approximately 00:30 hours was attacked by a Me 210 night fighter, which badly wounded the rear gunner Sergeant Philip B Aviet and shot away the elevator controls and trims, set fire to the H_2S and 6,000 rounds of ammunition and rendered part of the electrical equipment and intercom u/s. Humphries ordered the crew to put on parachutes and to try to put out the fire. Next he dropped the bomb load and turned towards base. The bomb load fell in a field next to Kærgade road in Vorup near Randers. It detonated and the explosion destroyed three houses and six civilians were killed; six were wounded severely while eleven were lightly wounded.

Upon discovering that the elevator controls were gone Humphries headed for Sweden, controlling the Lancaster by use of the throttles. Mid upper gunner Sergeant Dennis Fallon and W/Op Flying Officer Ronald K Stratford DFM were told to get Aviet out of his turret. They were losing height all the time and when down to 3,000 feet the crew were ordered to take up ditching positions. Fallon and Stratford had got Aviet out of the turret, but chose to stay with him. The ditching at about 01.00 hours north of the island of Anholt was successful, but the tail broke off and the Lancaster went down. Humphries was thrown about 20 metres out in front of the Lancaster and when he swam back he found Flying Officer T B MacNeill the Canadian navigator, bomb aimer Sergeant G D Walsh and flight engineer Sergeant S R Wild sitting on the Lancaster with the dinghy out. The three men in the tail had gone down with the aircraft.

The survivors entered the dinghy and in the early morning the dinghy was observed from the island of Anholt and a rescue launch sailed out and picked the flyers up. They were taken to the island where they were taken prisoner by the local *Wehrmacht* garrison. They then spent the next four days on the island before they were shipped to København by the weekly supply boat and from there they were sent to *Dulag Luft* for interrogation. After about a week Humphries and MacNeill were sent to *Stalag Luft I* Barth while Walsh and Wild were sent to *Stalag Luft VII* Bankau.

On 4 September the body of Ronald Stratford was found washed ashore on Vesterstrand beach on the island of Anholt. The *Wehrmacht* buried the body in Anholt cemetery the same day. Philip Aviet and

Dennis Fallon were found washed ashore on the Swedish west coast and both rest in Falkenberg Forest cemetery in Sweden.[9]

With the Allied armies advancing into France the Chief of Air Staff once again gained control of Bomber Command, which resumed area bombing and also mounted a new precision bombing campaign against oil and transportation targets. On the afternoon of 5 September in good visibility, 313 Lancasters, 30 Mosquitoes and five Stirlings carried out the first of a series of heavy raids on the German positions around the 400-year-old town of Le Havre, where the enemy was still holding out after being bypassed by the Allied advance. One of the French residents who survived the raid said that the Lancasters 'turned the sky black'. It was claimed that the raid was accurate and no aircraft were lost but when the raid was over, at least 2,000 French civilians were dead. Another 60 Lancasters and six Mosquitoes of 5 Group bombed gun positions outside Brest, whose garrison was also still holding out. Again no aircraft were lost.

On 6 September, Emden was bombed in daylight by 181 heavies escorted first by Spitfires and then American Mustangs, for the loss of one Lancaster on 7 Squadron, flown by the deputy Master Bomber, 23-year-old Flight Lieutenant Granville Wilson DSO DFC DFM, which suffered a direct hit from a flak shell. Wilson was killed instantly and the navigator and bomb aimer were killed also. The five others bailed out safely and were taken into captivity. The bombing was accurate and Emden was seen to be a mass of flames. This was the final Bomber Command raid of the war on the city. Le Havre was also bombed again, by 344 aircraft, over 300 of them Lancasters. All the bombers returned safely but two Lancasters on 101 Squadron crashed at Ludford Magna. One was *B-Bertie* piloted by Flight Lieutenant A Massheder.

Sergeant Gerhard Heilig, the special operator, recalls:

Our target was the German pocket of resistance. Bombing had to be extremely accurate lest we hit our own troops who were only a few hundred yards away from the enemy lines, and due to bad visibility we had had to abandon our mission. Jettisoning our load was out of the question over the Channel crowded with allied shipping and so we brought our bombs home. Back over England my duties were finished and I emerged from my post to enjoy the scenery from behind the pilot's seat. Our heavily laden state proved too much for the pneumatic system of the Lancaster and we had brake failure on landing. As the end of the runway loomed up at an alarming speed I saw the twisted wreckage of another aircraft beyond and we were about to join it. I curled up in a ball and waited for the imminent crash. As we overshot the runway the pilot pulled up the undercarriage and we slid to rest on our belly. I shot aft to the door and followed on the heels of my crew, running until we had reached what we considered a safe distance before the plane blew up. Well, it didn't. I found myself clutching two parachutes and two helmets, my own and the navigator's and I realised at what utter speed my mind had been working in the seconds following the crash. When I had picked myself up my first thought was to get out quick, abandoning my personal equipment which would be no trouble to get written off. Or would it? There would be no questions, but there would be forms to be filled in and the nuisance of going to stores and drawing replacements. I had never been a believer in unnecessary effort so why not take it along? On my way I decided to grab the navigator's 'chute and helmet as well, why not save a friend some bother? I had thought it all out quite logically but it could not have taken more than a split second, for I could not have got out of the aircraft any faster without climbing over someone's back – and that would have been another unnecessary effort to say the least. It was an amazing experience of how fast a human mind can work.

On 8 September, 304 Lancasters, 25 Mosquitoes and four Stirlings of 1, 3 and 8 Groups were dispatched on an early morning 'milk run' to Le Havre to bomb the German positions again. This would be the last occasion on which Stirlings were to carry out bombing operations. It was also Henry Baskerville's first operation since joining 460 Squadron. He recalls:

We were fortunate in that we arrived on the squadron just as the allied armies were consolidating their position on the French mainland and gearing themselves for the first great breakout at Falaise. At this time Bomber Command was under the control of the Supreme Commander and was being used as a tactical rather than as a strategic weapon. Accordingly we were directed to raid the various French ports, Calais and Le Havre, where German garrisons were still holding out. Our target was German troop positions on the outskirts of Le Havre. They were defending the port and were being gradually pushed back, by British and Canadian Divisions, towards the city, into which they eventually entered and managed to hold out for another three days. We were to take *U-Uncle* on our first operational flight. It had arrived on the squadron from 32 Maintenance Unit in August. The plane really belonged to Tony Willis who at the time was 'B Flight' commander. We all had planes which we considered our own and generally, when we flew on 'ops', we flew in our particular plane. Sometimes, however, the plane might be in for a service and we would be allocated another; sometimes, when we were not on the Battle Order, some other crew would take our plane. *Uncle's* ground crew was under the control of Flight Sergeant Harry Tickle, probably the most senior of the Australian

NCOs on the station. Each aircraft had its own ground crew to look after it: usually four aircraftmen under the control of an NCO. These men were responsible for maintaining the plane in a serviceable condition. One was an engine fitter; another was an airframe fitter and another a rigger and the NCO was probably a jack of all trades. Generally they acquired as much a proprietary interest in their plane as did the aircrew. Harry Tickle was quite an identity and the stories which were told concerning him became legendary. Eventually he flew home to Australia on *G-George*, which was put on permanent display in the Canberra War Museum.

I can still recall the look on Harry Tickle's face and the attitude of the other ground crew members as the tender disgorged our crew on the dispersal under the wing of *U-Uncle* on the morning of 8 September. To him and his men we were a 'sprog' crew, still wet behind the ears. In actual years we would have appeared to them as a bunch of boys. It was well known that the loss rate amongst crews during their first five 'ops' was higher than at any other time during their tour. This was due to inexperience in many areas. The pilot might have only a little over 10 hours flying time on the Lancaster; the other crew members were also just getting familiar with their equipment and their crew positions. None of them had any experience of battle conditions, of flying in a sky crowded with other aircraft to say nothing of enemy action: flak, searchlights and night fighters. What perverse fate had entrusted the plane of a veteran flier like Tony Willis DFC DFM to a team such as this?

We were to be part of a force of 333 aircraft, predominantly Lancasters, with 460 contributing 21 aircraft. We took off soon after seven o'clock in driving rain and climbed to our cruising height of 3,000 feet in cloud all the way. As we settled down on course to the south of England, I was unhappy about the conditions. There was nothing to be seen outside except the murk and I didn't know what other aircraft might be groping their way through it close to us. I climbed up a thousand or so feet but we were still in it. I decided then to come down and try to get under it. At 500 feet we were still in it. I crept lower and lower hoping for a break and conscious that I still had a hundred feet more than was shown on the altimeter to play with. Binbrook was a hundred feet above sea level and we always set our altimeters at zero on the tarmac before take-off. But at 300 feet there was no change and I felt that I was stretching my luck to go any lower so I climbed back to 3,000 feet and stayed there. This is another example of how inexperienced pilots can get into trouble. I was taking greater risks of collision with all my climbing and descending than I would by staying where I was. Eventually the cloud dissipated in the south of England and steadily climbing to reach our bombing height of 6,000 feet we crossed the coast in clear air except that there was higher overcast and poorer visibility towards the ground.

When we arrived at 08.15 we could see the markers which had been dropped by the Path Finders burning on the ground. Jack Trist immediately began to give directions for the bombing run. I opened the bomb doors and we dropped our load of 13 1,000-pounders and four 500-pounders. The bombs had hardly gone when we heard the voice of the Master Bomber declaring that the visibility was too poor to continue the attack and ordering all aircraft to take their bombs home.

When we got back and were being interrogated there was obvious concern on the part of the Intelligence Officer, Squadron Leader Leatherdale. He was a fine stamp of an Englishman and a pilot whose flying days were past because of his age. He fitted in well into the Australian scene and had an apparent sympathy for the young men who flew in peril of their lives. His concern arose from several facts: one, that we were an inexperienced crew on our first op; secondly, that the attack had been called off and yet we had bombed; and thirdly, that there had only recently been a disaster, when Bomber Command had dropped bombs on Canadian ground troops in the same area, with very serious repercussions. Whether or not the Command was culpable, stringent measures were taken to make us realise the magnitude of the error. All crews that participated in the raid were excluded from further daylight raids and confined to night operations and every Squadron Commander whose squadron was involved, lost his command. I think my first assembly in the briefing hut was when the whole squadron was gathered to hear Wing Commander John Keith Douglas DFC AFC make an emotional farewell address. Everyone felt extremely sorry for him but it was the old principle of the 'Captain being responsible for his ship' being worked out. After he left, Tony Willis assumed temporary command of the squadron until the arrival of Keith Parsons from Australia.[10]

So it was with some degree of apprehension that he awaited the target photo which would show where our bombs had dropped. Jack Trist was sure we had no cause for concern as he had definitely bombed on the markers. Nevertheless, we were there with controlled eagerness as soon as the photos were released and were relieved to be given a clean bill of health by an equally relieved Intelligence Officer.[11]

Another daylight raid, on eight different strong points at Le Havre on 10 September, involved 992 heavies and all the bombers returned safely. A follow up raid the next day also saw the return of all 218 aircraft involved. However, a Halifax on 346 *Groupe Guyenne* Free French Squadron piloted by the squadron commander, *Lieutenant Colonel* Venot, landed at Elvington at dusk after a daylight attack on a V-1 site at Octeville in Northern France. Just as he was taxiing there was a violent explosion, which sent shockwaves reverberating across the airfield. Unbeknown to Venot and his crew a 1,000lb bomb had hung up and fallen to the ground with the landing impact. Flames quickly enveloped the Halifax and with it, the crew. Miraculously, Venot, semi-conscious from the blast, had managed to lift the cockpit canopy and jumped several feet to the ground, just as the flames were licking at his face and hands. The remainder of the crew, stunned by the explosion were unable to get out. Only little Dominique Francois Biaggi MM CdeG, the rear gunner, recovered consciousness. He was screaming, imprisoned in his turret. Immediately in front of the Halifax was another piloted by *Capitaine* Jean Calmel (later *Général* Calmel, Vice Chief of the Air Staff of the French Air Force). He and his crew could do nothing. Helplessly, Calmel wept at the loss of Jules Joseph Kipferle, an Algerian, Marcel Louis Coupeau, Wilson Georges Finale and Biaggi. He had loved them like brothers.

A few weeks later Calmel was diverted while returning from a night operation to an American B-24 base in East Anglia. He cut the engines and went through the standard 'stop' procedures, one of which was to leave the bomb bay doors open on parking. While he operated the levers with Roux, his flight engineer, the American crews watched as the bomb bay doors opened. Calmel heard a sinister sound of crumbling metal followed by a dull thud. He knew instantly that a bomb which, like Venot's had hung up and had now fallen to the ground. Luckily, it had fallen quite flat without striking its fuse and it did not explode. Calmel dared to look up and saw 'everyone fleeing in all directions away from the aircraft like sparrows or throwing themselves to the ground behind any available shelter!'[12]

On Monday 11 September, 379 Halifaxes, Lancasters and Mosquitoes escorted by 26 squadrons of Spitfires, Mustangs and Tempests, pounded three synthetic oil plants in the Ruhr area. The Castrop-Rauxel refinery and the Bergkamen plant just north of Kamen were clearly visible and were accurately bombed but at Gelsenkirchen (Nordstern) a smoke screen hindered bombing and results were unobserved. German fighters were noticeable by their absence, though five Halifaxes of 4 Group and two Path Finder Lancasters were lost on the Nordstern raid and two Lancasters were lost to flak or to 'friendly' bombs at Castrop-Rauxel and Bergkamen. Another 218 aircraft that set out to attack German positions outside Le Havre in support of British divisions making an attack on the port was only partially successful. Bombs were dropped by just over 170 aircraft before the Master Bomber ordered the final wave to cease bombing because of smoke and dust. The German garrison in Le Havre surrendered a few hours later but the port was not cleared for Allied use until several weeks later. All of the bombers returned safely.

That night another 226 Lancasters and 14 Mosquitoes of 5 Group set out on a 900-mile round trip (which with the dog-leg deception course was nearer 1,083 miles) for an area attack on Darmstadt, a prosperous provincial town in the Land of Hessen, 15 miles south of Frankfurt-am-Main. Primarily a residential and small business centre set in rolling farmland studded with woods, Darmstadt had been the subject of a failed raid by 5 Group on 25/26 August when the Master Bomber had had to return early and his two deputies were shot down. The marker flares had been dropped too far west of the target and Mosquito marker aircraft failed to locate the target area. It was but a temporary reprieve for the town's 120,000 inhabitants, of which, only 18½ per cent of the workforce were engaged on war production.

The first Mosquito marker crew to identify the Marking Point was usually the first to break radio silence by shouting the time-honoured British hunting call, 'Tally Ho!' This was the signal for the rest of the Mosquito Marking Team to hold back, for within a second or two other crews would be in the same position and chaos could have ensued unless alerted. The first Flare Force had only just begun illuminating the target when one of 627 Squadron's circling Mosquitoes announced Tally Ho and dived to mark the *Kavallerie Exerzierplatz* with red TIs, aiming to drop them at about 600 feet to give time for the barometric fuse to operate and allow the red pyrotechnic to drift slowly to the ground. Wing Commander John Woodroffe the Master Bomber circling the target in another 627 Squadron Mosquito at 1,000 feet was satisfied and he ordered the rest of the markers to back up the red 'candles' now burning merrily away, with greens. All TIs were within 400 yards of the Marking Point. At 23.52 hours Woodroffe halted the second Flare Force in the midst of their run and a few moments later he sent all the marking aircraft home. At 23.56 hours and as 'H-hour' arrived, he called in Main Force to bomb the aiming points as briefed. For 51 minutes Woodroffe guided and encouraged the bomber crews and generally co-ordinated the way in which the raid progressed, until the last aircraft had dropped its bombs and set course for home. In that time 399 tons of HE and 580 tons of incendiaries were dropped by 218 bombers.

Jack Stephens wrote:

Monica and H_2S wiped (not used) as Jerry was homing on them.[13] 14 clusters of 41lb incendiaries and a cookie (4,000lb) from 14,750 feet. 800 aircraft made a wizard fire. Chemical and aircraft component factories. A perfectly clear night all the way. A bit of trouble with *Gee* on the way in. I saw everything from the astro hatch including a number of combats and kites going down. There was a little flak, hundreds of searchlights and plenty of fighters in spite of the fact that the Yanks had shot down 130 that day. Coming out of the target at 200 mph we passed through a gap between two main belts of searchlights so kept well over near one belt to keep clear of any fighters waiting there. Saw about 6 kites hit the deck, one about half way back to the French coast. 49 Squadron tried out their new remote controlled radar turrets and we had the ultra-violet equipment going. 12 kites lost and one from each of our squadrons.[14]

Clear weather conditions, combined with efficient marking methods resulted in a fierce fire area in the centre of the hitherto untouched city and the devastation was intense. Police stations reported that over 6,600 men, women and children, 492 foreign workers and 368 prisoners of war died in the conflagration, which spread to districts immediately south and east of the centre. Many deaths were not immediately reported by the 49,200 Darmstadters made homeless and who were evacuated, as most did not return until after the war, so the death total may have been 5,000 more. The US Strategic Bombing Survey in 1945 concluded that 'this was an area raid of the classic saturation type, which had so effectively razed Cologne and Hamburg ... The mechanics of the raid ... were almost perfunctory and as a consequence Darmstadt was virtually destroyed.'

More synthetic oil plants at Dortmund, Scholven-Buer and Wanne-Eickel were bombed the following day, Tuesday 12 September, by over 400 bombers. Münster too was raided by 119 Halifaxes of 4 Group and five Path Finder Lancasters. Two Halifaxes were lost and two more crashed at Woodbridge on their return. The attack on Dortmund was particularly successful but results were unobtainable because of smoke screens at the target. All aircraft returned safely from the raid but two Halifaxes and a Lancaster failed to return from the operation on Scholven and three Lancasters and a Halifax were shot down on the raid on Wanne-Eickel. The Halifax that was lost was *K-King* on 426 'Thunderbird' Squadron RCAF at Linton-on-Ouse. Sergeant P S Twynam the WOp recalled:

Apart from the flight engineer and me the crew were Canadians. We never made the target. At about 13.00 hours we were shot down by flak near Dordrecht in the Netherlands. Six of us were captured fairly quickly though our pilot, Flight Lieutenant Percy Lloyd Buck AFC later died from injuries received. Sergeant K J Dugdale the mid-upper gunner eluded capture for about three months before being apprehended on Christmas Eve.

On the night of 12/13 September Frankfurt and Stuttgart were heavily bombed. The northern and western parts of the centre of Stuttgart were wiped out and at Frankfurt the bombing caused severe destruction in the western districts of the city. Twenty-one Lancasters failed to return from the two raids. Main Force daylight raids on Gelsenkirchen, Osnabrück and Wilhelmshaven followed and then there was a resumption of night attacks on 15/16 September when over 480 Lancaster and Halifax crews were briefed for a raid on Kiel.

At Tholthorpe in Yorkshire Flight Lieutenant Vic Motherwell and his Halifax crew on 420 'Snowy Owl' Squadron RCAF were a standby crew and expecting to have the night off but due to illness in one of the other crews they found themselves on the Battle Order after all. Their aircraft was new and had recently been delivered to the Canadian squadron but the 'Hallybag' had suffered mechanical failure at the start of its last two operations and its crew had aborted. This time Motherwell's crew went all the way and they bombed the target. Much of the bombing by 1, 4, 6 and 8 Groups fell outside the port but the old town and modern shopping centre were devastated. Just after bomb release Motherwell's crew heard a loud bang and the hydraulic pressure dropped to zero. The bomb doors remained open and the wing flaps began to droop and the undercarriage partially lowered. Soon after clearing the enemy coast Motherwell headed for Cromer on the Norfolk coast in the hope that he could bail the crew out over England. They made it as far as 50 miles off Norfolk when Motherwell had to ditch in a heavy swell with 20 feet waves whipped up by a strong westerly wind. The Canadian pilot skilfully put the Halifax down on the sea and coolly crawled out of the top escape hatch above his cockpit and walked along the top of the fuselage to the tail. He and the seven members of his crew scrambled into the dinghy which had inflated and they waited for rescue. By late afternoon the following day a Hudson dropped a Lindholme Gear and, just as it was getting dark, they sighted a Walrus rescue aircraft on the horizon, which swooped down and landed on the rough sea. With a crew of two and ten passengers crammed into the Walrus it was impossible for the aircraft to take off and the pilot taxied slowly to the Norfolk coast before the bomber crew were transferred to a RML, which conveyed them safely to Great Yarmouth. Motherwell's Halifax was one of four Halifaxes that failed to return and two Lancasters were also lost.[15]

On 16/17 and 17/18 September, Bomber Command supported the landings by British, American and Polish airborne troops at Arnhem and Nijmegen in Holland. Operation *Market-Garden*, as it was called, ended in heroic failure and the British 1st Airborne Division was destroyed at Arnhem. At the end of September Bomber Harris wrote a letter to Winston Churchill pointing out that the Germans were still fighting hard and their defence would be even greater when the Allies reached the Rhine and crossed into Germany so this was the time to use overwhelming Allied air superiority and 'knock Germany flat'. However, his wish for an all-out attack was rejected by Churchill who did not rate the contribution of the air force as high as Harris did. The C-in-C maintained that bombing German cities to destruction could still win the war.

Night raids on Bremerhaven and the twin towns of Mönchengladbach and Rheydt by forces of Lancasters were carried out on the nights of Monday the 18th and Tuesday the 19th respectively. Just over 200 Lancasters of 5 Group carrying fewer than 900 tons of bombs devastated the centre of Bremerhaven and the port area and 30,000 people were rendered homeless. Jack Stephens flew on the Bremerhaven raid and wrote:

> Night attack from 15,000 feet with 14 cans of 4lb incendiaries. Bremerhaven an industrial town, docks, harbouring the 'Bremen' and 'Europia'. Went out at 1,000 feet over the Dogger Banks. Sun set as the English coast disappeared over the horizon. Carried a 2nd dickey pilot who had arrived on the squadron 4 hours before. No fighters. A bit of heavy and light flak and a few searchlights. Used delay bombing run. We left the target a seething white mass of flame and could see the glow 150 miles away. Landed H2100.

One Lancaster and a Mosquito were lost. Jack Stephens spent the next day 'gadding' about London. He and the rest of the crew were not 'on' that night when 227 Lancasters and ten Mosquitoes of 1 and 5 Groups claimed severe damage to of Mönchengladbach and Rheydt. The Master Bomber for this raid was Wing Commander Guy Gibson VC DSO* DFC* who was flying a 627 Squadron Mosquito. Gibson and his navigator, Squadron Leader James Brown Warwick DFC were killed when they crashed in Holland on the return.[16] Four Lancasters were also lost in action.

These attacks were followed by a daylight raid on Calais on 20 September. Squadron Leader French Smith DSO DFC RAAF was captain of an aircraft detailed to mark and attack a pinpoint target on the outskirts of Calais and in addition was appointed Master Bomber. As such he was required to make a reconnaissance of the target area before the main force arrived, mark this exact aiming point and then direct the main force throughout the attack. Weather conditions obliged him to fly below 2,000 feet to identify the target, in face of intense light AA fire. French Smith's aircraft was repeatedly hit. A shell exploded in the fuselage, rendering the bombsight unserviceable and making accurate dropping of his markers impossible. French Smith instructed the deputy master bomber to mark and make an assessment. This was done and thereafter, French Smith took over the direction of the attack, although his aircraft was still the target for AA fire. The attack was highly successful. French Smith got his badly damaged aircraft safely back to base and was awarded the DSO soon afterwards.

After an end of tour leave in September 1943, Sergeant Charles Cawthorne DFM on 467 Squadron had been posted with his Skipper Warrant Officer

Warren 'Pluto' Wilson, to 1668 HCU at RAF Balderton and later carried out staff engineer duties with 1660 HCU at RAF Swinderby. This was followed by ground instructor duties at the Lancaster Holding Unit at RAF Scampton. In July 1944, Cawthorne was called back to do a second tour of operations and he joined Flight Lieutenant Hugh Horsley's crew at 1661 HCU at RAF Winthorpe near Newark. They first flew together as a crew in a Stirling on 20 July. On 2 September they started Lancaster training at 5 Lancaster Finishing School, RAF Syerston and eight days later they were posted to 61 Squadron at RAF Skellingthorpe. On posting Horsley was promoted to Squadron Leader and immediately took command of 'A' Flight on 61 Squadron. On 17 September they flew their first operational sortie against the French port of Boulogne in veteran Lancaster EE176 *Mickey The Moocher* QR-M. It was the aircraft's 107th operation. Little did Cawthorne know that his second tour of operations was destined to end over Holland a week later.

On 24 September 1944, a BBC wireless news programme gave out brief details of the previous night's bombing operation carried out by 5 Group. In essence the news reader announced: 'Last night RAF Lancasters of Bomber Command carried out a successful attack on the Dortmund–Ems Canal. Fourteen of our aircraft failed to return to their bases.' At RAF Skellingthorpe near Lincoln, preparation for this raid started early in the day when ground crews on 50 and 61 Squadrons carried out routine maintenance and later loaded 14,000lb of HE bombs and 1,500 gallons of fuel aboard each aircraft. The main operational briefing for the aircrews started at 15.00 hours. They were told this was a 5 Group Operation and the objective was to breach the banks of the Dortmund–Ems Canal near Ladbergen, just north of Münster. The aiming point was the twin aqueducts over the River Grane where the level of the canal water is higher than the surrounding land. If the crews were successful in draining this section of canal it would halt the barge traffic for a while from carrying vital raw materials between the North Sea ports and the industrial Ruhr.

Take-off time for the 30 Skellingthorpe Lancasters was set to start at 19.00 hours and the route selected was a direct track of 350 miles on an easterly heading of 110 degrees. This took the heavy bombers over the North Sea to the Scheldt Estuary and then across Holland to the target area in northwest Germany. One of the Lancasters taking part in the raid was *K-King* on 61 Squadron, a comparatively new aircraft with only 45 hours flying time in its maintenance log, flown by Squadron Leader Hugh Horsley AFC. This was the crew's fourth operation together. After taking off at 19.17 hours they soon settled down in their crew positions on the first leg of the flight to join up with the main force of 135 Lancasters and five Mosquitoes heading out over the North Sea. By the time *K-King* had reached the Dutch coast it was flying at an altitude of 20,000 feet and ahead the crew could see occasional bursts of scattered flak and searchlights lazily roving across the night sky. Twenty minutes later in the Eindhoven area Sergeant Herbert William Jennings, the mid-upper gunner, saw a twin-engine night fighter coming in for an attack and opened fire with his twin Brownings while yelling out over the intercom: 'Skipper corkscrew port. Go!' Horsley immediately responded to the instruction by diving the aircraft to the left while the rest of the crew hung on in the blackness to whatever they could while the aircraft gyrated in this dramatic manoeuvre. Throughout this defensive action the two gunners reported the position of the fighter. Suddenly, after the fifth corkscrew, the Messerschmitt Bf 110 attacked again from the rear port quarter and opened fire with its 20mm cannon and machine guns, hitting the vulnerable Lancaster in the centre of the fuselage and port wing. Inside *K-King* the crew felt their aircraft judder from the fighter's devastating fire which left the mid-upper gunner and the wireless operator either dead or seriously wounded and a power loss on both port engines. Within seconds the Lancaster was coned by searchlights and this was quickly followed by a barrage of exploding shells from the Eindhoven flak batteries. Horsley responded to the danger by putting the Lancaster into a high speed dive to escape the searchlights and deadly flak. Unbeknown to him the aircraft had also sustained damage to the control system and it took all his strength to apply enough backward pressure on the control column before the aircraft responded and they were flying straight and level once again.

They were now down to 10,000 feet and after quickly weighing up the situation Horsley decided the best course of action was to abort the operation, lighten the aircraft and return to base. As navigator Flying Officer Jack Webber worked out a course for home, the bomb doors were opened and the bombs were quickly jettisoned over the Dutch country-side. Even after trimming the aircraft Horsley still found it difficult to control and with the two port engines shut down they continued to lose altitude at an alarming rate. The situation was now grave so Horsley had no alternative; he ordered 'GET OUT' and the crew abandoned the crippled aircraft. The first one out was Sergeant Reg Hoskisson the rear gunner, who was wearing a fighter pilot's parachute so all he had to do was unplug his oxygen pipe and intercom lead before rotating his turret to the right, opening its back doors and rolling out backwards into the aircraft's slipstream. Meanwhile, up front in the nose, bomb aimer Flying Officer Johnny Wheeler jettisoned the escape hatch in his compartment and quickly disappeared through the gaping black hole. Flight engineer Charlie Cawthorne should have been the next man out but was having problems locating his parachute under a pile of *Window* packages. In his panic a number of the bundles were thrown in the direction of Jack Webber who had just left his seat and was moving towards the forward escape hatch. Moments later in the darkness of the cockpit, he pushed past Cawthorne, who was in the process of clipping on his chute and rapidly departed through the hole in the bomb aimer's compartment floor. By this time Hugh Horsley had set the automatic pilot and was leaving his seat so without further delay Cawthorne pulled off his oxygen mask and helmet and dived head first through the hatch from the cockpit step and was quickly followed by his Skipper. *K-King* crashed near the village of Deurne in southeast Holland at approximately 22.30 hours on 23 September. Horsley, Cawthorne and Hoskisson evaded capture and all returned to operations. Webber and Wheeler were taken prisoner. Flight Sergeant George Twyneham the WOp/AG and Bert Jennings were killed.[17]

Daylight raids on German positions in and around Calais, which had begun on 20 September, were resumed on five successive days, 24–28 September. Henry Baskerville on 460 Squadron flew on these operations as he recalls:

We raided troop concentrations in the field and dropped bombs on the cross channel guns at Cape Gris Nez. These were all relatively short, low-level raids (say, from 3,000 to 10,000 feet) and were often conducted in murky weather where the target was not easily identifiable. Some of them were controlled by Master Bombers and on two occasions he made us take our bombs home because he could not be sure of the aiming point. On one occasion during this series of raids we were diverted to Spilsby, the home of 207 Squadron in 5 Group, because Binbrook was fogged in. Lyall Notley had received the base plate of a 1,000lb bomb back from the ground and into his port inner engine (we were bombing from 3,000 feet) and though he got home to Spilsby, his plane could not be flown back to Binbrook the next day. I was detailed to bring him and his crew home. Binbrook was still fogged in next day and we had to grope around in the murk looking for the ground. On two attempts I missed lining up with the runway and had to go round again. On the third as I was on the approach, peering ahead looking for the start of the runway, I suddenly saw it but over to my right. By this time I was determined not to go round again, so, on the approach, at about 500 feet, I put the plane into a steep turn to the right and then quickly again straightened up to land on the runway. In the event, I didn't judge it quite right and landed on the grass at the right hand side of the runway. Fortunately the ground was firm and I got away with it.

Tony Willis who was watching from the control tower was horrified when he saw this great bomber doing steep turns in the funnels and called for a report on the flying abilities of the pilot. The report, whatever it was, must have satisfied him because he said nothing to me at the time and only confided that he had taken such action when I was with him at High Wycombe many months later. 'Lucky you were in a Lancaster' he said. 'You would not have gotten away with it in any other plane.' Flying Officer Lyall Notley DFC who was strangely quiet throughout, also made no subsequent comment. His was the plane on the Kiel raid that was lower over the water than any other and drew comment from Arch Campbell's crew.

On 30 September, 209 Halifaxes and 46 Lancasters attempted attacks in daylight on oil plants at Sterkrade and Bottrop but both targets were cloud-covered and only 24 bomb aimers got their bombs away at Sterkrade and just one dropped his bombs on Bottrop. The rest of the force dropped on estimated positions of various Ruhr cities. One of their Halifaxes that took part was *F-Fox* – better known *as Friday The 13th* – which joined 158 Squadron at Lissett in March. It had been placed in the charge of ground crew chief Flight Sergeant Wicks, who was told by the pilot, Flying Officer Smith, who was beginning his tour, to name the aircraft and call it whatever he liked, as he was not superstitious. Wicks, or one of the ground crew chose *Friday the 13th*, which was painted on the port side of the nose below the cockpit.[18] Fred Allen, the rear gunner, who completed 38 ops, recalls:

The first time round the bomb aimer forgot to fuse the bombs. Next attempt he didn't open the bomb doors. When you didn't bomb you had to turn to port and go around again. Everybody else was turning starboard. The Jerries weren't much concerned with the ones that had bombed but they were with those that hadn't. It got a bit hot. The Skipper said, 'If you don't drop the buggers this time, I will' – meaning he'd use the jettison bar. We dropped them all right.[19]

Bernard Aves on 218 Squadron recalls:

Daylights were interesting as we were able to see what was going on. And I could not like what I saw – the odd aircraft upping its nose and then going straight down with a burst of flame and smoke as it hit the ground, you hoped and prayed we weren't going to be the next, but what could you do to avoid becoming the next casualty? The very odd kite got a direct hit which was not a pretty sight, orange flames and black smoke. These were more upsetting at night. Whilst on the subject of casualties, some descriptions I have read make out that the sky is full of aircraft being shot down, rubbish! You certainly saw the odd kite catch it but by no means several all at once and outside of daylights the only aircraft you would see being shot down would be a direct hit at night. It must be remembered that either day or night the op would normally be in three waves, (always endeavour to keep out of the second wave, that was the hottest – what am I talking about – you didn't have a choice anyway!) and perhaps 500 aircraft, which were on average travelling at 210 mph. Usually the raid time for all aircraft to pass over the target was 20 minutes or so and thus the distance between the first and last plane was 70 miles. Could anyone expect us to believe that they can see all these kites being shot down, both day and night? The fact is that you saw only a few shot down in your close vicinity and then at night only those which got a direct hit.

Notes

1. *RAF Bomber Command Losses of the Second World War Vol 5 1944*, by W R Chorley (Midland Publishing 1997).
2. S/L Arthur Llewelyn Williams DFC on 83 Squadron and S/L Stuart Martin Parkeshouse Parkes DSO* on 97 Squadron. Both were killed.
3. *218 Gold Coast Squadron Association Newsletter No. 17* edited by Margery Griffiths.
4. See *Out of the Blue: The Role of Luck in Air Warfare 1917–1966* edited by Laddie Lucas (Hutchinson 1985).
5. In the winter of 1945 and with the Germans in retreat, Jim Verran found himself on the move on more than one occasion. An 18-day forced march in bitterly cold weather led to his freedom when American tanks intercepted the prisoner of war column. At the time they were near Munich and had spent nights sleeping in fields. Never one to lack initiative, Verran and F/L E Creed, a Spitfire pilot, set off for Brussels in a Mercedes drop head coupe liberated by the Americans and presented to Jim. A friendly farmer agreed to store it in his barn until Verran could return to claim it, which he duly did. Verran's return to England was in a Mosquito piloted by an old friend who he had met in Brussels. Once back in England, the RAF hospital at Cosford again beckoned for yet more skin grafts. It took a year of convalescence before he was fit to resume duties. While at Cosford, Jim Verran received a bar to his DFC.
6. This raid was escorted by nine squadrons of Spitfires on the outward flight and seven squadrons on the withdrawal. *The Bomber Command War Diaries: An Operational reference book 1939–1945*. Martin Middlebrook and Chris Everitt. (Midland 1985).
7. 'We carried on ops to various places during September, October and November. After an op to Oberhausen on 4 December, I left for Chedburgh on the 5th. One op to Duisburg on the 8th December and we had completed our tour. In all we had done 33 trips and went on leave and then our separate ways.' *218 Gold Coast Squadron Assoc Newsletter*, No. 50, March 2008.
8. Ron Pate. See *At First Sight: A factual and anecdotal account of No. 627 Squadron RAF* researched and compiled by Alan B Webb (1991).
9. *Airwar over Denmark*, www.flensted.eu.com via Andy Bird.
10. Later Air Cdre K R J Parsons DSO DFC. In May 1944 Douglas had become, at age 22, the youngest RAAF officer to command a bomber squadron.

11. Harry Baskerville saw *U-Uncle* shot down over Emmerich on 7 October 1944. 'It received a direct hit from incendiaries falling from above which set its right wing on fire and, as it went cart-wheeling down, we counted seven parachutes opening as the crew bailed out; all of them became prisoners of war. F/L Eric Greenacre was the pilot on this occasion. He was on his second tour and this was their fourth operation. After the war Eric became a doctor and practised as a GP in Bathurst until the early 1980s. He died at Manly in December 1986.' *U-Uncle – My first Lancaster* by Henry Baskerville via Andy Bird.

12. See *Out of the Blue: The Role of Luck in Air Warfare 1917–1966* edited by Laddie Lucas (Hutchinson 1985). Bomber Command's two French Squadrons, 346 and 347, in 4 Group, suffered 79% losses of the original aircraft strength and 48% of the original aircrew strength, killed or missing, in the 11 months from June 1944 to 8 May 1945.

13. When in July following the capture of a Ju 88G-1, which landed by mistake at Woodbridge, it became known that *Flensburg* FuG 227/1 equipment was being used to home on to *Monica* and the FuG 350 Z *Naxos* to home on to H_2S radar bombsight transmissions, RAF bombers were ordered immediately to restrict the use of H_2S while *Monica* sets were removed from the Lancasters and Halifaxes. Virtually all the advantages enjoyed by the *Tame Boars* were lost.

14. Apart from the 12 Lancasters that FTR, three Lancaster minelayers were lost in the Kattegat.

15. See *Shot Down And In The Drink: True Stories of RAF and Commonwealth aircrews saved from the sea in WWII* by Air Commodore Graham Pitchfork (The National Archives, 2005). Noel Langdon, pilot of the Walrus was awarded the AFC at the end of the war having completed 65 ASR sorties. Motherwell was later promoted squadron leader and was awarded the DFC. All the crew survived the war.

16. See *Legend of the Lancasters* by Martin W Bowman (Pen & Sword 2009).

17. On 1 February 1945, the Lancaster flown by Squadron Leader Hugh Horsley crashed on take-off at RAF Skellingthorpe. Sgt Reg Hoskisson was the only survivor. See *Thundering Through The Clear Air: No. 61 (Lincoln Imp) Squadron At War* by Derek Brammer (Toucann Books, 1997).

18. *Handley Page Halifax: From Hell to Victory and Beyond* by K A Merrick (Chevron Publishing 2009).

19. See *Round The Clock* by Philip Kaplan and Jack Currie (Cassell 1993).

RAF Bomber Command Battle Order, 5 June 1944

Squadron	Station	Aircraft	Command
7	Oakington	Lancaster B/III	Bomber
9	Bardney	Lancaster BI/III	Bomber
10	Leeming	Halifax	Bomber
12	Wickenby	Lancaster BI/III	Bomber
XV	Mildenhall	Lancaster BI/III	Bomber
21	Gravesend	Mosquito FBVI	2nd TAF
35 'Madras Presidency'	Graveley	Lancaster BI/III	Bomber
44 'Rhodesia'	Dunholme Lodge	Lancaster BI/III	Bomber
49	Fiskerton	Lancaster BI/III	Bomber
50	Skellingthorpe	Lancaster BI/III	Bomber
51	Snaith	Halifax BIII	Bomber

Squadron	Station	Aircraft	Command
57	East Kirkby	Lancaster BVIII	Bomber
61	Skellingthorpe	Lancaster BI/III	Bomber
69	Northolt	Wellington XIII	2nd TAF
75 RNZAF	Mepal	Lancaster BI/III	Bomber
76	Holme-on-Spalding Moor	Halifax BIII	Bomber
77	Full Sutton	Halifax BIII/IV	Bomber
78	Breighton	Halifax BIII/IV	Bomber
83	Coningsby	Lancaster BI/III	Bomber
85	Swannington	Mosquito NFXII/XVII	100 Group
88 'Hong Kong'	Hartford Bridge	Boston III/IIIa	Bomber
90	Tuddenham	Stirling III/Lancaster BI/III	Bomber
97 'Straits Settlements'	Coningsby	Lancaster BI/III	Bomber
98	Dunsfold	Mitchell II	2nd TAF
100	Grimsby	Lancaster BI/III	Bomber
101	Ludford Magna	Lancaster BI/III	Bomber
102 'Ceylon'	Pocklington	Halifax BIII/IIIa	Bomber
103	Elsham Wolds	Lancaster BI/III	Bomber
105	Bourn	Mosquito BIX/XVI	Bomber
106	Metheringham	Lancaster BI/III	Bomber
107	Lasham	Mosquito FBVI	Bomber
109	Little Staughton	Mosquito BIV/IX/XVI	Bomber
115	Witchford	Lancaster BI/III	Bomber
138	Tempsford	Halifax BII	Special Duties
139 'Jamaica'	Upwood	Mosquito BIV/IX/XVI/XX	Bomber

Squadron	Station	Aircraft	Command
141	West Raynham	Mosquito NFIV/FBVII/NFXXX	100 Group
156	Upwood	Lancaster BI/III	Bomber
157	Swannington	Mosquito NFXIX/NFXXX	100 Group
158	Lissett	Halifax BIII	Bomber
166	Kirmington	Lancaster BI/III	Bomber
419 'Moose' RCAF	Middleton St. George	Lancaster BX	6 Group
420 'Snowy Owl' RCAF	Tholthorpe	Halifax BIII	6 Group
424 'Tiger' RCAF	Skipton-on-Swale	Halifax BIII	6 Group
425 'Alouette' RCAF	Tholthorpe	Halifax BIII	6 Group
426 'Thunderbird' RCAF	Linton-on-Ouse	Halifax BIII	6 Group
427 'Lion' RCAF	Leeming	Halifax BV	6 Group
428 'Ghost' RCAF	Middleton St. George	Lancaster BX	6 Group
429 'Bison' RCAF	Leeming	Halifax BIII	6 Group
431 'Iroquois' RCAF	Croft	Halifax BIII/V	6 Group
432 'Leaside' RCAF	East Moor	Halifax BIII/V	6 Group
433 'Porcupine' RCAF	Skipton-on-Swale	Halifax BIII	6 Group
434 'Bluenose' RCAF	Croft	Halifax BIII/IV	6 Group
460 RAAF	Binbrook	Lancaster BI/III	Bomber
463 RAAF	Waddington	Lancaster BI/III	Bomber
464 RAAF	Thorney Island	Mosquito FBVI	2nd TAF
466 RAAF	Leconfield	Halifax BIII	Bomber
467 RAAF	Waddington	Lancaster BIII	Bomber
487 RNZAF	Thorney Island	Mosquito FBVI	2nd TAF
514	Waterbeach	Lancaster BI/III	Bomber

Squadron	Station	Aircraft	Command
515	Little Snoring	Mosquito FBVI	100 Group
550	North Killingholme	Lancaster BI/III	Bomber
571	Oakington	Mosquito BXVI	Bomber
576	Elsham Wolds	Lancaster BI/III	Bomber
578	Burn	Halifax BIII	Bomber
582	Little Staughton	Lancaster BI/III	Bomber
608 North Riding	Downham Market	Mosquito BXX	Bomber (formed 1.8. 44)
617	Woodhall Spa	Lancaster BI/III	Bomber
618	Skitten	Mosquito BIV	Bomber
619	Dunholme Lodge	Lancaster BI/III	Bomber
620	Fairford	Stirling IV	38 Group
622	Mildenhall	Lancaster BI/III	Bomber
625	Kelstern	Lancaster BI/III	Bomber
626	Wickenby	Lancaster BI/III	Bomber
627	Woodhall Spa	Mosquito BIV	Bomber
630	East Kirkby	Lancaster BI/III	Bomber
635	Downham Market	Lancaster BI/III	Bomber
640	Leconfield	Halifax BIII	Bomber
644	Tarrant Rushton	Halifax BV	ADGB
692 Fellowship of the Bellows	Graveley	Mosquito BIV/XVI	Bomber
1409 Met Flight	Oakington	Mosquito	Bomber

Index

234